Martin Buber's Social and Religious Thought

REAPPRAISALS IN JEWISH SOCIAL AND INTELLECTUAL HISTORY

Martin Buber's Social and Religious Thought:
Alienation and the Quest for Meaning
LAURENCE J. SILBERSTEIN

LAURENCE J. SILBERSTEIN

Martin Buber's Social and Religious Thought

Alienation and the Quest for Meaning

NEW YORK UNIVERSITY PRESS
NEW YORK & LONDON

Library of Congress Cataloging-in-Publication Data
Silberstein, Laurence J. (Laurence Jay), 1936–
Martin Buber's social and religious thought : alienation and the
quest for meaning / Laurence J. Silberstein.
p.   cm. — (Reappraisals in Jewish social and intellectual
history)
Bibliography: p.
Includes index.
ISBN 0-8147-7886-0 (alk. paper)
1. Buber, Martin, 1878–1965.   I. Title.   II. Series.
B3213.B84S496   1989
296.3'092'4—dc19   88-25575
                          CIP

First published in paperback in 1990

Copyright © 1989 by New York University
All rights reserved
Manufactured in the United States of America

New York University Press books are printed on permanent and durable acid-free
paper, and their binding materials are chosen for strength and durability.

Book Design by Ken Venezio

p10987654321

This book is dedicated to my wife, Mimi, and our children, Devorah, Rachel, Uri, and Avi, who have taught me the most about genuine dialogue and have helped me to understand the meaning of Buber's words "Love is the responsibility of an I for a You."

Contents

Foreword by Robert M. Seltzer   ix

Acknowledgments   xiii

Note on Gender and Language   xvii

Introduction   1

1. Fin de Siècle Vienna: Cultural Context and Early Writings   18

2. Hasidism and the Renewal of Judaism   43

3. Revisioning Judaism   71

4. Edification and the Meaning of Personhood   104

5. Refining the Categories: From Relation to Dialogue   140

6. The Crisis of Community: Buber as Social Critic   168

7. Revisioning Religion: Between Person and the Eternal You   204

8. Living as a Jew   229

Concluding Reflections   264

vii

Notes   267

Bibliography   329

Index   347

Foreword

The academic study of Judaica has undergone a remarkable efflorescence in America during the last twenty years. The dream of the pioneers of *Wissenschaft des Judentums* in the early nineteenth century that Judaica would become accepted into the curriculum and research program of great universities has largely come to pass. As the modern study of Jewish history and literature spread east, west, and south of its original German home, the scholarly investigation of Judaica itself became far richer more varied, and far reaching. Still encompassing traditional disciplines of philology, literature, theology, biography, and traditional history, the study of the Jewish past and civilizations shows, since the late nineteenth century, the powerful impact of the perspectives and methodologies of the social sciences—sociology, economics, anthropology, and psychology—as well as new trends in social thought and literary criticism. A far more complex map of the Jewish heritage has emerged. Simplistic understandings of what was normative and what was nonconformist have given way to a more objective and more sensitive appreciation of historic Jewish subcultures, of intellectual and social tensions and cycles within the Jewish people, and of dissident and marginal forms of Judaism.

Equally important has been the astonishing, often traumatic history of the Jews since the first appearance of *Wissenschaft des Judentums*. In the 1820s the modern odyssey of the Jewish people and the Jewish tradition had barely commenced—indeed, the modern age (better, the sequence of modern ages) had just begun. More than a century and a half later, the academic study of Judaica includes not only ancient and medieval texts, practices, beliefs, and institutions but the dialectic of two centuries of modern challenges and response: ideological replies to liberalism, conservatism, anti-Semitism, and socialism, cultural reactions to the pressures of acculturation and assimilation, institutional reconstruction after the experience of migration, economic dislocation, and attempted genocide, secular and spiritual reactions to the vast technological and scientific changes occuring since the industrial revolution. The careful study of all these phenomena and more is indispensable for an adequate grasp of contemporary Jewish postures and mentalities. And modern Jewish studies has shown itself to be of immense value for comparative study of traditional and modern ethnic and religious groups everywhere on the globe.

This series, *Reappraisals in Jewish Intellectual and Social History*, seeks to contribute to the further growth and clarification of Jewish studies, especially in the early modern and modern periods, through a dedication to two tasks in particular. First, the books included will deal with topics which at one time were high on the agenda of Jewish research and now can be subjected to fresh appraisal in the light of newly discovered data or newly developed explanatory models. There are individuals, events, and movements whose exemplary significance are being illuminated through concepts and methodologies developed since the classical presentation or the authoritative treatment of the subject. Second, the series is intended to facilitate the reappraisal of topics in a broad comparative perspective. Works included will articulate the reciprocal influences and parallel developments that clarify the interrelationship of Jewish history and thought and the general context and further integrate Jewish studies into the contemporary academy.

Some publications in *Reappraisals in Jewish Intellectual and Social History* will be diachronic, tracing development through time, and others will be synchronic, cutting across the temporal process to look for other patterns of interrelationship. In common will be a bridging of the gap between highly specialized studies directed primarily to scholars working in the area and popular accounts for the general public through an up-to-date, fresh synthesis for students, teachers, scholars, and laypeople struggling to keep abreast of current knowledge. Some works will be collections of studies by groups of scholars who have met together in a preliminary conference for the initial phases of the development of the theme. Others will be monographs by a individual scholar on a subject of profound and intense interest to him or her for a number of years.

In light of these considerations, we are particularly pleased to inaugurate *Reappraisals in Jewish Intellectual and Social History* so auspiciously with Laurence Silberstein's broadranging, sensitive analysis of Martin Buber. By placing the range of Buber's thought in the context of late nineteenth-and twentieth-century intellectual trends and issues, Professor Silberstein enhances our understanding of one of the most fertile thinkers in twentieth-century Jewish and general philosophy. He thus enables us to see the sources and dynamics of the Judaism of our time more distinctly and profoundly, as Buber himself sought to revitalize Judaism through a reacquaintance with its living roots.

ROBERT M. SELTZER

Acknowledgments

The National Endowment for the Humanities provided me with a research fellowship that enabled me to undertake the initial research for this work. Mrs. Margot Cohn, private secretary to the late Martin Buber and the curator of the Martin Buber Archives at the Jewish National and University Library in Jerusalem, graciously provided invaluable assistance to me. Her readiness to assist me from afar as well as during my stay at the archives greatly facilitated my work. I am also indebted to Mr. Raphael Buber for warmly receiving me in Jerusalem and allowing me full access to his father's archives. All material from Buber's unpublished writings is quoted with the permission of the Martin Buber Archives and its director, Raphael Buber.

Nahum Glatzer, who first introduced me to the world of Jewish studies, inspired me to pursue a career in this field. Benjamin Halpern, a model of intellectual integrity for all of his students, was instrumental in helping me to understand the implications of social theory for the interpretation of Judaism. I was also fortunate to have had the opportunity to study both in Israel and in New York with Akiba Ernst Simon, one of Buber's great disciples.

Many friends and colleagues gave of their time to read and comment on earlier drafts of this work, either in part or in its entirety. I am grateful to Malcolm Diamond, Steven Dunning, Michael Fishbane, Arthur Green, Richard Matthews, and Jeffrey Stout for giving of their time and sharing their insights. An early draft of the section on the Buber-Scholem debate in chapter 2 was presented at the interdepartmental Interpretation Seminar at Lehigh University. I am grateful to the members of the seminar, especially Don Campbell, Michael Raposa, and Myra Rosenhaus, who shared their criticisms with me and helped me to unravel some of the problems in my argument. My colleague Norman Girardot helped me to understand the Taoist teachings as they relate to Buber's thought.

I owe a special debt to Michael Raposa. The epitome of colleagueship, he carefully read and patiently criticized two complete drafts of this work. Our frequent conversations did much to make me aware of the changes that were occurring in my interpretative framework during the course of my work on this book. Special thanks are also due to my friend and colleague Michael Fishbane who provided much-needed encouragement during my period of reentry into the academy after a four-year hiatus.

My daughter Rachel compiled and edited the original bibliography. Her efforts greatly facilitated the final preparation of the manuscript. Ms. Shirley Ratushny, my secretary at the Lehigh Valley Center for Jewish Studies, revised and retyped many sections of the book and, in the process, saved me from many errors.

I am fortunate to have had the opportunity to teach Buber's thought to students at the University of Pennsylvania, Swarthmore College, Haverford College, Princeton University, Lafayette College, and Lehigh University. Their enthusiastic response to Buber's thought has served as a continuing source of encouragement.

Philip and Muriel Berman, who established at Lehigh University the chair in Jewish studies that I currently occupy and who founded the Lehigh Valley Center for Jewish Studies, have been a constant source of encouragement during the past four years. It is rare to encounter two people who combine philanthropy, imaginative vision, and respect for the integrity of the academy.

Finally, I am deeply indebted to my wife, Mimi, who has continually supported me in my academic work in spite of the burden that this sometimes imposed on my family. Her constant encouragement during a period of professional uncertainty prevented me from abandoning the work I love the most.

I would also like to express my appreciation to the following publishers and individuals who have graciously granted permission to cite material from Martin Buber's writings:

The Estate of Martin Buber: *A Believing Humanism—My Testament, 1902–1965*, copyright 1967 Maurice Friedman, preface by Ruth Nanda Anshen, copyright 1967 Simon and Schuster; *Daniel—Dialogues on Realization*, copyright 1964 Holt, Rinehart and Winston; *Hasidism and Modern Man*, copyright 1958 Horizon Press; *Israel and the World*, copyright 1963 Schocken Books; *The Knowledge of Man—Selected Essays*, copyright 1965 Martin Buber and Maurice Friedman; *The Legends of the Baal Shem*, copyright 1955 Harper and Row, first Schocken edition, 1969; *Pointing the Way—Collected Essays*, copyright 1957, 1985 Martin Buber.

Rafael Buber: "Zarathustra," "Erziehung zur Gemeinschaft," and "Martin Buber Abende," from the Martin Buber Archives.

The Macmillan Publishing Company and Routledge & Kegan Paul: *Paths in Utopia*, copyright 1949 by Martin Buber, reprinted with permission of Macmillan Publishing Company; *Between Man and Man* (New York: Macmillan, 1947), reprinted with permission of Macmillan Publishing Company.

Oxford University Press: *A Land of Two Peoples: Martin Buber on Jews and Arabs*, copyright 1983 Oxford University Press.

Schocken Books, published by Pantheon Books, a Division of Random House Inc.: *On Judaism*, translated by Eva Jospe, copyright 1967 Schocken Books.

Scribner Book Companies and T. & T. Clark Ltd.: *I and Thou*, translated by Walter Kaufmann, copyright © 1970 Charles Scribner's Sons, reprinted with the permission of Charles Scribner's Sons, an imprint of Macmillan Publishing Co.

Chapter 2 incorporates some sections of my article, "The Buber-Scholem Debate Reconsidered: Modes of Discourse in Modern Judaism," *Soundings*, 71, no. 4, Winter 1988.

Note on
Gender and Language

Identifying with the efforts of feminists to correct the prevailing use of masculine language, I have endeavored to employ gender-free language throughout this work as much as possible, either through the use of the plural or through such terms as *person, human being, one,* and *people.* Whenever I found the usage of singular personal pronouns unavoidable, I have used *he or she* and *him or her.* Insofar as the use of male pronouns only exacerbates sexist images and attitudes that are deeply ingrained in our society, whatever awkwardness the approach generates is, I am persuaded, fully justified.

The titles of Buber's works, many of which include the word *mensch,* present a special problem. *Mensch,* in contrast to *mann,* is a gender-free term best translated as *person* or *human being.* However, insofar as the current English titles of Buber's works translate *mensch* as man *(Between Man and Man; The Way of Man; Hasidism and Modern Man; The Knowledge of Man),* replacing *man* with *person* would only confuse the reader. A similar problem exists in the current translations, which, following the conventional style of the times, translate *mensch* as *man.* Thus, while many quotes from these translations speak of man rather than person or human being, it should be clear that the latter is meant. Accordingly, in my discussion, I have tried to translate the term *mensch* consistently as person or human being. In future translations of Buber's writings these problems should be corrected and the titles changed to *Be-*

tween Person and Person, The Human Way, and *Hasidism and the Modern Person.* This, I am convinced, would be fully consistent with Buber's thought, which is devoted to helping all people—male and female—to actualize their unique potential.

Introduction

The nature and scope of Martin Buber's writings pose a number of problems for one seeking a coherent sense of his intellectual activity. In the current age of academic specialization, Buber's writings elude convenient categorization with regard to both form and content. Ignoring the disciplinary boundaries that characterize university life, Buber's work spans a number of conventional academic disciplines including psychology, philosophy, literature, religion, Jewish studies, art, politics, social theory, education, biblical studies, and philosophical anthropology. In addition, Buber wrote in many literary forms, including poetry, fiction, philosophical discourse, social theory, translation, textual commentary, and criticism.

As a result, many scholars are uncomfortable with Buber's thought. Contemporary philosophers, for example, especially those in the Anglo-American tradition, find his work obscure and ambiguous. As we shall see, Buber was concerned with the analysis of concepts, but his mode of analysis, grounded in existential experience, is far removed from that which prevails in current academic philosophy. And in sociology, a discipline in which Buber held a chair, one rarely finds reference to his works in the literature or on reading lists for sociology courses.[1] Similarly, while a number of practicing psychologists and psychiatrists find Buber's ideas to be fruitful in their own clinical practice, his work is virtually unknown among academic psychologists.[2]

I

If Buber's works have gained a serious place in university courses, it has been in the fields of religious studies and Jewish studies. Yet, in religious studies courses, which frequently use *I and Thou* and other of Buber's "religious" works, Buber's religious thinking is rarely situated within the context of Judaism from which it emerged. Moreover, scant attention is paid to his writings in social theory or philosophical anthropology.

Even works like *I and Thou* defy classification and invite diverse readings.[3] Subtly interweaving an analysis of concepts, existential phenomenology, psychology, social theory, cultural theory, theology, and philosophical anthropology, Buber combines poetry, philosophy, and religious discourse. To contemporary philosophers, the work lacks logical rigor, conceptual clarity, and precision. Theologians, drawn to the third section of the work, may be put off by his explorations of philosophical anthropology and social theory in the first two sections. The social scientist may find its religious tone and poetic style objectionable, while the poet may very well find its style too discursive and the content too philosophical.

It is clear, therefore, that Martin Buber's intellectual corpus eludes easy categorization. Is he to be read as a theologian or a philosopher, a religious teacher or a social theorist, a Jewish thinker or a general theologian? This uncertainty is exacerbated by the diverse frameworks that interpreters have applied to his works. In the anthology of critical essays published in the Library of Living Philosophers and in the discussion of his works in the volume *Philosophical Interrogations*, the diversity and variety of these interpretive frameworks clearly emerges.[4]

Another source of confusion to Buber's readers is the precise relationship between his general philosophical writings and his writings on Judaism. Deeply committed to the Jewish people and its historical heritage, Buber addressed the world from the doorway of his ancestral home. At the same time, his orientation to Judaism was rooted in a universalistic humanism. While his writings on Judaism provide little of the conceptual analysis found in his philosophical works, his philosophical writings are virtually devoid of references to Judaism. *I and Thou*, for example, makes reference to the Buddha and Jesus, yet makes no mention of Judaism or any figure from Jewish religious history.

As a result, whereas the general reader may find much of his writing too particularistic, his Jewish readers may fail to see the relevance of his general philosophical works. For example, students often see no connection between Buber's seminal work *I and Thou* and his writings on Judaism. Frequently, his Jewish readers ask, What is Jewish about Buber's philosophy? or, What makes him a Jewish thinker?

It is no wonder, therefore, that the question of Buber's place as a Jewish thinker is a particular source of controversy. Many have commented on the problematic nature of Buber's relationship to the Jewish community and his place within the history of Jewish thought. Long after achieving international renown as a representative Jewish philosopher, his place as a Jewish thinker was, particularly in Israel, still called into question. Ironically, until recently, Buber enjoyed a much wider and more sympathetic hearing among Christian theologians than among students of Jewish thought. While Christians regard Buber as one of the major representatives of modern Jewish thought, his name is missing from two basic studies of it.[5]

This appears all the more strange when we recognize that, during the first two decades of his literary career, Buber devoted the overwhelming bulk of his writings to Jewish issues. Long before he wrote *I and Thou*, his writings on Hasidism and his famous *Lectures on Judaism (Reden über das Judentum)* had earned him a reputation among western European Jewish intellectuals as a major Jewish thinker. Moreover, throughout his life, Buber wrote prodigiously and spoke out publicly on issues relating to Judaism and Jewish nationhood.

How, then, are we to understand the fact that Buber is frequently viewed as a "rejected prophet" among his own people? In Israel, where he settled in 1938, Buber's place in the social, religious, and cultural life of the country was marginal.[6] Apart from a small group of intellectuals of German origin, his university students, and a limited circle of kibbutz members, few Israelis are familiar with his teachings.[7] Although he played an active role in the rise and development of Zionism, Zionist leaders considered him to be, at best, a naive idealist removed from the realities of Israeli life.

Israeli religious traditionalists, offended by his abandonment of traditional Jewish religious practices, branded him a heretic. At the same time, secular Israelis were put off by the religious tone of his teachings and were frequently angered and offended by his controversial, outspoken position on Jewish-Arab relations.

Among the American Jewish community, Buber also holds an ambiguous place. Highly regarded by many American Jewish intellectuals, Buber was an anomaly owing to his unique interpretation of Judaism. Synagogue-oriented Jews, deeply rooted in organized liturgy and in the celebration of the traditional religious festivals, find little relevance in Buber's existential approach. Secular American Jews whose Jewish commitment is expressed primarily through organizational activities find Buber's highly personal religious interpretation of Judaism unhelpful.

Buber has had a serious influence on non-Orthodox Jewish religious thinkers in the United States.[8] Nevertheless, Conservative rabbis generally find Buber's antihalakhic Judaism unacceptable. Reform rabbis, while finding his religious writings inspirational, often have difficulty applying his anti-institutionalism to the synagogue or reconciling his existentialism with the Reform movement's traditionally rationalistic outlook.

Thus, in his introduction to a symposium on Jewish belief published in 1966, Milton Himmelfarb observed: "What has been Buber's influence on Jewish thought in America? From the evidence of these statements, hardly any. This is strange and needs explaining." Himmelfarb further noted that, in contrast to Franz Rosenzweig, whose influence on non-Orthodox Jewish theology is widespread, "It is Buber, who died full of years, and honored in Christian theology, whose influence on Jews is relatively slight. Some Jews read his books on Hasidism, more flocked to his lectures, and a few respected his work for rapprochement between Arabs and Jews. That is about all."[9]

Buber's standing as an interpreter of Hasidism, the Jewish movement of spiritual renewal that arose in eastern Europe in the eighteenth century, is also a subject of controversy. The author of numerous translations and interpretive essays, Buber has become widely known as one of the West's foremost interpreters of Hasidism. His Hasidic writings continue to enjoy a wide audience, and, in the minds of many readers, have supplanted the original Hasidic versions. In spite of this, the Jewish scholarly establishment has strongly criticized his interpretations. Led by Gershom Scholem, the foremost scholar in the fields of Jewish mysticism and the history of Jewish religion, scholars in Jewish studies have accused Buber of distorting the teachings of Hasidism to conform to his own personal religious and philosophical views.[10]

This work provides a framework in which to explore the ambivalent responses toward Buber and to elucidate the overall nature of his intellectual enterprise. I have thus focused on dimensions of Buber's thought long neglected in existing studies. First, in an attempt to answer the question of what fundamental problems occupied Buber throughout his life, I focus on the theme of alienation. Second, by applying selected categories from the fields of postfoundational philosophy and contemporary literary theory, I illuminate dimensions of Buber's thought previously ignored.

Alienation and the Crisis of Modernity

One of the important and neglected dimensions of Buber's thought is his concern with alienation. Yet, alienation is the underlying problem that links together Buber's diverse intellectual activities. Informing all of his writings is the concern for the growing estrangement of the modern person from other persons, from the divine, and from his or her own authentic self. At the same time, the concern with alienation, bridging his social and religious concerns, as well as his universal and his particular Jewish concerns, also helps to explain the diverse modes of discourse he employed.

Most studies tend to concentrate on Buber as the philosopher of dialogue.[11] While technically not incorrect, this emphasis, focusing on the irenic, consoling dimension of his thought, pays scant attention to the critical, deconstructive themes in his writings. Yet, Buber's concern for dialogue grows out of his profound awareness of the abysses that permeate human life. The crisis of human existence is a theme that recurs throughout his works.

From the beginning of his literary career, Buber portrayed the modern person as cut off from those humanizing forces necessary to his or her actualization as an independent self. This sense of the sickness of our age, evident in his earliest writings, continued to pervade his later thought. His writings on Judaism, art, society, education, and religion are all permeated by a sense of estrangement and alienation.

As Buber viewed modern life, a natural wholeness had been broken, a natural unity fragmented, and natural relations impaired. Unlike the academic philosopher or scholar whose concern is to contribute to an existing scholarly tradition, Buber, eschewing systematic thought, wrote in response to the fundamental social and cultural problems of his age. Buber sought to expose and criticize those conditions that suppress the innate drive of persons to actualize their authentic selves. Like other critics of alienation, he viewed the modern world as one in which "man is dehumanized by being conditioned to see himself, his products, his activities and other men in economic, political, religious and other categories—in terms which deny their human possibilities."[12]

In his effort to unmask the alienating conditions of modern life, Buber formulated a unique set of categories and concepts through which to illuminate the existential realities of the human condition. Like Rousseau, Nietzsche, and Marx before him, Buber believed that the human being possesses inherent tendencies and capacities whose nurturance is necessary to growth and creativity. For Buber, however, that capacity was located neither within the individual nor within the social group. Instead, walking the narrow ridge between existential philosophy's focus on the individual and the communal focus of contemporary social thought, he developed a relational view of human existence that revolved around the concept of the *Zwischenmenschliche* (the interhuman). This concept, first formulated by Buber in 1906 and subsequently elaborated through such concepts as I-Thou and dialogue, synthesized insights culled from such diverse sources as European existentialism, Christian and Jewish mysticism, Chinese thought, and German social theory.

Alienation thus serves as a useful category around which to organize and integrate Buber's diverse writings and social activities. Whether editing and interpreting Hasidic stories, translating the Bible, interpreting Judaism, writing about religion, inquiring into the nature of community, or reflecting on issues of philosophical anthropology, his primary concern was to arouse the consciousness of his audience to the alienating conditions of life and to indicate ways to combat these conditions.

Alienation also provides an illuminating category through which to view Buber's personal life. At an early age, when children first develop their sense of identity and trust in the world, Buber abruptly lost the support of both parents and his earliest writings express his profound yearning to overcome the isolation of human beings from one another. Moreover, both as a Jew and as a European, Buber experienced the sense of alienation that, in Charles Taylor's formulation, "arises when the goals, norms or ends which define the common practices or institutions begin to seem irrelevant or even monstrous, or when the norms are redefined so that the practices appear a travesty of them."[13] Finding that neither official Viennese society nor Jewish society provided the humanizing context he so eagerly sought, he grew estranged from both. Searching for an alternative form of life, he undertook a far-reaching revision of the basic assumptions of both European and Jewish thought and rendered a significant contribution to our understanding of the social and cultural forms of alienation.

Positing alienation as one of Buber's overriding concerns enables us to illuminate dimensions of Buber's thought previously neglected while rendering his intellectual career intelligible in a way fully consistent with his writings and his social commitments. Nevertheless, in using alienation as an organizing concept, I am in no way suggesting that Buber consciously addressed this crisis at all times. Not only are there multiple, frequently conflicting factors that come into play when a writer sits down to write, but at different points in his or her career as a writer, different concerns and perceptions come into play. Moreover, insofar as readers' interpretations of a writer's work are, to a significant degree, the product of their own encounter with a text, the concept of intentionality is highly problematic.[14]

It would be also misleading to suggest that the theme of alienation was explicitly addressed in his earliest writings, which, strongly influenced by Nietzsche, fin de siècle neoromanticism, *Lebensphilosophie*, and mysticism, are couched in the discourse of aesthetics, religion, and individual psychology. Only in the period following the First World War did Buber succeed in clarifying the social focus of his thinking and formulating the categories through which to articulate this move. With the publication of *I and Thou* in 1923, the theme of alienation, already latent in his earliest works, became explicit.

Buber as Social Thinker and Social Critic

The emphasis on alienation directs our attention to Buber's social thought, a subject conspicuously neglected in most existing studies.[15] American interpreters of Buber, such as Friedman, Herberg, Kaufmann, and Diamond, have tended to focus on Buber the existentialist. As they correctly point out, the nineteenth-century existentialists provide the backdrop for Buber's vision of the world. With his existentialist precursors, Nietzsche and Kierkegaard, Buber shared an underlying sense of alienation and loneliness, "a sense of the basic fragility of human life; the impotence of reason confronted with the depths of existence; the threat of Nothingness, and the solitary and unsheltered condition of the individual before this threat."[16]

However, Buber was also indebted to such German social thinkers as Tonnies, Simmel, and, in his later life, Weber.[17] From his earliest days, one finds an abiding concern for the social forms of alienation. Along with his existential concerns, Buber was a social thinker deeply concerned with the structures within which people relate to one another.

A basic theme in Buber's writings is the critical need for a renewal of authentic communal forms. Like Tonnies and Simmel, he decried the dissolution of organic communal forms that accompanied the spread of industrialization. In an effort to unmask the social forms of alienation, Buber formulated categories that provide an alternative way of understanding and coping with the crisis of modern social life. Through such concepts as relation, dialogue, and the interhuman *(das Zwischenmenschliche)*, he sought to move beyond the impasse created by psychologists and sociologists, and to formulate a conception of community appropriate to his understanding of the person as a relational being.

Buber viewed social thought pragmatically. Like Marx, he was concerned not simply to understand society, but also to change it. Viewing social thought as a critical enterprise, Buber used the concepts of relation and dialogue as the basis for his critique of modern society. In *Paths in Utopia* and other works, he formulated a vision of utopian socialism as an alternative to the prevailing forms of Western society. Integrating his socialist vision with his dialogical philosophy, he espoused a theory of social revolution based upon education as a distinct alternative to the Marxist conception of political revolution. His unique interpretation of social alienation addressed aspects of social reality neglected by Marx and other social critics.

Buber's activities as a social critic are most clearly evident in the last three decades of his life. Following his immigration to Palestine in 1938, he was an active participant in public debates concerning the fundamental social and political issues within the Jewish community. Repeatedly, he challenged the leaders, first of the Zionist movement, then of the new state of Israel. While Buber addressed himself to a variety of social and political issues, it was the Arab-Jewish conflict that served as the fundamental test of the truth of his philosophical and religious thought.

Buber's stand on social and political issues, grounded in his philosophy, isolated him from the mainstream of Israeli society and evoked sharp criticism and antagonism. With a small group of colleagues and disciples, he raised painful questions that subjected the basic assumptions of Zionism to a rigorous critique. Thus at a time when non-Jews regarded him as one of the powerful moral voices of his time, many of his own people viewed him with anger and disdain.

Buber as Edifying Philosopher

Philosophy constituted the core around which Buber's other intellectual activities were built: "I am not merely bound to philosophical language, I am bound to the philosophical method, indeed to a dialectic that has become unavoidable with the beginning of philosophical thinking" (*PMB*, 90).

At the outset of his career, Buber eschewed philosophical discourse, preferring literary modes such as essay, translation, and interpretation of traditional religious texts. However, he soon found that philosophizing was essential to his task:

Since I have matured to a life from my own experience—a process that began shortly before the "First World War" and was completed shortly after it—I have stood under the duty to insert the framework of the decisive experiences that I had at that time into the human inheritance of thought, but not as "my" experiences, rather as an insight valid and important for others and even for other kinds of men. . . . My communication had to be a philosophical one. It had to relate the unique and particular to the 'general', to what is discoverable by every man in his own existence. It had to express what is by its nature incomprehensible in concepts that could be used and communicated (even if at times with difficulties). (*PMB*, 689)

In contrast to mainstream or "normal philosophers" primarily interested in formulating a philosophical system that yields an accurate picture of reality, Buber, in the language of Richard Rorty, was an "edifying philosopher" who endeavored to uncover and diagnose the alienating conditions of modern society.[18] Like other edifying philosophers, Buber considered philosophy to be a liberating activity, the purpose of which is "to edify, to help their readers break free from outworn vocabularies and attitudes, rather than provide 'grounding' for the intuitions and customs of the present."[19]

By providing readers and listeners with new, creative ways of thinking, speaking, and living, the edifying philosopher, as described by Rorty, seeks to free them from the shackles of outmoded thinking and living. The ultimate purpose of this activity, however, is not simply to change our way of thinking, but, in Rorty's words, "to take us out of our old selves, by the power of strangeness, to aid us in becoming new beings."[20] Such an enterprise entails unmasking and deconstructing the prevailing thought systems. Like his precursors Nietzsche and Kierkegaard, Buber believed that the conventional ways of thinking and speaking engendered and intensified alienation. Accordingly, Buber formulated categories to help free his readers and listeners from the illusions that impede free choice, decision, and the actualization of the authentic self.

Philosophizing for Buber meant, first and foremost, the critique of language. The task of the philosopher, as he understood it, is to evaluate and criticize prevalent concepts, testing them against personal experiences, and then revising and refining them. For Buber, the basis of this critique is not reason, logic, social usage, or sense experience but the total existential experience of the individual in interaction with the world.

Buber doubted language's ability to capture the deepest levels of human experience adequately. In his view, there is an inherent gap between our concepts and categories and the basic human experiences they are meant to express. He was thus skeptical of language's capacity to reflect reality, sharing this view with medieval mystics, Taoists, Nietzsche, and contemporaries such as Hugo Von Hofmannsthal, Fritz Mauthner, and Gustav Landauer.

But Buber was not content simply to clarify concepts. In the spirit of Nietzsche and Kierkegaard, he criticized modes of life and thought conventionally viewed as normal and sought to awaken his readers to alternative, humanizing ones. The categories he employed in this effort grew out of his continuing struggle to uncover, elucidate, and define the fundamental crisis in the life of the modern person. Using such binary categories as religiosity/religion, I-You/I-It, relation/experience, dialogue/monologue, education/propaganda, he challenged the privileging of the second of these pairs. Thus, Buber engaged in a deconstructive activity which, "by disrupting the hierarchical relations on which critical concepts and methods depend, prevents concepts and methods from being taken for granted and treated as simply reliable instruments."[21] Whether discussing religion, community, education, Judaism, or philosophical anthropology, Buber endeavored to revise the prevailing way of thinking.[22]

For Buber, as for other edifying philosophers, philosophical activity is analogous to participating in a conversation: "I have no teaching, but I carry on a conversation" (PMB, 693).[23] For him, philosophy was not a precise science that uncovers the ultimate foundations of reality and establishes universal criteria of truth. The philosopher's task is not to transmit fixed truths but to free people from illusions and help them see more clearly the truth of their experience. Thus, philosophy is evaluated not by its capacity to mirror objective reality accurately but by its power to illuminate and direct our lives.

Ultimately, Buber considered his subject matter to be the "dynamics of lived life" (*PMB*, 691), that is, the lived reality of human existence in its totality and wholeness. To him, the specialized vocabulary of established academic disciplines only served to diminish the reality he was seeking to communicate. Although frequently labeled a theologian or religious thinker, Buber believed that such categorization distorted the actual character of his thought. Although his understanding of life was grounded in a personal religious faith, he denied any unique knowledge of the divine. As he saw it, he was "absolutely not capable nor even disposed to teach this or that about God" (*PMB*, 690). At the same time, in sharp contrast to Nietzsche, Buber considered the encounter with the divine to be a basic positive force in human existence. Accordingly, he was willing to accept the label of religious thinker so long as it was understood that religion is "a reality, rather the reality, namely, the whole existence of the real man in the real world of God, and existence that unites all that is partial" (*PMB*, 742).

In the final analysis, Buber's concerns were metaphilosophical. His ultimate goal was not simply to change the way that people think but to alter the way that they live their lives. Through conversation and dialogue, myths and legends, he endeavored to help his readers and listeners understand and clarify their own relationship to themselves, to the world around them, to other persons, and to the divine.

Like Kierkegaard and Nietzsche, Buber resisted all efforts to systematize his thought: "I build no towers, I erect bridges; but their columns are not sunk in 'isms' and their arches are not fitted together by means of 'isms'."[24] Like the artist and the poet, his primary concern was to help others see that which he had seen:

I must say it once again; I have no teaching. I only point to something. I point to reality. I point to something in reality that had not or had too little been seen. I take him who listens to me by the hand and lead him to the window. I open the window and point to what is outside. (*PMB*, 693)

Buber was convinced that the experience to which he bore witness, the reality to which he pointed, was shared by other people. Rather than presenting something new to his readers, his task was to awaken them to something that was already a part of their experience: "I say to him who listens to me: it is your experience.

Recollect it, and what you cannot recollect, dare to attain it as experience" (*PMB*, 693).

Primarily as a result of the breakdown of organic forms of community and the growing domination of technology, the modern person, according to Buber, has lost touch with the fundamental levels of life experiences. Consequently, many of his readers would find what he had to say incomprehensible. To restore the link between the individual and the deepest levels of existence, he considered it necessary to unmask the impediments that hamper people's capacity to see and to understand.

Buber and the Revisioning of Judaism

Although many of Buber's writings were addressed to universal problems of human society and culture, the historical experiences of the Jewish people and the teachings of the Bible and Hasidism provided the particular perspective from which he addressed these problems. The edifying impulse and the concern with alienation evident in his general philosophical works also informed his Jewish writings. Although deeply committed to the Jewish people, he found, like many of his Jewish contemporaries, that traditional Jewish categories and forms of life no longer provided the means for ordering his life in a meaningful way. His concern, therefore, was to reveal the inadequacies of these categories and replace them with new ones.

Harold Bloom's concept of revisionism provides a helpful tool for understanding Buber's activity as an interpreter of Judaism. Buber, in Bloom's terms, approached Judaism as a "revisionist" who sought to transform the framework of discourse within which the Jewish conversation was being carried out.[25] Rejecting traditionalism, reform, and assimilation alike, Buber endeavored to develop new categories with which to talk about Judaism. While identifying, at an early age, with the Zionist movement, he soon took issue with the movement's official ideology and formulated revised interpretations of such fundamental concepts as Zion, exile, and redemption.

Bloom's categories of strong reader and creative misreading provide an important perspective from which to understand Buber's controversial role as an interpreter of Hasidism, the eighteenth-century Jewish spiritual movement.[26] As mentioned earlier, Buber's interpretations of Hasidism were severely criticized by Jewish scholars. However, the debate over Buber's Hasidic writings was based upon a limited understanding of the processes of reading and interpreting. Contemporary literary theory's new appreciation for the multiplicity of discourse and the diverse modes of reading, opens the way to a renewed appreciation of Buber as an interpreter of Hasidism in particular, and Judaism as a whole.

Another of Bloom's concepts, that of the anxiety of influence, opens the way to a new understanding of the complex relationship between Buber and Nietzsche. Virtually all interpretations of Buber tend to minimize the Nietzschean influence, limiting it to an early stage of his life. These interpretations are based largely on Buber's stated rejection of Nietzsche's teachings. Such a reading, however, presupposes a theory of influence that Bloom has called "benign influence." According to this theory, prevalent in the history of ideas, a thinker adopts the ideas of a previous thinker, uses those that are valuable, and discards the rest. In Bloom's view, such a conception of influence ignores the agonistic nature of creative thought, which thinkers such as Nietzsche and Freud have uncovered,[27] and which is supported by Buber's own description of his relationship to Nietzsche.

The Structure of the Book

The cultural context for Buber's works and the early expressions of the theme of alienation are discussed in chapter 1. There, I situate Buber within the context of the issues and problems addressed by nineteenth-century existential thought and German social theory. In addition, I argue that the intense impact of Nietzsche's thought on the young Buber had a lasting influence different from that suggested by the standard interpretations. Juxtaposing Buber's own description of this relationship with Bloom's suggestive ideas, I posit the struggle with Nietzsche as a decisive factor that shaped Buber's subsequent thought long after he had consciously repudiated Nietzsche.

In the second chapter, I explore Buber's distinctive but controversial interpretation of Hasidism. Viewing the debate between Buber and Gershom Scholem in the light of contemporary literary theory, I show how the conventional scholarly reading of Buber's Hasidic works imposes upon him a framework of discourse that he, himself, rejected.

Moving from Buber's interpretation of Hasidism to his interpretation of Judaism in general, in chapter 3 I describe the premises on which Buber's unique approach to Judaism is based. Like his writings on Hasidism, Buber's writings on Judaism as a whole reflect his struggle against the modern Jew's alienation from Jewish tradition. Employing Bloom's category of revisionism, I argue that those who claim that Buber is not really a Jewish thinker or that his writings do not present an authentic Judaism have a narrow view of tradition. Imposing criteria that are foreign to Buber's own approach, his Jewish critics overlook that which is most powerful in Buber's writings on Judaism.

Buber's activity as an edifying philosopher is discussed in chapter 4. In contrast to those who wish to situate Buber's thought in the context of the history of systematic philosophy, I argue that Buber's philosophical writings are best understood in light of his edifying concerns, especially his effort to provide a conceptual framework for the critique of modern society. First set forth in *I and Thou*, this conceptual framework established the basic premises for all of his later writings, both Jewish and general.

Chapter 5 is devoted to a discussion of the ways in which Buber refined the basic categories of his philosophy of relation/dialogue in the decades following *I and Thou*, a process overlooked by most critics. Chapter 6 discusses Buber's social philosophy, which, in my view, comprises the core of his later thought. There I examine Buber's distinctive contribution to our understanding of alienation, previously neglected by his interpreters. Analyzing his interpretation of community, I show how it differs from that of his social-theory mentors.

Chapter 7 analyzes Buber's mature interpretation of religion and religious faith, which is shaped by his dialogical philosophy. Consistent with his edifying concerns, Buber wanted to liberate people from the conventional, alienating notion of religion and provide an alternative interpretation. His mature interpretation of Judaism, which is also rooted in his philosophy of dialogue and his social thought, is discussed in chapter 8. Buber evaluated his teachings in terms of their capacity to engender practical activities aimed at repairing basic injustices. In his own life, he applied this test through his activities as a social critic in Israel. As I show in chapter 8, the Arab-Jewish conflict was, for Buber, the ultimate testing ground of these teachings.

Buber's writings address issues of current critical importance. His focus on alienation touches upon basic problems that continue to plague Western society. While Buber's grasp of the factors contributing to our alienated condition was somewhat limited, he illuminated dimensions of the human situation still neglected by philosophers and social thinkers alike. Also, the growing emphasis by contemporary philosophers on dialogue and community makes Buber's contribution to these issues particularly significant.[28] While these writers rarely, if ever, cite Buber, his analysis of dialogue and community provides a corrective to the overly rational conception that is found in the writings of Rorty, Bernstein, Gadamer, and Habermas.

Buber's philosophical anthropology emphasizes dimensions of human existence that are increasingly attracting the attention of feminist psychologists and philosophers. In significant and suggestive ways, his concepts of relation and dialogue and his critique of power relations adumbrate the discussions of such writers as Carol Gilligan, Jean Baker Miller, and Marilyn French.[29]

Within the Jewish community, Buber still has not received an adequate hearing. Yet his revisionist approach to Judaism, when fully understood, comprises a significant alternative within the contemporary Jewish conversation. In addition, more than any other Jewish thinker, Buber has synthesized particularly Jewish concerns with the general concerns of humanity. No other Jewish thinker contributes as much to our understanding of the human condition and the realm of interhuman relations.

Buber's critical perspectives on Zionism, Hasidism, and Judaism provide stimulating and provocative alternatives to the conventional ways of thinking. At the very least, Buber forces one to recognize that all "isms" are linked to specific attitudes toward power. At this critical juncture in the life of the Jewish people and the state of Israel, Buber's critical perspective on Jewish-Arab relations and on the meaning and purpose of the Jewish state poses fundamental challenges that penetrate to the core of Jewish life and self-understanding.

I

Fin de Siècle Vienna: Cultural Context and Early Writings

Buber and the Crisis of Alienation

While the term *alienation* has held different meanings in the history of Western thought, it is generally used to describe a condition or experience in which a natural unity, wholeness, or relation in human life has been disrupted.[1]

The "facts" to which the term alienation refers are, objectively, different kinds of dissociation, break or rupture between human beings and their objects, whether the latter be other persons, or the natural world, or their own creations in art, science and society.[2]

The concept of alienation serves as a fruitful and illuminating category around which to organize and integrate Martin Buber's various writings and social activities. A careful reading of Buber reveals his ongoing concern for the meaningless, fragmented quality of life in the modern world. His books and lectures reflect his concern for the modern person's estrangement from nature, from other persons, from God, and from his or her own essential being. In his writings, one feels a profound sense of the loneliness, isolation, and meaninglessness of modern life. Throughout his life, Buber endeavored to educate his audience to the alienating conditions of modern life and to point them to the path of liberation from these conditions.[3] A vision of abysses permeates Buber's thought and is a common theme in both his Jewish and his general writings.

Buber's critique of the alienating conditions of modern life is best understood when read within the context of nineteenth-century existential philosophy and nineteenth- and twentieth-century social thought. Like his existentialist precursors, Kierkegaard and Nietzsche, Buber was deeply troubled by the dehumanizing effects of modern society. In *I and Thou* and subsequent writings, he sought to counter the reductionistic, functionalizing trends in modern life and restore the individual to his rightful place as a unique being.

Although these existentialists focused on the personal alienation of the individual, Buber, in the tradition of German sociology, was also troubled by the social forms of alienation resulting from the erosion of communal bonds and the fragmentation of social relations. Like the German social thinkers, he viewed the dominant social structures as conditioning the individual "to see his products, his activities and other men in economic, political, religious and other categories in terms which deny their human possibilities."[4] Deeply committed to the renewal of community and the facilitation of direct, confirming relations between people, Buber, like many of his contemporaries, believed that the forms and structures of modern Western society frustrated and impeded such relations.

In his writings on Judaism, Buber addressed the modern Jew's alienation from the traditions and forms inherited from the past. His discussions of the Bible, Hasidism, Jewish history, and Zionism reflect a profound concern for the modern Jew's estrangement from the spiritual power of authentic Judaism and reflect his search for an alternative, nonalienated form of Jewish life. In his youth, Buber became personally estranged from the values, norms, and ends that defined the common practices and institutions of traditional Jewish society. Although raised in a traditional Jewish environment, he, like many young Jews, found that institutionalized Judaism failed to instill in him a sense of the spiritual power of Jewish tradition or provide the framework for the communal life he so desperately sought.[5] Unable to find meaning in the forms and symbols of the

official Jewish community, he longed for a life that combined rootedness in an organic community and deep spirituality.

Fin de Siècle Vienna

Like many young intellectuals growing to adulthood in fin de siècle
Vienna, Buber found that the rational, liberal worldview in which
he had been socialized no longer served to order the sociocultural
reality around him meaningfully. Reason, which the older generation viewed as the key to all social and political problems, was, to
his generation, a harsh, divisive force that disrupted the unity and
wholeness of human existence. In addition, for many young intellectuals and artists, the culture based upon the liberal, rational
values of the nineteenth century lacked cohesion and direction. To
them, it appeared that all sense of firmness was gone, replaced by a
feeling of constant slippage and movement.[6]

Yearning for direct, emotional experiences, young artists and
intellectuals rebelled against the values bequeathed by their parents' generation:

The new culture-makers in the city of Freud thus repeatedly defined themselves in terms of a kind of collective oedipal revolt. Yet the young were
revolting not so much against their fathers as against the authority of the
paternal culture that was their inheritance. What they assaulted on a
broad front was the value system of classical liberalism in-ascendancy
within which they had been reared.[7]

Hungry for instinctual expression and satisfaction, a generation
of writers and artists, including Arthur Schnitzler, Hugo Von Hofmannsthal, and Stefan Zweig, rebelled against the rational ethos of
liberal society. The cultural movement known as Jung Wien, the
subject of Buber's earliest published essay, yearned for wholeness
and unity and eagerly sought to recover the primal forces of life
suppressed by the analytic spirit of Western rationalism.[8]

Two responses to the disillusionment with nineteenth-century
liberal life and rational thought were of particular significance for
Buber. In the cultural realm, the suspicion of rational forms led to
a growing skepticism regarding language. Writers and poets like

Hugo Von Hofmannsthal and Karl Kraus questioned the capacity of language to embrace the wholeness of human experience adequately:[9]

Images and concepts only lead back to themselves. They do not open any way to the nature of things and to individual life. They are a roundelay, similar to a circle in which everything is in tune, everything is in a state of harmony of beauty, but they are "eyeless statues" which surround him, forms without any genuine relation to existence.[10]

This skeptical view of language, common among circles of young Viennese intellectuals at the turn of the century, exacerbated their sense of isolation. Without language to provide an accurate reflection of reality, the gap separating the individual from the world appeared greater than ever. At the same time, this skeptical view of language undermined trust in the efficacy of communication, thereby widening the distance between one person and another.

The language skepticism of the Viennese intellectuals was shared by non-Viennese writers, such as Rilke, Kafka, and Musil. While Rilke and Kafka "formulated the problem of existence in terms of the limits of language and the encapsulation of the self," Musil shared a "pre-war concern with the incapability of language to explain men's innermost being to others."[11]

This skeptical attitude toward language was philosophically formulated by Fritz Mauthner, who had a profound influence on Buber's close friend and mentor, Gustav Landauer, and whose views are reflected in Buber's thought.[12] To Mauthner, philosophy was a theory of knowledge based upon a critique of language *(Sprachkritik)*:

Philosophy is theory of knowledge. Theory of knowledge is critique of language *(Sprachkritik)*. Critique of language, however, is labor on behalf of the liberating thought that men can never succeed in getting beyond a metaphorical description of the world utilizing either everyday language or philosophical language.[13]

The reaction against the modern, technologically ordered society was also expressed in the yearning for premodern, organic forms of community. Increasingly despairing of the social order, people turned to the artist and the architect in search of desperately sought truths. The quest for the irrational was expressed in poetry, art, literature, and science, while the newly emerging field of psychoanalysis was laying the foundations for a radical upheaval in Western thought.

Alongside the cultural response, the fin de siècle's felt need for values rooted in "an archaic, communitarian tradition"[14] evoked a powerful political response among many young European Jews, Buber included. To the chagrin of Jewish and non-Jewish liberals, a Viennese journalist, Theodor Herzl, declared that the hope for the successful integration of Jews into European society was futile. Herzl, whose teachings were to have a profound impact on Buber, proclaimed the failure of liberalism's program of emancipation and social integration of Jews and called for an independent Jewish homeland.[15]

Whatever little faith Buber and his contemporaries retained in the rational beliefs and liberal values inherited from the nineteenth century was destroyed by the trauma of World War I. Throughout Europe, men and women experienced the shattering of a dream. All hopes that individuals could rationally control either their impulses or their technological instruments seemed to disappear with the outbreak of the war:

August, 1914, shattered the foundations of that human world. It revealed that the apparent stability, security and material progress of society had rested, like everything human, upon the void. European man came face to face with himself as a stranger. When he ceased to be contained and sheltered within a stable social and political environment he saw that his rational and enlightened philosophy could no longer console him with the assurance that it satisfactorily answered the question What is Man?[16]

Alienation in Buber's Personal Life

The events of Buber's personal life, as described in his autobiographical recollections, contributed to his profound sense of alienation. Speaking shortly before his death of "moments that have exercised a decisive influence on the nature and direction of my thinking," (Schilpp and Friedman, *Philosophy of Martin Buber*, 3, hereafter referred to as *PMB*), Buber recalled an event that occurred in his fourth year. The memory, which remained vivid throughout his life, was of his forced separation from his mother following the divorce of his parents.

I still hear how the big girl said to me, "No, she will never come back." I know that I remained silent, but also that I cherished no doubt of the truth of the spoken words. It remained fixed in me: from year to year it cleaved even more to my heart. (*PMB*, 3–4)

The loneliness, anxiety, and sense of estrangement that are reflected in this passage appear to have shaped Buber's overall view of life. In his mind, the separation and estrangement he had personally experienced were characteristic of the lives of all people. Particularly in his later philosophy, this trauma of separation became a paradigm for the human condition:

But after more than ten years, I had begun to perceive it as something that concerned not only me, but all men. Later, I once made up the word "Vergegnung"—"mismeeting," or "miscounter"—to designate the failure of a real meeting between men. . . . I suspect that all that I have learned about genuine meeting in the course of my life had its origins in that hour on the balcony. (*PMB*, 4)

As Erikson has argued, the failure of a child to establish a trusting attitude toward the world can play a decisive role in shaping his or her subsequent psychic development. This trusting attitude is largely dependent on the nurturing love of parents in the early years.[17] Buber's mother, absent from his life during his entire childhood, played no part in his upbringing following the breakup of the marriage. Moreover, Buber saw his father only occasionally before going to live with him at the age of fourteen.[18] Although I am not suggesting that Buber's philosophy was solely the result of this traumatic moment in his life, the divorce of his parents obviously shattered the framework from which the young Buber derived his basic sense of trust and security.

Even in the last years of his life, Buber still recalled the decisive transforming impact of his parents' divorce. The childhood separation from his mother epitomized for him the fragility and precariousness of all human relations. Using Buber's own terminology, it served as a formative, memory-shaping event, a basic mythic moment in his life.[19] However, in describing the event as the source of his knowledge of genuine meeting, Buber appears to have repressed the negative traces of the experience. As his own words indicate, the event symbolized not meeting but "mismeeting," "miscounter," and "the failure of a real meeting between men." The formative, memory-shaping moment of childhood separation served as a paradigm of the mismeetings between people, the abysses that separate them from one another.

Buber's grandparents, acting as surrogate parents, did succeed in infusing his early life with stability and security, and his relationship to them was one of warmth, love, and mutual respect. Nevertheless, although the relationship to his grandparents appears to have mitigated the sense of absence brought about by the divorce of his parents, the longing for direct, need-free, loving, confirming relationships nonetheless permeates all of his writings and appears to be traceable in part to this tragedy in his life.

The stability of his grandparent's home, in which love of Western culture was combined with a reverence for the study of Torah, provided a viable framework of meaning for the young boy. His grandmother's humane urbanity and his grandfather's deep commitment to Jewish learning made a lasting impression upon him and had a formative effect upon his own life choices.[20] However, as a young adolescent, Buber came to feel estranged from the forms and structures of the traditional Judaism in which he had been raised. His grandfather's model notwithstanding, this alienation, which manifested itself shortly after the occasion of his becoming a bar mitzvah, culminated in a general alienation from Judaism and from religious faith in general.

So long as I lived with him, my roots were firm, although many questions and doubts also jogged about in me. Soon after I left his house, the whirl of the age took me in. Until my twentieth year, and in no small measure even beyond then, my spirit was in steady and multiple movement, in an alternation of tension and release, determined by manifold influences, taking ever new shape, both without center and without growing substance; it was really the "Olam HaTohu," the "world of confusion," the mythical dwelling place of the wandering souls. Here I lived, in virtual fullness of spirit, but without Judaism, without humanity, and without the presence of the divine. (HMM, 51–52)

Beset by turmoil and confusion, Buber grew increasingly alienated from the very forms of life and teachings that had once infused his life with order and meaning. While he subsequently renewed his relationship to the divine, alienation from the forms and structures of traditional Judaism remained a permanent part of his life. While, from the 1920s on, his early antagonism to the rabbinic tradition was somewhat muted, he continued to view traditional forms and structures as antithetical to authentic Judaism.[21]

Nietzsche as Precursor

Like many other young fin de siècle European intellectuals, Buber found Nietzsche to be the one writer who most effectively captured the spirit of the age. Nietzsche poignantly articulated the sense of alienation from the inherited social forms and cultural patterns that permeated the intellectual elite of fin de siècle Vienna. His works offered a dynamic, vital, creative critique of European culture, a sense of ending combined with a call for a new beginning; a sentence of death of old values and ideals combined with the proclamation of a new morality.[22]

Proclaiming the death of God, Nietzsche announced the demise of Christian values on the one hand and of the ideals of European liberalism on the other. The limits imposed by belief in a providential, moral God had been shattered once and for all. No longer could one find meaning or solace in the traditional religions or secular ideological and philosophical systems. Cut adrift from traditional sources of meaning and comfort, one could only turn inward in a desperate search to overcome isolation and alienation.

Unable to bear the sense of isolation and loneliness that such a vision entailed, according to Nietzsche, the modern individual seeks refuge and comfort in all kinds of intellectual and ideological systems. However, these systems only exacerbate our alienated existence. Only by confronting the truth of our situation can we reach the authentic sources of our own being and recover our authentic selves.

Refusing to replace the fallen faith of Christianity with modern, secular surrogates, Nietzsche applied his surgical skills to all systems of human thought and meaning, including science, philosophy, and historical inquiry. Even language, the staple of human culture that had once promised direct access to truth and reality, was, to Nietzsche, a system of elusive metaphors.

What, then, is truth? A mobile army of metaphors, metonyms, and anthropomorphisms—in short, a sum of human relations, which have been enhanced, transposed and embellished poetically and rhetorically, and which after long use seem firm, canonical and obligatory to a people; truths are illusions about which one has forgotten that this is what they are; metaphors which are worn out and without sensuous power; coins which have lost their pictures and now matter only as metal, no longer as coins.[23]

Stripping language of all permanence and stability, Nietzsche undercut all truth claims that it was employed to assert. What we know of reality is nothing more than a construction of the human imagination, a product of human valuation, and an expression of the human will.[24] Nietzsche rejected the idea that there exists some Archimedean point according to which we could test diverse truth claims. Only the individual willfully struggling to actualize his or her unique characteristics could serve as the measuring rod of truth.

For Nietzsche, being free meant freeing oneself from all illusory myths and recognizing ourselves as the authors of our own beliefs and actions, regardless of the cost.

For what is freedom? That one has the will to assume responsibility for oneself. That one maintains the distance which separates us. That one becomes more indifferent to difficulties, hardships, privation and even life itself. That one is prepared to sacrifice human beings for one's causes not excluding oneself.[25]

Nietzsche shifted the discussion of right and wrong from the framework of traditional morality to that of psychology. The true foundation of human existence is neither spirit nor soul, but the instinctual drives that constitute the true ground of our being. In Nietzsche's Dionysian vision, we fulfill our fundamental obligation to ourselves by acting out these instincts in our lives. Henceforth, good and bad are to be evaluated in terms of the relation of actions to our drives and instincts: "Every mistake in every sense is the effect of the degeneration of instinct, of the degeneration of the will; one could almost define what is bad in this way. All that is good is instinct—and hence, easy, necessary, free."[26] According to Nietzsche, life itself is the only authentic goal and source of values:

Saying yes to life even in its strangest and hardest problems, the will to life rejoicing over its own inexhaustibility even in the very sacrifice of its highest types—that is what I called Dionysian . . . that is what I guessed to be the bridge to the psychology of the tragic poet. Not in order to be liberated from terror and pity, not in order to purge oneself of a dangerous affect by its vehement discharge—Aristotle understood it this way—but in order to be oneself the eternal joy of becoming, beyond all terror and pity —that joy which included even joy in destroying . . . herewith I again stand on the soil out of which my intention, my ability grows—I, the last disciple of the philosopher Dionysus, I, the teacher of the eternal recurrence.[27]

For Nietzsche, history is not, as Western liberalism claimed, a story of progress, but a story of ongoing conflict between the forces of life and the forces of death. The individual's supreme responsibility, according to Nietzsche, is to become the self that one truly is. Like Zarathustra, our obligation is to develop those qualities that make us human in the deepest sense of the word. "The only absolute imperative a man should obey is that of his inward potential: whatever is given to a man to become, that should indicate the direction, and be the goal, of his intense striving, his will."[28]

By explicitly expressing what most people sought to suppress, Nietzsche led his readers to the brink of nihilism. Refusing to provide any comforting solution, he unmercifully forced the modern person to confront the reality of living in an age of the death of God. In work after work, Nietzsche deconstructed the philosophical, religious, and ideological premises upon which European society had been based. The old systems of meaning, including traditional religious faith, classical metaphysics, and modern science, rather than serve as bridges to reality, only alienate us further from the physical and psychological foundations of our existence:

It is we alone who have devised cause, sequence, for-each-other, relativity, constraint, number, law, freedom, motive and purpose; and when we project and mix this symbol world into things as if it existed "in itself," we act once more as we have always acted—mythologically.[29]

In place of the prevailing systems of meaning Nietzsche advocated life, creativity, vitality, and risk. However inspiring, this vision also led to the brink of despair:

Whither are we moving? Away from all suns? Are we not plunging continually? Backward, sideward, forward, in all directions? Is there still any up or down? Are we not straying through an infinite nothing? Do we not feel the breath of empty space? Has it not become colder? Is not night continually closing in on us? Do we not need to light lanterns in the morning? Do we hear nothing as yet of the noise of the gravediggers who are burying God? Do we smell nothing as yet of the divine decomposition? Gods too, decompose. God is dead. God remains dead. And we have killed him.[30]

In an unpublished essay on Nietzsche entitled "Zarathustra," written when he was only seventeen, Buber expressed his profound sense of estrangement, his "strong hatred for the loathsome air in which I lived, an antipathy for official morals, official culture and conventional smiles, a disdain for Catholicism and aestheticism."[31] Nietzsche's writings confirmed Buber's sense of confusion, anxiety, and alienation.

At the same time, in his encounter with Nietzsche, Buber experienced a powerful sense of inner liberation. Inspired by Nietzsche's skepticism and his radical deconstruction of Western thought and morality, he felt that the depths of his own consciousness had been penetrated and deeply buried feelings and attitudes uncovered: "And thus I came to believe in Nietzsche, I was compelled to believe in him who awakened that which slumbered in me and brought it out into the light."[32]

According to Buber, one had to be confused and alienated to truly appreciate Nietzsche's profound insights. Revising our conventional understanding of health and sickness, Nietzsche had insisted that what appeared to be sickness was actually health, and vice versa. "One must be sick for Nietzsche. The secret of all artistic sensitivity is health as counternature, and the artist should be prepared to create a god out of his illness" (Buber, "Zarathustra," 26–27). Like Nietzsche, Buber considered despair and alienation to be necessary prerequisites for genuine understanding. As Nietzsche had perceived, the truly sick were not the ones who felt alienated, but those who adjusted to the alienating conditions.

In a brief encomium published in 1900, Buber described Nietzsche as an apostle of life who came into the world at a time when man's relationship to the world and himself was in a critical state.[33] Nietzsche's great accomplishment was to have deconstructed the cherished values and institutions of Western culture, showing them to be rooted not in eternal truths, as conventionally believed, but in the drives and longings of the human psyche.

Nietzsche, for Buber, was a great psychologist who deserved a place alongside other students of the human psyche such as Shelley, Poe, Stendhal, and Baudelaire. Nietzsche, however, exceeded his predecessors in psychological insight:

He fought with the most subtle, noble weapons against the dominant metaphysics and morality, viewing them as the symptoms and the tools of a deteriorating life. He revealed the weak falsehood of our values and truths." (Buber, "Nietzsche und die Lebenswerte," 13)

For Buber, Nietzsche's deconstruction of Western values and thought was anything but negative. His critique of Western culture set the stage for the liberation of modern culture from the shackles traditional Christianity and modern liberalism had imposed:

. . . fresh grains of seed in the graves of dung—. . . uncovering and reshaping truths that had been buried in cultures long since dead; in place of a crippled, sterile altruism, Nietzsche brought a new egoism; in place of an effete sympathy he emphasized shared joy and action, elevating the earthly and bodily to their rightful significance. He portrayed life as neither painless nor comfortable, but rather as tumultuous and dangerous. (Buber, "Nietzsche und die Lebenswerte," 13)

Buber found Nietzsche's critique of Western values and thought invigorating. Replacing the static God of creation with a dynamic, becoming God, Nietzsche had restored the human being to the position of active participant in the ongoing process of creation: "Over and against the God of the world's beginning he set up a formidable adversary, the becoming God to whose development we can contribute, the envisaged product of future evolutions."[34]

Swerving away from the Precursor

Like many others in his generation, Buber came to feel that Nietzsche's ideas, pursued to their logical conclusion, led to the brink of nihilism. Alongside the excitement and challenge of deconstruction was danger and risk. Once the old systems were unmasked and their illusory nature revealed, all sources of continuity, stability, and meaning seemed to disappear. No longer able to find solace and comfort in the teachings and traditions of the past, Nietzsche's disciples were confronted with a world devoid of all firm foundations of meaning and value:

The sense of the utter bleakness of life, and the "devaluation" of all values, which is the immediate consequence of the modern loss of faith in God, is not just a casual insight. . . . To escape nihilism, which seems involved both in asserting the existence of God and thus robbing this world of ultimate significance, and also of denying God and thus robbing everything of meaning and value—that is Nietzsche's greatest and most persistent problem.[35]

Although initially overcome by euphoria and a sense of liberation, Buber soon concluded that Nietzsche's answers were in no way sufficient. Whereas Nietzsche appeared to have reveled in the nihilistic implications of his teachings, Buber was not satisfied simply to unmask the forces of alienation. Inspired by personal religious experiences and convinced of life's ultimate meaningfulness, Buber broke with his mentor and endeavored to bridge the abysses separating persons from one another, from nature and from the divine.

As Harold Bloom has recently argued, to emerge as an independent creative thinker, a writer must first struggle to liberate himself or herself from a precursor.[36] Moreover, the creative efforts of the disciple or ephebe are best understood in terms of the struggle with a precursor. This struggle is clearly evident in Buber's relation to Nietzsche. While many thinkers influenced Buber, including Kant, Kierkegaard, Feuerbach, and Boehme, only with reference to Nietzsche does he use the language of struggle and agon:

About two years after that the other book took possession of me, a book that was, to be sure, the work of a philosopher but was not a philosophical book: Nietzsche's Thus Spake Zarathustra. I say "took possession of me," for here a teaching did not simply and calmly confront me, but a willed and splendidly able utterance stormed up to and over me. This book, characterized by its author as the greatest present that had ever been made to mankind up till then, worked in me not in the manner of a gift, but in the manner of an invasion which deprived me of my freedom, and it was a long time until I could liberate myself from it.[37]

Metaphors such as "took possession of me," "stormed up over me," and "invasion" are clear indications of the strength of the Nietzschean influence. In order to emerge as an original creative force, Buber first had to break with the precursor whose teachings had originally exercised the greatest influence on him.[38] Reflecting back on his early encounter with Nietzsche, Buber spoke in terms of conflict, struggle, and seduction.

As I shall argue below, a number of Nietzschean themes continued to play a major role in Buber's writings. For example, Buber stressed the obligation to actualize oneself and viewed intellectual systems and institutional structures as hideouts that engender alienation from self, from others, and from nature. Like Nietzsche, he looked upon the prevailing forms of systematic thought, including theology, metaphysics, science, and historical scholarship, as impeding rather than facilitating the actualization of the self. Moreover, although in *I and Thou* Buber struggled to find an alternative to relationships built upon power, his concept of the ubiquity of I-It relationships serves as at least partial confirmation of the Nietzschean vision.[39]

However, although never abandoning the Nietzschean task of unmasking the sources of human alienation, Buber chose a path that sharply diverged from Nietzsche's. From the turn of the century, Buber's writings reflect a powerful yearning to transcend alienation. Increasingly, he struggled to formulate categories and concepts through which to articulate a nonalienated interpretation of the individual's relationship to the universe, to ultimate reality, and to self. This search, which led through mysticism, Zionism, Hasidism, and *Lebensphilosophie*, culminated in the philosophy of relation developed in *I and Thou*.[40]

The Quest for Community:
Alienation as a Social Phenomenon

As mentioned above, the young intellectuals of fin de siècle Vienna were moved by strong yearnings for a renewal of organic community. Although it was to be several years before this social concern became dominant in Buber's writings, from the outset his concern for individual self-actualization was balanced by a deep-seated yearning for community.

Buber's search led him to the writings of German social theorists. In contrast to the individualistic, existential orientation of philosophers like Nietzsche, social theorists like Tonnies and Simmel emphasized community as essential to the development of the individual self.[41] Their writings, analyzing the social and cultural forces that generate alienation, provided the ground for Buber's own social thought.

Marx, building upon Hegel, had laid the foundation for all subsequent social theories of alienation. Marx viewed the human being as a natural creator and worker who expresses and externalizes his or her uniqueness through the work of his or her hands. A natural bond exists between a person and the products of his or her own labor. In modern, capitalist society, however, this bond has been severed and the products of our labor transformed into commodities that are used to oppress the worker.

Cut off from the fruits of his or her own labor and deprived of a fundamental source of human development, the individual lives an alienated existence: "Since alienated labor: (1) alienates nature from man, and (2) alienates man from himself, from his own active function, his life activity; so it alienates him from the species."[42]

This alienation manifests itself on the social, cultural, and political levels. Natural relations between persons and groups have been sundered, and the relationship between social classes is characterized by continuous strife:

(3) . . . It alienates from man his own body, external nature, his mental life and his human life. (4) A direct consequence of the alienation of man from the product of his labour, from his life activity and from his species is that man is alienated from other men. . . . In general, the statement that man is alienated from his species life means that each man is alienated from others and that each of the others is likewise alienated from human life.

Human alienation, and above all the relation of man to himself, is first realized and expressed in the relationship between each man and other men.[43]

To overcome alienation, according to Marx, we must restore the bond between persons and the fruits of their productive labor. To achieve this, power relations, as manifested in the political and economic spheres, must be changed. In Marx's view, this change can only occur through sociopolitical revolution.

Following Marx, Tonnies, Weber, and Simmel directed their attention to the social and cultural manifestations of alienation.

Tonnies' writings offered a striking description of the destructive effects of modernization and of the alienation that it engendered in modern society. To Tonnies, the modern person is cut off from major sources of creativity and deprived of the satisfactions and solace previously provided by work, religious faith, politics, and interhuman relationships. This exposure to the chaos from which the premodern person had been shielded engenders in the modern individual a sense of alienation:

> The modern age, dominated by *Gesellschaft*, is characterized by separations and divisions. The separation of church and state, the division of labor, and the increasing disappearance of contractual relations between people had led, in turn, to the estrangement of people from their own potential selves, and the spiritual isolation of the individual cut off from the comfort of the church, the state, the nation and the local community as well.[44]

Tonnies distinguished between *Gemeinschaft* (community) and *Gesellschaft* (society) in terms of human will. While *Gemeinschaft* embodies the natural/essential will, or *Wesenwille*, which expresses our total, essential personality, *Gesellschaft* embodies the arbitrary will, or *Kurwille*. The germinal forms of *Gemeinschaft* are the natural love relationships between mother and child, lovers, and siblings.[45]

The theory of *Gemeinschaft* starts from the assumption of perfect unity of human wills as an original or natural condition, which is preserved in spite of separation.[46] In *Gemeinschaft*, relationships are natural, intimate, organic, mutual, and whole: "The relationships which come to us from nature are in their essence, mutual, are fulfilled in mutual performance. The relationships produce this mutuality and demand, require or make it necessary."[47]

Gemeinschaft can be rooted in blood relationship, physical proximity, or intellectual proximity. Accordingly, Tonnies spoke of a *Gemeinschaft* of blood, locality, and mind. Wherever human beings are organically related through their wills and affirm one another, we have one or another of these three types of *Gemeinschaft*.[48] Thus, *Gemeinschaft*, comprised of people living and working together in relationships of mutual sharing and concern, is manifested in such groups as guilds, fellowships, fraternities, religious communities, villages, peoples, and tribes.

In contrast to *Gemeinschaft*, *Gesellschaft*, a form of association rooted in an instrumentalist ethos, is characterized by the dissolution of intimate, direct communal relations. While *Gemeinschaft* is rooted in an a priori, natural unity, no such unity underlies *Gesellschaft*. The social forms of *Gesellschaft* are artificial constructions of human beings relating to one another in terms of the rational achievement of their own ends: "In *Gesellschaft*, every person strives for that which is to his own advantage, and he affirms the actions of others only insofar as they can further his interest."[49]

Insofar as people act out of the desire to achieve their own ends, *Gesellschaft* is marked by a sense of separation, isolation, and competition. With everyone striving for his or her own advantage, a negative relationship to others prevails. One gives to others only in exchange for equivalent gift or labor, with all relationships marked by calculation and anticipated benefits. Consequently, individuals come to view one another solely as means to an end and treat one another as "inanimate objects and tools."[50]

In Tonnies' view, *Gemeinschaft* was, prior to the modern age, the normal form of social life. However, rational, scientific thought requires a social form in which the individual is emancipated from all social and intellectual ties that impede independent rational calculation.[51] Accordingly, the rise of modern, industrialized society entailed a gradual displacement of *Gemeinschaft* by *Gesellschaft*.

Tonnies viewed the process of modernization as a mixed blessing. Although undermining the organic, mutual interactions of *Gemeinschaft*, *Gesellschaft* made possible intellectual accomplishments previously unattainable. Although the price for these accomplishments included "the fall of the communal household in villages and towns, of the agricultural community, and of the art of the town as a fellowship, religious, patriotic craft" and resulted in "the victory of egoism, impudence, falsehood and cunning, the ascendancy of greed for money, ambition, and lust for pleasure," it did bring about "the victory of the contemplative, clear and sober consciousness in which scholars and cultured men now dare to approach things human and divine."[52]

Nevertheless, Tonnies was sensitive to the inherent tragedy of modern life. While he considered the achievements of science and technology to be a great source of pride, he saw their cost as communal disintegration and the accompanying loss of calm, beauty, and dignity. Moreover, the deterioration of *Gemeinschaft* and the ascendancy of *Gesellschaft* were, in Tonnies' view, irreversible processes:

However, modern civilization is caught in an irresistible process of disintegration. Its very progress dooms. This is hard for us to conceive, and harder still to acquiesce in it, to admit it and yet to cooperate with it willingly and even cheerfully. We must bring ourselves to look upon tragedy, wrestling with both fear and hope so as to rid ourselves of them, and to enjoy the cleansing effect of the dramatic course of events. Scientific thought can do this if it has matured and transformed itself into philosophy, that is, wisdom.[53]

Georg Simmel, a teacher of Buber's who had a decided influence on him, expanded the analysis of the alienating effects of modern social and cultural forms.[54] Simmel, like Nietzsche, stressed the celebration of life. However, he perceived reality in terms of a perennial, dialectical conflict between life and form.

Life as such is formless, yet incessantly generates forms from itself. As soon as each form appears, however, it demands a validity which transcends the moment and is emancipated from the pulse of life. For this reason, life is always in latent opposition to the form. This tension soon expresses itself in this sphere and eventually, it develops into a comprehensive cultural necessity.[55]

Transposing the Marxian idea of reification and alienation to the sphere of cultural creativity, Simmel described art, science, religion, and law as the major forms in which the life impulse is objectified. As these forms acquire their own independent existence, they become rigid, stifling the very life forces that had originally given rise to them. In Simmel, the Nietzschean dichotomy of Dionysian and Apollonian forces reappears as the conflict between life and form.[56] The vital, dynamic, flowing forces of life are continually engaged in a struggle to overcome the stifling, rigid, static forms of culture:

I see the most capacious and far-reaching collision between society and individual, not in the aspect of particular interests, but in the general form of the individual life. Society aspires to totality and organic unity, each of its members constituting a component part. The individual, as part of society, has to fulfill special functions and employ all his strength; he is expected to modify his skills so that he will become the best-qualified performer of these functions.[57]

The impact of this conflict on the modern individual has been to generate a condition of alienation. In Simmel's view, modern man is a homeless, powerless stranger, alienated from the fundamental forces of life:

The individual is reduced to a negligible quantity, perhaps less in consciousness than in his practice and in the totality of his obscure emotional states that are derived from this practice. The individual has become a mere cog in an enormous organization of things and powers which tears from his hands all progress, spirituality and value in order to turn them from their subjective form into the form of a purely objective life.[58]

Weber, like Simmel and Tonnies, saw the modern person as having lost control of his or her own actions and destiny, a cog in the midst of an impersonal, rationalized bureaucratic system. Weber was ambivalent concerning Western society's prospects of escaping from the "iron cage" in which it was imprisoned. While conjecturing that a new prophet might emerge in the future to challenge the stifling forces of rationalization and bureaucracy, he nevertheless envisioned a society ruled by "specialists without spirit, sensualists without heart."[59]

To Tonnies' description of spreading *Gesellschaft*, Weber added a vision of growing rationalization and alienation. Weber, like Tonnies, believed that the modern individual had lost control over his or her own actions and, consequently, his or her destiny. Weber depicted the person in modern society as entrapped in a system in which "explicit, abstract, intellectually calculable rules and procedures are increasingly substituted for sentiment, tradition, and rule of thumb in all spheres of activity."[60]

Owing to the spread of the calculating, rational mentality the premodern relationship to the universe had disappeared. Instead of solace and consolation, the modern person found loneliness and isolation. In the modern, industrialized world, permeated by a rationalist ethos, routinization and institutionalization prevail. While Nietzsche spoke of the modern situation in terms of the "death of God," Weber preferred to speak of the "disenchantment of the world."

Zionism:
The Turn to Jewish Nationhood

Buber's affinity to German social thought is reflected in a speech delivered in 1899 to Neue Gemeinschaft, a group seeking alternative communal forms. Employing the rhetoric of *Lebensphilosophie*, Buber proclaimed community as the source from which life flows[61]: "All life emerges out of community and strives for community. Community is the well spring, the source of life (Buber, "Alte and Neue Gemeinschaft," 51)."[62] The individual, he insisted, could overcome alienation and actualize his unique potential only in the context of genuine community. Echoing a theme common to German academicians and social theorists, Buber denounced the profit-oriented, utilitarian values of Western society as the major obstacle to genuine community.

This speech contains the first clear expression of the anarchistic tendencies that characterized all of Buber's future writings. According to Buber, the institutional structure of modern society and the ethos that it generates have a stifling effect on the individual, cutting the individual off from immediate life experiences *(Erlebnisse)* essential to spiritual vitality and growth. Arguing that the crisis of modern society could not be resolved by the imposition of new forms or structures, he insisted that genuine community could only arise from within the individual, in a manner appropriate to each particular time and place. The tension between the experiences of the individual self and the drive to community, the antagonistic attitude to social forms, and the emphasis on the inner transformation of the individual all continued to characterize Buber's thought throughout his life.[63]

While Neue Gemeinschaft offered Buber the first outlet for his communal concerns, his involvement with the group was short-lived.[64] Before long, Buber's quest for community drew him to the newly emerging Zionist movement, a movement of Jewish national renewal, established in 1897 by Theodor Herzl. In Zionism Buber and his contemporaries found a vision of community rooted both in Jewish historical consciousness and in the ideology of nineteenth-century romantic nationalism. Attracted to the rapidly spreading

Volkish ideology, Buber and his contemporaries saw in Zionism the hope for the renewal and regeneration of the Jewish people.[65]

Buber's conception of Zionism was shaped by his quest for authentic individual and communal existence. Rejecting the prevailing sociopolitical conception of Zionism, he conceived of Jewish nationalism as the Jewish form of the universal human quest for spiritual renewal. For Buber, as for many others of his generation, Jewish nationalism offered a way to renew the broken bonds of community. Furthermore, Zionism offered the individual Jew the hope of inner liberation. Whereas Nietzsche had offered hope of liberation from the alienation that permeated European culture, Jewish nationalism offered escape from the alienation that pervaded Jewish life. As Buber was later to recall, "the first impetus towards my liberation came from Zionism. I can only intimate what it meant for me; the restoration of the connection, the renewed taking root in the community" (HMM, 57).

Buber's early writings on Jewish nationalism reflect a romantic yearning for wholeness, unity, and harmony and are, like his writings on community, infused with the values of Lebensphilosophie. Jewish nationalism offered the Jews a "broad, soul-filled view of nature" and a "warm, flowing life-feeling" that had been stifled by rabbinic scholasticism (Buber, Jüdische Bewegung 1:10). In the movement for Jewish national renewal, Buber found a spiritual, communal life experience that was a viable alternative both to the nihilistic, individualistic Nietzschean vision and the rationalist ethos of Western society:

To create new values and new works out of the depths of his own primordial uniqueness, out of the unique, incomparable force of his blood, which has been for so long imprisoned in the chains of unproductivity. This is the ideal for the Jewish people. (Buber, Jüdische Bewegung 1:42)

The new being of which Nietzsche had spoken would, according to Buber, emerge through the renewal of the Jewish people and its culture: "As one is drawn deeper into his own history, one recognizes that renaissance signifies not regression, but rebirth, a renewal of complete men" (Buber, Jüdische Bewegung 1:10).

The vitality of the Jewish community, like that of Western society, was endangered by rationalized, institutionalized structures that stifled the soul. In Buber's view, these structures were mainly the creation of the rabbinic tradition that had dominated the Jewish community for approximately sixteen centuries. In the traditional conception of Judaism, rabbinic Judaism is seen as the legitimate continuation and fulfillment of the written Torah. The rabbis, according to that view, were the authoritative interpreters of divine revelation, and their teachings defined the nature and forms of authentic Judaism.[66]

To Buber, however, the forms and structures of rabbinic Judaism distorted and suppressed the vital forces of life. The forms of behavior and principles of faith that had served as the foundations of traditional Jewish life were antithetical to immediate life experiences *(Erlebnisse)*. In harsh, caustic language, Buber characterized the rabbinic tradition as "a misunderstood, distorted, deformed religious tradition, the power of a hard, static system of obligations alienated from reality, that negated all light and joy, all thirst for beauty and flight, stifling feeling and imprisoning thought in chains" (Buber, *Jüdische Bewegung* 1:94).

Buber saw the rabbinic forms of life and modes of interpretation as detrimental to a healthy Jewish existence. Revising the prevailing traditional view, he linked the revitalization of Judaism to the overthrow of the rabbinic tradition and the recovery of the dynamic, creative, primal forces of Jewish life. Although this hostility to the rabbinic tradition, which Buber shared with many Jewish nationalists, was subsequently mitigated in Buber's writings, he never ceased to view the rabbinic tradition as suppressive. However, in contrast to most Jewish nationalists who wished to replace rabbinic Judaism with a secular national culture, Buber sought to replace it with a synthesis of existential religious faith and national culture.

Mysticism and the Quest for Meaning

Zionism, which offered Buber a means for actualizing his yearning for community, did not afford him sufficient spiritual satisfaction. His yearning for such satisfaction led Buber to the teachings of Christian mystics. In the works of such figures as Nicholas of Cusa,

Angelus Silesius, Meister Eckhart, and Jakob Boehme, Buber found accounts of profound personal spiritual experiences unlike anything that he had thus far found in Judaism.[67]

In his writings on mysticism, Buber focused his attention on the writings of Jakob Boehme, the primary subject of his doctoral dissertation.[68] Essentially bypassing Boehme's theology, he emphasized, instead, Boehme's insights into the existential human condition:

> Boehme's fundamental problem, on which all of his thinking concentrated, was the relationship of the individual to the world. . . . The world remains a puzzle. It works upon one and affects one, while remaining distant and alien. The individual is consumed by (verzehrt sich) mute, hopeless loneliness. (Buber, "Über Jakob Boehme," 251)

Of particular concern to Buber was the way in which Boehme and Nicholas of Cusa portrayed the human being's development from submersion in the organic unity of the universe to emergence as a separate, unique being.

Buber found in Boehme a dynamic conception of the universe in which all created beings are bound together by a dual drive for power and love. Like Nietzsche, Boehme assigned human beings an active role in the ongoing process of creation and considered the drive to power to be a basic force in the universe. However, in contrast to Nietzsche, Boehme balanced the drive for power with the drive for love, which linked the human being to God. Thus, Boehme provided an alternative to the Nietzschean will to power.

Boehme denied any sharp distinction between human beings and the rest of the universe. Absorbed into the universe as an integral part, each person embodies within himself or herself an entire universe. Boehme who, like St. Francis, "called the trees, the birds and the stars his brothers and sisters" (Buber, "Über Jakob Boehme," 251), spoke of the universe as an enormous pipe organ in which the multiplicity of tones was produced by a single movement of air.[69]

The idea of entelechy, a concept that played a fundamental role in his later thought, already appears in Buber's dissertation.[70] Boehme's view that each created being possesses the will and the capacity to actualize its unique potential and in so doing contributes to the actualization of God, played a key role in Buber's mature conception of religion.

Like his conception of Judaism, Buber's early understanding of mysticism was shaped by the categories of *Lebensphilosophie*. For Buber, all mystical experiences were grounded in the life experiences *(Erlebnisse)* of the mystics. In spite of the diversity of forms in which they are expressed and communicated, all mystical experiences derive from a fundamental experience of unity, in which all life drives culminate.

Introducing his anthology of mystical writings published in 1909, Buber described those texts as projections of inner *Erlebnisse* that were experienced by the mystics as unification with the divine.[71] Unable to differentiate between the surrounding world and his or her inner being, the mystic sees the origin of the experience of unity not within himself or herself, but in God.[72]

To the mystic, "ecstasy is beyond common experience. It is unity, solitude, uniqueness. It cannot be transmitted. It is the abyss that cannot be fathomed or expressed" (Buber, *Ekstatische Konfessionen*, xix). However, feeling compelled to speak about his experiences, the mystic turns to myth, which has an expressive power that is lacking in normal discourse: "Isn't the myth proclaimed by the Veda, the Upanishads, the midrash and the Kabbalah, Jesus and Plato, the symbolic expression of what the mystic experiences?" (Buber, *Ekstatische Konfessionen*, xxv).[73]

In Buber's early writings, we encounter many of the basic concepts and themes that were later to characterize his mature thought including a sense of alienation, a yearning for organic communal forms, and a thirst for immediate life experiences. Although Buber found the implications of Nietzsche's revaluation of European values to be too radical, Nietzsche's skeptical view of language and his suspicion of institutional forms and philosophical systems remained a permanent part of Buber's intellectual framework. Similarly, although he rejected Herzl's form of political Zionism, Buber remained convinced of the need for a Jewish national homeland throughout his life and devoted his energies to the actualization of that goal.

While Buber was eventually to break with the mysticism that had appealed to him in his early years, mystical motifs were to remain a basic part of his worldview. His mystical yearning for immediate relations with the world around him was to find its ultimate expression in the philosophy of relation first articulated in 1923 in *I and Thou*. First, however, Buber's mystical yearnings, his quest for community, and his commitment to the renewal of the Jewish people led him to Hasidism, a movement for Jewish spiritual and communal renewal.

2

Hasidism and
the Renewal of Judaism

Martin Buber was one of the best-known interpreters of the Jewish spiritual movement of Hasidism, which had emerged in eastern Europe in the eighteenth century. Through his translations and commentaries, which he began to publish in 1908, Buber brought the teachings of Hasidism to the attention of the Western world. The interpretation of Hasidism was one of Buber's lifelong central intellectual activities and the teachings of Hasidism provided him with fundamental insights around which he built his philosophical and religious positions. An analysis of Buber's interpretation of Hasidism and the controversy that it provoked among Jewish scholars provides significant insights into his intellectual development.

As indicated in the Introduction, Buber's position as an interpreter of Hasidism was highly problematic, and his approach distinguished him from the conventional interpreters of Hasidism of his day. As a child of modern culture nurtured by the teachings of existentialism and social theory, Buber did not consider affiliation with the Hasidic movement a viable option.[1] Yet, in contrast to scholars like Dubnow who wrote histories of the Hasidic movement, Buber found the historical mode of discourse inadequate to his purposes.

Neither an uncritical disciple nor an objective historian, Buber, motivated by deep, personal concerns arising out of the conditions

43

of modern life, approached Hasidism as a strong reader. Providing neither a literal transmission of texts nor a scholarly account of Hasidism, he engaged in what some modern literary critics refer to as "creative misreading."[2] Rather than trying to replicate the original meaning of the Hasidic texts or set them in their historical context, Buber used them to address the issues and concerns of the present creatively. Diverging from Jewish conventional scholarship, his interpretations of Hasidism made him one of the most controversial figures in modern Jewish thought.[3]

Although, as we saw in the previous chapter, the writings of the Christian mystics had served Buber as a source of religious inspiration, they could not satisfy his yearning for a uniquely Jewish form of spirituality. Similarly, while drawn to the Zionist program for a renewal of Judaism, he found that Zionism, focusing on political and diplomatic activity, lacked the power to effect a truly spiritual renewal. Thus, his search for a uniquely Jewish spiritual force led him to the writings of Hasidism, a traditional Jewish pietist movement with which he had had contact during his childhood.

In Hasidism, Buber found the vehicle for synthesizing his social and religious concerns into a way of life that could transcend the abysses of alienation. Through Hasidism, he could fulfill his yearning for community, life, and creative spirituality within the context of Judaism. In 1904, Buber disengaged himself from all official Zionist activities and invested himself full time in the study of Hasidic texts.[4]

While not abandoning the study of non-Jewish mysticism and spirituality, Buber now devoted his primary efforts to the study, translation, and dissemination of the teachings of Hasidism.[5] Through these endeavors, he hoped to find a way for the alienated Jews of his generation to bridge the gap separating them from the sacred. Moreover, Buber believed that Hasidism had the power not only to speak to the modern Jew but also to address the spiritual crisis of humanity in general. Thus through the teachings of Hasidism, Judaism could again speak to the world as it had done in the days of the prophets of Israel.

Buber found Hasidism to be an indigenous Jewish form of life with a spiritual power equal to that of the Christian mystics. Just as *Haskalah*, a movement of enlightenment among eastern Euro-

pean Jewry, had provided the secular foundation for Jewish national renewal, Hasidism could provide the spiritual foundation.[6]
While *Haskalah* had provided the secular, rational form of liberation from ossified Jewish tradition, Hasidism would provide the
religious, spiritual form.

Buber's turn to Hasidism may also be viewed as another manifestation of his basic antipathy to the liberal, rationalist ethos of post-
Enlightenment European culture. To Western Jews, Hasidism was
an atavistic vestige of medieval irrationalism and superstition. It
was viewed as an obsolete way of life that had to be discarded if
Jews wished to enter Western society.[7] Seeing Hasidism as an out-
dated mixture of mysticism, emotionalism, and anti-intellectual-
ism, Western Jewish scholars considered it to be antithetical to their
sense of the authentic rational spirit of Judaism. By publicly advocating and disseminating Hasidic teachings, Buber defied convention and repudiated the values and ideals espoused by modern,
Western Judaism.

It was precisely the antimodern, mythic elements in Hasidism
that most appealed to Buber. As an indigenous Jewish form of life
and thought, Hasidism offered an alternative to both the utilitarian
ethos of Western society and the arid rationalism and ritualism
that, according to Buber, prevailed in Jewish life. Opposing conventional Jewish scholarship that considered mysticism to be an anomaly in Judaism, Buber insisted that mysticism constituted an inherent, creative element in Jewish life. "The tendency toward mysticism
is native to the Jew from antiquity. . . . The strength of Jewish
mysticism arose from an original characteristic of the people that
produced it" (Buber, *Nachman*, 34).

Although admitting that, when compared with Christian mysticism, Jewish mysticism seemed trivial and confused, it was, he
argued, one of the world's great examples of ecstatic wisdom. Cele-
brating mystical experience and elevating personal spirituality to a
fundamental value, Hasidism viewed the mythic, folk elements of
Judaism as a unique source of life force.

An examination of Buber's writings on Hasidism is essential to
any overall understanding of his thought. On the one hand, the
teachings of Hasidism provided him with the mythic foundation
upon which his own philosophy was based. At the same time,

Buber's distinctive mode of interpreting Hasidism represents a significant alternative to the prevailing modes of interpretation in modern Jewish thought.

The Teachings of Hasidism

Bypassing theoretical writings, including biblical commentaries, liturgical tracts, sermons, and speculative theological treatises, Buber based his interpretation of Hasidism on stories and tales.[8] The myth of the broken vessels, a "creative misreading" of the biblical story of creation by the sixteenth-century Kabbalist Rabbi Isaac Luria and his disciples, formed the central motif in his interpretation.

Luria and his disciples, ignoring the conventional readings of the biblical texts, had formulated a radical interpretation combining motifs of cosmic alienation, catastrophe, and messianic redemption. To Luria and his followers, creation began with the self-contraction of God. The vessels into which the divine rays poured broke and the divine sparks were scattered. Thus, the primordial unity of God was shattered and the universe was plunged into a condition of cosmic alienation, with God fragmented and separated from his or her own essential being.[9]

The possibility of redemption was built into the Lurianic system through the process of *tikkun*, or repairing. By performing traditional commandments with the proper devotional attitude, Jews actively help to reunite the divine sparks. In Lurianic Kabbalah, the commandments are no longer seen as ends in themselves but as vehicles for effecting redemption.

Both Lurianic Kabbalah and Hasidism emphasized the experiential aspect of religious life. The performance of the commandments in the proper spirit leads to *devekut*, the cleaving of the person to God.[10] This culminating experience of the direct encounter with the divine is considered to be the ultimate goal.

Elaborating on a rabbinic motif, Lurianic Kabbalah and Hasidism both viewed the individual as a coparticipant with God in the creation and redemption of the world. In this conception of the Jew as actively engaged in the ongoing process of creating, Buber found an emphasis on human creativity that had so appealed to him in the teachings of Nietzsche and the Christian mystics: [11]

One day, I opened a little book entitled, *Zivaat HaRibesh — The Testament of Rabbi Israel Baal Shem*, and the words flashed towards me. "He takes upon himself the quality of fervor for he is hallowed and become another man and is worthy to create and become like the Holy One Blessed Be He, when he created his world." It was then that, overpowered in an instant, I experienced the Hasidic soul. The primally Jewish opened to me, flowering the new conscious expression in the darkness of exile. Man's being created in the image of God, I grasped as deed, as becoming, as task. (*HMM*, 59)

Hasidism, interpreting redemption as an inner, spiritual process rather than a historical one, neutralized the eschatological and catastrophic elements of the Lurianic myth. Redemption was seen not as the direct outcome of the individual's actions but as an outgrowth of spiritual processes set in motion by those actions that lead to the unification of the divine sparks with their primordial source.

In addition to mitigating the messianic implications of Lurianic Kabbalah, Hasidism also expanded the scope of redemptive activity beyond the limits of the traditional system of commandments to include relationships to nature and other persons.[12] However, the Hassidic expansion of the traditional framework in no way entailed a break with the rabbinic system. In Hasidism, as in Kabbalah, the observance of halakhah, the traditional rabbinic norms and patterns of behavior, remained a given.

Just as Hasidism had transformed Kabbalah into a new Jewish ethos, Buber, in his strong reading of Hasidism, transformed it into a humanistic religious teaching.[13] Recasting the myth of the broken vessels as the foundation of a new interpretation of person, community, and religion, Buber broadened and universalized the Hasidic concept of action. Whereas, for Hasidism, the fulfillment of the traditional commandments constituted the main path to redemption, Buber expanded the range of redemptive acts to include any action performed in the proper spirit.

Around each man — enclosed within the wide sphere of his activity — is laid a natural circle of things which, before all, he is called upon to set free. These are the creatures and objects spoken of as the possessions of this individual; his animals, his tools, his food. So far as he cultivates them and enjoys them in holiness, he frees their souls. (*HMM*, 105)

Echoing Kierkegaard, Buber asserted that the "how" of an action, the spirit in which it was performed, rather than the "what," the content, was decisive.[14] Similarly, he expanded the concept of *kavanah*, that is, inner feeling, concentration, and direction.[15] Whereas Hasidism related *kavanah* primarily to the performance of traditional commandments and prayers, Buber applied it to all actions and situations.

Buber transformed Hasidism into a theory of universal human spirituality. According to this theory, people live religiously not by fulfilling specific obligations imposed by a fixed tradition, but through the way in which they relate to creatures and things encountered in their daily lives. To be religious means to hallow the everyday. In Buber's reading, the entire range of one's activity has the potential for redemptive action. All beings and objects that one encounters in the course of one's daily life constitute paths to the divine. Thus, Buber's reading of Hasidism yielded a highly individualistic conception of religious life that encourages each person to develop his or her own way of serving God, unencumbered by prescribed practices or fixed beliefs. Breaking with rabbinic Judaism, Buber denied the authority of the traditional prescribed commandments.[16]

Whereas in the Hasidic version the sparks symbolize the dispersal of the divine in this world, in Buber's interpretation the sparks also symbolize the uniqueness of each person. Buber thus transposed the Hasidic idea that each person is obligated to nurture his or her own divine spark into the key of individualism and self actualization. A person's divine spark represents a "priceless treasure that is in no other" (*HMM*, 115). Each person is obligated to nurture his or her own unique qualities and to actualize his or her own unique self: "Every man shall know and consider that in his qualities he is unique in the world and that none like him ever lived, for had there ever before been someone like him, then he would not have needed to exist" (*HMM*, 111).

Moving well beyond the limits of rabbinic Judaism, Buber advocated a religious existentialism that conflicted with the premises of traditional Judaism.[17] Although Hasidism had simply extended the scope of rabbinic Judaism and encouraged people to emphasize particular deeds in their service of God, it never granted them the right to challenge the authority of tradition. Buber, however, insisted that no one had the right to prescribe for another person the appropriate way to serve God:

Only in his own way and not in any other can the one who strives perfect himself. "He who lays hold of the rung of his companion, and lets go of his own rung, through him neither the one nor the other will be actualized." (Buber, *Baal Shem*, 42)

While it was to be several years before Buber succeeded in synthesizing the individualistic and social elements in his thought, even in his early Hasidic writings the individualist ethic was balanced by an ethic of social responsibility.[18] Besides responsibility to oneself, Hasidism, in Buber's reading, teaches responsibility to the other. In addition to obligating people to nurture their own uniqueness, the myth of the sparks teaches that each one is responsible for one's fellow human beings: "In each man there is a priceless treasure that is in no other. Therefore, one shall honor each man for the hidden value that only he and none of his comrades has (Buber, *Baal Shem*, 45). Buber interpreted this to mean that each person is responsible for helping others to cultivate and actualize their own uniqueness. Love exists not only within the individual but also "exists in reality between the creatures, that is, it exists in God" (Buber, *Baal Shem*, 47).[19]

Buber related the themes of community and love to the idea of the organic interrelatedness of all creatures. Insofar as each creature embodies a divine spark, everyone is related to one another through the primordial divine unity "for each is a spark from the primordial soul, and the whole of the primordial soul is in each" (Buber, *Baal Shem*, 49). Since all creatures, human and nonhuman alike, are bound together in relationship, none can be regarded as "the other." To love truly, one has to live with the other in community.

For the community of the living is the carriage of God's majesty, and where there is a rent in the carriage one must fill it, and where there is so little love that the joining comes apart, one must love more on one's side to overcome the lack. (Buber, *Baal Shem*, 47)

Loving another does not mean simply feeling love but performing acts of love. Unlike acts of pity done to alleviate our own pain, genuine acts of love are done in order to alleviate the pain of the other.[20]

By 1908, Buber had begun to move away from his earlier mystical orientation toward an existential one. Unlike most forms of mysticism that subsume the individual being as an organic part of the cosmos, Buber emphasized the distinctiveness of the individual. In Kabbalah and Hasidism, when the spark is liberated the being that embodies it is annihilated. In Buber's reading of Hasidism however, the individual being, far from being annihilated, is actualized in all of his concreteness. Thus, the spark is not separate from the concrete being that embodies it but comprises this being's essence or soul. As the spark is liberated, the individual emerges as a unique being.[21]

To Buber, the myth of the sparks also presupposes a primal condition of organic connectedness. Anything that impedes or disrupts this connectedness engenders or exacerbates a condition of separation and estrangement. Buber thus transformed the Lurianic myth from a theological vision of divine self-alienation to an existential vision of human alienation in which persons are separated from one another, from nature, and from the divine:

All things were enveloped by the abyss, and yet the whole abyss was between each thing and the other. None could cross over to the other, indeed none could see the other, for the abyss was between them. (Buber, *Baal Shem*, 69–70)[22]

In Hasidism's vision of a world permeated by abysses, Buber found a view of existential and social alienation similar to that of Nietzsche and the social theorists. Like modern existentialism, Hasidism was conscious of the factors that impede our ability to commune with one another. As Luria had taught that cosmic alienation could be overcome through redemptive acts, Hasidism, in Buber's view, taught that human alienation could be overcome through acts of love and through communal existence. Thus, Hasidism carried a hope of redemption missing from Nietzsche.

Alongside individual redemptive acts, Hasidism taught a social form of redemption. The *zaddik*, the leader of the community, is the paradigm of a helping person, serving as the vehicle for bridging the abysses:

They saw one another through his eyes, and they touched one another through his hand. And since the things came to one another, there was no longer an abyss, but a light space of seeing and touching, and of all that was therein. (Buber, *Baal Shem*, 70).

Hasidism, combining a theory of alienation with the hope of redemption, offered Buber a way of avoiding the nihilistic implications of Nietzsche.[23] Nevertheless, in reading Hasidic texts, Buber used an individualistic, highly pragmatic mode of interpretation that resembled Nietzsche's. Like Nietzsche, Buber eschewed historical scholarship as well as conventional philology. Instead, he combed texts in search of those words that had the power to speak to the conditions of the modern world.

Coming to Hasidism as a passionate reader in search of a way out of the abyss of nihilism, Buber found a way out of the morass of modern alienation. In contrast to Nietzsche's naturalistic philosophy, Buber viewed reality through the lens of religious faith: "It seemed clear enough to me that I was concerned from first to last with restoring immediacy to the relation between man and God, with helping to end 'the eclipse of God'."[24]

In the spirit of turn-of-the-century neoromanticism, Buber turned to myth. Combining poetic sensibility, a yearning for direct life experience, and a longing for myth, Buber undertook to reshape the raw materials of Hasidic literature into a new Jewish mythos. Through its myths, Hasidism had the power to speak not only to Jews but to all humanity.

Situating himself within the tradition of Jewish mythos that had been suppressed by nineteenth-century scholarship, Buber undertook to uncover the spiritual power that had characterized Judaism in its most creative moments. "My object is not the recreation of this [historical] atmosphere. My narration stands on the earth of Jewish myth and the heaven of Jewish myth is over it" (Buber, *Baal Shem*, 10–11). Rather than transmit the myths benignly, Buber elicited new meaning from them:

I have told it anew as one who was born later. I bear in me the blood of those who created it and out of my blood and spirit it has become one. I stand in the chain of narrators, a link between links. I tell once again the old stories, and if they sound new, it is because the new already lay dormant in them when they were told for the first time. (Buber, *Baal Shem*, 10)

Buber's turn to myth and his divergence from historical scholarship are further indications of his affinity to Nietzsche. Nietzsche had characterized Western history as an ongoing conflict between the dynamic, creative Dionysian culture and the rationally structured Apollonian culture. Under the repressive power of the latter, the creative forces of life have been repeatedly driven underground. Only the periodic breakthrough of Dionysian forces has prevented the total stagnation of Western culture. Nietzsche believed that if modern society was to be saved from this stagnation a renewal of myth and artistic creativity was essential. "Every culture that has lost myth has lost, by the same token, its natural, healthy creativity. Only a horizon ringed about with myths can unify a culture. The forces of imagination of Apollonian culture are saved only by myth."[25]

Viewing all forms of expression as metaphor, Nietzsche abandoned scholarship in favor of imaginative, artistic creation.[26] If Western civilization was to recover from its current stagnation, art and imagination would have to replace historical scholarship, and a mythic conception of truth supplant the prevailing positivistic and idealistic conceptions.

In following Nietzsche's lead and embracing myth, Buber departed from the norms of modern Jewish thought and scholarship. To Jewish rationalist philosophers and scholars, myth was primitive, irrational, and antithetical to authentic Judaism. Breaking with prevailing paradigms of Jewish thought and scholarship, which identified myth with paganism, Buber saw myth as "the expression of the fullness of existence, its sign; it drinks incessantly from the fountains of life" (Buber, *Baal Shem*, 11).[27] Thus, Buber's turn to myth was a basic component of his revisionistic orientation to Judaism, which I shall discuss more fully in the next chapter.

Like Nietzsche, Buber saw objectivistic historical scholarship as contributing to the individual's alienation from the surrounding world. To recover the sources of authentic life, one must abandon objectivistic scholarship in favor of imaginative, artistic creativity. In contrast to historical scholarship, myth is the mode of discourse most closely related to the concrete reality of existential experience. For Buber, as for Nietzsche, myth is essential to a healthy culture.[28] In sharp contrast to the historical mode of modern Jewish scholarship, Buber saw a renewal of myth as a key to uncovering the power of Judaism.[29]

Interpreting Hasidism:
Buber vs. Scholem

Owing to his prodigious output of articles and books on the subject, Buber became widely recognized as one of the world's leading interpreters of Hasidism. Through his numerous translations, interpretive essays, and books, Buber helped to shape the view of Hasidism that continues to prevail among many Western readers.[30] Accordingly, when Gershom Scholem, the acknowledged dean of scholars of Kabbalah, the Jewish mystical tradition, unleashed a sharp critique of Buber's Hasidic writings, the battle lines were drawn between two radically different conceptions of the interpretive process.[31]

In questioning the validity of Buber's interpretive strategies and rejecting the readings that they produced, Scholem raised fundamental questions about the limits within which the modern interpretation of Judaism should be carried out. Buber, in his response, defended an interpretive approach that deviated from the scholarly norm. Accordingly, an analysis of that debate in the light of current conceptions of reading and interpretation will shed new light on Buber's interpretive activities and provide a deeper understanding of his significance as an interpreter of Judaism.

To Scholem, Buber's interpretation of Hasidism was a gross distortion of the historical reality that was Hasidism. Instead of revealing the genuine character of this religious movement, Buber, according to Scholem, imposed his own existential concerns and biases to produce a highly misleading depiction of Hasidic teachings. While not denying that Buber contributed something to our understanding of Hasidism, Scholem insisted that his disregard for historical evidence and his cavalier use of texts for his own purposes greatly undermined the value of this contribution.

Scholem publicly challenged both Buber's method and the substance of his interpretation in a 1961 article. According to Scholem, the fundamental task of the interpreter of Hasidism is to uncover what Hasidic teachings "really meant in their original context."[32] When viewed in this light, Scholem claimed, Buber's interpretation of Hasidism is totally unsatisfactory.

Buber's basic methodological error was his exclusive reliance on tales and legends and his neglect of such theoretical writings as Bible commentaries and theological treatises. Moreover, the legendary material upon which Buber relied was a product of later Hasidism and, consequently, does not reflect the reality of Hasidism in its original, formative stage. The result is a grossly distorted, historically untenable picture of Hasidism.

Scholem believed that the true character of Hasidism is revealed through its basic concepts.[33] These, however, are found in theoretical writings such as commentaries on the Bible and the Prayerbook, the very writings that Buber ignored. These writings, rather than the tales, constitute the

first and foremost authoritative representation of the meaning of this life, long before it was enveloped in legends. The identity of legends and life which Buber claims, is fictitious. . . . Life is reflected both in legend and in teaching, but it must be emphasized that, whereas the origins of this Hasidic life were deeply influenced and shaped by ideas laid down in the theoretical literature, its beginnings were certainly not influenced by legend.[34]

Buber's interpretation of Hasidism was "far too closely tied to assumptions that derive from his own philosophy of religious anarchism and existentialism and have no roots in the texts themselves." Ignoring those fundamental Hasidic teachings that were incompatible with his own philosophical leanings, Buber infused his interpretation with "very personal speculations."[35] An outstanding example is his distorted interpretation of the motif of liberating the sparks.

In Scholem's opinion, a careful analysis of Hasidic writings reveals a negative, destructive attitude toward concrete reality. Far from confirming the existential reality of individual beings, the act of liberating the sparks destroys concrete, everyday reality in favor of a higher, spiritual reality:

The actual and final realization of such a communion has a destructive quality. . . . As so many Hasidic writers like to put it: it is necessary to reduce things to their nothingness in order to restore them to their true nature.[36]

Blinded by his own existentialist biases, Buber erroneously attributed to Hasidism a positive attitude toward concrete, everyday reality. According to Scholem, however, an objective reading of Hasidic literature reveals that the key to liberating the sparks is to strip away corporeal reality, thereby annihilating the concrete. This is particularly evident in Hasidism's conception of the act of prayer as communion with God: "Here we have the clear and radical thesis: The actual and final realization of such a communion has a destructive quality."[37]

While not denying that a view similar to Buber's can be found among the Hasidim, Scholem dismissed it as merely a "popular or vulgar version" that reflected the mood of some followers but not that of the genuine leaders: "To call this the message of Hasidism seems to me far from the truth."[38] In the "real Hasidic teaching," the emphasis in the divine-human encounter is on "emptying the concrete phenomenon of its own weight and individual significance."[39]

Scholem further criticized Buber for ignoring the central position of institutionalized religious forms and structures in the life of the Hasidim. Whereas Buber, the existentialist, concerned himself only with the *how* of religious life, original Hasidism never hesitated to prescribe and proscribe specific forms and actions. While paying careful attention to the *how*, Hasidism also emphasized the *what*:

This tradition presents a teaching in which directions and decisions could be formulated, i.e., a teaching concerning *what* should be done. Only against this background can we understand in its true context the certainly emphatic interest of Hasidism in the *how* of such action. For Buber, this world of the *how* is all that has remained.[40]

Scholem attributed Buber's neglect of the structured, institutionalized character of Hasidism to his "religious anarchism":

To put it bluntly, Buber is a religious anarchist, and his teaching is religious anarchism. By this I mean the following: Buber's philosophy demands of man that he set himself a direction and reach a decision, but it says nothing about which direction and which decision.[41]

Thus, Scholem criticized Buber's interpretation of Hasidism on philosophical, methodological, and substantive grounds. Philosophically, Buber injected his own existential, anarchistic views of religion into his reading of Hasidism, thereby distorting its authentic teachings. Methodologically, Buber ignored the relevant texts in his effort to construct an accurate picture of Hasidism, while the texts upon which he did draw did not reflect authentic Hasidic teachings. Substantively, Buber attributed to Hasidism a concern for the concrete and the everyday where no such concern existed:

> The spiritual message he has read into these writings is far too closely tied to assumptions that derive from his own philosophy of religious anarchism and existentialism and have no roots in the texts themselves. Too much is left out of these descriptions of Hasidism and what is included is overloaded with very personal speculations. . . . If we would understand the real phenomenon of Hasidism, both in its grandeur and its decay, . . . we shall have to start again from the beginning.[42]

The year following the publication of Scholem's critique, Buber published a response in which he endeavored to clarify his position.[43] In that article, Buber responded to both the substantive and methodological criticisms. Substantively, Buber rejected Scholem's claim concerning the destructive character of the act of liberating the sparks. While the nihilistic, spiritualizing tendencies referred to by Scholem are to be found in Hasidism, they appear only in the later writings of the Maggid of Mezzeritch and reflect the growing influence of Kabbalistic doctrine.[44] However, in the teachings of the Baal Shem Tov, Hasidism's founder, and his immediate circle, the emphasis on concrete, everyday reality was already evident.

The main thrust of Buber's defense against Scholem's critique revolves around their different objectives as interpreters of Hasidism. Imbued with the spirit of nineteenth-century objectivistic historical scholarship, Scholem was primarily concerned with adding to our fund of historical knowledge.[45] Buber, on the other hand, clearly disavowed the goals of historical scholarship, which "addresses the past as an object of knowledge with the intention of advancing the field of historical knowledge" (Buber, "Interpreting Hasidism," 218).

While not denying the historical mode of inquiry a valid place,

Buber's concern was a totally different, edifying one, rooted not in the past, but in the present:

The other, and essentially different, way of restoring a great buried heritage of faith to the light is to recapture a sense of the power that once gave it the capacity to take hold of and vitalize the life of diverse classes of people. Such an approach derives from the desire to convey to our own time the force of a former life of faith to help our age renew its ruptured bond with the absolute. The scholar bent upon unearthing a forgotten or misunderstood body of teaching cannot accomplish this renewal even if he succeeds in establishing a new interpretation. (Buber, "Interpreting Hasidism," 218)

Buber valued the study of the past not for its own sake but because of its power to assist us in confronting the crisis of the present. In contrast to Nietzsche, Buber believed that the alienation from the divine is the key to the modern person's condition. Hasidism, he believed, has the power to help the modern person combat this alienation. Translating and interpreting Hasidic texts, he sought to help his age overcome the gap separating the modern person from the sacred: "I was concerned from first to last with restoring immediacy to the relation between man and God, with helping to end 'the eclipse of God' " (Buber, "Interpreting Hasidism," 224).

Buber described his approach to Hasidism as that of an artist. Like the artist, his major faculty was not cognition, but vision. Not what he thought, but what he saw was primary: "I had to tell the stories that I had taken into myself from out of myself, as a true painter takes into himself the lines of the models and achieves the genuine images out of the memory formed of them" (HMM, 61–62).[46]

Far from denying that his primary concerns were existential, Buber openly acknowledged these concerns and made them central to his writings on Hasidism. Unlike objectivistic historians, such as Scholem, who viewed such existential concerns as detrimental to the pursuit of objective truth, Buber considered them to be essential to such a pursuit. While never explicitly denying the validity of historical inquiry, Buber, like Nietzsche, held it to be an ineffective way to address the issues of the present.

While Scholem related to Hasidism as a system of theological concepts, Buber, in the spirit of existentialism and Lebensphilosophie, viewed it as a mode of life "that shapes a community and that is consonant with community by its very nature" (Buber, Origin

and Meaning, 24). Accordingly, while Scholem was primarily concerned with the key ideas of Hasidism, Buber emphasized the tales,
those literary expressions that, to him, best revealed Hasidism's
dynamic power:

> Because Hasidism in the first instance is not a category of teaching, but one
> of life, our chief source of knowledge of Hasidism is its legends, and only
> after them comes its theoretical literature. The latter is the commentary,
> the former the text. (Buber, *Origin and Meaning*, 27) [47]

The logically structured theoretical writings of Hasidism are, in
Buber's view, efforts to rework the original moments in the life of
the community into a rationalized literary form. Their effect, therefore, is to distance us from the actual lived experience of the community:

> I have not converted the message of Hasidism into solid concepts; I was
> concerned to preserve its mythical as well as its epic essence. I cannot
> concur with the postulate of the hour—to demythologize religion. For
> myth is not the subsequent clothing of a truth of faith; it is the unarbitrary
> testimony of the image-making vision and the image-making memory, and
> the conceptual cannot be refined out of it. (*HMM*, 41)

The predilection for myth was not limited to Buber's interpretation of Hasidism, but informed his interpretation of the Bible, and
of Jewish history as a whole. In sharp contrast to the majority of
Jewish scholars who denied that there was any mythic content in
the Hebrew Bible, Buber insisted that biblical narratives were best
understood as myth, "a corporeally real event that is perceived and
presented as a divine, an absolute event" (Buber, *On Judaism*,
103). [48] Moreover, according to Buber, myth was biblical Israel's
natural mode of expression:

> The Jew of antiquity cannot tell a story in any other way than mythically,
> for to him, an event is worth telling only when it has been grasped in its
> divine significance. All story-telling books of the Bible have but one subject
> matter: the account of YHVH's encounters with his people. (Buber, *On
> Judaism*, 105)

These myths, the memories of events experienced as revelatory
acts of God, shaped the consciousness of subsequent generations.
Rather than historicize myths by situating them in a continuum of

time, the Bible perceived historical events as divine acts. This, according to Buber, was the real stuff of history.

The emphasis on the mythic character of Judaism and the call for the renewal of myth were basic to Buber's revision of Judaism. Among Western Jews, myths were viewed simply as stories of the life of the gods and, as such, were alien to the authentic spirit of Judaism. To historians and philosophers alike, the central theme of the Bible was the displacement of pagan myth by monotheistic religion. In nineteenth and twentieth century interpretations, the antimythic character of Judaism was a given.[49]

For Buber, however, myth, which preserved the vitality of Judaism in the past, was a key to the understanding of the overall development of Judaism:

The history of the development of Jewish religion is really the history of the struggles between the natural structure of a mythical-monotheistic folk religion and the intellectual structure of a rational-monotheistic religion. I said 'a mythical-monotheistic folk-religion'; for it is not at all true that monotheism and myth are mutually exclusive and that a monotheistically inclined people must therefore be devoid of a myth making capacity. To the contrary, every living monotheism is filled with the mythical element and remains alive only so long as it is filled with it. It is to myth that Judaism owed its inmost cohesiveness in times of danger. (Buber, *On Judaism*, 99–100)

Unlike the prevailing contemporary worldview, which perceives reality in terms of empirical cause and effect, the primitive, mythic mind perceived experience as "a signum of a hidden, supracausal connection; of the manifestation of the absolute" (Buber, *On Judaism*, 104). Moreover, the tendency to mythicize is not a remnant from the archaic past. In every age, including our own, the mythic mode of perception continues, disclosing to us "a deeper, fuller truth than the causal" (Buber, *On Judaism*, 105).

History Deconstructed:
The Debate Reconsidered

When we read the Buber-Scholem debate in the light of recent discussions in the fields of philosophy and literary theory, it becomes clear that it is not simply a debate over method, evidence, and historical accuracy. What at first glance appears to be a debate among scholars over the correct interpretation of the past can now be seen as a debate that revolves around diverse interests, purposes, and background beliefs.

On the one hand, underlying the debate are such neglected issues as, What constitutes a valid interpretation of a movement or event from the past? What criteria does one employ to evaluate such interpretations? What is the relationship between creative, imaginative discourse and objectivistic scholarship? What are the goals of interpretation? What, if any, are the limits within which one must remain in interpreting Judaism?

On the other hand, the apparently epistemological questions concerning the interpretation of the Jewish past also entail questions concerning how we should live our lives. Insofar as a perspective or framework of interpretation presupposes a particular form of life or a particular attitude toward life, the issue is, as recognized by Stout and others, one of social values:

At the heart of the current debate over literary theory is the question of which normative aims one ought to have in studying literature. What begins seeming like a debate over the nature of meaning reveals itself before long as a struggle over what makes literature worth caring about and what kind of a society to strive for.[50]

Buber's interpretation of Hasidism challenged the prevailing modes of interpretation in the Jewish scholarly world. The freedom with which he appropriated and revised the Hasidic textual material offends the canons of Jewish scholarly discourse, which, since the emergence of Wissenschaft des Judentums (the historical school of Jewish scholarship) in the early nineteenth century, have privileged the historical mode of inquiry over philosophical and theological discourse. Alienated from the theological categories of traditional Jewish thought and seeking to legitimate a secularized form of Jewish national existence, Jewish scholars found in historical inquiry a way of talking about Judaism that was fully compatible with the secular, scientific ethos.[51]

Basic to this historical orientation is the value of "objectivity." Freeing himself or herself from all subjective concerns and eschewing all theories, a scholar must engage in an inductive process of interpretation.[52] While modern Jewish scholars may criticize the ideological foundations and methods of the original proponents of Wissenschaft des Judentums, they continue to share their view of the privileged place of history as an academic discipline.[53]

It is not surprising, therefore, that in the scholarly world, the Buber-Scholem controversy is conventionally seen as a debate over the accurate representation of the historical reality known as Hasidism. According to this reading, Scholem, an objective historian engaged in the dispassionate pursuit of truth, employed methods of critical scholarship in order to portray Hasidism as it truly was.[54] Buber, driven by subjective, theological concerns, violated the canons of historical inquiry and appropriated the teachings of Hasidism for his own ideological purposes. Whereas Scholem, according to the conventional reading, was concerned with Hasidism in and of itself *(wie es eigentlich gewesen ist)*, Buber was concerned only with disseminating his own existential brand of Judaism. Given Scholem's unchallenged reputation as the world's foremost authority on Jewish mysticism, it is not surprising that almost all scholars have sided with him.

Thus, as most scholars read the Buber-Scholem controversy, it revolves around the issue of objective truth. The key issue is, Which man offers the truer, more accurate picture of Hasidism? For Scholem and his disciples, the so-called historical method produces the truest depiction of Hasidism. According to this view, the historical mode of discourse offers the most valid way of talking about Judaism in general, and Hasidism in particular.[55] Insofar as Buber deviated from the canons of objectivistic historiography, he deviated from the truth.

In recent decades, however, the privileged conception of objectivistic historiography has been challenged by a growing number of writers, many of whom are disciples of Nietzsche.[56] Viewing different disciplines as different frameworks of discourse, students of literature and semiotics have denied the existence of objective criteria that could support the privileging of one framework of discourse over another. Different frameworks of discourse, utilizing different paradigms, serve the needs of different communities, each of which has its own set of purposes and goals. Accordingly, fields such as history, literature, or philosophy do not represent different levels in a hierarchy of truth but are simply different ways of framing and talking about reality.

Implicit in this view is the belief that there are no universal, "objective" standards by means of which to adjudicate between diverse interpretations. Different fields of inquiry, operating within different frameworks of discourse, pursue the interpretation of texts and data in different ways. All reading, historical and otherwise, is a constructive, creative enterprise; the historian, like the novelist or the poet, participates in constructing the reality that he or she describes.[57]

Theorists writing in the spirit of Nietzschean perspectivalism are in essential agreement that writing, reading, and interpretation are willful acts occurring within a distinct social setting and informed by pragmatic concerns.[58] To these antiobjectivists, the criteria for evaluating literary works are ultimately pragmatic and social. In the final analysis, the validity of any interpretation depends on how one wishes to use a given text and with which community of discourse one chooses to identify.

In light of these recent insights into the process of reading and interpretation, it is difficult to sustain the conventional reading of the Buber-Scholem controversy, which assumes that both men engaged in the same activity, operated with the same set of rules, and pursued the same goals.[59] While one can certainly say that both Buber and Scholem were engaged in the activity of interpreting Hasidic texts, a careful examination of their debate clearly reveals that their conceptions of reading and interpretation differ significantly.

In interpreting Judaism in general and Hasidism in particular, Buber and Scholem utilized different discursive frameworks and pursued different objectives. Accordingly, to evaluate their interpretations as if they were engaged in the same inquiry is to confuse two different kinds of interpretive activity. The central issue in that debate is not, as is commonly assumed, historical accuracy but the appropriateness of particular modes of interpretation. The question is not which writer most accurately depicted the "true" Hasidism but rather which mode of interpretation best illuminates the Hasidic texts. The answer to this question depends upon why we want to read and interpret Hasidic texts in the first place.

Buber's reading of Hasidism is best understood in the context of his fundamental edifying project. As I have indicated previously, his fundamental concern was to change the ways in which modern persons, Jews as well as non-Jews, think, talk, and, most importantly, live.[60] When seen in this light, his turn to Hasidism was motivated by a desire to help liberate his generation from the alienated condition in which it lived.

Buber was what Rorty refers to as a "strong textualist," who approaches texts out of a concern for present realities and reads them in a way that renders them useful in addressing these concerns: "The strong textualist simply asks himself the same questions about a text which the engineer or the physicist asks himself about a puzzling physical object: 'How shall I describe this in order to get it to do what I want?' "[61]

Furthermore, in situating himself within the tradition of Jewish myth making, Buber identified with a long line of strong readers. From rabbinic midrash to the daring "misreadings" of the Kabbalists, Jewish scholars did not hesitate to read the sacred texts of Judaism in daring, highly creative, imaginative ways:

We tend usually to think of reading as a passive occupation, but for the Jewish textual tradition, it was anything but that. Reading was a passionate and active grappling with God's living word. It held the challenge of uncovering secret, unheard of explanations, matters of great weight and significance. An active, indeed interactive, reading was their method of approaching the sacred text called Torah and through that reading process of finding something at once new and old.[62]

Scholem played a major role in making us aware of this active, creative, daring way of reading texts. To take but one example, in a superb essay on the concept of Torah in Kabbalah, he lucidly described the Kabbalah's pluralistic orientation to reading:

The ever flowing fountain has different sides, a front and a back. From this stems the differences and the conflicts among the varying conceptions regarding the prohibited and the permitted, the usable and the unusable as it is known to the mystics. . . . The implicit meaning of this secret is that it lets every scholar insist on his own opinion and cite proofs for it from the Torah. . . . Thus it is incumbent upon us to hear the different opinions, and this is the sense of "these and these are the words of the living God."[63]

Throughout his writings, Scholem repeatedly emphasized the propensity of the Kabbalists for strong reading. While analyzing passages from the Zohar, Lurianic writings, and other Kabbalistic texts, he questioned neither the validity of these interpretations nor the authors' right to appropriate the biblical texts in this way. For Scholem, the importance of the Kabbalists' interpretation was not that they read the text "correctly," but the fact that their interpretations infused new life into the texts and introduced new and powerful ideas into Judaism. To accuse the mystic of not being faithful to the original source would have been simply beside the point.

Scholem defended the most bizarre interpretations as authentic Jewish thinking. What might strike the conventional reader as alien to Judaism is, insisted Scholem, an authentic part of Judaism:

I do not hold to the opinion of those (and there are indeed many) who view the events of Jewish history from a fixed dogmatic standpoint and who know exactly whether some phenomenon is Jewish or not. Nor am I a follower of that school which proceeds from the assumption that there is a well-defined and unvarying essence of Judaism, especially not where the evaluation of historical events is concerned.[64]

Advocating a pluralistic approach to Judaism, Scholem resisted all efforts to distinguish between that which is authentically Jewish and that which is not.

Nevertheless, Scholem did not hesitate to accuse Buber of reading into the texts strange ideas inconsistent with authentic Hasidism. Although considering it valid for the Kabbalists to propound radical "misreadings" of biblical sources, Scholem considered it invalid for Buber, who situated himself in the tradition of Jewish myth making, to do so. Thus, in spite of Buber's repeated statements disavowing any identification with the discursive mode of historical scholarship, Scholem nonetheless insisted that Buber conform to the rules of that discursive mode.

A stronger form of the argument described above would claim that all readings are, by necessity, misreadings or interpretations that emanate no less from the reader than from the text. According to this argument, there exist no absolute, objective standards by means of which one can substantiate a claim that a reading is the correct one.[65] Reading is a dynamic activity involving author, reader, text, and context. No sooner is a text written than it must be read. Moreover, the author is often unaware of the various factors, conscious and unconscious, that shaped his or her text. Furthermore, there is no guarantee that an author will read his or her own text in the same way on different occasions. Consequently, Scholem's quest for a "correct" reading of Hasidism is based upon assumptions that can no longer be sustained.

Moreover, according to many theorists, insofar as any reader's access to Hasidism is, like Scholem's and Buber's, mediated through language, there is no Olympian perch from which to validate one reading over another. Language, the medium of communication between author and reader, displaces rather than reflects the reality being discussed. Accordingly, it makes no sense to speak of the "true meaning" or "real meaning" of any text. Whatever reality serves as the stimulus or referent, whether it is an experience, an idea, an event, an object, or a feeling, language displaces that reality and puts in its place a word. Thus, the connection between the word and that which it signifies is both arbitrary and elusive.

Yet another problem in Scholem's argument derives from his privileging of objectivistic, historical inquiry. As White has effectively argued, the gap between the historian and the writer of fiction is far more narrow than is commonly admitted. The historian, like the novelist, must shape the limitless mass of events into a coherent story:

Unlike the novelist, the historian confronts a veritable chaos of events already constituted, out of which he must choose the elements of the story he would tell. He makes his story by including some events and excluding others. This process of exclusion, stress and subordination is carried out in the interest of constituting a story of a particular kind. That is to say, he "emplots" a story.[66]

Like all reading, historical inquiry is best understood as a constructive endeavor that is as dependent on the activity of the reader as it is on the texts or evidence under study. Meaning is something that historians help to construct. Through the modes of "emplotment" that they bring to the material, historians prefigure the shape of their interpretations.

In addition, the very act of selecting data is a constructive activity. Whenever historians endeavor to make sense out of data, they must perforce select from an endless number of psychological and individual movements:

Every one of these movements expresses unconscious developments, and these, in turn, resolve themselves in cerebral, hormonal, or nervous phenomena, whose frame of reference is itself of a physical or chemical nature. . . . As a consequence, the historical fact is no more given than other facts. It is the historian, or the agent of the historical process, who constitutes it by way of abstraction, under the threat, as it were, of a regression to infinity.[67]

Any event involves an infinitely rich variety of physical and psychological moments, "each of which plays a role in the way he [the historian] experiences history and conceives it." In order to avoid the total chaos of a total history, "the historian and the agent of the historical process choose, make cross sections, and abstract."[68] Thus, the constitutive role of the historian is inherent in the situation.

Reading as a Perspectival Activity

Like any historical movement, Hasidism is an ideal type abstracted from a seemingly endless variety of individuals, social groups, texts, ritual acts, interpretive activities, and personal experiences. Whenever we seek to depict Hasidism, Judaism, or any other "ism," we must, of necessity, "choose, make cross sections and abstract." All such "isms," therefore, are mental constructs.[69]

While the historian must provide evidence to support his or her particular interpretation or reading of Hasidism, what is presented is partial and perspectival. The very act of determining which data is relevant is a function of the questions that we ask, and these questions, in turn, reflect our own concerns. Thus, the claim that Buber selected certain aspects while neglecting others or that his selection reflected his own value system applies to any interpreter of Hasidism, including Scholem.

When Scholem, or any other scholar, talks about Hasidism, he is talking about an abstraction that, of necessity, is shaped by a particular perspective. Like Buber, Scholem reworked the data of Hasidism, and of Judaism in general, into a coherent pattern that yields a particular kind of plot or story. In the case of Scholem, the form of the story is that of a dialectic: "As opposed to the harmonious idea of progress adopted by the nineteenth century historians, Scholem's vision of Jewish history is a stormy dialectic of constructive and destructive forces."[70]

As his own words make clear, Scholem's turn to historical scholarship cannot be understood apart from his ideological concerns for the then-present condition of Judaism: "I wanted to enter the world of Kabbalah out of my belief in Zionism as a living thing — as the restoration of a people that had degenerated quite a bit."[71] Scholem's particular concern was whether or not halakhic Judaism still retained enough strength to survive. While he did not personally accept the authority of halakhah, he nonetheless appreciated its historical power and sensed "that it might be kabbalah that explains the survival of the consolidated force of halakhic Judaism. That was certainly one of my obvious motives."[72]

As Biale has convincingly argued, Scholem's historiographical inquiries "are based on significant theological assumptions of his own."[73] Like Buber's, his historical investigation was undertaken out of a deep concern with the present.[74] Scholem, like his nineteenth-century precursors in Wissenschaft des Judentums, believed that the historical mode of discourse held the key to understanding the Jewish situation in his own time. Thus, in opposition to Buber's faith in myth stands Scholem's faith in the dialectical pattern of history.

Buber and Scholem undertook the interpretation of Hasidism, and Judaism in general, out of different concerns, interests, purposes, and background beliefs. Accordingly, at issue between them is not which interpretation of Hasidism most closely corresponds to some original or pure entity known as Hasidism, but rather, which interpretation of Hasidism best serves their respective concerns, interests, purposes, and beliefs:

Philosophical and literary texts often enter the humanistic canon because they provide uniquely valuable occasions for normative reflection. We lavish great interpretive care upon them, but not always in order to "get them right". Getting them right sometimes ceases to matter. We sometimes want our interpretations to teach us something new, not so much about the text itself, its author, or its effective history as about ourselves, our forms of life, our problems.[75]

Thus, one evaluates interpretations such as Buber's and Scholem's not through some objective standard that transcends our historical situation but through an interpretation of reality, a value system, and a form of life with which one identifies and according to which one chooses to live.

Buber's existential concerns and his interpretation of the condition of modern society led him to approach Hasidism through the framework of religious discourse. Accordingly, as Walter Kaufmann pointed out, rather than treat Buber's Hasidic writings as works of scholarship in the conventional sense, one should view them as a body of primary Jewish religious teachings. Just as one would not read religious scriptures such as Genesis or the discourses of the Buddha "as reports of 'how it actually happened'," one does not read Buber in this way either. "The ranks of these works does not depend on their positivistic accuracy but on their profundity. And that is true also of *Tales of the Hasidim*."[76]

In demanding that Buber's work conform to the canons of objectivistic historiography, Scholem and his colleagues, privileging history over other modes of discourse, evaluate one framework of discourse — that of myth — according to the rules of another.[77] However, the question of whether mythic discourse or historical discourse is preferable can only be answered in terms of the purpose for which the interpretation of Hasidic texts is being undertaken in the first place.[78]

The issues separating the objectivistic, progressivist view of scholarship from the perspectival view being advocated here has been effectively summed up by Richard Rorty:

There, then, are two ways of thinking about various things. . . . The first tradition thinks of truth as a vertical relationship between representations and what is represented. The second tradition thinks of truth horizontally — as the culminating reinterpretation of our predecessors' reinterpretation of their predecessors' reinterpretations. . . . This tradition does not ask how representations are related to nonrepresentations, but how representations can be seen as hanging together. The difference is not one between "correspondence" and "coherence" theories of truth — though these so-called theories are partial expressions of this contrast. Rather it is the difference between regarding truth, goodness and beauty as eternal objects which we try to locate and reveal, and regarding them as artifacts whose fundamental design we often have to alter.[79]

According to Rorty, scholarship, like any mode of intellectual inquiry, is not an ongoing process in which subsequent generations, building upon the work of their predecessors, come closer to a determinate truth. Historians, like any group of scholars, are participants in an ongoing conversation or debate. What such a conversation can achieve is not an accurate, objective description but a way of talking about the subject at hand that is appropriate to a given set of interests, concerns, purposes, and beliefs.

Seen in this light, the validity of an interpretation is not to be determined by its correspondence to some ideal reality. Instead, interpretations are to be evaluated in terms of whether or not they do the job we want them to do, whether we conceive of that job in political, aesthetic, or moral terms:

What makes a given interpretation good? That depends upon which interests and purposes are relevant to the case at hand. We should not expect the same answer in each case, unless somebody succeeds in establishing a hermeneutical equivalent of the categorical imperative — a criterion of adequacy one could usefully apply to interpretations of every sort.[80]

Accordingly, the ongoing interpretation of Judaism or Hasidism by historians and nonhistorians alike is best understood as an ongoing conversation or argument informed by the values, concerns, and intellectual premises of the participants.[81] Consequently, when confronted by a debate such as the one between Buber and Scholem over Hasidism, it simply makes no sense to ask which one is right if by right we mean which interpretation corresponds most closely to the truth. Instead, we are led to ask, which interpretation points to and gives support to the form of life and system of values with which we most closely identify.[82] Thus, the debate over interpretation is, at one and the same time, a debate over forms of life, interests, and values.

To say, therefore, that the issue between Buber and Scholem is not simply which man's reading of Hasidism is the correct one is not to say that there is no way of evaluating the debate. If the debate over interpretation is grounded in concerns that the interpreter brings to the text, one may inquire into these concerns and critically appraise them. In the case of the Buber-Scholem debate, we encounter two readers each approaching the Hasidic texts for his own purposes. In such a situation, we can explore these purposes and concerns, the beliefs they presuppose, and the social forms they evoke and support and critically assess them.

By viewing conflicting interpretations in light of the purposes for which they are being undertaken, the way remains open for a critical discussion concerning the appropriateness of a particular mode of discourse for particular purposes:

What is the goodness of an interpretation relative to? The interests, purposes and background beliefs of interpreters. But this does not imply what I would call relativism — the idea that any interpretation is as good as any other — for the interests, purposes and background beliefs relative to which we assess interpretations are themselves subject to rational assessment.[83]

Accordingly, in posing the issue of cross-perspectival validity, we shift from an epistemological framework to a moral framework having to do with beliefs, values, and behavior.

Buber's activity as an interpreter of Hasidism is fully consistent with his overall edifying concerns and his interest in a renewal of Jewish communal life. As Buber defined the primary issues facing his age, the approach adopted by conventional historians was inadequate and inappropriate. By focusing our attention on such questions as what really happened or what was the reality known as Hasidism, objectivistic historiography distracts us from the burning existential crisis of our age. Searching the Hasidic texts for insights that could assist in the effort to bridge the gap separating the human and the divine and to overcome the alienation between persons, Buber opted for a mode of inquiry that was appropriate to that task.

3

Revisioning Judaism

Like his interpretation of Hasidism, Buber's interpretation of Judaism as a whole was the center of much controversy among Jewish scholars and philosophers.[1] As in the case of Hasidism, Buber's critics based their approach on premises that Buber himself rejected and used a framework of interpretation that differed substantially from his. As I argued in chapter 2, the appropriate question for the reader of Buber is not whether Buber accurately describes an objective reality known as Judaism, but rather how he defines the Jewish problem and what mode of interpretation he employs to address that problem.

As we saw in the previous chapter, Buber approached the interpretation of Hasidism as a strong, creative reader whose primary concern was not to present an accurate historical picture but to uncover the distinct spiritual power of the Hasidic writings. Coming to the Hasidic sources neither as a detached scholar nor as a faithful disciple, but rather as a modern Jew overcome by a sense of alienation, Buber sought in the teachings of Hasidism a way out of this alienated condition.

This same stance marks his overall interpretation of Judaism. Deeply concerned with the alienated condition of Jewish life, he sought to unearth those spiritual forces within Judaism that had the power to generate spiritual renewal among Jewish youth. His primary concern, therefore, was not historical reconstruction but bridging the abyss that loomed between the contemporary Jew and the inherited forms of Jewish life and thought.

To Buber, the alienation that permeated Jewish life was, to a large degree, the result of an obsolete discourse that masked the contemporary Jew's estrangement from the vital sources of authentic Jewish spirituality. Approaching Jewish tradition as a revisionist, his primary concern was to bring about a radical change in the conventional ways of living and thinking about Judaism.[2] In contrast to the benign interpreter who acquiesces to the basic authority of tradition, the revisionist "strives to see again, so as to esteem and estimate differently."[3] Rather than benignly accept inherited ways of thinking and behaving, the revisionist "wishes to find his own original relation to truth, whether in texts or in reality (which he treats as texts anyway), but also wishes to open received texts to his own sufferings, or what he wants to call the sufferings of history."[4] To achieve this end, the revisionist subjects texts and traditions to a strong reading or, as discussed in the previous chapter, a creative misreading.

For all of Buber's attraction to the deconstructive elements in Nietzsche's thought, Nietzsche, who denounced religious traditions, could provide little help to Buber in his efforts to revise and renew the teachings of Judaism. Accordingly, forsaking the antireligious tenor of Nietzsche's writings, Buber turned to a thinker who, while engaging in a deconstruction of religious tradition, did so in the name of religious faith. Accordingly, in revising the conventional, official interpretations of Judaism, it was Kierkegaard, the believing Christian, rather than Nietzsche to whom Buber turned as a mentor.

Consistent with his own edifying concern, Kierkegaard had analyzed the ways in which alienation both manifested itself and was perpetuated by the social conditions of the time. The modern age, as Kierkegaard viewed it, is one in which passion, feeling, subjectivity, action, and faith are suppressed. He portrayed his age as "essentially one of understanding and reflection, without passion, momentarily bursting into enthusiasm, and shrewdly relapsing into repose."[5] Like Nietzsche, Kierkegaard believed that in the modern age, the concrete, feeling, existing individual has been swallowed up by the crowd.

Rather than act out of concrete decision, individuals act out of abstract principles. Consequently, moral action, which presupposes concrete choice, is reduced to abstraction. In modern society, persons do not relate to each other on the level of genuine, spontaneous decision but in a detached manner. They live as if they were playing a game rather than living real life. Communication has deteriorated into talkativeness, and speech is characterized by abstraction and objectivity.

In contrast to Nietzsche, who sought to liberate the individual from the alienating effects of religion, Kierkegaard believed that genuine religious faith offered the only hope for overcoming alienation. The existential philosophical task of rehabilitating the individual was, in fact, a religious task: "I was conscious of being a religious author and, as such, was concerned with the individual, a thought in which is contained an entire philosophy of life and of the world."[6]

To Kierkegaard, religion meant Christianity. Throughout his writings the recurring question is, How can I become a Christian? However, defining himself as a revisionist, Kierkegaard endeavored "to revise the definition of what it is to be a Christian."[7] To Kierkegaard, *Christianity* meant neither historical Christianity nor Christianity as currently lived. Instead, he distinguished between official, establishment Christianity, or Christendom, and authentic, subjective, existential Christianity which was rooted in the Christian Bible.[8] In Kierkegaard's writings, therefore, *Christianity* is a critical term employed dialectically to criticize conventional forms of religion and culture. Although a religious believer, he criticized the alienating power of religion.

Kierkegaard's solution to the crisis of alienation was to recover the original force and meaning of Christianity as lived by Christ. To be a Christian meant, first and foremost, to live as an individual, in complete subjectivity, without the consolation of fixed forms or objective certainty. The genuine individual lives in perennial uncertainty: "An objective uncertainty held fast in an appropriation-process of the most passionate inwardness is the truth, the highest truth available for an existing individual."[9]

Rather than seize onto objective systems, the authentic, religious individual suffers this anxiety and retains his or her freedom. Living in objective uncertainty, the person of faith risks himself or herself continually. To know God rationally, through objective knowledge, is the antithesis to genuine faith.

Without risk, there is no faith. Faith is precisely the contradiction between the infinite passion of the individual's inwardness and the objective uncertainty. If I am capable of grasping God objectively, I do not believe, but precisely because I cannot do this, I must believe.[10]

Accordingly, for Kierkegaard, "to live in the anxiety of freedom, without finite support or encouragement is to live by the power of God."[11]

Buber's revisionist stance toward Judaism parallels in striking ways the revisionist stance adopted by Kierkegaard toward official Christianity. Just as Kierkegaard revised the conventional definitions of Christianity, Buber revised the conventional definitions of what it was to be a Jew. Buber's distinction between official rabbinic Judaism and existential Jewish "religiosity" parallels Kierkegaard's distinction between official, establishment Christianity, or Christendom, and authentic, subjective, existential Christianity. Just as Kierkegaard had rooted authentic Christianity in Christian scripture, Buber turned to the Hebrew Bible for a model of authentic Jewish "religiosity."

Buber's emphasis on the existential experience of the Jew and his critique of the objectified, institutionalized forms of Jewish life were the distinctive components of his revisioning of Judaism. He believed that the conventional formulations of Judaism, couched in the discourse of rational philosophy or nationalist ideology, neglected the inner religious experience of the individual. Consequently, they were inadequate foundations for Jewish renewal.

The Crisis in Jewish Life

At the end of the first decade of the twentieth century, many young Jews in central Europe found Judaism to be a vapid, ineffectual form of life, lacking in both spiritual vitality and creative force. With the exception of the Orthodox community and the small number of active Zionists, the young Jewish intellectuals of Berlin, Frankfurt, and Prague were unconvinced of the ultimate meaning and significance of being Jewish.[12]

Young Jewish intellectuals found little that was inspiring in the official institutions of Jewish life. The overall ethos of these Jewish communities was shaped by a concern to integrate the Jews into the surrounding society and to combat anti-Semitism. Few of the activities of organized Jewish life succeeded in confirming the uniqueness or the value of Jewish life and culture. As a Jewish intellectual of that period put it, "we perceive the Jewish people, hardly a people any longer, as a worn out herd, fearful and cowardly, inactive and dull, surrendered to the everyday, in awe only of its dependence, and accepting its weakness as its norm."[13]

Yet many young Jews, particularly in central and Eastern Europe, had grown up in societies in which ethnicity still served as a powerful source of individual identity. Furthermore, anti-Semitism reinforced their awareness of the wall separating Jews from all others. Consequently, feeling the need to root themselves in a community, they found the Jewish community to be their only viable option. In Jewish culture, they sought fertile soil in which to nurture their ethnic roots.

For most young Jews whose primary education was European, Orthodoxy was not a viable option. Alienated from the sources of Jewish tradition, most of these Jews considered the theological premises of Orthodox Judaism to be obsolete. The alternatives to Orthodoxy included trying to assimilate completely into the surrounding culture, joining the movement for a Jewish national homeland, or identifying with the movement for religious reform.[14]

Unlike Orthodoxy, Reform Judaism, grounded in a developmental historical perspective, believed that rabbinic Judaism, while once valid, had, for the most part, outlived its usefulness. Nevertheless, Reform Judaism appropriated the framework of the rabbinic liturgical calendar and synagogue structure. Subjecting Judaism to a rational critique grounded in the moral and social values of European liberalism, the reformers did not hesitate to alter the rabbinic framework significantly.[15]

The reformers viewed the ritualistic and symbolic framework of rabbinic Judaism as the product of evolutionary processes. Specifically, the talmudic rabbis had introduced and preserved those forms and symbols that insured the continuity of the religious and moral teachings of ethical monotheism. These teachings and the accompanying moral principles constituted for the reformers the core of authentic Judaism.

While, to the reformers, the essential Jewish belief in a moral deity had remained constant, many of the external ritual forms that symbolized this belief had become obsolete. Those beliefs and practices that could not pass the test of Enlightenment rationalism or impeded the assimilation of the Jews into Western culture had to be either reformed or jettisoned. For the most part, the reformers did not wish to overturn the entire structure of rabbinic Judaism but simply wanted to make it more compatible both with modernity and with the spirit of prophetic teachings. Defending their proposed changes, reformers insisted that they were conforming to the authentic spirit rather than to the letter of rabbinic Judaism.

Rejecting the national conception of Judaism, the reformers sought to eliminate or neutralize all ethnic components as antithetical to full sociocultural integration. In their eyes, the Jews were solely a religious community, whose political and cultural loyalties were to those nations in whose midst they lived.[16] Viewing Jewish history as an evolutionary process characterized by adaptation and change, liberal Jews believed that Jews had a unique mission to disseminate ethical monotheism among the nations of the world. Thus, in contrast to both traditionalists and Zionists, the reformers viewed the dispersal of Israel among the nations not as a disaster but as a stage in the historical mission of the group.

Buber's objection to Reform Judaism was based upon three major factors: its evolutionist conception of Jewish history; its rationalistic orientation to religion; and its antinationalist ideology. In contrast to the evolutionist perspective of Reform Judaism, Buber, like Nietzsche, viewed history as an ongoing struggle between dominant and suppressed forces.[17] Thus, rabbinic Judaism, rather than constituting a natural stage in Israel's religious development, had repressed the creative, vital forces in Judaism.

Accordingly, simply to reform the existing structure of beliefs and practices was inadequate. What was required was a sudden and radical revision of the prevailing modes of Jewish life and thought. "By renewal, I do not in any way mean something gradual, a sum total of minor changes. I mean something sudden and immense — by no means a continuation or an improvement, but a turning and a transformation" (Buber, On Judaism, 35). Rejecting any interpretation of Judaism based upon theological or moral principles, Buber advocated a religious faith grounded in existential freedom, individual choice, and direct religious experience.

Consistent with his critique of modernity, Buber also objected to liberal Judaism's rationalistic outlook. Viewing the direct encounter with the divine to be the core of religious life, he believed that reformulating religious principles in a rational, ethical spirit only exacerbated the crisis of Jewish life. In acquiescing to the modern, rationalist spirit, the reformers were embracing elements in modern society destructive to the human spirit.

Buber considered the reformers' desire to integrate the Jews into the nations within which they lived contrary to the ethnic foundations of Judaism. In light of his nationalist convictions, Buber found the Reform movement's anti-Zionism to be totally unacceptable. To him, Jewish nationhood was an essential and nonnegotiable given.

As indicated in chapter 1, Buber, repelled by the pragmatic political orientation of Herzl and his followers, identified with the spiritual, cultural conception of Jewish nationalism espoused by the Hebrew writer Ahad Haam.[18] In contrast to Herzl, Ahad Haam considered the renewal of Jewish national culture to be a necessary stage prior to the social transformation sought by the Zionists. This message of Jewish cultural renewal inspired many of Buber's contemporaries:

Our Zionism was not a reaction to persecution, but under the influence of the German thought of the period, a search for "roots" . . . a turning inward toward the supposed center of our true self, which dated back, so we believed, over 2000 years to biblical times.[19]

For Ahad Haam, the fundamental crisis in Jewish life was spiritual and cultural. The basic problem was the deterioration of Jewish culture and the spiritual stagnation that it engendered. As a result of the conditions of exile, Jewish culture no longer had a direct connection with the life of the people. Simultaneously, the people felt alienated from the culture. The Jews, originally a creative, "literary people," had been transformed into a "people of the book," a community that was enslaved to the written word:

It has surrendered its soul to the written word. The book ceases to be what it should be, a source of ever new inspiration and moral strength; on the contrary, its function is to weaken and finally to crush all spontaneity of action and emotion, till men become wholly dependent on the written word and incapable of responding to any stimulus in nature or in human life without its permission or approval.[20]

In the spirit of the eastern European Jewish Enlightenment, or *Haskalah*, Ahad Haam denounced the alienation that permeated traditional Jewish culture.[21] A committed nationalist, he associated this alienation with the conditions of exile and believed that only the establishment of a Jewish homeland could overcome it. This homeland, in which Judaism could grow and flourish in a normal social and cultural environment, would serve as a spiritual center for Jews throughout the world, renew their Jewish consciousness, and inspire cultural creativity.

Effecting a Copernican revolution within Jewish thought, Ahad Haam transposed the discussion of Judaism from a theological to a secular-nationalist framework. Inspired by European positivism and by sociologists such as Spencer and Tarde, he formulated a secular, antitheological conception of Judaism. In his view, Judaism is not a set of divinely revealed religious beliefs and activities but the national culture of the Jewish people, created by the nation out of its will to survive and stamped with a unique national spirit: "Judaism was created not only for the Jews, but by the Jews themselves. They devoted their best energies for thousands of years to its creation and preservation."[22]

From Ahad Haam's perspective, Judaism was fully compatible with secularism. In the Jewish homeland, a new, secular form of Judaism, rooted in humanistic values, would supplant the now-obsolete religious forms. To be a Jew, in Ahad Haam's terms, meant to identify with the Jewish people, speak its language, and identify with its literature and history. Religion, an outgrowth of an inherent moral spirit, was valued for its historical function in preserving the nation.

Ahad Haam believed that the essence of Judaism was a unique national spirit derived from the moral vision of the prophets of Israel. The sanctity of the Bible derived not from its supposed divine origin but from the fact that it embodied the values and ideas of the Jewish people. Declaring the historicity of biblical figures to be irrelevant, Ahad Haam formulated a mythic interpretation rooted in nationalist values: "I care not whether this man Moses really existed; whether his life and his activity really corresponded to our traditional account of him; whether he was really the savior of Israel who gave the people the Law."[23] For Ahad Haam, the important point was not the historical Moses who lived at a particular time but rather the mythic figure of Moses as it was created and transmitted in the life of the community: "In other words, what manner of thing is the national ideal that has its embodiment in Moses?"[24]

Criticizing the efforts of liberal western European Jews to legitimate Judaism through the idea of chosenness, Ahad Haam characterized being Jewish as analogous to being a member of a family. "I, at least, know why I remain a Jew — or rather, I find no meaning in such a question anymore than I would in the question why I remain my father's son."[25]

Ahad Haam's interpretation of Jewish nationalism attracted Buber, who became one of his strong supporters.[26] Sharing Ahad Haam's humanistic conception of nationalism, Buber viewed Jewish national renewal in terms of the general humanistic awakening occurring throughout Europe. Like Ahad Haam, Buber viewed "exile" as a spiritual phenomenon. Owing to the unnatural conditions of exile, rabbinic tradition, which had gained the ascendancy in Jewish life, was choking the life forces essential to the survival of the nation. The best way to release these creative Jewish life forces was through national renewal.

Buber agreed with Ahad Haam that the heart of the modern Jewish problem was spiritual. By focusing on the spiritual problem of Judaism, Ahad Haam had formulated a much-needed corrective to the Herzlian view. Nevertheless, Buber found Ahad Haam's position to be inadequate.

First, Buber rejected the secularist interpretation of Judaism. In contrast to Ahad Haam and the majority of cultural Zionists, Buber considered religious faith to be an essential element in Judaism. In addition, Ahad Haam had focused on the social group to the neglect of the individual. Finally, Ahad Haam's evolutionist model of history diverted attention from the necessary radical transformation in the life of the individual and the community.

While strongly nationalistic, Buber was deeply troubled by the chauvinism within the Jewish national movement that elevated the nation to a level of absolute priority. To Buber, the nation must always be subordinate to what he called the power of the spirit. Nations that deny the sovereignty of the spirit ultimately destroy one another and themselves.

> We must be willing to subordinate ourselves to the spirit in order that through our means it may become reality. Only so long as we are of the spirit do we carry within ourselves the seed of true life; on the day we become like the other nations, we shall indeed deserve to be no more than that. (Buber, *On Judaism*, 136)

Buber was convinced that the solutions proposed by the existing religious groups only exacerbated the problem. These solutions derived from their definition of the problem. Traditionalists viewed the crisis as the result of widespread deviation from traditional norms and beliefs. To reverse this process, Jews must be brought back to the faith of their fathers and to the patterns of behavior as prescribed by the rabbis. The reformers, on the other hand, saw the problem in terms of outmoded practices and beliefs. To them, the very beliefs and rituals that the traditionalists endorsed had to be revised or eliminated in the light of rational and ethical principles.

Like the reformers, Buber rejected the rabbinic tradition's claims of eternal validity. However, whereas the reformers based their critique on rational evaluation, Buber's position was existential. It is not that traditional beliefs and observances were archaic and irrational; they were not authentic expressions of the individual's encounter with the divine. Like all institutional forms, the institutions of traditional Judaism impeded authentic life experiences.

Revisioning Judaism:
Religion, Nation, Tradition

The method that Buber employed to carry out his revision of Judaism was consistent with his general philosophical method, which, as I shall discuss in chapter 4, is based upon a critique of language. Focusing on key concepts, such as tradition, religion, and nation, Buber endeavored to demonstrate the inadequacies of the conventional understanding of these terms. By revealing the problems inherent in the traditional conceptual framework conventionally used to interpret Judaism, Buber opened the way to an alternative reading.

An example of this method is found in the first of three lectures that Buber delivered before a group of young Jewish intellectuals in Prague in 1909.[27] Buber began his first lecture by asking his audience to reflect on the very conditions of their Jewish identity:

The question that I put before you, as well as before myself, is the question of the meaning of Judaism to the Jews. I want to speak to you not of an abstraction, but of your own life, of our own life; not of life's outer hustle and bustle, but of its authenticity and essence. Why do we call ourselves Jews? Only out of inherited custom — because our fathers did so? Or out of our own reality? (*Buber, On Judaism*, 11)

Whereas conventional discussions of Judaism took as their starting point objectified forms such as religious or ideological principles, Buber began with the existential experience of the individual Jew. His were not academic questions amenable to scholarly inquiry. They originated in and penetrated to the heart of one's innermost being. To answer them, his listeners would have to look within.

In his lectures and writings on Judaism, Buber undertook to revise conventional concepts and categories so as to alter the way in which his audience thought about them. This intellectual strategy is clearly reflected in his lectures to the Bar Kokhba group in Prague, delivered between 1909 and 1911. Rather than take such concepts as tradition, community, and history as self-explanatory, Buber insisted on scrutinizing each of them to determine what existential force they had in the life of his listeners and readers. Upon introducing a concept, he questioned its adequacy in the light of his listeners' personal experience. In this way, he hoped to awaken his hearers or readers to the dissonance between conventional understanding and their personal experience.[28]

The starting point for Buber's critique of official Judaism was the general sense of alienation from European and Jewish society that permeated his audience, a condition, as we have seen, in which he shared:

Intellectualization, in the making for centuries and accomplished within recent generations, has brought a depressing loneliness to the youth of present day Europe. By intellectualization, I mean the hypertrophy of intellect that has broken out of the context of organic life and become parsasitic, in contradistinction to organic spirituality, into which life's totality is translated. . . . This intellectualization begets loneliness . . . the negative loneliness of the abyss experienced by the lost and the forlorn. Out of the anxiety and depression of such a state of mind, modern Europe's youth longs for community. (Buber, *On Judaism*, 158–59).

Owing to the "anomaly of *galut* life," that is, life in exile, the alienation and loneliness of Jewish youth was more intense than that of their non-Jewish contemporaries. Cut off from the roots of national existence, yet not fully integrated into general European society, young Jews lacked the organic group ties that could assuage their longing for community. Like Kierkegaard, Buber believed that alienation and loneliness could serve as the starting point for a renewal of spiritual life.

Only those who were willing to risk themselves could find in Judaism the answers that they were seeking. To break free of current alienated existence, as Kierkegaard and Nietzsche had both argued, one must first surrender the security that the familiar forms and categories provided and confront the world stripped of all artificial supports.[29]

. . . the members of Jewish youth who genuinely participate in the evolving religious awareness of an evolving generation. By this I mean those young men and women who are concerned not with acquiring security in the chaos of our time by conforming to the tested order of the knowable and doable but solely with confronting, unwaveringly, the impact of the unconditional at this hour of twilight, an hour of death and birth. (Buber, *On Judaism*, 168)

Many young Jews identified with Buber's interpretation of the crisis. Buber was one of the few who simultaneously appealed to them as both Jews and human beings. Inspired by his vision of Judaism as an alternative to existential loneliness and alienation, they were drawn to Buber's new way of talking about Judaism.[30] In his depiction of a renewed Judaism, they found a model of organic communal life for which they so deeply yearned.

Sharing his audience's conviction that current forms of Judaism were ineffective, Buber sought to persuade them of Judaism's great spiritual power and of the possibility of renewing that power. Not only was Judaism potentially vital, but it comprised a viable alternative to the overly rationalized, dehumanized, instrumentalist culture of the West. In Buber's words his young listeners discovered a conception of Judaism that went beyond the conventional theological principles, moral exhortations, and ritual patterns; a creative, vital Judaism grounded in their own existential experience.

His effort to transpose the Jewish question from a historical one into an existential one is clearly evident in his early lectures between 1909 and 1912. In his opening lecture, Buber articulated a series of questions that were to serve as the basis for all of his subsequent writings on Judaism. Buber broke down the issues confronting the modern Jew into four specific problems: the meaning of Jewish identity, the meaning of Jewish tradition, the meaning of Jewish community, and the meaning of Jewish history. Thus, Buber posed to his audience four fundamental questions: What does it signify when one identifies himself or herself as a Jew? What is the meaning of Jewish tradition? What is the nature of the group with which the Jew identifies? What, if any, are the goals and purposes of the Jewish people's historical career.

Buber's distinctive approach is reflected in his discussion of the concepts of tradition, religion, and nation. For many of Buber's contemporaries, the concept of tradition best expressed their sense of Jewishness. Buber, using a form of deconstructive strategy, argued that the concept of tradition not only did not resolve the dilemma of his generation but was, itself, the source of the problem:[31]

What meaning does this tradition have for us, this name, watchword, marching order: Judaism? What sort of a community is this we bear witness to when we call ourselves Jews? What is the significance of this journey of ours through the abyss — do we fall through the millennia's nebulous space into oblivion, or will some power carry us to fulfillment? What does it mean for us to want perpetuity, not merely as human beings — human spirit and human seed — but, in defiance of both Time and particular time, as Jews? (Buber, On Judaism, 11–12)

From the outset, Buber made it clear to his audience that tradition did not constitute a viable answer to the contemporary Jewish problem.[32] Tradition was a double-edged sword that "constitutes the noblest freedom for a generation that lives it meaningfully. But it is a most miserable slavery for the habitual inheritors who merely accept it, tenaciously and complacently" (Buber, On Judaism, 11).

Rather than accept tradition as a given as the Orthodox insist, we must subject it, like all inherited systems, to the test of existential meaning. Denying the inevitability of reification, Buber insisted that a person retains the capacity to choose and the responsibility to act. To evade that responsibility by refusing to choose is to do evil. In this sense, evil does not refer to an external force or power that affects human life, but rather to our readiness to surrender our power of decision in exchange for a safe, but passive existence.[33]

When, instead of uniting them for freedom in God, religion keeps men tied to an immutable law and damns their demand for freedom; when, instead of viewing its forms as an obligation upon whose foundation genuine freedom can build, it views them as an obligation to exclude all freedom; when, instead of keeping its elemental sweep inviolate, it transforms the law into a heap of petty formulas and allows man's decision for right or wrong action to degenerate into hair splitting casuistry — then religion no longer shapes, but enslaves religiosity. (Buber, On Judaism, 91–92)

To demonstrate further the problematic nature of tradition and to challenge the conventional assumptions of his audience, Buber critically analyzed the two terms most commonly used to define Judaism, *religion* and *nation*. Questioning the adequacy of these conventional definitions, Buber sought to persuade his listeners of the need to revise both the prevailing interpretations of Judaism and the prevailing forms of Jewish life.

As an alternative to the conventional interpretation of religion as a system of principles, dogmas, and/or practices, Buber, as mentioned earlier, proposed the concept of religiosity. Whereas *religion* connotes objectified forms of thought and behavior, *religiosity*, for Buber, evoked a sense of inwardness and personal experience:[34] "Is there an inherently Jewish religiosity? Is there, not dogma or norm, not cult or rule, but alive in men of today and manifest in a community of Jews a unique relation to the unconditioned which can be called essentially Jewish?" (Buber, On Judaism, 12).[35] Implicit in the *religion/religiosity* distinction is the premise that any authentic discussion of Judaism must begin with the existential experience of the individual.

The replacement of a conventional term, *religion*, by an uncommon one, *religiosity*, was typical of Buber's deconstructive strategy.

Aware of the extent to which thinking was determined by language, he was forever concerned with liberating people from conventional habits of thought.[36] Insofar as language is a necessary, although insufficient means of communicating our innermost experience, it is essential that people be liberated from the constraints imposed by conventional habits of speech. This means introducing alternative concepts. However, the ultimate issue was not language. Insofar as concepts reflect modes of living, the introduction of new concepts helps to foster alternative modes.[37]

Buber's revisionism is most clearly reflected in his attitude toward the rabbinic tradition. If Nietzsche was the antagonist against whom Buber struggled in formulating his general philosophical stance, the rabbis were his major antagonists in his struggle to formulate a viable interpretation of Judaism.[38] Although raised in a traditional Jewish household, Buber's critique of religion in his early lectures reflects a virulent, hostile attitude toward traditional Judaism.

Rabbinic Judaism, with its complex system of commandments and laws, constituted the prevailing form of Jewish life throughout the medieval period and remained dominant among eastern European Jewry at the end of the nineteenth century. The categories and concepts formulated by the rabbis set the parameters for both the behavior and thought of the community and established the framework within which the authoritative interpretation of scripture was carried out. Thus, the teachings of the rabbis had provided both the legitimations and the plausibility structure of Jewish life.[39]

Buber's attitude toward traditional Judaism was not dissimilar to that of many eastern European enlightened Jews who had been influenced by the main currents of eighteenth- and nineteenth-century European thought. Not only had traditional Judaism outlived its usefulness, but it represented to Buber all that was destructive and repressive in Jewish life. Having been raised in a traditional environment, Buber, at an early age, rebelled at what he felt to be the repressiveness of tradition.[40] While he rejected Reform as being a distortion of authentic Judaism, his most acerbic barbs were reserved for traditional rabbinic Judaism.

His primary objection to traditional Judaism was based upon premises derived from the turn-of-the-century school of thought known as *Lebensphilosophie* (philosophy of life).[41] While the philosophers associated with *Lebensphilosophie* differed among themselves in fundamental ways, they all spoke of *Leben* (life) as the fundamental level of existence. To them, the fundamental human experience was the immediate encounter with life, which they spoke of as life experience *(Erlebnis)*.[42] As Simmel put it, "the purest expression of life as a central idea is reached when it is viewed as the metaphysical basic fact, as the essence of all being. . . . Every object becomes a pulse beat of absolute life."[43]

According to the advocates of *Lebensphilosophie*, the antinomy of life and form was manifest in all spheres of human existence: cultural, social, and religious. On all levels of being, life struggles against the forces that seek to entrap it in fixed, static forms. The task of the individual, therefore, is to liberate life from the stifling, deadening forces of rational form and structure and restore it to its rightful position as the vital, dynamic force in human society.

Valuing unity and wholeness, the advocates of *Lebensphilosophie* rejected the atomistic, reductive orientation of science. In contrast to the rational analytic approach of modern positivism, advocates of *Lebensphilosophie* espoused a direct, intuitive approach. Like Nietzsche and Simmel, they wished to bring philosophy back to concrete reality, to life itself. To achieve this goal, they focused their attention on the lived experience *(Erlebnis)*. This experience, which is prior to all rational reflection and language, is fundamental to human thought and culture. Consequently, the ultimate test of an idea, its truth, consists of its capacity to serve life and enhance life.[44]

As we saw in Chapter 1, the antithesis between life and form was basic to the thought of Buber's teacher, Georg Simmel.

Life perceives the form as such as something which has been forced upon it. It would like to puncture not only this or that form, but form as such, and to absorb the form in its immediacy, to let its own power and fullness stream forth just as it emanated from life's own source, until all cognition, values and forms are reduced to direct manifestations of life.[45]

According to Simmel, religious life reflects the general cultural conflict between form and life. As religious faith becomes objectified in dogma, it stifles the life impulse that originally gave rise to it. In religion, as in all cultural spheres, "life is condemned to assume forms. Creation implies objectification, and each object is encased in a form. But life must revolt against forms, for forms inhibit the free expression of life."[46] The mystic, engaged in a quest for direct life experiences, epitomizes for Simmel the struggle against reified form.

Sharing Simmel's views on the basic antithesis between life force and structure, Buber viewed the institutionalized forms and structures of rabbinic Judaism as stifling genuine Jewish religious spirit. Authentic Judaism was not to be found in a system of laws and rituals but in the genuine moments of divine human encounter, that is, in religiosity.

Neither strict adherence to tradition nor rationalization of that tradition could alleviate the alienation that pervaded the life of large numbers of young Jews. To alter this condition and alleviate the crisis, a new intensity of faith and experience was necessary.

Where is there . . . a community dominated not by Jewish inertia (called tradition), nor by Jewish adaptability (that "purified," that is, "soulless" Judaism of a "humanitarianism" embellished with "monotheism"), but by Jewish religiosity in its immediacy, by an elemental God consciousness? (Buber, On Judaism, 12–13)

As a revisionist, Buber did not see himself as introducing something new into Judaism. He was simply recovering the essential elements that had been suppressed: "I shall try to extricate the unique character of Jewish religiosity from the rubble with which rabbinism and rationalism have covered it" (Buber, On Judaism, 81).

Buber's early discussion of religion and religiosity reflects the dichotomous thinking that characterized all of his subsequent writings. Throughout his career, Buber tended to analyze problems in terms of polar concepts, a method that the psychologist Albert Rothenberg has found to be common to creative thinkers.[47] While, as Rothenberg has argued, polar, or Janus, thinking is an effective way of generating creative insights, it also carries the danger of oversimplified bifurcation and tends to overlook gradations and complexities.[48]

The religion-religiosity dichotomy also reflects Buber's tendency, in the tradition of Lebensphilosophie, to distinguish sharply between experience and form. As mentioned earlier, Buber, like Simmel and Nietzsche, considered life (Leben) to be the underlying stratum of human existence and life experience (Erlebnis) the basis of all knowledge. Like Nietzsche and Simmel, he believed that the objectification of life into fixed forms and structures stifled the vitality of society and culture.[49] In the tradition of mysticism, existentialism, and *Lebensphilosophie*, Buber considered individual experience to be prior to all forms and structures. In religious life, this meant the priority of religiosity over religion. Fixed forms and structures were epiphenomenal, arising only as a response to the immediate encounter with the divine.

However, religiosity was not only known from personal experience. Classical sources of Judaism, such as the Bible and the writings of Hasidism, present many instances of religiosity. One early example cited by Buber was Jacob's struggle with the angel. In later Jewish history, religiosity was expressed in movements like the prophets, the Essenes, pre-Pauline Christianity, Kabbalah, and Hasidism.

Whereas traditionally the priesthood and later the rabbis were considered to be the legitimate bearers of Judaism, in Buber's revisionist perspective this is contested. To him, the priests and the rabbis are the bearers of institutionalized patterns of behavior and thought, which are the outgrowth of objectification and reification. To the official Judaism of the priesthood and the rabbinate, Buber juxtaposed an underground Judaism that embodied Jewish religiosity.

Religiosity, the legitimate form of Judaism, was not simply a matter of inner experience; the encounter with the unconditioned must be transposed into deed. In addition to experience, Judaism entails both the will to actualize this encounter through action, as well as action itself. However, in keeping with his existentialist premises, Buber refused to prescribe the forms this action must assume.

While many Jews defined Judaism in terms of religion, others defined it according to the category of nationhood. Accordingly, Buber's revision of Judaism also required a critique of the conventional usage of the concept of nation. In Buber's view, *nation*, like *religion*, does not adequately convey the uniqueness of Jewish existence. As in the case of religion, one must distinguish between the outer manifestations and the inner experience of nationhood.

As mentioned earlier, Buber was not satisfied with the political definition of *nation* advocated by Herzl and his followers. For Buber, to be a Jew meant much more than dedication to the struggle for a Jewish homeland or involvement with cultural forms, such as the Hebrew language, Hebrew literature, and a common history. The key to being a member of the Jewish nation was located in the experience and consciousness of the individual:

At the hour when he envisions the line of fathers and mothers that had led up to him, he perceives then what commingling of individuals, what confluence of blood has produced him, what round of begetting and births has called him forth. He senses in this immortality of generations, a community of blood, which he feels to be the antecedents of his I, its perseverance in the infinite past. To this is added the discovery that, promoted by this awareness, that blood is a deep rooted nurturing force within individual man; that the deepest layers of our being are determined by blood. (Buber, *On Judaism*, 17) [50]

To be a Jew is to be aware that one is shaped and formed by the Jewish people and its history. The negative side to this experience is the awareness of exile and alienation. "In the stillest of hours, when we sense the ineffable, we become aware of a deep schism in our existence" (Buber *On Judaism*, 18). Unlike "normal" nations that live in their national homeland and speak their national language, Jews live in foreign lands, amidst an alien culture, speaking a language that is not that of their natural "blood community."

Neither the land he lives in, whose nature encompasses him and molds his senses, nor the language he speaks, which colors his thinking, nor the way of life in which he participates and which, in turn, shapes his actions, belongs to the community of his blood; they belong to another community. (Buber, *On Judaism*, 16–17)

Buber's interpretation of Jewish nationhood entailed a unique understanding of the concepts of exile and redemption. [51] To Herzl and his followers, *exile* meant socioeconomic oppression and political persecution. To be in exile is to suffer anti-Semitism and its effects. To Ahad Haam, *exile* was a condition of social fragmentation and cultural stagnation. In contrast to both of these views, Buber described exile as an inner condition of the individual that manifests itself in the individual's consciousness and shapes the individual's perception of reality. To be in exile, according to Buber, means that the Jew lives with a profound consciousness of estrangement from his physical environment and separation from his natural environment.

Thus, the Jew experiences a distinct form of multiple alienation. On the one hand, the Jew is estranged from the forms and structures of Jewish tradition, which have lost the power to infuse life with order and meaning, and at the same time, is cut off from the natural environment that could nurture national and communal identity. Consequently, the Jew is forced to make choices that other people are not compelled to make:

He finds himself inescapably confronted by a choice between the world around him and the world within him; between the world of impressions and the world of substance; between environment and blood; between the memory of his lifespan and the memory of millennia; between the objectives of society and the task of releasing his own potential. (Buber, On Judaism, 19)

Unlike the majority of Jewish nationalists, Buber did not perceive the culture of the diaspora as inherently destructive to Jewish existence.[52] While life in exile had generated distorted forms of Judaism, the solution was not to discard one culture in favor of another but to acknowledge one as primary. The question of priority, a personal question that confronts all Jews, must be discovered and answered within.

Insisting that the conventional concepts of religion and nation distort our understanding of Judaism, Buber endeavored to formulate alternative concepts that would more adequately convey Judaism's dynamic character and spiritual quality. In his early lectures, he employed the concept of spiritual process:

When we view it as a religion, we touch only the more obvious fact of its organizational form; we arrive at a deeper truth when we call it a nationality; but we must still look deeper to perceive its essence. Judaism is a spiritual process documented in the internal history of the Jewish people as well as in the works of the great Jews. . . . Only by grasping this process in its total magnitude, in the wealth of its elements and the manifold transmutations of its historical revelation, can we understand the meaning of what I here call renewal. (Buber, On Judaism, 39–40)

By revealing the inadequacy of conventional concepts, Buber hoped to help free Jews from distorted conceptions of Judaism. Only in this way could Jews acquire a genuine understanding of their problems

and a valid conception of Jewish renewal. Although both nationalists and reformers had advocated programs of Jewish renewal, their
programs, grounded in a misunderstanding of the nature of Judaism,
were inadequate.

The reformers' "rationalization of faith, simplification of dogma,
modification of ritual law," (Buber, *On Judaism*, 37) failed to penetrate to the existential core of the crisis. Ahad Haam's cultural
orientation, as appealing as it was, ignored the essential role of
personal religious faith in the revitalization of Judaism. Accordingly, while Ahad Haam's strategy could lead to an intellectual
awakening, it could not, in Buber's view, effect the radical inner
transformation necessary to genuine renewal.[53] Like the religion-
ists, Ahad Haam had failed to grasp the necessity for a total, existential transformation in the inner life of the individual:

Indeed, just as I believe that in the life of individual man there may occur
a moment of elemental reversal, a crisis and a shock, a becoming new that
starts down at the roots and branches out into all of existence, so do I
believe that it is possible for such an upheaval to take place in the life of
Judaism too. (Buber, *On Judaism*, 35)

The Nature and Course of Jewish History

The same artistic vision that informed Buber's interpretation of
Hasidism also informed his general interpretation of Jewish history.
As in his interpretation of Hasidism, his concern was not to paint a
historically accurate portrait of the Jewish past but to capture and
reveal its creative power and vitality. Ultimately, he wished to
transform his readers' view of the Jewish present and the Jewish
future.

Buber's indebtedness to Nietzsche, which I emphasized in my
discussion of Hasidism, is further evident in his overall approach to
the Jewish past. In contrast to the developmental, progressive model
of history that characterized nineteenth-century European thought,
Nietzsche had opted for a conflict model. Contrasting the rational,
structured Apollonian culture with the dynamic, creative Dionysian culture, Nietzsche depicted Western history as an ongoing
struggle between these two forms of life. Under the repressive power

of Apollonian culture, the Dionysian forces were repeatedly driven underground. Only the periodic breakthrough of Dionysian forces had insured the survival of Western culture. History is not, as Western liberalism claimed, a story of progress but a story of ongoing conflict between the forces of life and the forces of death.[54]

Applying this model to Jewish history, Buber depicted it as an ongoing struggle of conflicting forces. Just as the individual encounters impediments to the actualization of inherent growth tendencies, so does the nation.[55] In the case of the Jews, the conflict took the form of a recurring struggle between the powerful, repressive forces of "official Judaism" and the authentic forces of "underground" Judaism. While alternately designating the creative force as myth, religiosity, the striving for authentic community, and the actualization of unity, deed, and future, Buber consistently identified official, repressive Judaism with the priests and rabbis.

Particularly in his early lectures, Buber accused rabbinic Judaism of impeding the actualization of the authentic Jewish ethos. In the struggle to preserve the Jewish nation amidst the conditions of exile, the rabbis had reduced Judaism to a system of reified legalistic norms and patterns of ritual:

With the destruction of the Jewish commonwealth the creativity of the fight for the sake of the spirit was diminished. All spiritual strength was now concentrated on preserving the substance of nationhood against external influences; on closely fencing in one's own realm in order to keep out the influx of alien tendencies; on the codification of all values in order to prevent any displacements; and on an unequivocal, not-to-be misconstrued —that is, an invariably rational—formulation of religion. Increasingly, the God-permeated, commanding, creative element was being replaced by the rigid, merely preserving, merely continuing, merely defensive element of official Judaism. (Buber, *On Judaism*, 74)[56]

Under rabbinic Judaism, elements within the nation that struggled for spontaneity and creativity were deemed heretical. Increasingly, Judaism was dominated by a spirit of "detached intellectuality that, as out of touch with the fundamental roots of natural life as with the functions of a genuine fight for the sake of the spirit, was neutral, devoid of substance, and dialectical" (Buber, *On Judaism*, 74). At times, the underground authentic Judaism found its expression in such movements as prophecy, the Essenes, pre-Pauline

Christianity, Kabbalah, and Hasidism.[57] For the most part, however, the repressive forces of official Judaism prevailed.

In the spirit of German nationalism and romanticism, Buber believed that nations possess an underlying ethos, or innate predispo-
sition that manifests itself in a complex of actions and values.[58] In
striving to actualize unity, the Jewish people duplicated a process
fundamental to the consciousness of each individual. Just as each
individual is conscious of the duality of existence, so is the nation.
In the case of Israel, its career expresses the ongoing effort to overcome this duality and actualize unity in the world. Especially in
the Bible, we find fundamental insights into the nature of duality,
an awareness of disunion, and a striving for unity.

It is this striving for unity that made the Jew creative. Striving to evolve
unity out of the division of his I, he conceived the idea of a unitary God.
Striving to evolve unity out of the division of the human community, he
conceived the idea of universal justice. Striving to evolve unity out of all
living matter, he conceived the idea of universal love. Striving to evolve
unity out of the division of the world, he created the messianic ideal, which
later, under the guiding participation of Jews, was reduced in scope, made
finite and called socialism. (Buber, On Judaism, 28)

Judaism, as Buber viewed it, embodies a continual effort to overcome the polarities that fragment the universe and shatter its primordial wholeness and unity. The entire career of the people of
Israel can best be understood through the metaphor of unity. Even
the Jewish conception of God is to be understood in terms of the
quest for unity. The basic ideas of Judaism emerged out of the
striving to overcome duality and achieve unity. To Buber, ideas
such as monotheism, universal justice, love of humanity, and mes-
sianism all can be traced back to this fundamental striving.[59]

Consistent with this interpretation of Jewish history, Buber defined the current crisis in Judaism as one of spiritual stagnation.
Overcome by rationalization and reification, the vitality of Jewish
life has been stifled. Only "a new shape, a new form, a new actualization all merging into a new attitude toward the world," could
change the situation (Buber, On Judaism, 54). However, faithful to
his individualistic, existential orientation, Buber refused to prescribe the specific requirements of this new form of life. The individ-

ual Jew's primary responsibility was to be conscious of the innate tendencies of authentic Jewish existence and prepare to actualize them in his or her own individual life. Beyond that, no specific prescriptions could be given. For the individual Jew, the shape of the future is unknown.

For Buber, the Hebrew concept *teshuvah* provided a viable alternative to the widespread belief that alienation was irreversible.[60] Interpreting the concept to mean a total reversal in the stance of the individual and a complete alteration of the basic direction of his or her life, Buber argued that *teshuvah* implied that freedom and the responsibility to choose was inherent in the human condition. Insofar as we adhere to systems of thought or behavior in a vain effort to escape from the anxiety of insecurity and disorder, we evade this responsibility. Consequently, ideational or behavioral systems, insofar as they relieve us of the need to exercise choice in each situation, threaten our freedom.

Another indication of Buber's revisionist perspective is his effort to link Judaism to the religions of the Far East. The prevailing Jewish view presumed the compatibility of Judaism and Western culture. To traditionalists and reformers alike, living as a Jew was fully congruent with participation in European culture.[61] Buber, however, took a different position.

The cultures of the East, eschewing metaphysical speculation and theologizing and stressing concrete behavior, had great appeal to Buber and many of his contemporaries. Unlike the West's penchant for control, power, and domination, the cultures of the East emphasize inner contentment. Moreover, the Eastern cultures espoused a dynamic, relational concept of the universe, seeing the world in constant motion and becoming, and viewing all creatures as related to each other.

Utilizing a vague conception of group psychology to isolate the distinguishing characteristics of Far Eastern cultures, Buber used a highly general, simplified typology to identify Judaism with the cultures of the East:

From this point it can be seen that of all the Orientals, the Jew is the most obvious antithesis of the Greek. The Greek wants to master the world, the Jew, to perfect it. For the Greek, the world exists; for the Jew, it becomes. The Greek confronts it; the Jew is involved with it. The Greek apprehends it under the aspect of measure, the Jew as intent. For the Greek, the deed is in the world, for the Jew, the world is in the deed. (Buber, *On Judaism*, 66)

In Oriental culture, Buber found the same emphasis on inwardness and immediate experience he had found in Hasidism. Moreover, it was precisely the Oriental qualities in Judaism that held out the promise of renewal. In a world in which Western imperialism fosters hostility in East-West relations, the Jews, comprising a unique link between the Orient and the Occident, could play a unique role in preserving an ethos that is in danger of being eradicated.[62] Thus, Buber further challenged the prevailing assumptions of Western Jewry.

Torah:
Judaism as Teaching and Living

Buber's critique of tradition and his universal, humanistic worldview left his audience with many unanswered questions. If the forms and structures of rabbinic Judaism impeded rather than facilitated the religious quest, what could be the new form of Judaism? Also, if the problem of redemption was universal, why should young Jews pursue the struggle for redemption within the particular framework of Judaism? Finally, if religiosity was a universal human phenomenon, what value was there in preserving a distinctly Jewish form of religious life? In sum, what legitimation was there for the continued existence of a uniquely Jewish mode of living?

As discussed previously, Buber had, in his earlier lectures, suggested one answer. Being Jewish is a condition rooted in the individual's inner substance—his or her "blood." One could not simply choose to be or not to be Jewish; history and heredity had already dictated that choice. The only choice confronting the individual Jew was how to allocate his or her priorities in the struggle between inner identity and natural environment. Moreover, Judaism embodied a distinctive religiosity.

In a 1918 lecture entitled "Herut" (freedom), Buber elaborated upon his earlier interpretation of Judaism and Jewish identity. In that lecture, Buber sought to walk a middle path between the traditionalism that he rejected and the romantic, psychologized view of religion that he detected among young Jews. These Jews, finding the existing forms and structures of Jewish life to be spiritually unsatisfying, turned inward in search of religious experience.

Insofar as Buber had repeatedly emphasized the importance of inner feeling and experience, it was easy for his listeners to conclude that, when all was said and done, religion was ultimately a psychological experience, as writers like Feuerbach had earlier argued. Buber, however, argued that religion is more than just an inner feeling. The younger generation's move toward romantic religion was a flight from their innate religiosity. Moreover, to reduce God to a psychological experience was to distort authentic religious faith.

In a decisive move away from the *Lebensphilosophie* that permeated his earlier writings, Buber now criticized all religion that was based solely on inner experience.[63] Such religion, in which a person simply wallowed in his or her own feelings, lacked the power to effect long-lasting changes (Buber, *On Judaism*, 153). To counter the dangers of romantic religion, Buber advocated a rootedness in one's ethnic community. The inherited symbols and forms of life of this community prevent one from slipping into an insipid romanticism and enable one to channel one's basic religiosity in creative directions:

The man who is truly bound to his people cannot go wrong, not because he has at his disposal the symbols and forms of life that millennia of his people's existence have created for envisioning as well as for serving the unconditional, but because the faculty to create images and forms flows into him from this bond to his people. (Buber, *On Judaism*, 154)

This passage contains one of Buber's rare positive statements concerning inherited forms and symbols.[64] While continuing to insist upon individual responsibility and choice, he now acknowledged the value of traditional symbols. Even the founders of new religions utilized existing symbols to express and communicate their insights. Thus, spiritual creativity is not something that occurs *de nova* but depends upon the effective appropriation of existing culture. From the literature, history, and historical consciousness of one's ethnic community, one acquires the language through which to express religiosity.

Only rootedness in their natural community, the community of Israel, could save young Jews from a destructive psychologizing of religion that leads to illusory religious faith. Only through the Jewish community could they avoid the dangers of rationalism, romanticism, and existential loneliness.

Nevertheless, Buber never ceased to question the adequacy of the prevailing symbols, forms, and interpretations of Jewish life. While young Jews desperately needed forms and symbols from which to draw, the existing ones, as then interpreted, were not adequate. Whereas, in Buber's view, traditional Judaism was stagnant and lifeless, Reform offered only a set of abstract principles severed from the life of the community. However, ritual forms, moral principles, or theological doctrines could not capture the primal power of Judaism. Authentic Judaism was, in Buber's view, a dynamic process of spiritual creativity and response that manifests itself in changing life situations and experiences (Buber, *On Judaism*, 164).

In an effort to resolve the tension between forms and structures on the one hand and dynamic spiritual power on the other, Buber distinguished between two aspects of the concept of Torah: Torah as teaching and Torah as law. While Jewish teachings embody the spiritually creative, dynamic forces necessary for a genuine Jewish renewal, law (halakhah) only perpetuates the processes of stagnation. Consequently to recover the primal forces of Judaism, the Jew must engage in a study of Jewish literature and culture, the "records and forms in which the effect of the unconditional upon the spirit of the people has become manifest during the four millennia of its path" (Buber, *On Judaism*, 171).

Buber, of course, did not advocate an uncritical approach to Jewish tradition. The Jew has to approach the literature in a stance of openness, conviction, choice, and will in order to uncover the primal forces of Judaism that remain buried beneath the institutionalized tradition:

As we have seen, we cannot commit ourselves to an acceptance of Jewish teaching if this teaching is conceived of as something finished and unequivocal; nor can we commit ourselves to Jewish law if this law is taken to mean something closed and immutable. We can commit ourselves only to the primal forces, to the living religious forces which, though active and manifest in all of Jewish religion, in its teachings and its law, have not been fully expressed by either . . . They are the eternal forces that do not permit one's relationship to the unconditional ever to wholly congeal into something merely accepted and executed on faith, the forces that, out of the total of doctrines and regulations, consistently appeal for freedom in God. (Buber, *On Judaism*, 168–69)

Since Judaism did not offer prepackaged answers to the spiritual dilemmas of the present, the individual Jew had to be selective.

While not denying the usefulness of historical inquiry, myth, and poetic interpretation, Buber insisted that one had ultimately to move beyond these modes to the "suprapoetic element which transcends all forms"; only in this way would the contemporary reader experience the primal forces out of which a new religiosity could grow and thrive (Buber, *On Judaism*, 172).

Whatever his knowledge of old or new exegesis, he will search beyond it for the original meaning of each passage. No matter how familiar he is with modern biblical criticism's distinction between sources, he will penetrate beyond this criticism to more profound distinctions and connections. (Buber, *On Judaism*, 172)[65]

While Buber also encouraged his readers to study postbiblical Jewish texts, at this point in his development such statements appear to be half-hearted. In contrast to traditional Judaism, Buber bypassed rabbinic interpretation. To recover the unconditional's effect upon the people, the modern reader must circumvent all accrued interpretation, modern as well as traditional, and directly encounter the existential force of the text. Bypassing rabbinic Judaism, Buber made the biblical text the focal point of his revised interpretation of Judaism.

Similarly, while advocating the study of beliefs and customs of the community, Buber personally devoted little time to such study, concentrating almost exclusively on biblical and Hasidic texts. Translating and interpreting these texts, he attempted to provide the modern Jew with a bridge over the abyss separating the individual Jew from the divine and from the corpus of Jewish teaching.

Buber was careful to point out that the crisis of modern Judaism was not to be equated with secularization. First, the crisis derived from processes of reification inherent in religion itself. Second, the very concept of secularization presupposed an untenable distinction between the religious and the nonreligious. In Judaism, the important distinction is not between the sacred and the profane, but between Jewish law and teaching viewed as a closed, reified system and the primal forces that are prior to this reification. By differentiating between the sacred and the profane we distort the original spirit of Judaism. Accordingly, the task of the Jew is to strive continually to reunite the sacred and the profane, "the unification of the spiritual and the worldly; the actualization of the spirit and the hallowing of the worldly, the sanctification of the relationship to all things" (Buber, *On Judaism*, 169).

Challenging the conventional religious definition of Judaism as a body of sacred teachings and practices, Buber insisted that true religion, in the spirit of Hasidism, entails hallowing the worldly and rendering all of life sacred. Accordingly, we should not conceive of religion as a special sphere of our life, demarcated by fixed boundaries.

From Religiosity to Community

As I shall discuss more extensively in chapter 4, a decisive shift is evident in Buber's thought following the end of World War I. Central to this change was the shift in focus away from the experience of the individual to the social life of the community. While the significance of this shift for Buber's general philosophy will be explored in the next chapter, let us, at this point, briefly consider its significance for his developing conception of Judaism.

For the present discussion, the most significant dimension of this shift is the displacement of individual religiosity by community as the essential component of Judaism: "[Judaism's] goal is not the creation of a philosophical theorem or a work of art but the establishment of true community" (Buber, *On Judaism*, 113).

Further indication of the switch in Buber's interpretation of Judaism is the way in which he characterized the historical manifestations of authentic Judaism. Whereas previously he had portrayed the prophets, the Essenes, pre-Pauline Christianity, and Hasidism as models of religiosity, after 1917, he portrayed them as models of true community. Similarly, the criteria of authentic Judaism was no longer religiosity but the nation's success or failure in actualizing community. Finally, the longing for God, which had earlier been depicted as the individual's quest for religiosity, was now identified with the will to create genuine community.

The change in Buber's thought is also reflected in his changing interpretation of Jewish identity. In his earlier lectures, to be a Jew meant to combine a national consciousness with a personal relationship to God. After 1917, however, being Jewish entailed devoting oneself to actualizing genuine community, thereby actualizing the divine:

Its [Judaism's] longing for God is the longing for a place for him in the true community; its consciousness of Israel is the consciousness that out of it the true community will emerge; its wait for the Messiah is the wait for true community. (Buber, *On Judaism*, 110–11)

The shift to community also entailed a different critique of Jewish ideologies. Whereas Buber had previously evaluated movements within Judaism in terms of their religious orientation, he now evaluated them in terms of their attitudes to the task of building a true community.

In order to distinguish his form of nationalism from that of the official Zionist movement, Buber coined the phrase "Hebrew Humanism".[66] This term highlighted the fact that Israel's problem was but a distinct form of the universal human problem. Accordingly, the task of Israel as a distinct nation was inexorably linked to the task of humanity in general.

Buber's social turn is also reflected in other writings from this period. In a brief autobiographical essay published in 1918, "My Way to Hasidism," he described Hasidism's original impact upon him in terms of community. Brought as a young child to a Hasidic prayerhouse in a village near his grandparents' home, he emerged from this visit with a profound sense of leadership and community:

The Prayerhouse of the Hasidim with its enraptured worshipers seemed strange to me. But when I saw the rebbe striding through the rows of the waiting I felt, "leader," and when I saw the Hasidim dance with the Torah, I felt, "community." At that time there rose in me a presentiment of the fact that common reverence and common joy of soul are the foundations of genuine human community. (*HMM*, 53)[67]

According to his recollection of 1918, this presentiment was embedded in his unconscious even during his adolescent period of alienation. Viewing his childhood experiences from the perspective of his clearly emerging social orientation, the concepts of leader and community now loomed the largest.

In the concept of community Buber found the answer to the question of Jewish meaning posed in his opening lecture on Judaism nine years earlier. The essential meaning and purpose of Jewish existence is the drive to actualize genuine community. The history of Israel is the story of its quest for genuine community. It is this quest that epitomizes its existence.

The Jew can truly fulfill his vocation among the nations only when he begins anew, and, with his whole, undiminished, purified original strength, translates into reality what his religion taught him in antiquity: rootedness in his native land; leading the good life within narrow confines; and building a model community on the scanty Canaanite soil.[68]

As the community attempted to render its encounter with the unconditional comprehensible, it necessarily used symbols and concepts. In the course of time, symbols and teachings turn into reified dogmas and rules that stifle and distort the personal religious experiences.

Man's mind thus experiences the unconditional as that great something that is counterposed against it, as the Thou as such. By creating symbols, the mind comprehends that which is in itself incomprehensible; thus, in symbol and adage, the illimitable God reveals Himself to the human mind, which gathers the flowing universal currents into the receptacle of an affirmation that declares the Lord reigns in this and in no other way. Or man's mind captures a flash of the original source of light in the mirror of some rule that declares the Lord must be served in this and in no other way. (Buber, *On Judaism*, 150)

Ultimately, all religious symbols generate a distorted understanding of God: "It is not God who changes, only theophany—the manifestation of the Divine in man's symbol-creating mind—until no symbol is adequate any longer, and none is needed" (Buber, *On Judaism*, 151).[69]

Buber's interpretation of Judaism, distinguishing between Torah as teaching and Torah as law, was sharply challenged by Buber's contemporary and collaborator in the Bible translation, Franz Rosenzweig. In a long essay, "The Builders," and in a subsequent exchange of letters, Rosenzweig insisted that, in rabbinic Judaism,

Torah incorporates both halakhic and nonhalakhic expressions. To separate "teaching" from law, as Buber sought to do, was to distort the concept of Torah.[70]

In addition, argued Rosenzweig, there was no justification for Buber's assumption that God could be revealed in the act of studying a text but not in the act of observing the Sabbath or any other sacred act. According to Rosenzweig, in the very process of fulfilling a "commandment" one could encounter the Commander. Rosenzweig further argued that at no time in Jewish history was the divine origin of the law the basic factor motivating Jews to observe it.

Distinguishing between *law* and *commandment*, Rosenzweig insisted that just as one, through one's inner power, could transform the biblical text into a living teaching, one could also translate the law *(Gesetz)* into a living link to the divine. While agreeing with Buber that revelation is never given in the form of law, Rosenzweig insisted that the law that emerged from the human side has the power to be transformed into commandment *(Gebot)*, an authentic bond between the divine Commander and the commanded person.

Buber's response was to fall back on his personal experience. While agreeing with Rosenzweig that God commands, Buber rejected the claim that commandments take the form of laws. If, in his personal encounter with the divine, he had experienced the law as commandment, he would have committed himself to fulfilling it. Having had no such experience, however, he could do only that which he was commanded to do.[71]

Thus, Buber and Rosenzweig parted company on the issue of the possibility of the law's being transformed, through one's doing, into God's law. Rosenzweig, who assumed a critical, yet conservative attitude to tradition, insisted, based upon his personal experience, that through one's doing, law could become commandment. At the same time, he acknowledged one's right, insofar as one did not experience law as commandment, to refrain from fulfilling it. What he insisted upon, however, and what Buber was unwilling to give, was the same stance of openness to the halakhah that Buber had urged toward the biblical teachings.

From the perspective of consistency, Buber's position appears to be unassailable. If, as Rosenzweig acknowledged, revelation is not law, why should Buber take seriously the claim of the rabbinic system? From Rosenzweig's perspective, however, once Buber acknowledged the seriousness of the Bible's claim to being sacred scripture, he opened himself to the criticism of inconsistency.

Teaching is, no less than law, susceptible to reification and rationalization. How, therefore, could Buber encourage youth to remain open to the "teachings" while rejecting a similar demand with regard to the law? Certainly, the claim that the divine will is expressed through a canonized body of texts and teachings conflicts with the demand for total freedom in responding to revelation. Certainly, the same tendencies to alienation and reification that so disturbed Buber in the law also inhere in a body of teachings.

Apart from Rosenzweig's criticism, Buber's distinction between teaching and law presumes a distinction of thought, speech, and action that contemporary philosophers would find unacceptable.[72] To many philosophers, speaking is a form of action. Accordingly, speaking and learning the Torah entail action no less than observing the Sabbath or the dietary laws. Consequently, Buber's readiness to accept one form of action as valid while rejecting the other as alienating is problematic.

While never abandoning his objections to the halakhah, Buber denied that he opposed tradition per se. His critique, he insisted, was aimed at those who embraced the law without believing that it embodied the divine will. However, Buber's protestation notwithstanding, it is difficult not to conclude that he was hostile to institutionalized religion in any form. If form and structure are basically antagonistic to life, we must consider all institutionalized religion as an impediment to genuine life and to an authentic dialogical relation with God. Given Buber's perspective, any traditional system interferes with the quest for the divine: "We shall resist those who, invoking the authority of an already existing law, want to keep us from receiving new weapons from the hands of the living God" (Buber, On Judaism, 128).

4

Edification and the
Meaning of Personhood

Buber, in his earliest writings, had sensed that the alienation that pervades modern society is rooted in the basic modes of human interaction. However, it was not until the period immediately following World War I that he succeeded in formulating the concepts through which to carry out a sustained critique of these alienating conditions. Increasingly he came to see that these alienating modes of interaction are grounded in a mistaken concept of personhood. This flawed vision was, in turn, rooted in and helped to sustain the dominant alienating modes of discourse that prevailed in modern life. If modern individuals were to be effectively awakened to the conditions of their existence, the conceptual, discursive, and social processes that engender alienation would have to be unmasked.

Originally, Buber had eschewed philosophical discourse, choosing instead to achieve his edifying goal through other means such as translating and disseminating Hasidic teachings. However, while never abandoning these activities, he soon recognized their inadequacy. If his thinking was to reach a broad audience, another mode of discourse—a philosophical discourse—was necessary:

My communication had to be a philosophical one. It had to relate the unique and particular to the "general," to what is discoverable by everyman in his own existence. It had to express what is by its nature incomprehensible in concepts that could be used and communicated (even if at times with difficulties).[1]

While Buber considered his mode of discourse as philosophical, it is clear that his philosophical approach differs significantly from the dominant tradition of Western systematic philosophy. Unlike those whom Rorty calls "normal" philosophers, Buber had no system; his purpose was to testify to experience:[2]

No system was suitable for what I had to say. Structure was suitable for it, a compact structure but not one that joined everything together. I was not permitted to reach out beyond my experience, and I never wished to do so. I witnessed for experience and appealed to experience. (PMB, 693)

While such an enterprise touches upon issues basic to normal philosophical discourse, Buber's concern for these issues was pragmatic rather than theoretical. Moreover, his philosophical style, as reflected in *I and Thou*, resembled poetic meditation rather than rational, critical discourse.

Rorty's distinction between edifying and mainstream, or normal, philosophizing provides a useful way of situating Buber's philosophical activity. Rejecting the enterprise of philosophical system building, the edifying philosopher carries on a conversation in hopes of "finding new, better, more interesting, more fruitful ways of speaking."[3] The edifying philosopher rejects the claim of objectivism and "the more concrete absurdity of thinking that the vocabulary used by modern science, morality, or whatever has some privileged attachment to reality which makes it more than just a further set of descriptions."[4] Moreover, the edifying philosopher engages in a deconstructive activity in which he or she endeavors to reveal the problematic nature of the common-sense concepts we employ to define reality: "Edifying philosophy is not only abnormal, but reactive, having sense only as a protest against attempts to close off conversation by proposals for universal commensuration through the hypostatization of some privileged set of descriptions."[5]

The edifying philosopher also rejects all essentialist claims. "By proclaiming that we have no essence," he or she questions the privileged status conventionally accorded to the descriptions of human beings offered by natural sciences, considering such descriptions "as on a par with alternative descriptions offered by poets, novelists, depth psychologists, sculptors, anthropologists and mystics."[6] Overall, edifying philosophy entails "a distrust of the notion that man's essence is to be a knower of essences." Rejecting the idea of a human essence, the edifying philosopher continually reflects on what it is that constitutes being human. Thus, the edifying philosopher endorses "our 'existentialist' intuition that redescribing ourselves is the most important thing we can do."[7]

In the attempt to edify ourselves and others, the philosopher may engage "in the 'poetic' activity of thinking up such new aims, new words, or new disciplines, followed by, so to speak, the inverse of hermeneutics: the attempt to reinterpret our familiar surroundings in the unfamiliar terms of our new inventions."[8] This activity is edifying, but it is not constructive in the sense of a normal, systematic research program. "Edifying discourse is supposed to be abnormal, to take us out of our old selves by the power of strangeness, to aid us in becoming new human beings."[9]

The characteristics of the edifying philosopher outlined by Rorty are fully consistent with Buber's philosophical activity. In *I and Thou* and in subsequent philosophical discussions, he undertook to unmask the prevailing discursive and social frameworks and to formulate an alternative view of language and society that would make possible nonalienating relationships between persons, persons and nature, and persons and the divine. While his primary task was to challenge the prevailing modes of human discourse and relationship and to awaken his readers to an alternative way of viewing them, his ultimate goal was to change ways of thinking in order to change ways of living.[10]

Buber criticized the modern objectivistic discursive framework, in which persons are viewed as separate individuals who relate to the world and other persons as subject to object.[11] This discourse, which privileges detachment, objectification, and rational analysis, is grounded in and simultaneously legitimates modes of social relationship that impede human growth and actualization. By awakening his readers to the categories that shape our discourse and social relations, Buber endeavored to point a way beyond the perennial alienation that characterizes modern life.

As stated above, Buber eschewed philosophical systemization. Refusing to provide fixed principles and solutions, he, as an edifying philosopher, insisted that his task was to carry on a conversation. "I have no teaching: I carry on a conversation" (*PMB*, 693). Moreover, he rejected the notion that one could ever permanently fix the validity of the concepts one utilizes:

A final validity can never be accorded them, although each of the great explanations claims for itself the character of final validity, and clearly must claim it. But in all genuine philosophy, analysis is only a gateway, nothing more. . . . I must philosophize; there is no other way to my goal, but my goal cannot be philosophical. (Rome and Rome, *Philosophical Interrogations*, 17)

Rejecting the reductionistic definitions of personhood offered by the social sciences, Buber endeavored to rethink the human enterprise. In *I and Thou* and other works, he continually struggled to redescribe the human being. Combining insights from existential philosophy and social theory, he formulated a dynamic conception of the human being. Utilizing a poetic discourse, he deconstructed the conventional concepts used to describe human existence and formulated new ones in an effort "to take us out of our old selves by the power of strangeness, to aid us in becoming new human beings."[12]

The Path to I and Thou

The edifying concerns that provide the context for Buber's philosophical writings emerge most clearly during the period between 1913 and 1923. Before turning to *I and Thou*, therefore, I shall briefly describe the context in which Buber undertook the work. In doing so, I shall depart from the conventional interpretations that situate the book in the context of Western systematic philosophy or religious thought. As we saw above, Buber's philosophical enterprise was an edifying one. Moreover, while religious issues form a significant part of the discussion in *I and Thou*, the basic concern of the work was to unmask the basic alienating forms of social life and provide an alternative way of thinking about them.

As Buber himself acknowledged, the period between 1913 and 1923 was decisive in his struggle to develop the categories through which to carry out his edifying project:

Since I have matured to a life from my own experience—a process that began shortly before the "First World War" and was completed shortly after it—I have stood under the duty to insert the framework of the decisive experiences that I had at that time into the human inheritance of thought, but not as "my" experiences, rather as an insight valid and important for others and even for other kinds of men. (*PMB*, 689)

Buber characterized his intellectual development as an ongoing effort to "clarify," "elaborate," and "bear witness to" a crucial vision, "a vision that had afflicted me since my youth, but had always been dimmed again" (Buber, *I and Thou*, 171).[13] Like the mystics whose testimonies he had published in 1909 in *Ekstatische Konfessionen*, he considered himself a witness who testified to experience in the hope that he could bring his readers to recollect their own experience: "I witnessed for experience and appealed to experience" (*PMB*, 693).

During this period, the basic concepts of Buber's mature philosophy began to emerge. These were first articulated in *Daniel*, published in 1913, and in a series of postwar essays and lectures. This period is marked by an increasing shift away from his individualistic focus toward social concerns.

Daniel represents Buber's initial attempt to deconstruct the conventions of Western thought that engender misleading language and experience. In a work that reminded some of his readers of Nietzsche's *Zarathustra*, Buber argued that to live authentically we must move beyond rational thought and embrace life in all of its fullness.[14] By defining our relationships to other people and to nature in terms of rational, goal-oriented categories, we suppress the life forces and creative drives within us, thereby fostering the conditions for our own alienation.[15]

In a metaphor reminiscent of both Simmel and Wittgenstein, Buber described the plight of the modern individual as that of a person arriving in a new city for the first time.[16] Hearing no sounds and seeing no one, he or she is overtaken with anxiety:

Because he longs for security, he needs, above all else this one thing: to know his way about. What sort of city is this? Where does this street lead? How do I get out of this sinister place? To know one's way about, this is the key to salvation and health, to security itself. (Buber, *Daniel*, 89)

Like a stranger, the individual in modern society, anxious over the apparent meaninglessness of his or her existence, becomes increasingly aware of the surrounding chaos and the ever-present abysses "between thing and thing, between image and seeing, between the world and me" (Buber, *Daniel*, 86). Impelled by this anxiety, the modern person grasps at the security offered by the scientific, rational worldview. Employing such categories as space and time, the individual seeks to alleviate anxiety and to overcome alienation by orienting himself or herself in reality. However, as Nietzsche had recognized, the effort proves to be empty and without meaning:

They have aims, and they know not how to attain them. They have an environment, and they have information about that environment. . . . They also have spirituality of many kinds, and they talk a good deal. And all of this outside the real. They live and they do not realize what they live. Their experience is ordered without being comprehended. They experience of it what component parts it has in common with other experiences and are oriented. . . . Their limitation is so closely cut to the body that they are glad and proud of it, and call it by elegant names, such as culture, or religion, or progress, or tradition, or intellectuality: Ah, the unreal has a thousand masks. (Buber, *Daniel*, 87)

Although philosophers, psychologists, and theologians offer cures for this anxiety, the price exacted is estrangement from immediate life experiences and from the vital sources of existence. In an effort to escape from this abyss, we create institutions and conceptual systems that only serve to exacerbate our alienation and impede our access to authentic existence.[17]

In the end, our own inner experiences reveal the emptiness of the alienated forms of our lives and point us to other possibilities: "But what good does it do me that they deny what I have experienced with my being? Shall the truth verify itself to me in a finished agreement, instead of in the totality of my life experience?" (Buber, *Daniel*, 87).

In *Daniel*, Buber took an important step toward clarifying his vision of alienation. Like Tonnies and Simmel, Buber viewed the city as a symbol of alienation. Urban dwellers, cut off from the authentic life experience, are unreal people who "hunt, storm after their aims, and, like the demiurge, their aims stride before them and dupe them; but they plunge after, running and sliding past one another like an anarchic dance of spectres" (Buber, *Daniel*, 75–76).

Imprisoned in urban fortresses, the modern individual is oppressed by the forces of technology:

These millions of men—not a number, Ulrich, forget the number, not a crowd, break up the crowd—all these individual men, naked underneath their clothes, bleeding underneath their skin, all these whose uncovered heartbeat united would drown out the united voice of their machines. These men are wronged, Ulrich, wronged in the right of rights, the gracious right of reality. (Buber, *Daniel*, 75)

Dominated by the drive to produce and oppressed by the techniques of production that society has developed, the modern person is alienated from other people and from his or her cultural creations. The root cause of this alienation is the instrumentalist ethos. Only by stripping away the protective devices that mask the underlying structure of this ethos can we hope to confront the chaos that threatens us. As Nietzsche had argued, all systems of thought, including philosophical and ideological systems, must be unmasked. Our task is to "tear down the dam of theories, of programs, of parties and shake the innermost soul" (Buber, *Daniel*, 78).

In contrast to the prevailing ethos, which views productivity as the measure of human worth, Buber insisted that productivity is illusory if it is not rooted in the immediacy of life experiences (Buber, *Pointing the Way*, 8). Genuine creativity begins in life experiences *(Erlebnisse)*, which are subsequently formulated into thoughts. These thoughts are, in turn, expressed in words, which eventually are written down and shared. However, as a result of our instrumental concerns, that which we have created assumes an objectivity of its own, independent of the life experience that first gave rise to it. Applying the productivity/creativity dichotomy to the encounter between persons, Buber distinguished between one who relates to another as an observer with a conscious aim, and one who relates as a friend who can either surrender to his feelings or exploit them.[18]

Daniel was Buber's first effort at formulating categories through which to articulate his critique of alienation. Referring to the conventional, rational, goal-directed mode of consciousness and life as *orientation*, Buber introduced an alternative mode, *actualization*. In contrast to the orienting person, who relates to reality through rational conceptual systems, the actualizing person, foregoing the security of orientation, immerses himself or herself directly in pure life experience *(Erlebnis)*.[19] These categories were the forerunners of those that Buber was later to formulate in *I and Thou*.[20]

The actualizing person is aware that life is fluid, dynamic, and, therefore, elusive. We cannot grasp life experiences any more than we can grasp a flash of lightning or a waterfall. To experience life, the underlying foundation of existence, we must not seek to order our experiences into rational systems. Instead, we must embrace life in all of its immediate fullness:

All life experience is a dream of unification; orientation divides and sunders it, actualization accomplishes and proclaims it. Thus, all reality is fulfilled unification. Nothing individual is real in itself; everything individual is only preparation. (Buber, *Daniel*, 72)

At this point, it appears that Buber still conceived of the alternative to alienation in terms of a mystical vision of unity. Like the mystics of all ages, he seemed to say that it is the quest for unity, rather than logical analysis, that brings us close to actual reality. Instead of gaining access to reality, rational inquiry only impedes that access.

However, although *Daniel* is usually identified as reflecting the mystical period in Buber's life, a careful reading makes it clear that by the time he wrote the book Buber had already begun to move away from his mystical orientation. In contrast to the mystic's celebration of solitude and individual meditation, Buber insisted that genuine life is only achieved through the immediacy of human relationships as expressed in "life of community and of human fellowship; for in genuine community as in genuine solitude, it is immediacy which makes it possible to live the actualizing as real" (Buber, *Daniel*, 78).

In an essay written shortly after *Daniel*, Buber further articulated his move away from mysticism:

I still grant to reason a claim that the mystic must deny to it. Beyond this, I lack the mystic's negation. I can negate convictions, but never the slightest actual thing. The mystic manages, truly or apparently, to annihilate the entire world, or what he so names, all that his senses present to him in perception and in memory—in order, with his disembodied senses or with a supersensory power, to press forward to his God. But I am enormously concerned with just this world, this painful and precious fullness of all that

I see, hear, taste. I cannot wish away any part of its reality. I can only wish that I might heighten this reality. (Buber, *Pointing the Way*, 28) [21]

The existential concern with the concrete and the growing emphasis on relationship are indicative of the new direction Buber was taking. Alongside the idea of unity, a favorite theme of mystical writings, Buber, in contrast to mystical traditions, emphasized active engagement with the world as the path to this unity:

Every true deed is a loving deed. All true deeds arise from contact with a beloved thing and flow into the universe. . . . Unity is not a property of this world, but its task. To form unity out of the world is our never ending work. (Buber, *Pointing the Way*, 30)

In *Daniel*, Buber also introduced the concept of dialogue that was to become central to his later thought. Here, for the first time, he expressed the view that to attain actualization a person requires a "Thou." Only to another Thou can we pour out our anxiety and restlessness in the face of the abyss "between thing and thing, between image and being, between the world and me" (Buber, *Daniel*, 86). [22]

In contrast to the mystic for whom solitude is a sufficient condition for achieving spiritual goals, Buber insisted that at some point in our lives, finding solitude to be no longer sufficient, we seek out the Thou. In Daniel's response to Ulrich, who is embarrassed at having revealed his personal dilemma to another person, we find evidence of the shift that was occurring in Buber's thinking. Moving away from both mysticism and *Lebensphilosophie*, Buber put the following words in Daniel's mouth:

Just speak, you are right in doing so. So long as one is in the calm of his becoming, the Thou that he bears in himself may be enough for him. But when the flood comes to him, then his need and summons is to find the Thou to whom he can speak in the world. (Buber, *Daniel*, 82)

Viewed in this light, *Daniel* may be read as yet another landmark on the road to the philosophy of interhuman relation. For the next three years, greatly distracted by the outbreak of the war, Buber deferred discussing the social implications of his writings. By 1916, however, he began to formulate the concepts that were later to be articulated in *I and Thou*. [23]

The Turn to the Interhuman

World War I confirmed Buber's conviction that the modern person lives in a condition of homelessness and alienation. The breakdown of organic communal forms was accompanied by an intensification of human solitude and insecurity. Attempts to create new social forms that would restore a sense of community and security had failed:

All that happens is that the increased sense of solitude is dulled and sup-pressed by bustling activities; but wherever a man enters the stillness, the actual reality of his life, he experiences the depth of solitude, and con-fronted with the ground of his existences experiences the depth of the human problematic. (Buber, *Between Man and Man*, 158)

The crisis of homelessness was exacerbated by a growing sense of powerlessness. The war had taught Western people how deeply they were enslaved to the technology they had created. What had once appeared to be progress was now perceived as a creeping enslave-ment, in which human beings no longer felt themselves to be the masters of the institutions and technical structures they had cre-ated.[24]

Man faced the terrible fact that he was the father of demons whose master he could not become. And the question about this simultaneous power and powerlessness flowed into the question about man's being, which received a new, and tremendously practical significance (Buber, *Between Man and Man*, 158–59)

The First World War was the catalyst that crystallized and final-ized Buber's shift from an individualistic-existential framework to a social-interactional framework.[25] By 1916, Buber had begun work on a philosophical prolegomenon out of which would emerge the conceptual framework for a synthesis of his social and religious thought.[26]

Several postwar texts offer clear evidence of Buber's social turn and reveal the issues in response to which he formulated the philo-sophical position articulated in *I and Thou*. These texts include an essay, "The Holy Way," first delivered in 1918 and published in 1919; *Worte an die Zeit*, a two-part pamphlet published in 1919; and a short statement, "The Task," published in 1922. Buber's growing social concern is further reflected in his autobiographical essay, "My Way to Hasidism," published in 1917, and a brief essay, "What Is to Be Done?" published in 1919 in the wake of the violent death of his friend and mentor, Gustav Landauer.[27]

The first clear indication of the decisive shift in his thought is found in "The Holy Way":[28]

The Divine may come to life in individual man, may reveal itself from within individual man; but it attains its earthly fullness only where, having awakened to an awareness of their universal being, individual beings open themselves to one another, disclose themselves to one another, help one another; where immediacy is established between one human being and another; where the sublime stronghold of the individual is unbolted, and man breaks free to meet other (sic) man. Where this takes place, where the eternal arises in the Between (im Dazwischen), the seemingly empty space; that true place of actualization is community, and true community is that relationship in which the Divine comes to its actualization between man and man. (Buber, On Judaism, 110)

Here, for the first time, Buber asserted that the locus for the divine-human encounter is found not in the experience of the isolated individual but in the interaction between persons.[29] God is to be sought not in moments of individual ecstasy, as Buber had previously indicated, but wherever people relate to one another in love and concern. In the meeting of person with person, we find the meeting of person with God.

The preceding statement is an explicit expression of Buber's break with Kierkegaard, Lebensphilosophie, and the German mystics. In subsequent years, Buber continued to privilege personal experience and faith over religious institutions and the experience of the individual Jew over the forms and structures of rabbinic Judaism. However, unlike Kierkegaard, he now believed that the divine-human encounter could only be fully actualized in the context of relations with other persons. Consequently, to speak of religion is to speak of interhuman relations.

In the next year, Buber applied this insight concerning the interhuman to humanity at large. In a two-part pamphlet, Worte an die Zeit,[30] he resumed the critique of Gesellschaft first raised in his 1900 lecture "Alte und Neue Gemeinschaft." Buber's starting point was

Tonnies' view that the fundamental problem of modern life is the displacement of organic, voluntary communities by depersonalized, mechanical, technologically oriented social structures. As Tonnies had correctly perceived, this process engenders the alienation of people from the social forms essential to their well-being.

To overcome this crisis, Buber argued, we must restore the possibility of direct, unmediated relationships between persons. However, the present institutional structure, embodied in state and church, precludes such relationships. The modern state has drained the blood out of communal life and frozen human relationships into rigid structures and organizations. Consequently, modern society is a ghostly organism of dead cells dominated by a utilitarian ethos and a mechanical functionalism.

Acknowledging that a return to premodern social forms is impossible, Buber advocated a new, organic model of community. The basis of this new form of community was to be the belief in the total connectedness and relatedness of all existing beings, an idea derived from the teachings of Boehme and Hasidism.[31] In the new community, this cosmic connectedness was to find its social actualization through helping relationships.

Helping relationships, first mentioned in *Legends of the Baal Shem*, are relationships that enable us to grow in self-discovery and self-awareness and to become, like God, creators.[32] Helping relationships are also educational relationships in that we help others to draw out *(zu erziehen)* and actualize their own innate predispositions.[33] Through such relationships, we contribute to the actualization of community.

The general guidelines for communal life that Buber set forth in "The Holy Way" and in *Worte an die Zeit* closely resemble those of his friend Gustav Landauer.[34] Genuine community presupposes shared ownership of land; shared labor; mutual aid and support, material as well as spiritual; and spiritual leadership. In the new form of social organization, local cooperative communities would serve as the basic cells of a commonwealth of communities.

To Buber, authentic political forms depend upon relationships formed in the nonpolitical spheres.

The healing and renewal can only occur from within, through the revitalization of the web of cells. The community must be filled, in all of its forms, with the reality of immediate, direct, pure, just relationships between person and person. Thus, a genuine communal system will emerge out of the combination of true communities . . . as the rusty wheelwork collapses piece by piece into a pile of rubble. (Buber, *Worte* 2: 16–17) [35]

Whereas Landauer located the starting point of this revitalization in the inner transformation of the individual, Buber located it in the realm of human relationships: "To bring about a true transformation of society, a true renaissance, human relationships must undergo a change" (Buber, *On Judaism*, 147).

During this immediate postwar period, Buber's writings acquired a new sense of urgency, reflecting a social critic struggling against the perils that threaten human society. Thus, in a 1919 essay entitled, "What Is to Be Done?" Buber wrote:

You, imprisoned in the shells in which society, state, school, economy, public opinion, and your own pride have stuck you, indirect one among indirect ones, break through your shells, become direct; man, have contact with man.

Ancient rot and mould is between man and man. Forms born of meaning degenerate into convention, respect into mistrust, modesty in communicating into stingy taciturnity. Now and then men grope towards one another in anxious delirium—and miss one another, for the heap of rot is between them. Clear it away, you and you and you! Establish directness, formed out of meaning, respectful, modest directness between men! (Buber, *Pointing the Way*, 109)

A brief essay, "The Task," published in 1922, provides a direct bridge between Buber's growing social emphasis and the philosophical discussion initiated in *I and Thou*. In that essay, Buber identified the source of the modern person's alienated condition as the utilitarian ethos that pervades public and private relationships. He was primarily concerned that the modes of discourse and the forms of relationship engendered by technological society had come to prevail in all realms of human life. This dominant discourse, which he labeled "the political," was the discourse of utility, power, control, and domination. It defined people as "Its," as objects to be manipulated.

It goes back to a basic relation of man to man which one can designate as the political. In it, one sees the other beings around one as centers of productivity which need to be recognized and employed in their specific capacities, as bundles of experienceable, influenceable, manageable, usable properties. Each one is to him a He or a She, constituted thus and thus, bearing in himself such and such possibilities of which those are to be furthered in their unfolding that can be made useful for the utilitarian goal. (Buber, *Believing Humanism*, 99)

The reduction of human beings to usable, manipulatable objects, the "primal evil of modern man, which is already preparing to annihilate him and his world" (Buber, *Believing Humanism*, 99), is attributed by Buber to the political orientation to society. The modern individual, when viewed within this framework, is reduced to a functional cog. The power executed through the political framework of discourse and through political structures condemns the contemporary individual, who yearns for direct, self-affirming relationships, to a condition of alienation and loneliness. This, according to Buber, is particularly evident in capitalist societies where the objectivist, goal-oriented, utilitarian mode of relation dominates all human relationships.

However, our propensity to view others as commodities, as "Its," is sporadically interrupted by "cursory vistas of love, friendship, comradeship, fleeting revelations of the Thou" (Buber, *Believing Humanism*, 99). Unfortunately, these fleeting moments are quickly replaced by periods of loneliness and alienation that characterize modern society. Our task, therefore, is to restore directness into human relationships. Only through the immediacy of direct relationships can we combat the conditions that reduce persons to dehumanized, manipulatable objects.

Buber's goal was to formulate an alternative discourse and an alternative mode of relating to others that was noncompetitive, noncontrolling, nonpurposeful, and nonutilitarian. An important step toward that goal was his distinction, first formulated in 1922, between relating to others as "Thous" and relating to them as "Its." In opposition to the primal evil of modern society, there are brief moments in which we can hear the message, "not your It, but your Thou is what is essential, though not surveyable" (Buber, *Believing Humanism*, 100). In contrast to the utilizable It, the Thou offers possibilities for opening up persons one to another, for beholding one another, and realizing one another.

I and Thou:
The Philosophical Critique of Alienation

Although many scholars have called attention to Buber's indebtedness to German social theory, the overwhelming majority of existing studies focus on the theological or ontological dimensions of his thought while neglecting his social concerns.[36] While there is no doubt that Buber was deeply concerned during the years immediately preceding the publication of *I and Thou* with religious issues, it was the social conditions of modern society that troubled him the most.

By 1923, Buber was convinced that the alienated condition that characterizes modern life was rooted in and sustained by the prevailing modes of discourse and social relationships that had come to be accepted as normal and given. Consequently, if one is to combat effectively the social forces supported by these patterns of thought and speech, one first has to deconstruct them, thereby revealing their inherent lack of meaning. For Buber, this meant a critique and "revision of concepts," which, he recognized, entails "a necessary destruction if the new generation is not to be the lifelong slave of tradition" (Buber, *Believing Humanism*, 153). An understanding of Buber's deconstructive strategy is essential to an understanding of *I and Thou*.[37]

The close analysis and criticism of concepts was the basic component of Buber's philosophical discourse:

An ever renewed analysis of basic concepts appears to me to be a central task of thought because it is the presupposition for an ever renewed confrontation with reality. Concepts, the grandiose instruments of human orientation, must repeatedly be clarified. (Rome and Rome, *Philosophical Interrogations*, 17)

Buber rejected the notion that rational conceptual frameworks give us access to concrete reality. The task of philosophers is to clarify concepts by repeatedly testing them against our own existential experience to determine whether or not they conform to that experience:[38]

Concepts become problematic because they do not show a concrete context that can be controlled. Every abstraction must stand the test of being related to a concrete reality without which it has no meaning. (Buber, *Believing Humanism*, 153)

We have already seen in chapter 3 an example of this deconstructive critique applied to the conventional notions of Judaism. Taking such concepts as tradition, religion, and nation, Buber sought to demonstrate that they did not simply reflect reality. Instead, these and other similar concepts, the products of social and intellectual processes, are rooted in a particular set of assumptions that both sustain and are sustained by particular sociopolitical forms of life.

Buber clarified his understanding of concept analysis in a series of unpublished lectures on community delivered in 1924.[39] There he specifically referred to his method as "concept criticism" *(Begriff-skritik)*. When we analyze a concept such as community, we must ask what is the actual reality, the living presence to which we are referring? "This question," which has to do with the existential grounding of speech, "can only be answered from one's innermost experience."[40]

As mentioned above, Buber acknowledged that his view of philosophizing precluded absolute certainty. Insofar as concepts can only approximate reality, they can never attain to absolute validity. Accordingly, while philosophical inquiry in the form of language analysis is essential, it is not sufficient. At the end of every philosophical analysis is uncertainty.

Responding to a critic's call for objective criteria by means of which we can distinguish "true from false, the true I-You relation from the alienated world of I-It," Buber, in the spirit of edifying philosophy, responded:

I would have to be untrue to my basic experience, which is an experience of faith, if I should seek to establish such "objective" criteria. I do indeed mean an "insecurity," insofar as criteria are concerned, but I mean—I say once again—a holy insecurity. (Rome and Rome, *Philosophical Interrogations*, 58)

In *I and Thou*, the basic target for Buber's critique is the common-sense concept of experience *(Erfahrung)* that prevails in modern Western society, and the concepts of person and community that derive from it. These concepts are rooted in our basic tendency to view the world around us, including our social world, as objects to be manipulated and exploited for our own purposes. To experience the world, or to experience other persons, we assume the stance of subjects standing over and against objects.

The common-sense, everyday world was designated by Buber as the "It" world. We experience this world as an object to be manipulated, used, and controlled. Our relationship to it is instrumental and is rooted in our need to possess, control, and dominate. Buber designated this mode of relating to the world, and to other persons, as the I-It mode.

The world experienced as It, perceived through rational, logical categories, is measured, ordered, and stable. It appears to us as structured and permanent.[41] To experience the world in this way presupposes a subject-object stance. In speaking the basic word *I-It*, we stand back from the world, view it objectively, break it down into component parts, and analyze it.

The paradigm of the I-It mode is objectivistic, scientific thought.[42] It is a way of thinking and speaking that is essential to material progress, and in no way should be equated with bad or evil.[43] Without the realm of It, without measurement, analysis, and quantification, scientific and technological progress would not be possible.

However, in modern society, the I-It mode of thinking and speaking, appropriate to commerce and industry, has expanded to dominate all aspects of our lives. As a result, we relate to other persons in the same way that we relate to objects or things. Moreover, we equate experience in general with the I-It mode. As a result, we approach everything that we encounter, including other persons, through the discourse of objectivity, quantity, and measurement.

One of Buber's basic concerns in *I and Thou* and subsequent philosophical discussions was to unmask the inadequacy of this mode of discourse and relation for human life:

The life of a human being does not exist merely in the sphere of goal directed verbs. It does not consist merely of activities that have something for their object.

I perceive something, I feel something, I imagine something, I want something, I sense something, I think something. The life of a human being does not consist of all this and its like. (Buber, *I and Thou*, 54)

Although we tend to take the common-sense world of I-It as given, there is, Buber argued, another way of being in the world, another mode of relating. Buber designated this alternative mode of being by the categories of *relation (Beziehung)* and I-You.[44] Unlike *experience*, the I-It mode of relating, *relation* is nonpurposeful, nonpossessive, and nonutilitarian. When we stand in relation to something, we no longer perceive it as an object apart from ourselves, to be used or manipulated to our own ends. Neither power, in the conventional sense, nor possession enter into this relationship.

Whoever says You does not have something for his object. For wherever there is something there is also another something; every It borders on other Its; It is only by virtue of bordering on others. But when You is said there is no something. You has no borders. Whoever says You does not have something; he has nothing. But he stands in relation. (Buber, *I and Thou*, 55)

In relation, we neither view reality through temporal or spatial categories nor compare or contrast. Although such activities have their use, in the I-You relation they are fused together in the immediacy of the encounter: "There is nothing I must not see in order to see, and there is no knowledge that I must forget. Rather is everything, picture and movement, species and instance, law and number included and inseparably fused (Buber, *I and Thou*, 58).

Unlike the I-It form of relating, which is mediated through concepts and categories, *relation*, the I-You mode of relating, is immediate and direct: "The relation to the You is unmediated. Nothing conceptual intervenes between I and You. No prior knowledge and no imagination. . . . No purpose intervenes between I and You, no greed and no anticipation" (Buber, *I and Thou*, 62–63).

Buber's new philosophy of relation arose "out of the criticism of the concept of *Erlebnis*, to which I adhered in my youth, hence, out of a radical self-correction" (*PMB*, 712). As his social concerns became more prominent, the inadequacy of his previous intellectual frameworks of *Lebensphilosophie* and mysticism became clear. Engaging in a process of self-criticism, he formulated new categories, such as I-You/I-It and relation, with which to carry on his critique.

The category of *Erlebnis*, grounded in the private experience of the individual, could not accommodate the social nature of human life. By limiting itself to the inner experiences of the individual, *Lebensphilosophie* renders all meaning psychological. This reductionism, or, as Buber referred to it, "psychologism," was one of the major impediments to a correct understanding of human existence.

Modern philosophy and psychology, represented by such diverse thinkers as Descartes, Freud, and Jung, are permeated by this psychologism. Yet this way of thinking about ourselves and others, emphasizing separation and isolation, prevents us from grasping the inherently relational nature of life. As a result, we define our needs in terms of individual satisfaction rather than interhuman relationships.

In the context of modern society, psychologism encourages us to distance ourselves from others and view them in terms of our own needs and satisfaction. According to Buber, psychologists and therapists mistakenly assume that sicknesses of the soul are rooted in the individual. Yet, as Buber understood it, we can only begin to heal the breaks in the human spirit when we recognize that the sickness of the individual is a function of the sickness that permeates our broken relationships with others.

Since Descartes, modern philosophy has been dominated by a tendency to reduce all experience to inner, psychological experiences, a tendency that Buber referred to as "psychologizing of the world":

"Psychologizing of the world" is the inclusion of the world in the soul, the transference of the world into the soul, but not just any transference but only that which goes so far that the essential is thereby disturbed. (Buber, *Believing Humanism*, 144)

Buber's own philosophical analysis of the human condition was grounded in a dissatisfaction with existing views. Buber saw a direct correlation between the way in which persons view themselves and the way in which they relate to one another. To change human behavior, we first have to change the way in which we understand human existence. To achieve a clear understanding of the human condition, we must first formulate a clear conception of what it means to be human, that is, we must develop a philosophical anthropology.

Philosophical Anthropology:
Toward a Concept of Person

According to Buber, an effective analysis of human relationships presupposes an adequate concept of the human being. As Kant had recognized, the study of person constitutes the central task of modern philosophy. However, although Kant had recognized that an understanding of human existence entails an inquiry into science, art, and religious faith, he had, according to Buber, failed to shed light on the meaning of human existence.

To Buber, post-Hegelian thinkers such as Feuerbach, Kierkegaard, and Nietzsche had contributed the most to our understanding of the human condition. Both Kierkegaard and Nietzsche had criticized the dominant modes of inquiry utilized by Western thinkers. Emphasizing direct, subjective experience, they questioned the adequacy of all positivistic, objectivistic thought. For each, the conventional objectivistic paradigm was not only misleading but contributed to the deactualization and alienation of the human being, which they had wished to avoid. Thus, although they, too, had erred in significant ways, an adequate philosophical anthropology, according to Buber, must begin with a critique of their views.

In the wake of the First World War, philosophers had increasingly turned their attention to the problematic nature of human existence. Men like Husserl, Heidegger, and Scheler had developed a new analysis of the anthropological condition. Their philosophizing was not an abstract, academic endeavor but an undertaking of the most urgent and practical consequences.

Buber believed that the objectivistic mode of knowing derived from the Greeks has had a fragmenting and alienating effect on our thinking: "All scientific and philosophical thinking tears asunder not merely the wholeness of the concrete person, but also God and man from each other" (Buber, *Believing Humanism*, 131). While purporting to save us from the anxiety of uncertainty and risk, objectivistic thought actually perpetuates the very alienation from which we seek to flee.

According to Buber, the Bible provides a relational mode of knowing that contrasts with the abstract, subject-object mode of knowing that prevails in the West. The verb *to know* in Hebrew presupposes direct relation. Thus, when we read the statement, "Adam knew his wife Eve," "the relationship of being to being is meant in which the real knowing of I and Thou takes place" (Buber, *Believing Humanism*, 130). Similarly, when the Bible speaks of knowing God, it does not refer to an objective, detached knowledge, but a relation of an I to a You.

Unlike objectivistic thought, which precludes immediate contact with the world around us, relational thought, as reflected in the Bible, bridges the abyss separating us from the world and thereby restores our wholeness as persons.

The individual man for himself does not have man's being in himself, either as a moral being or a thinking being. Man's being is contained only in community, in the unity of man with man—a unity which rests, however, only on the reality of the difference between I and Thou. (Feuerbach, quoted in Buber, *Between Man and Man*, 147–48)

Feuerbach, criticizing the idealistic metaphysics of Hegel, had made a decisive contribution to philosophical anthropology. Eschewing theological concepts, he had based his analysis solely on the fundamental needs of the living person. In this way, Feuerbach instituted a "Copernican revolution" in modern thought that paved the way for philosophical anthropology.

Feuerbach's writings had provided the young Buber with "a decisive impetus" (Buber, *Between Man and Man*, 148). Nevertheless, Feuerbach had, according to Buber, neglected the realm of the interhuman and had focused on the individual at the expense of the interhuman. Marx, on the other hand, while emphasizing the social realm, had neglected the interhuman in favor of the collective.[45]

As Kierkegaard and Nietzsche had understood, self-reflection was the starting point for an inquiry into the meaning of human existence. Kierkegaard had been a pioneer in the existential inquiry into human life.

Two ways, in general, are open to an existing individual; either he can do his utmost to forget that he is an existing individual . . . or he can concentrate his entire energy upon the fact that he is an existing individual. It is from this side, in the first instance, that objection must be made of modern philosophy; not that it has a mistaken presupposition, but that it has a comical presupposition, occasioned by its having forgotten, in a sort of world-historical absent mindedness, what it means to be a human being.[46]

Like Kierkegaard, Buber insisted that, unlike the objectivist who distances himself or herself from the situation under investigation, the philosopher must personally engage his or her subject.

In a number of studies, Kierkegaard had undertaken one of the most far-reaching inquiries into the human psyche by any nineteenth-century thinker. Plumbing the depths of human consciousness and emotion, he provided a psychological underpinning for such religious categories as sin and guilt. Transforming stages and conditions of human life, such as guilt, fear, despair, and decision, into the subjects of metaphysical inquiry, Kierkegaard, according to Buber, "lifts them beyond the sphere of purely psychological consideration . . . and looks at them as links in an existential process, in an ontic connection with the absolute, as elements of an existence 'before God' " (Buber, *Between Man and Man*, 162–63).

To Kierkegaard, the inner life of the individual is not secure but is beset by angst, or anxiety. Moreover, in spite of the efforts by the modern person to flee into the security of abstract, objective certainty, this is not a condition from which it is possible to escape. The very alienation that one experiences in both philosophy and society is built into the individual psyche: "Self-estrangement is to him primarily a process going on in one's self, not an external, but an internal relation, based on one's attitude to oneself.[47]

Buber criticized Kierkegaard's inquiry on two counts. First, Kierkegaard had introduced theological concepts into the anthropological discussion. While Buber's own anthropology was buttressed by his religious faith, he nevertheless insisted that one had to distinguish between inquiry into the human condition, which was the domain of anthropology, and inquiry into the divine, which was the province of theology. Moreover, theology, insofar as it purports to make objective descriptive statements about the divine, perpetuates objectivizing modes of thought.

Second, Buber found Kierkegaard's individualistic conception of person inadequate. Penetrating the despair and insecurity that mark the life of the isolated individual, Kierkegaard had provided an important corrective to Feuerbach's simplistic conception of person. Nevertheless, as Feuerbach had correctly recognized, persons do not live their lives in isolation but in relation to others.[48]

Nietzsche, in Buber's view, had made a distinctive contribution to our understanding of the human condition.[49] More than any of his predecessors, Nietzsche had understood the problematic nature of human existence: "In elevating, as no previous thinker has done, the questionableness of human life to be the real subject of philosophizing, he gave the anthropological question a new and unheard of impulse" (Buber, *Between Man and Man*, 153).

Viewing himself as a psychologist, Nietzsche, like Kierkegaard, was "one of the first to pursue psychology in the modern sense."[50] In particular, Nietzsche was deeply concerned about the ways in which modern thought stifled the human drive to self-actualization:

The man who would not belong to the mass needs only to cease taking himself easily; let him follow his conscience which calls to him: Be yourself! All you are now doing, thinking, and desiring is not you yourself.[51]

According to Nietzsche, the task of the philosopher, like that of the educator, was to help liberate the person from the chains of illusion within which he or she has been imprisoned by philosophy and religion, especially Christianity. In sharp contrast to Kierkegaard, Nietzsche denied all transcendental claims upon the self:

We are responsible to ourselves for our own existence: consequently, we want to be the true helmsman of this existence and refuse to allow our existence to resemble a mindless act of chance. One has to take a somewhat bold and dangerous line with this existence.[52]

Buber found two fundamental problems in Nietzsche's views. First, Nietzsche was so concerned with the human being's rootedness in and relationship to the animal world that he neglected the unique quality of human culture. For Buber, however, the essential question was not what links us to the animal world but what differentiates us. How did a being arise who developed a knowledge of the universe, the categories of space and time, and a reflective self-awareness?

Nietzsche's thought suffered from a second shortcoming. Although he had rightly removed the inquiry into the meaning of *person* from a theological discursive framework, he had, like Kierkegaard, failed to understand the social nature of human existence. Neglecting the essential realm of the interhuman, he perpetuated the fundamental error of the Western philosophical tradition.

Buber insisted that neither the individual nor the group is the proper starting point for understanding the human situation. The correct starting point is the relation of one person to another and of the individual to the community:

The individual is a fact of existence insofar as he steps into living relation with other individuals. The aggregate is a fact of existence insofar as it is built up of living units of relation. The fundamental fact of human existence is man with man. What is particularly characteristic of the human world is above all, that something takes place between one being and another, the like of which can be found nowhere in nature. (Buber, *Between Man and Man*, 203)

In the opening section of *I and Thou*, devoted to philosophical anthropology, Buber undertook to address a number of problems such as (*a*) What are the distinctive traits of humanness? (*b*) How can a person actualize his or her humanity? (*c*) What factors interfere with this actualization? and (*d*) What are the alternatives to the use-oriented, pragmatic, instrumental way of relating to others and to the natural world?

Buber was convinced that any interpretation of the condition of the modern person had to be grounded in a philosophical anthropology. One of his primary objectives was to develop an adequate conception of human existence. To achieve this goal, he employed a form of existential phenomenology, delving into the deep levels of human experience. Unlike his existentialist precursors, however, Buber's starting point was not the isolated individual but the individual in relation to other persons.

Rejecting the prevailing views of persons as individual entities essentially concerned with satisfying basic needs and gratifying instincts, Buber conceived of human life as grounded in relation. To Buber, a person is as he or she relates. We become what we are, we actualize our humanity, through the relations into which we enter. When, for purposes of analysis, we break down the universe, society or the person into component parts, we distort reality. This, in turn, generates and perpetuates a condition of alienation.

Buber, like Nietzsche, held a dynamic conception of person. Rather than being made up of fixed qualities that define his or her character, a person, in Buber's view, is in a continual state of becoming. Through the relationships into which he or she enters, through the stances that he or she assumes and the basic words that he or she speaks, a person becomes. However, in contrast to Nietzsche, Buber translated this dynamic conception into a relational, existential philosophy of human existence that emphasized the ultimate meaningfulness and sacredness of life. At the same time, particularly in his later writings, he, unlike Kierkegaard, tried to argue the case for this meaningfulness without recourse to theological categories.

In contrast to the individualistic, atomistic conception of person that prevails in Western thought, Buber advocated a relational view of the human being; a person exists not in isolation from others, but only through relationships. We are as we relate; how we relate is a function of the attitude we assume; that attitude is shaped by the basic words we speak.

There is no I as such, but only the I of the basic word I-You and the basic word I-It.

When a man says I, he means one or the other. The I he means is present when he says I. (Buber, *I and Thou*, 54)

In Buber's philosophical anthropology, human beings are not seen as isolated, independent entities, separate from one another and from the world. To speak of a person is to speak of his relation to something or someone. To speak of a person is to speak of modes of relation to the world of nature and to other persons. Moreover, the kind of a person that one is is a function of the mode through which one relates.

Diverting our attention from the realm of the interhuman, psychologism conditions us to view our relation to the other in subject-object terms. This stance, which is basic to the technological consciousness, enables us to gain control over our environment, including other persons. At the same time, it impedes both the actualization of the individual and the actualization of genuine community.

Speech both engenders and expresses a mode of relation. This mode of relation, in turn, shapes our existence and determines who we are. Apart from a mode of relation there is no existence. Buber, however, did not restrict speech to spoken words:

The linguistic form alone proves nothing. After all, many a spoken You really means an It to which one merely says You from habit, thoughtlessly, and many a spoken It really means a You whose presence one may remember with one's whole being although one is far away. (Buber, *I and Thou*, 111; cf. 85)

Words, devoid of intention, have little force. Thus, it is possible for one to say "I-You" while meaning "I-It," and vice versa. Speech, attitude, and intention are organically related. We separate them only for purposes of analysis.[53]

Although skeptical of the ability of language to conceptualize and communicate the depths of human experience adequately, Buber nevertheless had a profound respect for its power to shape human perceptions, attitudes, and actions: "Being I and saying I are the same. Saying I and saying one of the two basic words are the same. Whoever speaks one of the basic words enters into the word and stands in it" (Buber, *I and Thou*, 54).

Accordingly, in order to change the way that people live and relate to one another, we must alter their patterns of speech. Individual words, such as *I*, *You*, and *It*, incorrectly convey a world of separation and fragmentation in which beings are independent of one another.[54] So long as we utilize this atomistic language, we distort human existence.

In order to speak about a world grounded in relation, we require an alternative language form. Accordingly, Buber introduced the idea of word pairs. Rather than speak of *I* and *You*, which would reinforce an atomistic view, Buber spoke of the basic forms of relation using the word pairs *I-You* and *I-It*. Unlike individual words, word pairs convey relation.[55]

Consistent with his intellectual predilections, Buber formulated his understanding of person in terms of polar dichotomies.[56] Basically, he argued, there are two ways in which human beings relate to reality. "The world is twofold for man in accordance with his twofold attitude. The attitude of man is twofold in accordance with the two basic words he can speak" (Buber, *I and Thou*, 53).

One of the ways in which Buber differentiated the I of experience from the I of relation is through the category of presentness. In an I-It experience, neither I nor the other can be fully present. By objectifying that which stands over and against me, I reduce its fullness, relating only to a particular dimension or aspect of the other. At the same time, I hold back a part of myself. However, when I stand in relation, I am fully present, withholding nothing of myself and confronting the other as a whole: "The basic word I-You can only be spoken with one's whole being" (Buber, *I and Thou*, 42).

To distinguish further between the two basic modes of being human, Buber used the concepts of person and ego. *Person* refers to one who stands in relation. Although conscious of their own subjectivity, persons do not perceive themselves as subjects in relation to objects or experiences. In contrast, *ego* refers to one who is conscious of himself or herself as the subject of an action or experience. Unlike the person who enters into relation without predetermined goals or purposes, the ego steps back and stands apart in order to use or experience.[57]

When one stands in relation as person, one actively participates "in a being that is neither merely a part of him nor merely outside of him" (Buber, *I and Thou*, 113). In the mode of relation, all subject/object, internal/external distinctions fall away. Ego, on the other hand, knows himself or herself neither in relation to another nor through participation in the actuality of the between, but "by setting himself apart from others."

The ego does not participate in any actuality nor does he gain any. He sets himself apart from everything else and tries to possess as much as possible by means of experience and use. That is his dynamics: setting himself apart and taking possession—and the object is always It, that which is not actual. (Buber, *I and Thou*, 114)

Buber was careful to point out that the categories of person and ego are ideal types that do not refer to actual individuals. However, while no individual is either pure person or pure ego, each person gravitates toward one or the other of these poles:[58]

How much of a person a man is depends on how strong the I of the basic word I-You is in the human duality of his I. The way he says I—what he means when he says I—decides where a man belongs and where he goes. The word "I" is the true shibboleth of humanity. (Buber, *I and Thou*, 115)

Buber's philosophical anthropology rested upon the assumption that a longing for relation is innate in all people. In the womb, the child exists in a state of pure relation and bodily reciprocity. The child emerges from the womb with an innate longing for relation, a drive to panrelation:

It is not as if a child first saw an object and then entered into some relationship with that. Rather the longing for relation is primary, the cupped hand into which the being which confronts us nestles; and the relation to that, which is a wordless anticipation of saying You, comes second. (Buber, *I and Thou*, 78)

The innateness of relation is also evident in the life of primitive tribes. Primitive persons first experience the world in an I-You mode. Only subsequently do they detach themselves and perceive themselves as distinct I's.

Buber agreed with Kant that the human being grasps reality through innate forms or categories. For Buber, however, the primary mode of human experience is the mode of relationship rather than thought, consciousness, or ideas such as space, time, or causality. What distinguishes the human being and serves as the basic moving force in life is the longing for and the capacity to enter into unmediated, need-free, relation: "In the beginning is relation—as the category of being, as readiness, as a form that reaches out to be filled, as a model of the soul; the *a priori* of existence; *the innate You*" (Buber, *I and Thou*, 78).[59]

Buber believed that the category of relation was not unknown to his readers. His task, therefore, was not to introduce them to something new but to help them recover their forgotten existential roots:

The clear and firm structure of the I-You relationship is familiar to anyone with a candid heart and the courage to stake it, it is not mystical. To understand it, we must sometimes step out of our habits of thought. (Buber, *I and Thou*, 177)

It must be emphasized that, for Buber, the I-You relation is not a state of being that once achieved endures. Speaking of "the sublime melancholy of our lot" (Buber, *I and Thou*, 68), he insisted that every I-You relation necessarily reverts to an I-It relationship: "Every You in the world is compelled by its nature to become a thing for us or at least to enter again and again into a thinghood" (Buber, *I and Thou*, 147; cf. 68, 89, 101). However, that which has become It for us can again become You: "Whatever has thus been changed into It and frozen into a thing among things is still endowed with the meaning and the destiny *(Bestimmung)* to change back ever again" (Buber, *I and Thou*, 90). Moreover, although I-It relationships are inevitable, I-You relations are essential for actualizing our humanity: "And in all seriousness of truth, listen: without It, a human being cannot live. But whoever lives only with that is not human" (Buber, *I and Thou*, 85).

Life, as Buber understood it, is a process in which we continually move toward or away from the actualization of our innate drive to relation. Through the ways in which we relate to others, our basic human capacity is either actualized or deactualized. Each time we enter into relation, the innate You is actualized. By entering into relation, I become a complete person, an I.

Thus, personal development is a process in which the drive to relate is either actualized or thwarted. A person becomes actualized and develops into a complete human being through the I-You relations into which he or she enters. On the other hand, failure to enter into such relations contributes to the deactualizing of the person. Every person oscilates between these two poles in a rhythm of actualization and latency.[60]

Just as we require others to actualize our inherent potential for growth, the other requires us:

The concentration and fusion into a whole being can never be accomplished by me, can never be accomplished without me. I require a you to become; becoming I, I say You. All actual life is encounter. (Buber, *I and Thou*, 62)[61]

Certain historical personalities epitomize the relational mode of being in different spheres of life. In Socrates, Buber saw the epitome of relation as it pertains to human conversation. In dialogues and discussions, Socrates personified the I-You mode of being. Goethe, on the other hand, was the "I of the pure intercourse with nature." In their own ways, both of these men were models of "adequate, true and pure I saying." In the sphere of religious life, Buber viewed Jesus as epitomizing "the I of the unconditional relation in which man calls his You 'Father' in such a way that he himself becomes nothing but a son" (Buber, *I and Thou*, 116).

If Socrates, Goethe, and Jesus represent the historical embodiment of relation, Napoleon epitomized the "demonic You for whom nobody can become a You" (Buber, *I and Thou*, 117).[62] Totally incapable of stepping into relation either with others or even himself, Napoleon was outside of the categories of either person or ego. Unlike an ego, he no longer had the potential for relation:

To be sure, he views the beings around him as so many machines capable of different achievements that have to be calculated and used for the cause. But that also is how he views himself (only he can never cease experimenting to determine his own capacities, and yet never experiences their limits). He treats himself, too, as an It. (Buber, *I and Thou*, 228)

Thus, to Buber Napoleon epitomized demonic power, lacking both subjectivity and self-consciousness. In him and in all who seek to imitate him, the capacity for relation, the innate humanizing capacity, has been stifled together with the capacity to choose. Napoleon, therefore, is the example of a dehumanized individual locked in a perpetual state of self-contradiction from which he can no longer extricate himself.

As we have already seen, Buber developed his categories in order to uncover a dimension of reality, a mode of relating, that had been neglected by conventional disciplines. He was aware, however, that given the inherent limitations of language, his terms were somewhat ambiguous. Insofar as the I-You mode of relation is discontinuous, the term *Begegnung* (meeting) might have been more appropriate. *Begegnung* would have conveyed the sense that the I-You relationship cannot be sustained over time but necessarily reverts back to an I-It relationship.

The term *Begegnung*, however, indicates a one-time event and seems to preclude any kind of continuity. Yet, in Buber's view, in all relationships an I-You relationship always remains a latent possibility. Accordingly, in order to convey the idea that, in any relationship between persons, relation remains a possibility, Buber used the term *Beziehung* (relation). At the same time, he was fully aware that, owing to the inherent inadequacy of language, any terms that he might select would be imprecise:

One can only try to overcome the lack of an adequate designation through using the "skeleton word" relationship *(Beziehung)*, always according to the context, next to other, at once more concrete and more limited terms, such as meeting *(Begegnung)*, contact, communication; none of them can be replaced by any of them. *(PMB*, 705)[63]

An I-You relation cannot be planned and depends upon what Buber described as grace. Yet, while one can never be certain of entering into an I-You relation, the stance that one assumes does play a role. While the I-You relation cannot be sought out or planned in advance, one can assume a stance of openness and readiness:

The You encounters me by grace—it cannot be found by seeking. But that I speak the basic word to it is a deed of my whole being, is my essential deed. Thus the relationship is election and electing, passive and active at once. (Buber, *I and Thou*, 62)

It is only by means of encounters that I can actualize my own humanity. Accordingly, genuine existence begins with encounters. To the extent that we live in isolation, devoid of encounters, we forfeit the opportunity to actualize our humanness.

To elucidate the two basic modes of relating, Buber used the example of a tree. I can view the tree as a picture, deriving satisfaction and pleasure from its beauty; or, using the categories of mathematics and science, I can measure it, assign it to a species, or situate it within the framework of natural law. In each of these instances, which represent the ways in which people conventionally encounter nature, I assume an objective stance. I am the subject, and the tree is my object. For me the tree is a thing, an object among objects, which exists for my pleasure or curiosity. "Throughout all of this the tree remains my object and has its place and its time span, its kind and it condition" (Buber, *I and Thou*, 58).

In these situations, I relate to nature to enhance my power, my pleasure, or my self. In contrast, in the I-You mode, I do not relate to the tree as subject to object nor impose categories or concepts. Instead, I enter into an immediate, direct relation, where all categories are fused into one. At this moment, "the tree ceases to be an It":

Whatever belongs to the tree is included; its form and its mechanics, its colors and its chemistry, its conversation with the elements and its conversation with the stars—all this in its entirety. (Buber, *I and Thou*, 58)

The category of relation presupposes the same sense of organic relation to nature that Buber had earlier found in Boehme and St. Francis.[64] However, whereas most forms of mysticism absorb the individual into a greater entity or dissolve his or her individuality in a moment of mystical union, Buber insisted that in "relation" the integrity and concreteness of the individual is preserved:

The tree is no impression, no play of my imagination, no aspect of a mood; it confronts me bodily and has to deal with me as I must deal with it—only differently. One should not try to dilute the meaning of the relation: relation is reciprocity. (Buber, *I and Thou*, 58)[65]

The I-You encounter with the tree is not merely an aesthetic experience nor a product of the imagination. When I enter into relation with the tree, I encounter it bodily, as a living presence. However, when I seek to express this relationship, the conventional categories of empiricism and rationalism prove to be inadequate.

Relation is prior to all categories and presupposes reciprocity. Something or someone acts on me even as I act. It does not follow, however, that a tree has consciousness. Such an attribution, insisted Buber, is only the result of our inclination to analyze and divide.

Buber was careful to distinguish between reciprocity and mutuality. Any I-You relation is reciprocal insofar as each partner acts upon the other: "My You acts on me as I act on it. Our students teach us, our works form us" (Buber, *I and Thou*, 67). Relation of sorts can occur, according to Buber, even if the one to whom I say "You" does not hear it in his on her experience. "For You is more than It knows" (Buber, *I and Thou*, 60).

Mutuality, however, refers to a more limited situation in which each partner experiences the encounter in the same way, with each standing in the same relation to the other. While mutuality is possible in an I-You relation, it is not necessary. Moreover, whereas mutuality occurs in a relation between persons, it goes beyond our experience to speak of mutuality in our encounter with nonhuman beings or inanimate things.[66]

Another example employed by Buber to explain his views is the act of artistic creation. For the artist, the creative act entails a direct, personal encounter with the material that confronts us. Rather than assume a detached, objective stance, the artist must enter into a direct relationship with his or her materials. The intention of the artist, according to Buber, is neither to experience nor describe, but to draw out and actualize the form that is inherent in the material. Rather than impose a shape that is the product of the artist's own imagination, the artist uncovers or reveals the innate form of the other: "As I actualize, I uncover. I lead the form across into the world of It" (Buber, *I and Thou*, 63).

Ironically, in the act of artistic creation, the You is transformed into an It, an object which we can observe, a thing alongside other things. However, when we approach the material object that has been created with the proper attitude of openness, we can enter into relationship with it and bring to life the dynamic force that is prior to objectification.

Philosophy of Relation:
Mythic Roots

In his quest for a viable alternative to the prevailing individualistic and objectivistic conceptions of experience in Western culture, Buber had been drawn to Hasidism and to the religion of China. The Hasidic idea that divine sparks dwell in each living thing presupposes the organic unity of all existence and the priority of relation. Everything in creation, animate and inanimate, is related by virtue of the common bond to the divine. Consequently, all sharp divisions between person and nature fall away, and everything is viewed as organically connected. In *I and Thou*, Buber transposed this Hasidic view of reality into philosophical terms.

According to Buber, the Hasidic idea of the penetration of all spheres by the divine also implies the redemptive power of everyday human actions:

They [the teachings of Hasidism] can be summed up in a single sentence: God can be beheld in each thing and reached through each pure deed. But this insight is by no means to be equated with a pantheistic worldview, as some have thought. In the Hasidic teaching the whole world is only a word out of the mouth of God. Nonetheless, the least thing in the world is worthy that through it God should reveal Himself to the man who truly seeks Him; for no thing can exist without a divine spark, and each person can uncover and redeem this spark at each time and through each action, even the most ordinary, if only he performs it in purity, wholly directed to God and concentrated in Him. (*HMM*, 49) [67]

Hasidism, in Buber's reading, makes no distinction between life in general and religious life. All situations are religious situations, and all actions and all relationships have cosmic significance. The conception of religion implicit in the Hasidic myth of the sparks teaches that we fulfill our human task by hallowing the everyday.[68]

Therefore it will not do to serve God only in isolated hours and with set words and gestures. One must serve God with one's whole life, with the whole of the everyday, and the whole of reality. (*HMM*, 49–50)

Buber's concept of human action was also shaped by the teachings of Taoism.[69] In such texts as *Tao Te Ching* and *Chuang Tsu* Buber found a conception of action that was an alternative to the prevailing rational, instrumental, objectivistic Western conceptions: "I believe that we can receive from China in a living manner something of the Taoist teaching of 'non-action,' the teaching of Lao Tsu" (Buber, *Believing Humanism*, 189–91).[70]

The category of I-You relation is clearly influenced by the Taoist concept of *wu wei*. In the words of one modern commentator, *wu wei*

refers to the absence of purposive activity. The events that occur in the universe because of Tao are not consciously or purposively done, as could be said of the natural events decreed by an anthropomorphic deity; they simply unfold in accordance with the laws of change. Similarly, there should be no goal-directed conduct by men. . . . The man who models himself on Tao should also be disinterested and impartial.[71]

Wu wei connotes "a course of action that is not founded upon any purposeful motives of gain or striving," is spontaneous rather than calculated, and is natural rather than forced.[72] Nevertheless, the Taoist sage is not simply an inactive vegetable. His activity "can be described as toleration and accommodation." Once the sage understands Tao, he recognizes the temporal nature of particular attributes and can "accord with the naturalness of things" and accept them.[73]

Buber found in the concept of *wu wei* a corrective to the conventional Western conceptions of action and success. Like *wu wei*, the I-You relationship "is election and electing, passive and active at once" (Buber, *I and Thou*, 62). Moreover, both the I-You relation and *wu wei* connote an action that is seemingly passive and that is carried out with one's whole being.

For an action of the whole being does away with all partial actions and thus, also with all sensations of action (which depend entirely on the limited nature of actions) — hence, it comes to resemble passivity.

This is the activity of the human being who has become whole; it has been called not-doing, for nothing particular, nothing partial is at work in man and thus nothing of him intrudes in the world. (Buber, *I and Thou*, 125; cf. 62)

In the West, effectiveness is understood in terms of the exercise of power and the achieving of goals. Accordingly, one is deemed to be effective as a person to the extent that one succeeds in imposing one's will on others and in achieving one's goals. Thus, success is measured in terms of possessions and achievements.

In contrast to the Western view, Taoism teaches a concept of effectiveness based upon noninterference:

Opposed to it [the Western view of effectiveness] stands the changing of men through the fact that one effects without interfering. It is, I believe, in the commencing knowledge of this action without doing, action through nonaction, of this powerfulness of existence, that we can have contact with the great wisdom of China. (Buber, *Believing Humanism*, 190)

Unlike the ethos of success and power that prevails in the West, Lao Tsu's concept of action, like Buber's concept of *relation*, is noninterfering and nonaggressive. In both cases, we do nothing to impose our views on another. Instead, we accommodate ourselves to another's values and perspectives.

Effectiveness, from this perspective, is measured in terms that are alien to the Western world:

And there we come into contact with something genuinely and deeply Chinese, though not to be sure Confucian: with the teaching that genuine effecting is not interfering, nor giving vent to power, but remaining within one's self. (Buber *Believing Humanism*, 190)

The Taoist sage "adapts to any environmental circumstance, no matter how distressing it appears." Neither welcoming nor object-ing to anything, he seeks "the calmness of passive acquiescence in all matters." Ultimately, the aim of the sage is to achieve "tran-quility, and a sense of union between self and something beyond the self."[74] This something beyond takes the form of either an intellectual realization of the unity of all separate objects or a physical union between the person and the One.[75]

Several contemporary scholars have found in Taosim a social motif previously neglected.[76] These interpretations indicate that Buber's social interpretation of *wu wei* has a legitimate basis in the Taoist texts. Nevertheless, there is a clear difference in emphasis between Buber's social philosophy and the teachings of Taoism. Emphasizing biblical ideals such as sanctity of the individual and responsibility to the other, ideals that recur in existentialist writings in a secular form, Buber appropriated the Taoist teachings for his own social purposes.

Through the category of relation developed in *I and Thou*, Buber transposed the concept of *wu wei* into terms that were understandable to the Western reader. However his basic concern, the relationships between persons, does not occupy a prominent place in the Taoist teachings. Although he espoused a nonpurposive, noncontrolling mode of relationship, Buber's goal was decidedly social, that is, to alter the alienating conditions in which we find ourselves. Rather than accommodate oneself to the alienating conditions of the society in which we live, Buber believed that we must strive to combat this alienation through our relation to others.

These differences notwithstanding, Buber considered the concept of "action without doing, action through nonaction," to be a much-needed alternative to the Western conception of effectiveness and success. Unlike the prevalent Western mode of relating, the I-You relation is based not on power as conventionally understood, nor on practical benefit, nor on the satisfaction of needs. All thought of deriving benefit from the relationship is transcended. Rather than impose my own ideas, beliefs, and values, I accept and confirm you. To the extent that I influence you, I do so not by imposing myself on you but by helping to draw out your own unique qualities. Thus, in both *wu wei* and in an I-You relation, one acts effectively not by imposing values or wishes but by helping that which is innate in the other to emerge.[77]

5

Refining the Categories:
From Relation to Dialogue

As we saw in the previous chapter, Buber's concern in *I and Thou* was an edifying one. On one level, he wished to elucidate the realm of the interhuman, which, he believed, constituted the essential sphere of human existence. At the same time, he undertook this task in an effort to unmask the sources of alienation and liberate the individual. Consequently, the effectiveness of his categories had to be measured in terms of their utility and applicability to concrete everyday situations.

Buber's basic concern was not to contribute to systematic philosophic inquiry but to reach out to people suffering the effects of alienation. His words were not directed to an intellectual elite but to everyday people in everyday situations:

Yes, precisely him I mean, him in the factory, in the shop, in the office, in the mine, on the tractor, at the printing press. . . . I have him in mind, the yoked, the wheel treading, the conditioned. (Buber, *Between Man and Man*, 35)

As much as possible, Buber wished to avoid unclarity and abstraction, which would have impeded his communication to everyday people. His ultimate concern was to alter the ways that people think and talk and to open up the possibilities of alternative, unalienated modes of living.

The life of dialogue is no privilege of intellectual activity like dialectic. It does not begin in the upper story of humanity. It begins no higher than where humanity begins. There are no gifted or ungifted here, only those who give themselves and those who withhold themselves. (Buber, *Between Man and Man*, 35)

To succeed in his task, it was necessary to find a way of talking about what had become unfamiliar in a manner that was understandable to the masses. Like the Hasidic masters, Buber wanted to reach down to people imprisoned in the dull, repressed conditions of modern society and help lift them out of these conditions:

I am not concerned with the pure; I am concerned with the turbid, the repressed, the pedestrian, with toil and dull contrariness—and with the break-through. With the break-through and not with a perfection. . . . With the breaking through from the status of the dully-tempered disagreeableness, obstinacy, and contrariness in which the man, whom I pluck at random out of the tumult, is living and out of which he can and does at times break through. (Buber, *Between Man and Man*, 36)

Impelled by this edifying, liberating goal, Buber endeavored to clarify and refine his key concepts and apply them to changing circumstances. In the decades following the publication of *I and Thou*, he continually revised his concepts in an effort to render his ideas more accessible and more useful:[1]

Some time after I had earned the appropriate diction that permitted me to write the book in its definitive form, it appeared that a good deal remained to be added—but in its own place, independently. Thus, several shorter works came into being: I found occasions to clarify the crucial vision by means of examples, to elaborate it by refuting objections, and to criticize views to which I owed something important but which had missed the central significance of the close association of the relation to God with the relation to one's fellow-men, which is my most essential concern. Later, other discussions were added: of the anthropological foundations and of the sociological implications. (Buber, *I and Thou*, 171)[2]

This process of clarification and refinement helped to make Buber's writings more useful to a growing number of students of human society and human behavior. As a result, the categories that he formulated in the four decades following the publication of *I and Thou* have been appropriated by a number of practitioners in the field of psychotherapy.[3]

When viewed in the light of Buber's edifying concerns, *I and Thou* leaves the reader with at least four unresolved problems.[4] First, although, as Buber stated in 1919, the basic problem confronting the modern person in the wake of growing disillusionment is, what are we to do? *I and Thou* fails to provide a clear answer to this question.[5] The concept of relation, like the Taoist concept *wu wei*, offered the reader little guidance for specific action.

Yet according to Buber, it is precisely in the everyday world of interhuman relations that a person actualizes himself or herself. Insofar as the category of relation offers little guidance to concrete action, it does not teach us how to live and meet our responsibilities in that everyday world. Thus, although written to influence our relationship with the other, *I and Thou* offered little guidance regarding what, specifically, we were to do in the course of such encounters. Consequently, in order for the concept of relation to provide an adequate guide to action, it had to be revised. If the "interhuman" was to serve as the basis for a new conception of person and community, a more active conception had to be developed.

A second problem in *I and Thou* derives from Buber's polar way of thinking. As he described it, relation and experience appear as mutually exclusive, polar opposites. Each pole appears to be absolute, with no room for gradations. Consequently, relationships are either I-You or I-It, with nothing in between. However, this sharp dichotomy does not correspond to the complex actualities of human relationships as we experience them. Few relationships seem to conform solely to I-You or I-It. Most relationships, over time, seem to embody I-You or I-It in varying degrees. *I and Thou*, however, says little about this.[6]

A third problem in *I and Thou* relates to the question of mutuality and reciprocity. In several places, Buber said that genuine relation is mutual, insofar as it is experienced by both persons in a similar way. But what of those relationships that cannot be not fully mutual? As he, himself, acknowledged, there could be an I-Thou relation without full mutuality. Moreover, if mutuality is a precondition, how could one speak of an I-Thou relation with a tree or an animal?

A fourth problem that confronts the reader is the seemingly unrealistic, abstract nature of the discussion. Insofar as Buber, in *I and Thou*, failed to apply the discussion to concrete sociohistorical situations, his concerns seem to be far removed from normal, everyday reality. Moreover, as Buber himself acknowledged, when viewed from the perspective of the rational, goal-oriented ethos that prevails in modern life, the I-You relation appears to be most impractical. While I-You relationships may be appropriate within the confines of a religious community, they appear to be decidedly out of place in the factory or business office.

Buber, however, repeatedly rejected any firm division between the world of the sacred and the world of the everyday. Religious existence, which for Buber meant essentially all of human existence lived from a particular standpoint, was not a distinct, separate sphere. Religious life—human life—means hallowing the everyday.

The Concept of Dialogue

Between 1923 and his death in 1965, Buber tried to clarify further the dynamics of the interhuman, an effort that took place in several stages. In the first stage, during the 1920s and 1930s, Buber introduced the concept dialogue in place of the concept relation as his root metaphor.[7]

I proceed from a simple, a real situation: two men are engrossed in a genuine dialogue. I want to appraise the facts of this situation. It turns out that the customary categories do not suffice for it. I mark: first the "psychical" phenomena of the two speaking and gesturing men, second, the "psychic" phenomena of it, what goes on "in them." But the meaningful dialogue itself that proceeds between the two men and into which the acoustic and optical events fit, the dialogue that arises out of the souls and is reflected in them, this remains unregistered. What is its nature, its place? My appraisal of the facts of the case cannot be managed without the category of the between. (Schilpp and Friedman, *Philosophy of Martin Buber*, 706–7; hereafter referred to as PMB)

In contrast to the categories I-You and I-It, Buber's discussion of dialogue places greater emphasis on action and movement. Early in his discussion of dialogue, Buber described two basic or primal movements in human interaction: moving toward others through dialogue, or away from them and back to ourselves through monologue:

> I do not think of this as happening in time, as though the single action preceded the lasting attitude; the latter rather has its truth in the accomplishing, over and over again, of the basic movement, without forethought but also without habit. (Buber, *Between Man and Man*, 21–22)

Buber also expanded on the dialectical connection between our actions and our attitude, speaking of a "circle of essential action and essential attitude" (Buber, *Between Man and Man*, 22). Just as our actions determine our basic attitude, our attitude simultaneously shapes the way that we act. Thus, each acts on the other and, at the same time, is acted on.

Through the Hebrew concept of *teshuvah* (turning), Buber emphasized the element of choice and responsibility in interhuman encounters. When encountering other people, one can either turn to the other in order to enter into relation, or one can turn back to oneself, a movement Buber termed "reflexion" *(Ruckbiegung)*. Reflexion can take place solely on the level of consciousness, or it can incorporate action and/or emotion as well.

In contrast to the sharply dichotomous discussion of relation and experience in *I and Thou*, Buber now introduced the element of gradation into his discussion by speaking of different degrees of reflexion. Moving away from the other and turning back upon oneself, one can focus on oneself, stroke oneself, delight in oneself, or weep over oneself. Moreover, one can idolize oneself by transforming oneself into an object of self-worship.

Similarly, Buber spoke of different stages or degrees with regard to our movement toward dialogue with the other. One can simply focus attention on the other; one can act so as to make the other present; or one can enter into a full dialogical relation with the other and, through the act of "inclusion" *(Umfassung)*, experience the situation from the position of the other as well as from one's own position.

Dialogue entails a process of address and response. In our daily lives, we continually encounter signs that address us and call forth a response. Like the divine sparks in the Hasidic myth, these signs are imbedded in the ordinary events and encounters of everyday life: "Signs happen to us without respite, living means being addressed, we would need only to present ourselves and to perceive" (Buber, *Between Man and Man*, 10).

However, this process of dialogue, of address and response, does not require spoken language. Two strangers passing on the street can "reveal to one another two dialogical natures," without ever exchanging a word (Buber, *Between Man and Man*, 5). Similarly, two people sitting silently on a bench can commune with one another nonverbally, through appropriate thoughts or gestures.

Our responsiveness to being addressed by everyday situations is the key to transcending our alienated condition. According to Buber, to live authentically is to recognize and respond to the signs of address that surround us. However, while address is inherent in the human condition, not everyone is aware of it, for "each of us is encased in an armor whose task is to ward off signs" (Buber, *Between Man and Man*, 10). The person who is unaware that he or she is addressed and fails to see the other as one with whom he or she can commune lives a monological existence. Such a person fails to actualize the fundamental human drive, which Buber now referred to as the drive to commune *(Betrieb der Verbundenheit)*.

Like the I-You relation, genuine dialogue is immediate, unenduring, and lacking in structure. In our anxious quest for stability, security, and continuity, we erect elaborate defenses in the form of structured thought systems of categories and topologies that conceal the immediate moments of encounter. These systems of ideas or beliefs divert our concentration from the concrete, everyday events in which the sacred depths of existence are revealed. As a result, we become mired in monological existence, cut off from the possibilities of actualizing our authentic selves. According to Buber, humankind's task is to break down these defenses and open the way to genuine encounters between persons.

Confirming the Other

Throughout the 1930s and 1940s, little change was evident in Buber's discussion of dialogue. By midcentury, while Buber influenced many religious thinkers, his discussion had no noticeable impact on the fields of psychology or sociology. Thus, his hope to render a decisive contribution to the understanding of human relationships had not been realized.[8] In the 1950s, however, Buber was presented with several opportunities to enter into conversation with psychologists in the United States.

The essays derived from these lectures reflect a discourse far more appropriate to existentially minded psychiatrists and psychologists. In contrast to the poetic and somewhat esoteric language that characterized his discussion of dialogue during the 1920s and 1930s, these later essays are written in a more lucid, explicit, precise discursive mode. Moreover, the influence of German philosophy and romanticism is less evident, and one senses his clear desire to formulate his ideas in a manner more conducive to the human sciences.[9]

Theological discourse, so apparent in *I and Thou*, was absent from the essays of the 1950s. This does not mean that Buber no longer grounded his view of humanity in religious faith. On the contrary, religious faith continued to occupy his attention, and he devoted many writings to it. However, in his later writings on dialogue and the interhuman, he no longer found it necessary to support his philosophical-anthropological and social position by recourse to religious rhetoric. His writings therefore became more useful to social scientists and psychologists.[10]

When he first introduced the concept the interhuman (das Zwischenmenschliche), Buber had hoped to illuminate a new category of human existence (Buber, *Knowledge of Man*, 72). Insofar as the concept of the interhuman, or "the between," is essential to understanding personhood, one would expect it to be a major concern of psychologists and sociologists. However, as it is neither a feeling nor a social form, the interhuman eludes the normal categories of the human sciences. Consequently, psychologists tend to reduce the relation between persons to the level of feelings or emotions, thereby distorting what Buber saw as its true nature.

Buber eventually came to recognize the basic ambiguity in the concept of relation. Relation could easily be taken to refer to "a lasting disposition which is actualized in those happenings between [two individuals] as comrades, but also a lasting disposition which is actualized in those happenings and which even includes psychological events such as the recollection of the absent comrade" (Buber, *Knowledge of Man*, 75). Through the concepts of dialogue and the interhuman, Buber was able to distinguish between a relationship in this broad sense and the process by means of which actual or potentially mutual interaction between people occurs:

By the sphere of the interhuman I mean solely actual happenings between men, whether wholly mutual or tending to grow into mutual relations. For the participation of both partners is in principle indispensable. The sphere of the interhuman is one in which a person is confronted by the other. We call its unfolding the dialogical.[11]

For Buber, interhuman relations are not primarily a matter of feeling but consist of actual lived encounters, including glances between strangers in a streetcar and the encounter of opponents:

The only thing that matters is that for each of the two men, the other happens as the particular other, that each becomes aware of the other and is thus related to him in such a way that he does not regard and use him as his object, but as his partner in a living event, even when it is no more than a boxing match. (Buber, *Knowledge of Man*, 74)[12]

In several essays written in the 1950s, Buber sought to clarify the concept of dialogue by introducing such terms as *regard, accept,* and *confirm*. These essays represent the latest stage in Buber's effort to clarify his philosophical anthropology and educate his readers to the kinds of activities entailed in a dialogical encounter.

As a prerequisite to genuine dialogue, one must turn to another, *regard* the other as a unique individual, *accept* the other in his or her differentness, and *address* the other as the very person that he or she is. For genuine dialogue to occur, one must confront another in genuine openness:

Only he who himself turns to the other human being and opens himself to him receives the world in him. Only the being whose otherness, accepted by my being, lives and faces me in the whole compression of existence brings the radiance of eternity to me. Only when two say to one another with all that they are "It is Thou," is the indwelling of the Present Being between them. (Buber, *Between Man and Man*, 30)

Yet, this process of turning, regarding, accepting, and addressing does not presuppose agreement with the other. One can accept a person as a distinct and separate other, while disagreeing with him or her. If, in spite of a conflict of views, we relate to the other as a full person, genuine dialogue may emerge. Genuine dialogue can even occur between enemies as long as we perceive the other as a complete person and refrain from simply manipulating him or her for our own ends. As long as we recognize the other's uniqueness, dialogue can occur in spite of our disagreement: "I confirm him as creature and as creation, I confirm him who is opposed to me as him who is over against me" (Buber, *Knowledge of Man*, 79).[13] However, insofar as, in an effort to avoid conflict, we withhold our genuine feelings and opinions, we prevent dialogue from occurring.

Whereas, in earlier discussions, Buber had spoken of the fundamental human drive as the drive to relate and commune, he now spoke of the fundamental need to confirm and be confirmed:

The basis of man's life with man is twofold, and it is one—the wish of every man to be confirmed as what he is, even as what he can become, by men; and the innate capacity in man to confirm his fellow men in this way. . . . Actual humanity exists only where this capacity unfolds. (Buber, *Knowledge of Man*, 67–68)

Buber maintained that this need to confirm and be confirmed is what differentiates the human from other animals.

Buber distinguished between confirming and accepting another. In accepting the other, a person simply accepts what appears to him or her at the moment. To confirm, however, the person must penetrate behind appearances to the actual, vital self of the other. Thus, confirmation is a dynamic process that entails the growth of the other:

Confirmation can be misunderstood as *static*. I meet another—I accept and confirm him as he now is. But confirming a person *as he is* is only the first step, for confirmation does not mean that I take his appearance at this moment as the person I want to confirm. I must take the other person in his dynamic existence, in his specific potentiality. How can I confirm what I most want to confirm in his present being? This is the hidden, for in the present lies hidden what he can become. His potentiality makes itself felt to me as that which I would most confirm. (Buber, *Believing Humanism*, 170)

The concept of confirming the other represents an important development in Buber's later thought. First, it reflects a more active interpretation of human relationships. Unlike the verbs *relate* and *commune*, the verb *confirm* is transitive. When we confirm another, we act upon him or her directly, thereby helping the other to draw out his or her unique potential.

As indicated in chapter 1, Buber's interpretation of human existence presupposes the notion of entelechy. According to this view, which had roots in the philosophy of Aristotle, life is a dynamic process in which we grow from what we actually are at a given moment to what we are meant to become. The idea of becoming is basic to this view. A person is never simply what he is at any given moment. We must always view others in terms of that which they are capable of becoming.[14] Insofar as I accept another just as he or she is with no intention of changing him or her, I do nothing to help to actualize his or her potential. Mere acceptance, therefore, is insufficient. A person's responsibility is not simply to accept others but to confirm them as well. This occurs not when a person relates to them as they are at this given moment, but as they can become:[15]

And now I not only accept the other as he is, but I confirm him, in myself, and then in him, in relation to this potentiality that is meant by him and it can now be developed, it can evolve, it can answer the reality of life. (Buber, *Knowledge of Man*, 182)

The concept of confirming the other is further clarified by the idea of "imagining the real." This is done by identifying with the other person and imagining what he or she may be experiencing at that very moment:

Applied to the intercourse between men, "imagining" the real means that I imagine to myself what another man is at this very moment wishing, feeling, perceiving, thinking, and not as a detached content, but in his very reality, that is, as a living process in this man. (Buber, *Knowledge of Man*, 70)

However, to attain genuine dialogue, we must go beyond "imagining the real" and engage in what Buber called "making present."

For the inmost growth of the self is not accomplished, as people like to suppose today, in man's relation to himself, but in the relation between the one and the other, between men, that is, pre-eminently in the mutuality of making present—in the making present of another self and in the knowledge that one is made present in his own self by the other—together with the mutuality of acceptance, of affirmation and confrontation (Buber, *Knowledge of Man*, 70)

To make another present, I must actually experience that which the other is experiencing at a given moment. Thus, it is not sufficient merely to experience the other as this particular one, but I must also "experience, in the particular approximation of the given moment, the experience belonging to him as this very one" (Buber, *Knowledge of Man*, 71).

An example of making present is to actually feel the pain of the other. When this occurs, something new comes into being. This is not simply psychological, but ontological. It is not simply that the other becomes a self for me, but he or she becomes a self "with me." Dialogue becomes "ontologically complete" only when the experience is mutually shared. For this to occur, the other must know that he or she is made present by me and experience "inmost self becoming." (Buber, *Knowledge of Man*, 71)

Buber drew upon the concept of confirming the other to clarify further his understanding of love. In his earlier discussion of love in *I and Thou*, Buber had emphasized the responsibility of an I for a You. In these later essays, he discussed love from the perspective of entelechy. While each accepts the other as he or she is, this does not mean that neither wants the other to change. To love another is to recognize and address the other's potential for growth. Accordingly, each says to the other: "Just by my accepting love, I discover in you what you are meant to become" (Buber, *Knowledge of Man*, 182).

In his writings of the 1950s, Buber sought to clarify the concept of mutuality.[16] In *I and Thou*, it will be recalled, Buber had distinguished between reciprocity and mutuality. While he used the former to refer to any situation in which each being acts upon the other, he spoke of mutuality as a situation in which one experiences an event both from one's own side and from that of the other.

In his later writings, however, Buber acknowledged that there were degrees of mutuality. Thus, in the case of our relationship to inanimate matter, we can speak of reciprocity only insofar as the living wholeness and unity of, for example, the tree is manifest to the person who says "You" to it. The You-saying person gives the tree the opportunity to manifest its wholeness and unity, and "the tree that has being manifests it" (Buber, *I and Thou*, 173). To ascribe consciousness to the tree, however, would be to step beyond the bounds of our experience. Thus, Buber referred to our relationship to inanimate matter as standing on the prethreshold of mutuality.[17]

In contrast to inanimate matter, animals are capable of spontaneous, active, direct responses. However, unlike humans, animals are incapable of the twofold relationship of the basic words *I-You* and *I-It*. Accordingly, Buber spoke of the relations between persons and animals as being on the threshold of mutuality. Regarding our relationship to creations of the human spirit, such as works of art or literature, Buber spoke of the "over threshold," or lintel, of mutuality. If one turns to a text with one's whole being, one can hear the voice of a dead master speaking. Similarly, one can, in an encounter with a Doric column, experience something that borders on mutuality.[18]

The concept mutuality, therefore, only applies to relations between persons. Only in the interhuman realm can two beings, fully capable of speaking the basic words, enter into a mutual relation with one another. However, there are at least two kinds of relationships in which such mutuality is precluded: the relationship between a teacher and student, and that between a psychotherapist and client.

In both of these relationships, one partner acts upon the other so as to accomplish a specific goal. Accordingly, one expects the therapist and the teacher to experience the situation in an inclusive, embracing way that one cannot expect of the patient or the student:

In order to promote coherently the liberation and actualization of this unity in a new situation in which the other person comes to terms with the world, the therapist, like the educator, must stand not only at his own pole of the bipolar relationship, but also at the other pole, experiencing the effects of his own actions. (Buber, *I and Thou*, 179)

Mutuality is, for Buber, a prerequisite for full dialogue. Confronting the other as a distinct person is necessary but not sufficient. By accepting a person and confirming his or her otherness, we open the way to trust. However, for genuine dialogue to occur, mutual address must also take place.[19]

To be aware of a man, therefore, means in particular to perceive his wholeness as a person stamped by spirit; it means to perceive the dynamic centre which stamps his every utterance, action and attitude with the recognizable sign of uniqueness. (Buber, *Knowledge of Man*, 80)

In his later discussions of dialogue and monologue, Buber elaborated further on the forms of human behavior that impede genuine relations. Frequently, in conversation with another, while seeming to be fully present, we calculate the effect or impact of our words on the other. In so doing, we actually hold ourselves back from being fully present and from confirming the other as the one that he or she is. Moreover if, in our relations with others, we absolutize ourselves while relativizing the other, we preclude the mutuality that dialogue requires. In both of these instances, we have monologue pretending to be dialogue.

In distinguishing between genuine dialogue and pretense, we must look beyond the terms employed to characterize the relationship and examine the attitude with which we enter into it. Genuine dialogue entails a unity of heart, mouth, and mind, of feeling, intention, and action. For example, what appears to be the conversation of lovers may mask the desire for self-aggrandizement and self-glorification. In such a situation, what purports to be love is simply the desire of one or both persons to satisfy a yearning or need of his or her own, with little, if any, concern for the actualization of the other.

Similarly, acts that appear to be altruistic can actually be monological. For example, if a person engaging in an act of charity fails to address the other as a complete being, the relationship is monological. In acts of charity, as in any relationship, a person may be primarily concerned to enhance his or her own power or sense of worth, with little or no concern for the self of the recipient. In such an instance, when one is primarily concerned with the satisfaction of one's own needs, regardless of the category used to describe the activity, genuine dialogue is thwarted.

Another impediment to genuine dialogue occurs whenever we assume an analytic, reductive, objective stance to another person. By focusing on an aspect of the other rather than on his or her total being, we reduce and restrict the other's wholeness. Similarly, we impede genuine dialogue whenever we seek to influence the way in which the other perceives us. Buber demonstrates this by contrasting "being" to "seeming." Whereas the "being" person is spontaneous and unreserved, the "seeming" person contrives a particular appearance in order to appear in a particular way, to present a particular image, or to have a particular effect.

Buber was careful to point out that not all seeming is inappropriate. For example, there is a "genuine seeming," in which one imitates a hero. On the other hand, the seeming or pretending that springs from our desire to affect the other rather than relate to him or her obstructs genuine dialogue. Thus, when two people confront each another, one can differentiate between their intended appearance, their actual appearance, and their bodily existence. When intended appearance prevails, when one of them presents himself or herself not as he or she is but as he or she wishes to be seen, then genuine dialogue is blocked:

Whatever the meaning of the word "truth" in other realms, in the interhuman realm it means that men communicate themselves to one another as what they are . . . letting no seeming creep in between [themselves] and the other. (Buber, *Knowledge of Man*, 77)

As this passage and others like it make clear, Buber's concept of truth is situational. In his view, truth does not have one unchanging meaning, but assumes different meanings in accordance with the sphere of human existence under discussion. In the sphere of the interhuman, truth is synonymous with authenticity and genuineness. A relationship is true or genuine when one relates to another without pretense.

Another development that one sees in Buber's 1950s essays is a more positive attitude toward the realm of I-It. Revising his earlier interpretation of the twofold movement that informs our relationship with the world and with other persons, he contrasted "primal setting at a distance" with "entering into relation" (Buber, *Knowledge of Man*, 60). Whereas, in earlier works, Buber appears to have only begrudgingly assigned the I-It stance a positive function, he now acknowledged its importance. In order to be able to enter into relation fully, a person must first engage in the act of setting the other or the world at a distance. By remaining in a state of primitive union with the world, or, in the case of our human relations, with the mother, we remain unaware of its (her) wholeness and unity and, consequently, cannot step into relation with it. This act of setting apart or distancing is unique to human beings:

Rather is this the peculiarity of human life, that here and here alone a being has arisen from the whole, endowed and entitled to detach the whole as a world from himself and to make it opposite to himself, instead of cutting out with his senses the part he needs from it, as all other beings do, and being content with it. (Buber, *Knowledge of Man*, 63)

The process of distance and relation further distinguishes people from animals. Like the animals, we make use of the things around us. However, unlike animals, we are capable of setting things at a distance so that they acquire a certain independence and duration.

Relation and Healing:
Psychotherapy and the Self

From his earliest days, Buber felt a strong affinity for the field of psychotherapy, which he understood as a process devoted to repairing our damaged capacity for relation.[20] Avoiding the prevailing objectivistic psychotherapeutic discourse, he interpreted psychotherapy from the perspective of relation and dialogue. The therapist, like the educator whom I shall discuss in chapter 6, is engaged in a relationship that aims to help another person to actualize his or her unique potential. Like the teacher-student relationship, the relationship between psychotherapist and patient cannot be one of full mutuality and inclusion can only be achieved by one of the partners. One person, the helper, assumes a greater responsibility for the other.

Buber was critical of the dominant Freudian model of the psyche. Although acknowledging the reality of the unconscious, Buber refused to reduce it to either a physiological or a psychical phenomenon. Instead, he viewed the unconscious as the foundation from which the psychic and the physical both emerged. The term *unconscious* refers to the fact that "there are things that influence our life and that come out in certain conscious states" (Buber, *Believing Humanism*, 156). When we speak of a "psyche," however, we simply reify "that non-phenomenal unconscious that dissociates itself into the physiological and psychological" (Buber, *Believing Humanism*, 156).

In contrast to Freud's conflict model in which the basic human drive for pleasure conflicts both with other aspects of the psyche as well as with culturally imposed limits, Buber's relational model emphasized the human need to actualize one's basically humanizing capacities. In addition, whereas Freud conceived of love in terms of the discharge of basic instinctual energy expressed in the sexual drives, Buber viewed love existentially in terms of the responsibility of I for a You.

Understandably, Buber also rejected the Freudian model of therapy in which the therapist, assuming a stance of total objectivity and detachment, serves as the catalyst to reactivate repressed forces. For Freud, the therapeutic relationship centers around the process of transference. Acting out one's relationship to one's parents through one's relationship to the therapist, the patient exposes repressed feelings by reliving earlier experiences. In the process, unconscious feelings and attitudes are raised to a level of consciousness, or reactivated.

Buber believed psychological illnesses result from impaired or broken relationships between persons: "A soul is never sick alone, but there is always a between-ness also, a situation between it and another existing being" (Buber, *Believing Humanism*, 142). According to Buber, conventional psychiatry, viewing psychological illness as emerging from within a person, denies the interhuman reality of life.

Buber's conception of person led him to formulate a totally different view of the therapeutic process. Buber understood therapy as a healing relationship modeled on the concept of dialogue. The "abyss" of the patient calls out to the self of the doctor, "that selfhood that is hidden under the structures erected through training and practice" (Buber, *Believing Humanism*, 140). While the therapist may resort to specific methods, he or she is not an objective observer, but a human being who has been addressed by another.

As a healer, the doctor must strive to break free of all theoretical systems and methods and enter "into the elementary situation between one who calls and one who is called" (Buber, *Believing*

Humanism, 140). In the process of address and response, the therapist is changed through the "genuine personal meetings in the abyss of human existence between the one in need of help and the helper" (Buber, *Believing Humanism*, 140).

Only by entering into a genuine, albeit nonmutual, dialogue with the client can the therapist help the client to heal himself or herself. As the therapist stands before the client as a fully present human being, "a transformed, healed relationship must and can be opened to the person who is sick in his relations to otherness—to the world of the other which he cannot remove into his soul" (Buber, *Believing Humanism*, 142).

For Buber the fallacy of conventional psychotherapy is revealed in the way in which it copes with the problem of guilt. Like all psychic phenomena, guilt, for Buber, is not the outcome of conflict within the individual, but results from fractured relations between persons. Thus, guilt is an indication of a damaged relationship with another:

Existential guilt occurs when someone injures an order of the human world whose foundations he knows and recognizes as those of his own existence and of all common existence. (Buber, *Knowledge of Man*, 127)

Guilt is one thing that distinguishes the human being from other animal forms: "Man is the being who is capable of becoming guilty and is capable of illuminating his guilt" (Buber, *Knowledge of Man*, 146). Through selective memory, the individual tries to filter out this guilt, so that it does not enter consciousness as such.[21] Throughout history, human beings have repeatedly and unsuccessfully tried to resist this illumination by suppressing their guilt.

However, guilt is always accessible to consciousness. By overcoming inner resistance, the individual can attain self-illumination. But self-illumination is only the first step in the process. Insofar as guilt always entails an act against another, it can only be assuaged through reconciliation:

Reconciliation means here, first of all, that I approach the man toward whom I am guilty in the light of my self-illumination (insofar as I can still reach him on earth) acknowledge to his face my existential guilt and help him, insofar as possible, to overcome the consequences of my guilty action. (Buber, *Knowledge of Man*, 147)

The function of the therapist is not to bring salvation to the sinner, but to further the process of healing. To accomplish this, he or she must recognize the existential reality of guilt, and help the other bring it out into the open. Through the relationship between person and person, the healing process can occur:

The utmost that can be expected of him, as I have said, is only this: that reaching out beyond his familiar methods, he conduct the patient, whose existential guilt he has recognized, to where an existential help of the self can begin. (Buber, *Knowledge of Man*, 148)

The Teachings Applied:
Buber and Contemporary Psychotherapy

Buber, the edifying philosopher, conveyed his insights into the human condition in a speculative or theoretical mode, unsupported by clinical data or empirical evidence. Nevertheless, the clinical value of Buber's insights has been recognized by a number of contemporary therapists.[22] Their works reflect the ways Buber's writings have been used clinically to interpret and heal the modern alienated individual. Drawing extensively from their own professional practice, these therapists provide a clinical context missing from Buber's discussions. Moreover, applying Buber's insights to actual therapeutic situations, they have succeeded in elaborating and expanding his original insights.

Given Buber's basic orientation, it is not surprising that he attracts psychotherapists who approach the human condition from an existentialist perspective.[23] The writings of R. D. Laing, Robert F. Hobson, and Irvin Yalom clearly reflect three ways in which Buber has shaped their understanding of psychotherapy. First, each finds that Buber's insights regarding the primacy of need-free, loving relations provides a fruitful way of talking about the process of human development. Second, each finds the concept of dialogue to be a valuable metaphor in understanding health and illness. Finally, each finds that the concepts of genuine relation and dialogue provide a paradigm for the therapeutic relationship.

Buber's influence is clearly evident in Yalom's seminal study *Existential Psychotherapy*.[24] Citing Buber, Yalom insists that the most important lesson for the psychotherapist is "it is the relationship that heals."[25] Agreeing with Buber that the relationship makes it possible for the I to change through discovering new aspects of the self, Yalom stresses individual choice and responsibility. The goal of psychotherapy is "to bring the patient to the point where he can make a free choice."[26]

Yalom also applies Buber's distinction between the educator and the propagandist to psychotherapy.[27] In contrast to the propagandist, who imposes his attitudes and opinions on others, the psychotherapist, like the educator, seeks to "help another to discover his or her own dispositions and experience his or her own 'actualizing forces.' "[28] While agreeing with Rogers that empathy, genuineness, and positive, unconditional regard are essential elements in effective psychotherapy, Yalom warns against mistaking these qualities for a technique.

Yalom's interpretation of the therapist-client relationship is modelled on the I-You relationship. Like Buber, Yalom urges the therapist "to enter the patient's world and to experience it as the patient experiences it."[29] Moreover, as in the I-You relation, the therapist must be fully present and "disclose himself or herself as a person."[30] This, in turn, requires that the psychotherapist divest himself or herself of all presuppositions and avoid judging or stereotyping the patient.[31]

Like Buber, Yalom is deeply concerned with the alienation and isolation that permeates human existence:

Existential isolation refers to an unbridgeable gulf between oneself and any other being. It refers, too, to an isolation even more fundamental—a separation between the individual and the world.[32]

In describing this alienation and isolation, Yalom uses Buber's categories. With the increasing loss of institutional settings that facilitate intimate relationships, the modern individual increasingly relates to others "as toward tools or equipment. The other, now no longer an 'other' but an 'it', is placed there, within one's circle of world, for a function."[33]

As an alternative to these alienated I-It relationships, Yalom advocates need-free relationships in which one surrenders self-consciousness and self-awareness in order to enter wholly into a direct relationship. This entails knowing and experiencing the other as a total person and helping the other to actualize his or her potential. Rather than view love in terms of the satisfaction of needs, Yalom, like Buber, argues that love entails an active caring for the other that grows out of one's own positive being rather than one's needs or deficiencies.

Like the I-You relation, need-less caring is reciprocal. As one brings the other to life, one becomes more fully alive. Thus, while such need-free, confirming relationships bring rewards, "these rewards flow from genuine caring; they do not instigate it." Moreover, "the rewards ensue but they cannot be pursued."[34]

Acknowledging his indebtedness to Buber, Yalom writes, "I have cited Buber extensively because his formulation of a need-less love relationship is vivid and gripping."[35] Yalom, like Buber, wishes to unmask the hideouts through which we seek to escape from our human condition. Although "each of us craves perdurance, groundedness, community and pattern . . . we must all face inevitable death, groundlessness, isolation and meaninglessness."[36] Like Buber, Yalom argues that neither purposive activity nor self-actualization are sufficient to satisfy our inherent yearning for meaning. To find oneself, one must look beyond oneself to the other. Citing one of Buber's Hasidic tales, he concludes:

Buber's essential point is that human beings have a more far-reaching meaning than the salvation of individual souls. In fact, through excessive preoccupation with gaining an advantageous personal place in eternity, a person may lose that place.[37]

Buber's categories were also used by the Scottish therapist R. D. Laing. Although heavily indebted to Sartre, Laing has described Buber's writings as helpful in clarifying the human relationships he encounters in his clinical practice. Laing, in a radical move, has endeavored to understand the situation of schizophrenic patients through dialogue and inclusion. Rejecting the objectivistic discourse of contemporary psychiatry, Laing seeks to see the world through their eyes.[38]

Like Buber, Laing analyzes human relationships in terms of their capacity to confirm or disconfirm the participants. "One can think of action and interaction as more or less, and in different ways, confirmatory or disconfirmatory."[39] However, expanding on Buber's discussion, Laing is concerned with the ways in which forms of interaction "vary in intensity and extensity, quality and quantity."[40] Rather than view relationships as either fully confirming or disconfirming, Laing finds that relationships can be confirming on some levels while not on others. In any given relationship, one can confirm some aspects of another person while failing to endorse others.

According to Laing, a smile, a tactile response such as a handshake, and an auditory response such as an expression of sympathy all confirm the other in different ways. Moreover, a person's action may be confirmed on one level while disconfirmed on another. Even rejection can be confirmatory if it is direct and "recognizes the evoking action and grants it significance and validity." Such direct rejection differs from "the mocking or otherwise invalidating" character of an indifferent or impervious response. Thus, "some forms of disconfirmation may be more destructive of self-development than others."[41]

Laing also adds a developmental dimension to Buber's categories. As he sees it, there are times during the course of our lives when one area of our being cries out for confirmation more than others. For example, the kinds of responses required by an infant for confirmation differ from those required by an adult. Moreover, the qualities and capacities confirmed or disconfirmed will differ in accordance with who the other is, be it one's father, brother, sister, friend, or a stranger.

Laing believes that it is even possible to confirm false dimensions of our being or false aspects of our identity. In families of schizophrenics, for example, lack of genuine communication "takes the form of actively confirming a false self, so that the person whose false self is confirmed and real self disconfirmed is placed in a false position."[42] This, in turn, generates a sense of guilt, shame, or anxiety.

Laing also considers it to be disconfirming when a person, focusing on something that is merely tangential to the other, fails to endorse the activity of the other as the other perceives it. According to Laing, this "tangential response" engenders frustration in the other. If, for example, a boy approaches his mother with a worm and she expresses neither approval or disapproval, but instead focuses on something that the boy has not considered and which is not immediately important to him, the boy's feelings are disconfirmed through deflection.

Laing, like Buber, distinguishes between being and seeming, or genuine presence and pretense.[43] Whenever two people interact, each has four different faces: the image of oneself as one wishes to appear to the other; the way in which one actually appears to the other; the image that each has of himself or herself; and the bodily self. In Buber's words: "two living beings and six ghostly appearances, which mingle in many ways in the conversation between the two. Where is there any room for any genuine interhuman life" (Buber, *Knowledge of Man*, 77). Laing speaks of this as "counterfeiting a relation."[44]

When a disjunction arises between the way we wish or need to be seen and the way that the other actually sees and responds to us, we are likely to respond with "anger, anxiety, guilt, despair, or indifference."[45] Moreover, if there is an incompatibility between the way we wish to be taken by the other and the way in which the other wishes to be taken by us, both parties may go along with the pretense through collusion:

Collusion is always clinched when self finds in other the other who will "confirm" self in the false self that is trying to make real, and vice versa. The ground is then set for prolonged mutual evasion of truth and true fulfillment. Each has found an other to endorse his own false notion of himself and to give this appearance a semblance of reality.[46]

Laing has expanded Buber's categories by describing the way in which various aspects of a person can be confirmed or disconfirmed; the different kinds of confirmation or disconfirmation appropriate to different stages of life; and the way in which the intensity of confirmation or disconfirmation may vary according to the source of the confirming or disconfirming action. Working extensively with schizophrenics, Laing tended to focus on disconfirming, dehumanizing relationships. Nevertheless, he has found that Buber's categories help to reveal the dynamics of destructive as well as constructive human relationships.

In contrast to Yalom and Laing, the British psychiatrist Robert F. Hobson, in his study *Forms of Feeling*, focuses on the linguistic dimension of psychotherapy.[47] Developing what he calls a "conversational model" of psychotherapy, Hobson defines the task of the therapist as helping the patient to find the appropriate words through which to express his or her deepest feelings, wishes, and fears.

Hobson has been strongly influenced by British philosophy of language.[48] Accordingly, he focuses on the relationship between our existential experience and the language that we employ in conceptualizing and communicating that experience.[49]

To Hobson, I-Thou and I-It are best understood as Wittgensteinean forms of life. The basic forms of human life—that is, the relationships between person and person (I-Thou) and the relationship between person and thing (I-It)—entail different modes of discourse. When we wish to describe our relationship to things, discursive and linear language is appropriate. However, when describing our relationship to another person, another mode of discourse is required, a language of the heart or what Hobson calls "feeling language."

Like Buber, Hobson finds stories to be one of the most appropriate forms for communicating human experience.[50] In contrast to the dry, discursive language of objectivistic description, stories characterize human experience through images, sensations, emotions, and actions. Insofar as human experience is prelinguistic and preconceptual, language can never adequately mirror the reality of our inner experiences. Yet different modes of discourse have the power either to draw us closer to or to distance us from the world of our innermost feelings. By helping the patient to formulate the appropriate metaphors through which to express these feelings, the psychiatrist can help the patient to bridge the gap separating the patient from his or her own experiences and feelings.

Like Yalom, Hobson views the therapeutic relationship as a personal dialogue that "expresses and promotes a relationship of aloneness-togetherness."[51] In the therapeutic relationship, "two experiencing subjects commit themselves to a meeting" and disclose themselves to one another in the appropriate language.[52] Therapy is required when a person either suppresses the personal quality of his or her experiences or lacks the appropriate skills to talk about them. In therapy, as understood by Hobson, the therapist functions as a translator, helping the patient to discover "a precise expression for personal feeling, for a 'felt-meaning' in, and between, himself and his client."[53]

Hobson differentiates normal dialogical encounters from the therapeutic dialogue. In normal dialogue, I-You discourse suffices. In contrast, "a therapeutic dialogue involves the use of varied languages."[54] To truly know their patients, therapists must use the language of interhuman dialogue. However, in order for therapists to apply their specialized training and expertise to the problems presented by their patients, they must step back, analyze, and classify in language appropriate to the I-It form of life:

The fabric of a relationship is a tapestry woven by the weft of person language and the warp of thing language. A psychotherapist needs to learn to work the loom of language.[55]

Hobson follows Buber in tracing psychological disorders to disturbances in human relationships. For Hobson, however, these disturbed relationships result from "the inability of persons to use and/ or learn certain types of language." Accordingly, it is not enough for the psychiatrist to enter into relation with the patient. He or she must also perform an educative function, teaching the patient the appropriate linguistic skills: "Psychotherapy is concerned with the detection, exploration and correction of such disturbances. It is a matter of learning how to use a new language."[56]

Concepts such as wholeness, presentness, and becoming, which recur throughout Buber's writings, are essential to Hobson's conversational model. In relating to the patient, the therapist must be able "to 'be' with him 'as a whole': to value and respect his potentialities for growth towards a state of being-himself, of going on becoming a person."[57] Hobson also agrees with Buber's claim that the experience of relating is always of the present: "Experiencing is always 'now' and is always 'in relation to'—especially to persons who stand over and against me."[58]

Hobson, like Buber, speaks of the oscillating character of life. However, whereas Buber spoke of the movement between distance and relation, Hobson, borrowing from John Bowlby, speaks of relation and separation, bonding and loss, and togetherness and aloneness. Also, whereas Buber privileged relation over separation, Hobson, like Yalom, acknowledges the important role of separation and loneliness in human development.[59]

Between Person and Creations of Spirit

While primarily concerned with the relationships between persons, Buber also recognized the alienation that was manifest in our relationship to products of the human spirit, normally subsumed under the category of culture. Like his teacher, Simmel, Buber believed that the objectification of human creativity in cultural forms contributed to the alienated condition of the modern person. Accordingly, viewing cultural creativity to be an essential component in our actualization as persons, Buber applied his philosophical categories to this realm as well.

Culture, for Buber, is neither an objective realm nor a product of inner consciousness. Artistic creation is not, as Dilthey and Feuerbach claimed, the result of the externalization of inner experiences. Instead, cultural phenomena result from our encounter with the world around us and with the material through which we seek to express this encounter.

In *I and Thou* Buber used artistic creation as a paradigm for our relations to the world and to other persons. The artist does not impose his or her will upon the material. The relationship between artist and medium is not one of power and domination but one of mutual interaction. Encountering a block of marble, the sculptor draws out of the object the form that is inherent in it.

The concept of entelechy, basic to Buber's conception of person, was also important to his discussion of cultural creativity. In interhuman relations, we draw out and actualize the unique qualities of the other through relation. In the act of artistic creation, we seek to draw out and actualize the reality inherent in nature and in the inanimate world:

To all unprejudiced reflection it is clear that all art is from its origin essentially of the nature of dialogue. All music calls to an ear not the musician's own, all sculpture to an eye not the sculptor's, architecture in addition calls to the step as it walks in the building. They all say, to him who receives them, something (not a "feeling" but a perceived mystery) that can be said only in this one language. (Buber, *Between Man and Man*, 25)

Art is neither an expression of human consciousness nor an imprint of the outer world, but rather an event of relation, of the between: "It is the work and the witness of the relation between the substantia humana and the substantia rerum, it is the real of 'the between' which has become a form." The creation of a work of art is "a relational event which takes place between two entities that have gone apart from one another" (Buber, *Knowledge of Man*, 66).[60]

While most persons have the capacity to see the world figuratively, the artist is able to transform what he or she sees into a form or image. In contrast to common acts of perception, whereby we draw out of the world what we need, the artist elevates perception to vision and art that transcends need. Thus, the artist's transformation of the world into form and image is not a result of need but "discovery through figuration" (Buber, *Knowledge of Man*, 161).

Like knowledge, love, and faith, art is a means through which we can overcome our alienation from the world. Seen in this way, art is an expression of "the longing for perfected relation or perfection in the relation":

The imperfect relations belong to the world of needing and getting, or to its play annexes. But the human person desires more than this. He does not content himself with the measure and degree of the development of relations that are required for the mastering of the needs of daily life and for entering into the regulated freedoms of play: the higher wish appears. (Buber, *Knowledge of Man*, 163).

Through art, we transcend the sphere of the useful and "experience and actualize the perfection of the relation to the substratum of the sense things: through the figuration in the vision and in work" (Buber, *Knowledge of Man*, 164). With one exception, all forms of art entail an act of "elemental renunciation" in which we limit our response either to the visual or the acoustical. Poetry, in contrast to other art forms, rises above any single sense. In the tradition of romanticism, Buber viewed poetry as a unique sphere, rooted in "the primal structure of man as man" and expressed through language that transcends space and time (Buber, *Knowledge of Man*, 162).

For Buber, all knowledge arises in our encounter with the world, rather than within human consciousness. An insight, originating through basic relation, is grasped, limited, and compressed into an independent, conceptual form. It is then placed within an order of conceptual forms where it is expressed and clarified through language. This process is a dialogical one in which the thinker tests his or her insight against the basic relation. The testing of the idea takes place not in monologue with self but in dialogue with others. As Feuerbach had correctly observed, "genuine dialectic is not a monologue of the solitary thinker with himself, but rather a dialogue between heaven and earth" (Buber, *Between Man and Man*, 27). To conceive of this process as a "colloquy with the self is to err" (Buber, *Between Man and Man*, 26).

The dialogue that produces knowledge is not limited to cognitive processes but entails a meeting of whole persons. Accordingly, the process that culminates in knowledge is not a mental process but an existential process that transpires "not between minds, but between whole persons, who stand before us as concrete, bodily beings" (Buber, *Between Man and Man*, 28).

Buber also interpreted our knowledge of literary texts in terms of relation and dialogue. Rejecting both the objectivistic and subjectivistic view of meaning, Buber insisted that "we do not find meaning lying in things nor do we put them into things, but between us and things it can happen" (Buber, *Between Man and Man*, 36). On the one hand, Buber admitted that there is no way of attaining the correct meaning of a text. All reading, as Nietzsche had taught, is interpretation. Nevertheless, a text has its particular language, texture, structure, and rhythm, all of which communicate meaning and merit careful study. Accordingly, in the act of reading, the consciousness of the reader encounters the concrete reality of the text.

To teach a text, therefore, is not simply to present the student with the correct interpretation. The teacher leads the student to the text, seeking to "make visible the working forces of the text" that the teacher has experienced (Buber, *Pointing the Way*, 101). Thus, as reflected in Buber's transmission of Hasidic writings, the teacher acts as a kind of filter or facilitator.

As we have seen, from the publication of *I and Thou* until his death in 1965, Buber engaged in an ongoing process of clarification and refinement of categories. The result was his mature conception of dialogue, which he articulated in its final form during the 1950s. In the process, Buber presented a more complex notion than the dichotomous one he had first articulated in 1923. In addition, Buber assigned the I-It, or distancing, stance a more positive role.

The concept of dialogue formulated from the 1920s to the 1950s provided several psychiatrists with a useful and insightful way of understanding psychological growth and the therpeutic process. Working in the everyday world of human suffering, they were able to expand and elaborate Buber's categories in new and creative ways. At the same time, through their work, Buber's desire to bridge the abysses separating persons and to heal the pain of alienation was translated into practical processes of healing.

6

The Crisis of Community: Buber as Social Critic

Social Thought: The Task Defined

In the previous chapters, I have presented Buber as an edifying philosopher who, moved by the alienated condition of modern society, sought to formulate an alternative way of viewing human existence. *I and Thou*, as we saw in chapter 5, represented a turning point in Buber's lifelong effort to construct a set of categories that would enable his readers to revise radically the ways in which they perceive themselves and their relationships to other persons and the world around them.

In *I and Thou*, Buber utilized a philosophic-poetic mode of discourse to formulate and transmit his ideas, but his primary concern was to alter the social framework within which we live. As Walter Kaufmann has correctly observed, "the aim of the book is not to disseminate knowledge, but, at least in large measure, to diagnose certain tendencies in modern society."[1] Thus, although Buber devoted major sections to philosophical anthropology and religion, ultimately, *I and Thou* is an attempt "to indicate how the quality of life might be changed radically by the development of a new sense of community." Accordingly, "it speaks to those whose primary concern is not at all with religion, but with social change."[2]

In this chapter I shall consider the work in the context of Buber's social thought.[3]

As Kaufmann noted, the second, and central section of *I and Thou*, is devoted to a critique of the alienating forces in modern society and culture.[4] In that section, Buber set forth his basic understanding of the forms of human association and cultural creation. In subsequent works, such as *Between Man and Man*, *The Knowledge of Man*, and *Paths in Utopia*, and in several unpublished lectures, Buber elaborated on this discussion.

Strong support for reading Buber as a social critic is found in Buber's own formulation of social theory first articulated in a 1938 lecture. Identifying with a position articulated by Tonnies, Buber approached sociology as "social philosophy," rather than an empirical inquiry.[5] According to Buber, sociology, or social thought, did not emerge from a concern with abstract forms and structures but grew, instead, out of "the meeting of the spirit with the crisis of human society that occurred at the beginning of the nineteenth century" (Buber, *Pointing the Way*, 178).

Rather than adopt a detached, objectivistic stance, the sociologist stands within the crisis and actively participates in the search for a solution:

Modern sociology as an independent science was originally critical and demanding. Its earliest representative was Saint Simon, who as a social critic, perceived the inner contradiction of an age and designated scientific knowledge of social conditions as the decisive step towards its overcoming. (Buber, *Pointing The Way*, 177)[6]

Buber's conception of sociology parallels his interpretation of the philosophical enterprise. Like the philosopher, the sociologist engages in a critique of language. The sociologist's primary task is not to describe the norms of human interaction or the forms of communal life but to engage in "a genuine philosophical comprehension and clarification of basic social concepts" (Buber, *Pointing the Way*, 178). This critique entails three tasks: to formulate and clarify the categories of social life; to distinguish the social from the other spheres of human life; and to understand the meaning of social existence.[7]

The first task of the sociologist is concept clarification: "Amid the confusion and obliteration of basic social concepts, human knowledge of society must today, in many respects, begin anew with a new conceptual clarification, a new cleansing of the type" (Buber *Pointing the Way*, 191).[8] This process of clarification requires differentiating the social realm from the other realms of group life. On the one hand, this entails distinguishing between the social, the political, and the cultural spheres. It also requires, as Tonnies stressed, clarifying the difference between the social and the communal. For Buber, the key to this clarification is the concept of the interhuman.

In Buber's view, social philosophy entails valuation, criticism, and demand. In contrast to the value-free orientation to sociology, commonly but problematically ascribed to Max Weber, Buber envisioned a critical investigation of problems to which the sociologist is existentially committed.[9] Concerned with far more than description, the sociologist's responsibility is to inquire into the human meaning of social life in order to help shape that life:[10]

But this is a question of knowing a world in crisis, and the knowing spirit knows that it stands with the world in crisis. Not as if this spirit were merely a piece of social reality. Rather it is its partner, destined to learn from what is and to show it in return what should be—the crisis embraces them both together. (Buber, *Pointing the Way*, 178)

Only by experiencing social life from the inside can the sociologist hope to understand it: "Without genuine social binding there is no genuine social experience, and without genuine social experience there is no genuine sociological thinking" (Buber, *Pointing the Way*, 180–81).[11] Ultimately, as Marx had recognized, the concern of the social thinker is not simply to understand the world but to help change it.

As we saw in chapter 4, Buber, in keeping with the antiobjectivism that has characterized much of modern philosophy, was convinced that objectivity, in the conventional sense, is unattainable.[12] Like any critical thinker, the sociologist lacks an olympian perch from which to look down and see things independent of his or her own perspective. Sociologists who adopt the objectivistic orientation prevalent in the world of science dehumanize the sociological task.

In the relationship of a man to the truth he has discovered, freedom and obligation, vision and blindness, are always merged. Our concern is only this—to will with all the power of our spirit to achieve this free vision. On the basis of the knowledge thus won, the sociological thinker may value and decide, censure and demand, when the urgent question approaches, without violating the law of his science. Only so can the spirit preserve itself in the crisis that embraces it and historical reality together. (Buber, *Pointing the Way*, 181)

Insofar as the sociologist's existential reality conflicts with the experience of the group, he or she must be prepared to engage in an "ascetic act" by assuming a critical stance and questioning the validity of the prevailing forms and institutions. At no time, however, should the sociologists allow himself or herself to be submerged in the social reality he or she is studying:

No one becomes a sociological thinker if his dream and his passion have never mingled with the dream and passion of a human community; but in the moment of thinking, itself, as far as it stands in his power, he must exist only as person, the person open to the subject of thought. If this relation is maintained, he need not unduly trouble himself with the question of how far his knowledge was determined against his will by his membership in a group. (Buber, *Pointing the Way*, 181)

Striving to be value-free, sociologists often subordinate their own independent judgment to the will of the group. However, according to Buber, this destroys the critical spirit and engenders passivity. By assuming a purely descriptive stance, the sociologist becomes, in effect, the spokesman for organizations and institutions. In Buber's view, this politicization of sociology is disastrous.

Since the sociologist's goal is to transform social reality, "the social thinker who understands his office must ever again pose the question: 'How can the spirit influence the transformation of social reality?' " (Buber, *Pointing the Way*, 182). To transform society, for Buber, means to transform persons:

Man must change himself in the same measure as the institutions are changed in order that these changes may have their expected effect. If the new house that man hopes to erect is not to become his burial chamber, the essence of living together must undergo a change at the same time as the organization of living. (Buber, *Pointing the Way*, 179)

Thus, the sociologist's task, like that of the philosopher, is an edifying one that entails a critique of the existing forms of association. The social critic uncovers the ways in which the existing social structure is destructive to the human spirit. It is hoped that this critical process will educate people to alternative social forms conducive to their growth and actualization.

If the representative of the spirit of this new sociological view has merely succeeded in politicizing sociologicially, then that is lost which he and he alone can give to reality—he is lost. He must also educate sociologically, he must educate men in living together; he must educate man so he can live with man. (Buber, *Pointing the Way*, 179)

Sensitive to the obvious similarities between his view of the sociologist and the conventional view of the prophet, Buber took care to distinguish between these two forms of social criticism.[13] Prophets and social critics operate within different frameworks of meaning.[14] The prophet is the bearer of a divine message who comes armed with the certainty of divine revelation. Consequently, the prophet cannot be challenged by rational criticism but only by accusations of false prophecy or by an alternative revelation. The social philosopher, however, armed only with his or her teaching, engages in conceptual analysis and criticism. To challenge the philosopher one employs criticism and argumentation:

The social thinker is not a prophet, but a philosopher. He does not have a message, he has a teaching. But for the transformation of the social reality he intends that which is decisive. This is no Platonic task, no erection of a universally valid image of perfection; it is the prophetic task of criticism and demand within the present situation. Where an urgent question impinges, he cannot, of course, express criticism and demand as a message, but he can certainly express them on the basis of his knowledge. (Buber, *Pointing the Way*, 190)

Thus, although the social thinker, like the prophet, is a social critic, the grounds of his critique and the discourse that he employs are thoroughly secular.

Buber's efforts at social theory were clearly rooted in his own existential experience. As described in the previous chapter, his starting point was the vision of social reality which flowed from that experience. Disturbed by the gap between the existing sociocultural reality and his own sense of personhood, Buber sought to cope with the threat that the alienating conditions of modern life posed to the individual's basic drive to actualization.

Social theory, according to Buber, originates not in the quiet of the scholar's study but in the crisis of modern life. Unlike empirical sociologists who strive to suspend or suppress their own existential concerns in the name of scholarly objectivity, Buber viewed social theory as arising out of existential concerns. Like the philosophical anthropologist, the sociologist is personally engaged in the very issues that he or she investigates.

Thus, Buber's conception of social thought is fully compatible with the following description by the late sociologist Alvin Gouldner:

Social theorizing, then, is often a search for the meaning of the personally real, that which is already assumed to be known through personal experience. Basing itself on the imputed reality of the ordinarily experienced, much of theory work begins with an effort to resolve unresolved experiences: here the problem is not to validate what has been observed or to produce new observations, but rather to locate and to interpret the meaning of what one has lived. . . . Much of theory work is initiated by a dissonance between an imputed reality and certain values, or by the indeterminate value of an imputed reality. Theory making, therefore, is often an effort to cope with threat; it is an effort to cope with a threat to something in which the theorist, himself, is deeply and personally implicated and which he holds dear.[15]

Buber's Social Thought

Buber's activities as a social thinker follow the pattern set down in his 1938 lecture discussed previously. As I have repeatedly pointed out, "cleansing the type," that is, critically analyzing social categories in an effort to formulate a critique of the sources of alienation, was one of Buber's primary concerns. Both in Germany and in Israel, Buber drew upon his conception of person and community to challenge the political and social authorities repeatedly.[16]

From the outset of his public career, Buber had questioned the privileging of the prevailing social forms of life.[17] In his 1906 introduction to *Die Gesellschaft*, he had initiated a critique of the conventional categories of the human sciences utilizing his original category of the interhuman *(das Zwischenmenschliche)*. By the end of World War I, the crisis of community had emerged as a fundamental theme in his works:

This, however, is what is most critically problematic for humanity in our time; wherein the destruction of community by institutionalized society is unequivocally proclaimed, that even where one participates in public life, this life is alienating and fictitious. (Buber, *Worte* 1:22)

Insofar as the basic institutions of modern society both reflect and foster alienation, a critique of these institutions is central to the critique of alienation.

In the second section of *I and Thou*, Buber laid the foundations of his critical social theory. Based on the philosophical categories developed in the opening section of the book, Buber went on to criticize modern culture and society, articulating the crisis of the modern age in a new and illuminating way.

Buber acknowledged that the It world is necessary to human material progress. The processes of invention and production require a certain degree of objectification. Analyzing, measuring, and categorizing are all essential in our quest for scientific knowledge and technological development. Moreover, to be able to enter into dialogue fully, one first had to acquire sufficient distance.

In the modern age, however, we have confused material progress with human progress and have erased the boundaries separating the technological and nontechnological dimensions of our lives. "However the history of the individual and that of the human race may diverge in other respects, they agree in this at least: both signify a progressive increase of the It-world" (Buber, *I and Thou*, 87).

The modern age, in contrast to earlier periods, is characterized by the progressive encroachment of the It world into all corners of our social and our cultural lives. This increased domination is clearly evident in political, economic, and cultural spheres. The structures of the modern state and economy are grounded in the perception of others as objects who fulfill a particular function. If the economic and political leaders were to cease viewing those around them as Its and begin to view them as Yous, their world would "come crashing down upon them."

But isn't the communal life of modern man bound to be submerged in the It-world? Consider the two chambers of this life, the economy and the state. . . . If the I that experiences and uses holds sway here—in the economy, the I that uses goods and services; in politics, the I that uses opinions and aspirations—is it not precisely to this absolute dominion that we owe the extensive and firm structure of the great "objective" fabrics in these two spheres? Doesn't the form-giving greatness of leading statesmen and businessmen depend on their way of seeing the human beings with whom they have to deal not as carriers of an inexperienceable You, but rather as centers of services and aspirations that have to be calculated and employed according to their specific capacities? (Buber, *I and Thou*, 96)

The I-It objectifying mode of discourse that dominates the political and economic spheres also dominates our cultural lives. Although the creations of the human spirit and mind, including all forms of knowledge and art, originate in I-You encounters with the world, the products of these encounters are quickly objectified and frozen into the It world:

When a culture is no longer centered in a living and continually renewed relational process, it freezes into the It world which is broken only intermittently by the eruptive, glowing deeds of solitary spirits. From that point on, common causality, which hitherto was never able to disturb the spiritual conception of the cosmos, grows into an oppressive and crushing doom. (Buber, *I and Thou*, 103)

Intellectually, a biological and historical determinism threatens our freedom to act. Subsuming our lives under social, psychological, and cultural laws, we become convinced "that man is yoked into an inescapable process that he cannot resist, though he may be deluded enough to try" (Buber, *I and Thou*, 105). Increasingly, we view the universe as a mechanism in the process of running down, leaving us no room for freedom. "The dogma of running down offers you only one choice as you face its game: to observe the rules or drop out" (Buber, *I and Thou*, 106).

The "despotism of the proliferating It" has created a condition of all-pervasive alienation in which the state and the economy have achieved an independent power of their own and currently control the people who create them. The modern age, according to Buber, is a sick age in which "the It-world, no longer irrigated and fertilized by the living currents of the You-world, severed and stagnant," is rapidly becoming "a gigantic swamp phantom" that threatens to overpower us. Estranged from these reified social, cultural, and political forms, we attempt to cope by bifurcating our lives into two realms, the private and the public. Whereas we define our personal lives through inner feelings and experiences, our public lives are defined by utility, domination, and control.

But the severed It of institutions is a golem, and the severed I of feelings is a fluttering soul bird. Neither knows the human being: one only the instance and the other one only the "object." Neither knows person and community. (Buber, *I and Thou*, 93)

In creating this artificial division, however, we have overlooked the fact that genuine humanizing relations bridge the gap between inner experience and outside reality. In genuine, actualizing relations, public and private, outer and inner are joined.

Buber acknowledged that it would be absurd to attempt to reverse the basic processes that define modern society: "If one could bring off this absurdity, the tremendous precision instrument of this civilization would be destroyed at the same time" (Buber, *I and Thou*, 97). Yet modern society had reached a critical point and could no longer continue along its current path. Only with a fresh interpretation of communal life could genuine dialogue and community be recovered and the modern world extricate itself from this crisis of dehumanization.

In acknowledging that in modern society the I-It mode of relationship has eclipsed virtually "every trace of a life in which human beings confront each other and have meaningful relationships" (Buber, *I and Thou*, 97), Buber moved closer to Nietzsche than previous interpreters have recognized. Insofar as the I-It mode is one in which we use, possess, and control others, I-It relations are rooted in our will to power and control. Accordingly, Buber has, to a greater degree than he recognized, confirmed Nietzsche's view regarding the ubiquity of the will to power in our lives. Although we can achieve breakthroughs into the I-You mode of relation, the reversion to the I-It mode is inevitable. Standing over and against our ability to relate to persons in a nonutilitarian, need-free way is our recurring need to possess and control.

Unlike Nietzsche, Buber believed that through dialogue we could at least temporarily escape from this framework of power. Although we are unable to eliminate I-It relationships completely, he believed that we can, and must, provide enhanced opportunities for I-You relations. Unwilling to surrender us to a condition of endless power relations, Buber, seeking alternative social frameworks, pressed on with his edifying activity.[18]

What Is Community?

Buber's effort to "cleanse the type" is evident in his attempt to clarify the meaning of the concept community. Buber's understanding of community is rooted in his assumption that people are relational, dialogical beings. What is essential to genuine community is not spatial proximity, shared feelings, or common interests. According to Buber, community refers to a life situation in which persons stand in direct relation to one another and to a common center.

True community does not come into being because people have feelings for each other (though that is required, too), but rather on two accounts: all of them have to stand in a living, reciprocal relationship to a single living center, and they have to stand in a living, reciprocal relationship to one another. (Buber, *I and Thou*, 94)

The "center" to which Buber referred has been alternatively defined by his interpreters as a leader, such as the Hasidic rebbe; a common experience, such as the liberation from Egypt or the revelation at Sinai; or God, the Eternal You.[19] Buber used the term in each of these ways in various contexts. In each instance, however, he wished to argue that a group of people among whom I-You relations have been established does not yet constitute a community. For community to come into being, the presence of a center to which the members have a common relationship is also essential:

The real essence of community is to be found in the fact—manifest or otherwise—that it has a center. The real beginning of a community is when its members have a common relation to the center overriding all other relations; the circle is signified (*gezeichnet*) by the radii, not by the points of the periphery. (Buber, *Paths in Utopia*, 135)[20]

Although the relationship to the center is essential for genuine community, it is not sufficient. The members of a community must also engage in reciprocal relations. To clarify what he meant by this, Buber used the analogy of marriage, which he saw as the prototype of community.

Buber distinguished between the feeling dimension and the existential relational dimension of love. Whereas a person has feelings, love occurs between persons. As distinct from the eroticism that prevails in the modern age that is based primarily upon using others for self-enjoyment, "love is a responsibility of an I for a You" (Buber, *I and Thou*, 66). Marriage, based upon the metaphysical and metapsychical fact of love between an I and a You, "can never be renewed except by that which is always the source of all true marriage: that two human beings reveal the You to one another" (Buber, *I and Thou*, 95). Likewise, genuine community requires relationships of responsibility among its members.

In the years following the publication of *I and Thou*, Buber elaborated on the conception of community. In both published and unpublished lectures, he applied his method of "concept criticism" *(Begriffskritik)* to the concept of community, asking his audience, "What do we mean when we speak of community?"[21]

Like *relation* and *dialogue*, *community*, according to Buber, refers not to a static form or structure but to a dynamic process. Like relation, community is unstable, characterized by an ongoing ebb and flow in which direct relations are repeatedly actualized and deactualized. Community, therefore, is a concrete, existential situation, "the moment's answer to a moment's question" (Buber, *Believing Humanism*, 88).

Buber resisted formulating his concept of community into an ideological principle for he believed that community arises in response to a situation and not as the actualization of an abstract idea or principle: "The realization of community, like the realization of any idea, cannot occur once and for all time: always it must be the moment's answer to the moment's question, and nothing more" (Buber, *Paths in Utopia*, 134). As long as there are direct relations among members of a group and with a common leader, one can speak of community; when these direct relations decline, so does community.

In an unpublished lecture delivered in 1929, Buber set forth three prerequisites for community.[22] First, it requires direct, unmediated relations between people. Second, people must relate to one another wholly and not exclude from the outset any dimension of their lives. Thus, one must relate to others with the totality of one's being, including all of one's qualities, capacities, and potentialities. Finally, genuine community is based upon relations that are need-free and nonpurposive.

In community, one does not relate to others as means to an end but as persons who stand over against another person and are actually present for that other person. "A person cannot be a means for the other, in order to achieve his goal, but must be present for him as a living being . . . as a being for whom I am there even as he is for me" (Buber, "Erziehung zur Gemeinschaft," 10). Thus, the prerequisites for community parallel the prerequisites for I-You relation.

For Buber, community is less a matter of intimacy than of openness. It is possible to speak of community even if people are not continually together. Just as a love relationship does not require constant togetherness, neither does community. So long as people "have mutual access to one another and are ready for one another" (Buber, *Paths in Utopia*, 145), the basis for a community exists.

To clarify the concept of community further, Buber contrasted it with two other categories, society and the interhuman. *Society* refers to group life in its basic form:

We may speak of social phenomena wherever the life of a number of men, living with one another, bound up together, bring in its train shared experiences and reactions. But to be thus bound up together means only that each individual existence is enclosed and contained in a group existence. It does not mean that between one member and another of the group there exists any kind of personal relation. (Buber, *Knowledge of Man*, 72)

The category of the interhuman, on the other hand, indicates an existential relation between two persons.[23] This existential relation, for which the participation of both partners is indispensible, may either be mutual or may grow into a mutual relation. Buber referred to the process by means of which the sphere of the interhuman unfolds as the dialogical.

While the social context sets the stage, it is not the equivalent of community. Community arises only when there are direct and total relations. Accordingly, *community*, as Buber used the word, refers simultaneously to a social context and an existential situation between persons. By no means a utopian dream, genuine community can be actualized through the everyday relationships and occupations in which we are engaged.[24]

The concept of confirming the other, which Buber first articulated in 1950, enabled him to clarify further his interpretation of community. As mentioned in chapter 5, Buber spoke of the twofold basis of human relations: A person wishes to be confirmed as what he or she is, or even as what he or she can become, and has an innate capacity to confirm others. According to Buber, "actual humanity exists only where this capacity unfolds" (Buber, *Knowledge of Man*, 68–69), and one may judge the humanity of any social structure according to whether or not it facilitates this unfolding:

In human society at all its levels, persons confirm one another in a practical way to some extent or other in their personal qualities and capacities, and a society may be termed human in the measure to which its members confirm one another. (Buber, *Knowledge of Man*, 67)

To achieve genuine community and to actualize the idea of community, we must create the social conditions that facilitate dialogue—that is, the mutual confirmation of human beings by one another.

Buber insisted that the physical setting is an important factor in creating community, and he advocated an environment designed to allow persons to confirm and be confirmed by others,

not merely in the family, the party assembly or in the public house, but also in the course of neighborly encounters, perhaps when he or the other steps out of the door of his house or to the window of his house. (Buber, *Believing Humanism*, 95)

Accordingly, he believed that, architects' plans should encourage the possibility of genuine encounters between persons:

If the world of man is to become a human world, then immediacy must rule between men, and thus also between human house and human house. And, as in everything else, so also here the institutional and the educational influence must supplement each other. The secret longing of man for a life in reciprocal mutual confirmation must be developed through education, but the external conditions it needs in order to find its fulfillment must also be created. The architects must be set the task of also building for human contact, building surroundings that invite meetings and centers that shape meeting. (Buber, *Believing Humanism*, 95)[25]

Buber's conception of community differs from those of Tonnies, Simmel, and Weber, which I discussed in chapter 1. Buber moved beyond each scholar's interpretation by drawing on both social and existential components. While accepting Tonnies's overall interpretation of modern society, Buber adopted a different interpretation of community. Tonnies grounded *Gemeinschaft* in human will. Weber, on the other hand, rooted community in "a subjective feeling of the parties, whether affectual or traditional, that they belong together."[26] Buber, however, denied that either will or feeling constitutes a sufficient foundation for community.[27]

Although, as Tonnies had recognized, specialized organizations and small associations such as Bunds or trade associations facilitate direct relations, such groups encompass only a limited part of the members' lives. Community, on the other hand, is an all-encompassing social form, embracing the totality of the lives of its members, in all aspects and activities (Buber, "Erziehung zur Gemeinschaft"). Similarly, although Simmel had focused on the significance of the dyadic relationship and defined this relationship in terms of proximity, Buber defined it in terms of dialogue and confirmation.

As a consequence of his existential emphasis and his resistance to structure, Buber's conception of community is, from the perspective of contemporary sociology, highly elusive. Nevertheless, the anthropologist Victor Turner considered Buber's conception to be a viable and significant alternative to the prevailing structural view of society. In *The Ritual Process* Turner distinguished between societas and communitas as two distinct models for human interrelatedness:

The first is of society as a structured, differentiated, and often hierarchical system of politico-legal-economic positions with many types of evaluation, separating men in terms of "more" or "less." The second, which emerges recognizably in the liminal period, is of society as an unstructured or rudimentarily structured and relatively undifferentiated *comitatus*, community, or even communion of equal individuals who submit together to the general authority of the ritual elders.[28]

Unlike society, "communitas has an existential quality; it involves the whole man in his relation to other whole men."[29]

According to Turner, "Buber lays his finger on the spontaneous, immediate, concrete nature of communitas as opposed to the norm-governed, institutionalized, abstract nature of social structure."[30] Moreover, Turner believed that Buber's concept of *das Zwischenmenschliche* captured the essence of communitas, "the 'quick' of human interrelatedness."[31]

Turner conceived of communitas as built upon relationships between historical individuals who "are not segmentalized into roles and statuses but confront one another rather in the manner of Martin Buber's 'I and Thou'."[32] Like Buber, Turner acknowledged that communitas could not be maintained for long and that, like the I-You relationship, it reverts to a structure characterized by norm-governed relationships. For Turner, as for Buber, social life is a dialectical process in which individuals move between the poles of communitas and structure.

No society, in Turner's opinion, can operate without this dialectic in which communitas continually "breaks in through the interstices of structure."[33] Moreover, communitas represents "what is essentially a human social need—the need to be fully together with one's fellows and not segregated from them in structural cells."[34] According to Turner, when the human need for communitas is suppressed, people can actually go crazy.

Rethinking Alienation

In addition to providing much-needed insights into the existential dimension of community, Buber significantly contributed to the discussion of alienation.[35] Tonnies, as we saw in chapter 1, described the modern condition as one in which the natural, organic wholeness of *Gemeinschaft* (community) has been replaced by a depersonalized, artificial, mechanical social structure called *Gesellschaft* (society). Consequently, the modern person is cut off from sources of meaning and comfort previously provided in *Gemeinschaft*. A recovery of *Gemeinschaft* is necessary in order to overcome this situation, but Tonnies, fearing the inevitable continued spread of *Gesellschaft*, was pessimistic about this prospect.

Simmel, as we saw in chapter 1, portrayed the individual in modern society as a cog at the mercy of vast, impersonal forces that control his or her destiny. The individual is reduced to a functionary by the growing power of social structures and institutions. Simmel, like Tonnies and Weber, held out little hope to the modern person entrapped in a system over which he or she has no control.

To Weber, secularization and the rapid spread of a bureaucratized, rationalized social system had rendered the individual virtually powerless. In the modern, capitalist society, we are

bound to the technical and economic conditions of machine production that today determines the lives of all individuals who are born into this mechanism, not only those directly concerned with economic acquisition, with irresistible force.[36]

Identifying with the critiques of modernity contained in these writings, Buber perceived the modern person as a mere functionary in a bureaucratic state that regarded the individual as an object to be used in the pursuit of profit and power. However, rather than undertake to examine specific historical social forms and structures, Buber, like Nietzsche and Kierkegaard, focused on the existential condition. Synthesizing a phenomenological analysis of the human condition with a description of the interhuman, Buber's discussion of alienation provides an existential depth missing from the writings of the social critics.

While Marx, Tonnies, Simmel, and Weber all contributed to the understanding of the human condition, they had failed, according to Buber, to identify the interhuman as the key to alienation. According to Buber, what distinguishes humankind is not the capacity to externalize ourselves through labor and/or other creative activity but the unique capacity for relation and dialogue. Consequently, whatever prevents us from entering into dialogical relations alienates us from our true selves.

Seen in this light, alienation is a condition that blocks our drive for genuine dialogue and mutually confirming relations with others. For Buber, insofar as this basic drive is thwarted or impeded, we are alienated from other persons, and, consequently, from ourselves. To the extent that the prevailing social and discursive frameworks within which we live encourage and even compel us to view others as objects to be analyzed, measured, and utilized for our own ends, they breed and foster alienation.

Thus, modern social and cultural systems, insofar as they objectify human beings and impede our drive to relation, foster a condition of alienation. To unmask the causes of this alienation, Buber maintained, we must focus our attention on interhuman relations. Even if we succeed in overthrowing the social and political structures that turn human labor into a commodity, we will not have succeeded in eliminating the forces that engender alienation. Similarly, while *Gesellschaft* and bureaucracy may be expressions of alienation, they are not the cause. Underlying the spread of *Gesellschaft* and bureaucracy are the modes of discourse and relation that militate against dialogue.

Insofar as every You necessarily reverts to being an It, alienation, according to Buber, is inherent in the human condition. Without I-It relations, we could not survive. At the same time, Buber recognized that in certain social contexts more than others, I-It relationships thrive and multiply; and in some historical situations, the drive to relation is stifled more than in others. Human history is an ongoing movement between centralizing and liberating tendencies.

The modern age, according to Buber, is a sick age in which the domain of I-It has spread so that it now infuses all dimensions of our lives. The basic attitude toward people inherent in technological and bureaucratic enterprises has spilled over into all parts of our lives:

In our age, the I-It relation, gigantically swollen, has usurped, practically uncontested, the mastery and the rule. The I of this relation, an I that possesses all, makes all, succeeds with all, this I that is unable to say Thou, unable to meet a being essentially, is the lord of the hour. (Buber, *Eclipse of God*, 129)

The type of relationship appropriate to technological enterprises and bureaucratic structures has contaminated our relations to people and to nature, fostering alienating relationships in all spheres of life. Moreover, objectifying discourse, the discourse of I-It, is presented to us as natural, while dialogue is relegated to the realm of romantic longing. Although there is no way to eliminate I-It relationships from our lives permanently, we must, Buber believed, struggle to limit their power to appropriate situations.

Buber acknowledged the inherent conflict between his view of a community based on genuine relations and the prevailing forms of life in industrialized society. Speaking in the voice of his critics, he wrote:

All that you speak of takes place in the never-never land, not in the social context of the world in which we spend our days, and by which anything of reality is defined. . . . Is the business employee to communicate himself without reserve to his colleagues? Is the worker on the conveyer belt to "feel himself addressed in what he experiences?" Is the leader of the gigantic technical undertaking to "practice the responsibility of dialogue?" (Buber, *Between Man and Man*, 34–35)

Yet, Buber rejected the criticism that his view was sentimental and impractical. Everyday, the individual is confronted with opportunities to transcend alienating conditions. In factories as well as offices, in schools and in the consulting room, one encounters repeated opportunities to enter into dialogical relationships:

When one of them steps for some reason or other, steps really as an individual into the circle of his vision and the realm of his decision, he is aware of him without strain not as a number with a human mask, but as a person. (Buber, *Between Man and Man*, 38)

Buber clearly recognized that, insofar as institutional structures define persons instrumentally, they are destructive of the very forms of relationship necessary to genuine community and the actualization of the self. He was also keenly aware that contemporary economic and political structures both presuppose and foster a functionalist, utilitarian view of person. If genuine community was to be restored to its rightful place in the modern world, industrial and political life as we know it would have to be drastically altered.

Nevertheless, Buber eschewed all messianic hopes and identified himself as a meliorist. Acknowledging that we can never achieve an ideal society free of alienation, he insisted on a gradualist strategy in which we work toward creating greater opportunities for genuine dialogue and community:

I am very far from thinking that there can be an ideal dialogic relationship if one could only "restructure society." I never thought an ideal dialogic relationship possible in our world as it is. I am a meliorist and not an idealist, and so I want only as much dialogic element as can be realized in human life here and now.[37]

Just as a person is always in a state of becoming, living in the ebb and flow of experience/relation, or monologue/dialogue, society continually moves between two poles—the political and the social. The political principle, which dominates modern life, is reflected in the modern tendency to absolutize the state. The social principle, on the other hand, is reflected in the recurring efforts to establish small communes that facilitate mutual responsibility and direct relationships between persons.

Buber acknowledged that the political principle is necessary to modern life. If we are to adjudicate and resolve conflicts between groups and communities, a state appears necessary. What Buber opposed, however, is "political surplus," the extension and application of power and centralized authority beyond what is necessary. The task, therefore, is to modify and restrict the degree of centralized authority. However, Buber resisted the temptation to prescribe how this was to be done. Insofar as our choices are situational, no fixed plan is possible. Instead, we have no alternative but continually to make choices in accordance with the dictates of each situation.

Recognizing that alienation is a result of our attitude and stance toward others, Buber insisted that the altering of social or political structures is not sufficient to bring about the necessary change. As the Russian Revolution of 1917 demonstrated, one can alter the forms of government without eliminating the propensity for viewing and relating to others as objects or things.[38] Moreover, changes in the sociopolitical structure would not necessarily alter relationships on the immediate, dyadic level.

In spite of this pessimistic picture, Buber never lost faith in the individual's potential for dialogue. Within each of us, there remains the capacity to be open to and enter into humanizing, I-You relations.

What is decisive, is whether the spirit—the You-saying, responding spirit —remains alive and actual; whether what remains of it in communal human life continues to be subjected to the state and the economy, or whether it becomes independently active; whether what abides of it in individual human life incorporates itself again in communal life. (Buber, *I and Thou*, 99)[39]

There are, Buber believed, three ways in which we can carry out the struggle against alienation and the accompanying oppression. Through edification, we can deconstruct the prevailing objectifying discourse and uncover alternative ways of defining human relationships. A second way to combat alienation is to transform the social frameworks within which we live through a process of education. Finally, we can establish communal settings which facilitate and encourage dialogical relations between persons.

I have in chapters 4 and 5 already discussed Buber's edifying strategy. Accordingly, I shall devote the remaining sections of this chapter to a discussion of Buber's view of education and his conception of a viable communal model.

Education for Community

It is clear that Buber's critical analysis of modern society and its political and economic ethos contains radical implications. If, as he claimed, the structure of the modern state and the modern economy rests upon the spread of the I-It world then a radical renewal of genuine community would undermine that structure. Accordingly, in calling for a renewal of dialogue and of genuine community, Buber was, in effect, calling for the radical restructuring of modern society as we know it:

Don't we find that modern developments have expunged almost every trace of a life in which human beings confront each other and have meaningful relationships? It would be absurd to try to reverse this development; and if one could bring off this absurdity, the tremendous precision instrument of this civilization would be destroyed at the same time. (Buber, *I and Thou*, 97)

To achieve the possibility of nonalienating conditions of life as he envisioned them, the current social, political, and economic framework would have to be radically changed.

However, Buber rejected the revolutionary program espoused by the Marxists.[40] To Marx and his followers, any far-reaching changes in the social forms of modern society required a radical transformation in the structure of that society. Such structural changes could only be instituted through political action. While Marx advocated the education of the proletariat as a necessary ingredient in the revolutionary program, education alone was inadequate.

To Marx, the consciousness of the masses was itself a byproduct of the sociopolitical structure of the state. To alter that consciousness and liberate the masses from the illusory ideology of bourgeois capitalism, political revolution was necessary. Changes effected through education alone would only be neutralized by the power of the existing socioeconomic structure. According to Marx, revolution would only succeed when sufficient development had occurred within the society to "facilitate the realization of the revolutionary objectives so that the proletariat would be ready when circumstances would make this realization unavoidable."[41]

Buber agreed with Marx and his followers that socioeconomic relationships in capitalistic society foster alienation. Yet the socialist experiment in the Soviet Union had only succeeded in creating an oppressive centralized state. Unlike the Marxists, Buber opposed all such efforts to transform the sociopolitical structure through revolution. Instead, he defined the task as increasing the possibilities for relation, dialogue, and community by focusing our attention on the realm of the interhuman, the realm of genuine listening and response.

In his critique of Marxist social thought, Buber distinguished between two fundamental attitudes to social change, the apocalyptic and the prophetic. To the apocalyptic thinker, history is determined by forces beyond human influence. The prophet, on the other hand, believes in the effectiveness of human action. Therefore, the prophet holds out to the community the possibility of choice and sets before it a demand for decision. To the prophet, the future depends upon the actions of people.[42]

For the apocalyptic thinker, history will end with the sudden, radical transformation of society. For the prophet, history is a slow, gradual process that unfolds in the everyday life of the community.[43] Accordingly, for the prophet, change is effected through changes in everyday relationships while the apocalyptic believes that change is the result of external, superhuman causes.

Viewing Marx as a paradigm of the apocalyptic thinker, Buber identified with the prophet. The renewal of genuine community could not be effected by political revolution, but through education.[44] However, Buber rejected the conventional conceptions that viewed education in terms of the acquisition of knowledge or the transformation of the inner life of the individual. For Buber, the goal of education is to alter the ways in which persons relate to one another.[45] By nurturing our capacity for direct, dialogical relationships, education has the potential to counteract the power of alienation.[46]

Buber's concept of education, like his concept of community, was grounded in his assumptions concerning the nature of personhood. Although recognizing the importance of the child's capacity for creativity, he denied that it was the fundamental human drive. However basic the instinct to create and invent may be, the capacity to enter into dialogue with others remained the essential human characteristic.[47] However intelligent and creative a person may be, he or she could still relate to the world and to others as "Its," as subject to object. If education is to serve as the effective humanizing force in modern life, it must cultivate the fundamental drive to relate to or commune with others *(der Trieb der Verbundenheit)*:

The being of the world as object is learned from within, but not its being as subject, its saying of I and Thou. That teaches us the saying of I and Thou is not the originative instinct, but the drive for communion. (Buber, *Between Man and Man*, 88)[48]

While each person is born with this innate drive to commune, it must be nurtured and cultivated. The utilitarian, technological world of modern life, institutionalized in the modern state, stifles this drive and prevents it from being actualized. If we are to counter this effect, we must, through education, draw out and nurture this drive.

Buber clarified his concept of education by contrasting it with propaganda. *Education* refers to a process in which a person's basic, innate inclinations and qualities are drawn out and actualized in life situations.[49] The educator sees "each of these individuals as in a position to become a unique, single person, and thus the bearer of a special task of existence which can be fulfilled through him and through him alone" (Buber, *Knowledge of Man*, 83). In contrast, the propagandist subordinates the individual to the goals or program of the party. Viewing others solely as means to achieving his or her own political goals, the propagandist imposes his or her will.[50] Consequently, the propagandist dehumanizes those with whom he or she comes into contact.[51]

Buber's conception of education entails a revisioning of the conventional conception of teaching. According to prevailing views, a teacher either transmits knowledge or instills or facilitates habits and values. According to this view, knowledge is either comprised of a permanent body of truths or a set of habits and skills necessary to democratic living. In the latter view, espoused by Dewey, the function of the teacher is to help the student acquire the skills to apply creative intelligence to problem situations.[52] Insofar as both of these conceptions of teaching depend upon mastery and control, they presuppose a subject-object, I-It relationship to the world.

To Buber, however, such a view of education simply perpetuates the mentality of the It world, in which possessing and achieving are the prevalent goals. For genuine education to occur, the teacher-student relationship must be grounded in genuine dialogue. Insofar as people actualize themselves by relating to the world and others in a confirming way, the primary task of the teacher is to model confirming relations. By relating to the student as an I to a You, the teacher helps the student to actualize the inherent capacity to relate dialogically to the world and to other people. The teacher, therefore, assumes the role of the "reliable counterpart," giving and withholding and alternating between intimacy and distance.

Buber often spoke of the task of education as being "education for community." To achieve genuine community, young people must gain competence in relation:

I believe that education for community is competence in relation. By relation, I mean direct, non-purposeful relation. Therefore, education for community is competence in relating to the people with whom one lives. (Buber, "Erziehung zur Gemeinschaft," 19)

In the final analysis, "education for community is only possible when there exists a commonality through which one is educated to community" (Buber, "Erziehung zur Gemeinschaft," 15). Just as one learns relation by relating, one learns community by participating in one.

Insofar as education is the means by which to struggle against the centralizing tendencies of the modern state, it was, for Buber, political. Through education, we can combat the "political surplus" of the state whereby power exceeds the needs of the hour:

Social education seeks to arouse and to develop in the minds of its pupils the spontaneity of fellowship which is innate in all unravaged human souls and which harmonizes very well with the development of personal existence and personal thought. This can be accomplished only by a complete overthrow of the political trend which nowadays dominates education throughout the world. (Buber, *Pointing the Way*, 176)

Buber believed that we educate people to certain modes of behavior by creating the conditions in which this behavior is actualized and modeled.[53] Education aims to establish conditions in which the student experiences dialogue and genuine relation. The key to this process is the relationship that exists between the teacher and the learner. Accordingly, Buber objected to the exercise of compulsion and power in education. To compel a student is simply to perpetuate forms of relation that breed alienation:

Compulsion in education means disunion, it means humiliation and rebelliousness. Communion in education is just communion, it means being opened up and drawn in. Freedom in education is the possibility of communion. (Buber, *Between Man and Man*, 92)

Submission to any person, theory, ideology, or program subverts the student's capacity for free and genuine communion.

Buber acknowledged, however, that discipline is necessary in order to educate the drive to commune or relate. The teacher, serving as a link between the student and the outside world, functions as critic and instructor:

The educator gathers in the constitutive forces of the world. He distinguishes, rejects and confirms in himself, in his self which is filled with the world. . . . The educator educates himself to be their vehicle. (Buber, *Between Man and Man*, 101)

In Buber's view of education freedom is never a goal in and of itself but a springboard to a further goal, a means to an end. The end is communion and genuine dialogue. Genuine freedom is not freedom from all restraints and responsibilities but the personal act of accepting responsibility:

Let us realize the true meaning of being free of a bond; it means that a quite personal responsibility takes the place of one shared with many generations. Life lived in freedom is personal responsibility or it is a pathetic farce. (Buber, *Between Man and Man*, 92)

Education, therefore, cannot be prescribed in the form of recipes or plans, but occurs through a natural process of relation in which the educator is "really there," really present to the child. Thus, the person of the educator, rather than his or her "knowledge" or "skills" serves as the educative force.

According to Buber, the teacher-student relationship precludes full mutuality. As mentioned previously, a fully mutual relationship necessitates that each live through the "common event from the standpoint of the other," a condition that Buber referred to as *Umfassung* (inclusion). The teacher-student relationship, which is inherently unequal, presumes inclusion on the part of the educator only. The educator must learn the changing needs of the student, feel the way in which the student is responding, and, accordingly, acquire a deepening understanding of what a human being requires in order to grow. In the process, the educator is also educated.

The major impediments to effective education are eros and the will to power. It is incumbent upon the educator to practice what Buber called a "lofty asceticism," forfeiting both the will to power and eros "for the sake of the responsibility for a realm of life which is entrusted to us for our influence, but not for our interference" (Buber, *Between Man and Man*, 95). Whenever the educator uses the educational situation as a source of his or her pleasure or power, genuine education is precluded.

In describing the educational process, Buber used language similar to that used in *I and Thou* to describe revelation.[54] Like the recipient of revelation, the student emerges from the encounter with the person of the educator with a powerful sense of trust and meaning:

Trust, trust in the world, because this human being exists, that is the most inward achievement of the relation in education. Because this human being exists, meaninglessness, however hard pressed you are by it, cannot be the real truth. Because this human being exists, in the darkness the light lies hidden, in fear salvation, and in the callousness of one's fellow men the great love. (Buber, *Between Man and Man*, 98)

Just as he did not deny the value of the It world, Buber did not deny the value of conventional, objectivistic, pragmatic knowing for maintaining continuity and cohesion in the life of the individual. However, knowledge as conventionally conceived is insufficient. To the extent that education is limited to the conceptual knowledge of philosophy and science, it fails to penetrate to the essential core of human existence. Philosophical and scientific knowing, abstracted from the immediacy of the concrete situation, commence in an act of looking away from the concrete to the general. In contrast, *knowing*, in the biblical sense, means "the relationship of being to being" (Buber, *Between Man and Man*, 130).

By relying on rational discourse as its major vehicle, education runs counter to its goal. Insofar as it removes us from the immediate, concrete situation, rational discourse, rather than serving as the vehicle for relation, actually has an estranging effect, separating us from other persons:

In conceptual speech lies the tension of falling away from one another: we do not mean the same thing by our concepts, and so basically, we do not understand one another. Therefore, philosophy is incapable of forming community. (Buber, *Believing Humanism*, 134) [55]

Utopian Socialism and the Kibbutz:
An Experiment in Genuine Community

While the edifying and educational enterprises are essential to our struggle against alienation, the ultimate goal is to construct communities that foster direct, mutually confirming relations among their members:

The primal hope of all history depends upon a genuine, hence thoroughly communally disposed community of the human race. Fictitious, counterfeit, a planet-size lie would be the unity that was not established out of real communal living of smaller and larger groups that dwell or work together and out of their reciprocal relationships. (Buber, *Believing Humanism*, 87–88)

The issue, however, is not one of either or. The choice is not between destroying existing institutions or surrendering the ideal of community. The state is a network of relationships that can be altered through decision and action.

Buber insisted that a renewal of genuine community is possible within the framework of an urbanized, highly rationalized society:

In opposition to this mixture of correct evidence and distorted conclusions, I espouse the rebirth of the commune. Rebirth, not restoration. It cannot be restored in fact, although it seems to me that each breath of neighborliness in the apartment building, each wave of a warmer comradeship during the rest period in a highly rationalized factory means a growth of communal-mindedness of the world, and although at times an upright village commune pleases me more than a parliament, it cannot be restored. But whether a rebirth of the commune takes place out of the waters and spirit of the approaching transformation of society—by this, it seems to me, the lot of the human species will be determined. An organic communal being —and only such is suitable for a formed and articulated mankind—will never be erected out of individuals, only out of small and the smallest communities: a people is community to the extent that it is communally disposed. (Buber, *Believing Humanism*, 91)

Buber, the existentialist, rejected absolute principles focusing, instead, on concrete situations. In our struggle for genuine community, we must continually redraw the "line of demarcation that separates the action that is necessary at a particular moment from that which is not."[56] However, he did not totally neglect the issue of parameters. Through such categories as dialogue and community, actualization and deactualization, confirmation and disconfirmation, he set forth a framework in which to distinguish just from unjust actions.

Buber repeatedly criticized the growing centralization of political power in the modern state as stifling genuine existence and genuine relation. Whereas he originally had directed his critique against the forces that thwart individualism, he eventually turned his attention to the forces that impede relation and community. The danger, which he had earlier defined in terms of psychologism, he later defined in terms of collectivism:

In the monstrous confusion of modern life . . . the individual clings desperately to the collectivity. . . . He is all too willing to let himself be deprived of personal responsibility: he only wants to obey. And the most valuable of all goods—the life between man and man—gets lost in the process; the autonomous relationships become meaningless, personal relationships wither; and the very spirit of man hires itself out as a functionary. The personal human being ceases to be the living member of a social body and becomes a cog in the "collective" machine. (Buber, *Paths in Utopia*, 132)

Buber, like Landauer, viewed the state as a system of relationships based upon power and compulsion that posed a fundamental threat to human freedom.[57] While, in Buber's opinion, most post-Hegelian thinkers considered the state the epitome of human society, Buber, following the socialists, differentiated between state and society. The aim of the state is to increase the centralization of power and authority and to exercise control over the citizenry. In the modern state, relationships between persons are based upon utility and power. Citizens, lacking direct participation in government, depend upon representatives with whom they have, at best, a distant, impersonal relationship. In Buber's terms, the state is I-it institutionalized.

In contrast to the state, genuine society is comprised of a network of decentralized, individual communities. Thus, the struggle for community entails rebelling against the state and its growing power. Revolution, to Buber, did not mean the sudden overthrow of existing political structures but the gradual displacement of the state by genuine communities based upon mutual production and direct relations.

The modern state, with its propensity for destruction, represents the nonactualization of *Gemeinschaft:*[58]

Interhuman relations are ruled by the false, by the relationship based upon use and functionality rather than genuine relation. What is needed is a genuine relation between the voters and their representatives. This means a fundamental relationship between persons and an actual inner state which does not yet exist. (Buber, "Abende," 10)

Thus, if the domination of instrumental, functional relations is to be prevented, we must combat the political domination of the state.

Buber was a socialist who insisted that, whenever possible, the means of production should be transferred into the hands of the local communes.[59] In addition, he supported direct representation based upon common activity and experience. However, he offered no absolute prescriptions as to how this would be accomplished.

Buber was well aware that the social vision he was espousing would appear to many as naive and unrealistic, particularly to the Marxists who would view it as unscientific. Nevertheless, Buber did not hesitate to identify with that strain of socialism that Marx had pejoratively referred to as "utopian."

The picture that I have hastily sketched will be put on the shelf of "utopian socialism" until the storm turns over the leaves again. Just as I do not believe in Marx's "gestation" of the new form of society, so I do not believe in Bakunin's virgin birth out of the womb of revolution. (Buber, *Believing Humanism*, 92)

In *Paths in Utopia*, which contains Buber's most extensive presentation of his social philosophy, he identified with the tradition of utopian socialism represented in the thinking of such nineteenth-century writers as Lorenz Von Stein, Proudhon, Fourier, and Peter Kropotkin, a tradition that was carried on by his contemporary Landauer. These thinkers, differentiating the social from the political, criticized the centralizing tendencies of the modern state. To Buber, their writings provided the foundations for a contemporary theory of social change.

In *Paths in Utopia*, Buber reiterated his suspicion of fixed structures and ideologies. Buber described authentic socialism as a dynamic process of perennial becoming rather than an absolute structure:

Socialism can never be anything absolute. It is the continual becoming of human community in mankind, adapted and proportioned to whatever can be willed and done in the conditions given. Rigidity threatens all realization, what lives and glows today may be crusted over tomorrow and, become all powerful, suppress the strivings of the day after. (Buber, *Paths in Utopia*, 56)

In Buber's view, previous efforts to formulate a theory of socialism and to establish socialist communities suffered from basic shortcomings. Some lacked a proper balance of mutual production and consumption. Others, such as the Marxist effort, paid inadequate attention to the need for inner change and transformation and the importance of direct, need-free relations.

To Buber, Landauer had come the closest to espousing a comprehensive and humanistically grounded socialist vision. Landauer had, in Buber's view, most effectively formulated the principles of utopian socialism, which Buber described as "a revolutionary conservation."[60] Landauer espoused "a revolutionary selection of those elements worthy to be conserved and fit for the renovation of the social being" (Buber, *Paths in Utopia*, 50). He also proposed a network of socialist villages and communes that combined common production with common consumption.

Landauer had recognized that all efforts to solve social problems with political means produced societies not very different from those that they displaced. The utopian, non-Marxist socialist must utilize means commensurate with his ends: "To put it more precisely: he believes in a continuity within which revolution is only the accomplishment, the setting free and extension of a reality that has already grown to its true possibilities" (Buber, *Paths in Utopia*, 13).

Building on Landauer's teachings, Buber defined the crisis of modern society that utopian socialism had to address:

Just as his degenerate technology is causing man to lose the feel of good work and proportion, so the degrading social life he leads is causing him to lose the feel of community—just when he is so full of illusion of living in perfect devotion to his community. (Buber, *Paths In Utopia*, 132)

In the East, the dream of a socialistic society had been crushed under the burden of totalitarian centralization. At the same time, in the West, the politically centralized state and the highly rationalized social structure stifled personal relations. Accordingly, the issue was not, as conventionally formulated, a choice between East and West. The new society had to surpass all current social structures in quest of a different form of life.

While the East, represented by Russia, had absorbed the individual into the collective, the West, under capitalism, had created a society marked by atomization and isolation. Society, however, is neither a totality nor a body of isolated individuals but a network of associative units composed of local communes joined together in an overall confederation:

The prime conditions for a genuine society can be summed up as follows: it is not an aggregate of essentially unrelated individuals, for such an aggregate could only be held together by a "political," i.e., a coercive principle of government; it must be built up of little societies on the basis of communal life and of the associations of these societies; and the mutual relations of the societies and their associations must be determined to the greatest possible extent by the social principle—the principle of inner cohesion, collaboration and mutual stimulation. (Buber, *Paths In Utopia*, 80)

New laws, new institutions, and changes in the distribution of power cannot by themselves bring about the necessary changes in society. The change must come, Buber repeatedly emphasized, from within, beginning in the realm of interhuman relations.[61] The "utopian socialist" works for "the maximum degree of communal autonomy possible in a restructured society" (Buber, *Paths in Utopia*, 14–15).

Buber singled out the kibbutz as a concrete example of what he meant by authentic community. The cooperative communal settlements established in Israel beginning in the early part of the century most closely approximated the model of genuine community that he espoused. Of the various modern attempts to prevent the domination of the social by the political, only the kibbutz has avoided failure:

As I see history and the present, there is only one all-out effort to create a Full Cooperative which justifies our speaking of success in the socialistic sense, and that is the Jewish Village Commune in its various forms as found in Palestine. . . . Nowhere else in the history of communal settlements is there this tireless groping for the form of community life best suited to this particular human group, and nowhere else is there this continual trying and trying again, this going to it and getting down to it, this critical awareness, this sprouting of new branches from the same stem and out of the same formative impulse. (Buber, *Paths in Utopia*, 142)

Unlike communities that are based upon fixed doctrine, the kibbutz, according to Buber, developed in response to a particular situation. Combining ideas drawn from Russian communes, utopian socialism, and the Bible, the kibbutz movement represented a unique social experiment.[62] However, Buber did not regard the kibbutz movement as an unqualified success. The failure to unify the various communes into a larger structure that would link them together created many inequities. Thus, he preferred to speak of it as a "signal non-failure" (Buber, *Paths in Utopia*, 148). Nonetheless, the kibbutz movement represented a high point in the human effort to achieve community:

But that the men of the Jewish communes have labored so strenuously with one another and against one another for the emergence of a communitas communitatum, that is to say, for a structurally new society—this will not be forgotten in the history of mankind's struggle for self renewal. (Buber, *Paths in Utopia*, 147–48)[63]

Genuine Dialogue and
the Possibilities of World Peace

Endeavoring to elucidate and apply his philosophical categories to new situations in ever-widening circles, Buber turned his attention to the world scene, and, in particular, to the prevailing strife among nations. During the twenties and thirties, increasingly troubled by the growth of fascism and the increasing centralization of power, he criticized the political power of the modern state, on the one hand, and the dehumanizing effects of industrialization on the other.[64]

In Germany, Buber experienced first hand the totalitarian forces that threatened both individual and community. During this period, and throughout the remainder of his life, he focused his critique on the collectivistic tendencies that dominated the political life of Europe. Having previously drawn upon Kierkegaard when formulating his interpretation of Judaism, Buber now turned to Kierkegaard as a much-needed corrective to these collectivistic or totalitarian tendencies.

Kierkegaard had focused our attention on the thinking, feeling, anxiety-ridden self.[65] The genuine individual feels deeply and engages life with passion and commitment. Willingly accepting the responsibility of moral decision, the individual risks uncertainty rather than take refuge in false certainty and objectivity. However, the modern world, plagued by alienation on a number of different levels, stifles our yearning for authentic existence:

The individual no longer belongs to God, to himself, to his beloved, to his art or to his science, he is conscious of belonging in all things to an abstraction to which he is subjected by reflection, just as a serf belongs to an estate.[66]

Venturing into the area of social criticism, Kierkegaard attacked society's leveling effect. Swallowed up in the crowd and cut off from his or her deepest emotions, the individual is prevented from experiencing the passion that is necessary to genuine decision and action. In modern society, action has been displaced by advertising and publicity. As a result, revolutionary activity necessary for restoring the individual to his or her rightful place is precluded.[67]

Writing in the shadow of the Nazi authorities in 1936, Buber drew upon Kierkegaard's teachings about the individual to attack the basis of totalitarianism. In pointing out the dangers of the collective, or as he called it, the crowd, Kierkegaard provided an important weapon in the struggle against totalitarianism. His description of the active, responsible, choosing individual challenged the assumptions of fascistic, collectivistic societies.

Man in a collective is not man with man. Here the person is not freed from his isolation, by communing with living beings, which thenceforth lives with him; the "whole" with its claim on the wholeness of every man, aims logically and successfully at reducing, neutralizing, devaluating and desecrating every bond with living beings. That tender surface of personal life which longs for contact with other life is progressively deadened or desensitized. (Buber, *Between Man and Man*, 201)

According to Buber, Kierkegaard's authentic individual was a prelude to the emergence of true community, which "will be actualized only to the extent that the single ones become actual out of whose responsible life the body politic is renewed" (Buber, *Between Man and Man*, 82). However, Buber criticized Kierkegaard for having ignored the interpersonal dimension of human life.[68] Kierkegaard had neglected our relationship to other persons in favor of our relationship to God and ourselves.[69]

Thus, while Kierkegaard's category of the single one had significant social and political implications, it was, in the final analysis, insufficient. As Buber had learned from Hasidism, our relationships to other persons and to the world are the channels for our relationship with God. Whenever we accept responsibility for others and respond to their address, we respond to God as well. Similarly, the dangers of collectivistic societies that militate against genuine individuals and genuine communities are best countered not by the individual alone but by the individual in relation to others.

In the decades following World War II, Buber increasingly applied his philosophy of dialogue to the world scene.[70] Criticizing the existential mistrust that permeates the relationships among persons and nations, he insisted on the need for direct relations even on the international level. The basic attitude of suspicion espoused by Marx, Freud, and Nietzsche is indicative of "the progressive decline of dialogue and the corresponding growth of universal mistrust"

(Buber, *Pointing the Way*, 225).[71] In the absence of genuinely dial-ogical situations, people either turn inward in search of self-confir-mation or immerse themselves in the collective.[72] Having surren-dered genuine dialogue and mutual relations in the vain hope of finding a refuge, the modern person settles for illusory confirmation.

In order to cut through the existential mistrust that pervades the world, it is necessary to criticize partial, reductionistic views like those of Marx and Freud. While uncovering important aspects of human life, Marxists and Freudians erroneously identify these as-pects "with man's total structure instead of inserting it in this structure" (Buber, *Pointing the Way*, 226). While eros and class ideology are important dimensions of modern life, they are, by no means, the total picture. Missing from the writings of modern critics is the holistic philosophical anthropology of which Buber had spo-ken in 1938. The question is still "the simplest of all questions, yet inviting many difficulties: What does man need, every man, in order to be man?" Through such an examination, we will recognize the truly dialogical nature of human existence. This, in turn, will open the way to "the renewal of dialogical immediacy between men" (Buber, *Pointing the Way*, 228).

Overwhelmed by existential mistrust, people are no longer able or willing to carry on genuine conversation. The results, on the international level, are catastrophic:

The debates between statesmen which the radio conveys to us no longer have anything in common with a human conversation: the diplomats do not address one another but the faceless public. Even the congresses and conferences which convene in the name of mutual understanding lack the substance which alone can elevate the deliberations to genuine talk: can-dor and directness in address and answer. What is concentrated there is only the universal condition in which men are no longer willing or able to speak directly to their fellows . . . because they no longer trust one another and everyone knows that the other no longer trusts him. (Buber, *Pointing the Way*, 237)

Buber remained convinced of the power and the possibility of direct relation and dialogue in the arena of international relations in which "each of the partners, even when he stands in opposition to the other, heeds, affirms, and confirms his opponent as an existing other" (Buber, *Pointing the Way*, 238).

As a self-proclaimed meliorist, Buber did not foresee the total elimination of conflict. Injustice, conflict, and the exercise of political power are perennial factors in human life. Like I-It relationships, they are ever recurring. However, like the I-It relationship, the existential mistrust between nations could, if only sporadically, be contained and transcended.

In the life of groups, as in the life of the individual, one begins with the immediate situation at hand. Before confronting the situation and beginning the conversation, one cannot know the limits of what is attainable. Just as, on the individual level, one cannot strive for relation but only hold oneself open for it, on the social level, "one cannot produce dialogue, but one can be at its disposal" (Buber, *Pointing the Way*, 206).

The possibility of *teshuvah*, of turning or inner transformation, was an important component of Buber's social thought. Buber recognized that his position was ultimately grounded in faith, or, as he translated the Hebrew term *emunah*, trust. However, one can attain such trust only through struggle: "Existential mistrust cannot be replaced by trust, but it can be replaced by a reborn candor" (Buber, *Pointing the Way*, 206).

To his critics, Buber's attempt to apply his existential categories to world politics was far too abstract.[73] Admittedly, insofar as Buber did not analyze the complexities of concrete historical situations, he is vulnerable to this criticism. However, by focusing on dialogue and the interhuman, Buber believed he was addressing the genuinely concrete, existential realities of human life neglected by most social critics. At the same time, he avoided the ideological rhetoric and slogans that characterized most discussions of the Cold War and distorted the actual situation:

I have appealed just from politics, from its perspective, its speech and its usages, but not to any kind of philosophy. Rather I appealed directly to the genuine concrete, to the actual life of actual men which has become smeared over and crusted with the varnish of political fictitiousness. (Buber, *Pointing the Way*, 230)

Characteristically, Buber sought to revise the way in which political realities were conventionally analyzed. Most analyses, rooted in the detached, objectivistic perspective of the I-It stance, only succeed in achieving a partial understanding of the situation. Only by penetrating to the level of the concrete, lived, existential reality of the interhuman, he insisted, can one get to the heart of the problem.

That not everyone considered Buber too abstract is confirmed in a speech delivered by the then secretary general of the United Nations, Dag Hammarskjold. Speaking to an audience at Cambridge University in 1958, Hammarskjold quoted at length from Buber's speech "Hope for this Hour."[74] Upon concluding his quotation, Hammarskjold, who was engaged in translating *I and Thou* into Swedish at the time of his untimely death, explained: "I excuse myself from having quoted at such length from this speech. I have done so because, out of the depth of his feelings, Martin Buber has found expressions which it would be vain for me to try and improve."[75]

7

Revisioning Religion: Between Person and the Eternal You

The relational philosophy first articulated in *I and Thou*, which provided the categories for Buber's conception of person and community, also served as the basis for his mature conception of religion. Employing the language of relation and dialogue, Buber formulated an alternative way of talking about religion. Buber's formulation yielded a new and powerful interpretation of God, worship, and idolatry.

In his early writings on Hasidism and in his early lectures, published as *On Judaism* (Reden über das Judentum), Buber had advocated a highly individualized, personalized faith. By 1918, however, he had come to recognize the inadequacies of his earlier interpretations of religion. No longer satisfied to view religious faith in terms of individual experience, he began to speak of religion as a social phenomenon for which the locus is the interaction between persons. Thus, beginning with "The Holy Way," he focused on the realm of the interhuman as the locus of the full actualization of the divine. Moreover, as he stated in *Worte an die Zeit*, the renewal of religion and the renewal of community are intertwined.

Buber believed that the everyday world in which we live was infused with a divine presence:

God speaks to man in the things and beings that He sends him in life; and man answers through his action in relation to just these things and beings. All specific service of God has its meaning only in the ever renewed preparation and hallowing for this communion with God in the world. (Buber, *Origin and Meaning*, 94)

However, the same human propensity to objectification and reduction that distorts our understanding of person and community also produces a distorted, alienated view of the divine-human relation. Estranged from the dynamic, living reality of the divine-human encounter, human beings, in pursuit of certainty and security, construct systems of beliefs, norms, and actions that they call "religions."

Yet, rather than link us to the divine, these religions, with their routinized patterns of celebration and worship, replace genuine divine-human encounters with artificial systems and structures. The result is a perversion of authentic faith: "The largest part of what is today called religion is perverted—not perhaps in the individual details of its contents, but in its whole structure" (Buber, *Believing Humanism*, 110).

Instead of bridging the abyss between the human and the divine, religions, in Buber's view, enlarge it. Thus, religions are a form of exile that separates people not only from the divine but also from the people of other religious communities. Institutionalized religion, antithetical to and destructive of authentic religious faith, is a manifestation of alienation:

But there is a danger, in fact, the utmost danger and temptation of man, that something becomes detached from the human side of this communion and makes itself independent, rounds itself off, seemingly perfects itself to reciprocity, yet puts itself in the place of real communion. The primal danger of man is religion. (Buber, *Origin and Meaning*, 94)[1]

According to Buber, the artificial modern division between the sacred and the secular only exacerbates the inherently alienating effect of organized religion. This separation of the sacred from the secular contributes to "the sickening of our contact with things and beings," which Buber designated as the proliferation of the It world.

Buber believed that religion as it was conventionally understood had to be revised:

What is meant by religion is not the massive fullness of statements, concepts and activities that one customarily describes by this name and that men sometimes long for more than for God. Religion is essentially the act of holding fast to God. (Buber, *Eclipse of God*, 123)

Unlike hostile critics of religion, such as Feuerbach, Nietzsche, and Freud, Buber insisted that the existential core of religion was authentic and essential to human existence. However, as a description of cultural reality, Buber considered Nietzsche's proclamation of the death of God accurate.[2] Institutionalized religions and modern thought conspire to estrange us from the divine and, consequently, from other persons and from ourselves.

Buber accepted the ontological claim of religious faith. Far from being an illusion, genuine faith derives from an encounter with something outside of ourselves, affording us the deepest insight into the meaning and significance of human existence. Accordingly, paralleling Buber's critique of religion is a constructive project.[3] Not satisfied, like Nietzsche, simply to unmask the alienating effects of religion, he wished to help reveal the power of religious faith to the modern person. This entailed revising the conventional views.

To revise the prevailing understanding of religion, Buber engaged in a critique of such concepts as God, revelation, faith, and sacred scripture. In formulating this critique, Buber drew upon the teachings of Hasidism. Accordingly, I shall turn, once again, to his interpretation of Hasidism as a prelude to discussing his critique of religion.

Hasidism and the Contemporary Crisis of Faith

Hasidism, according to Buber, contributes important insights into the contemporary crisis of alienation. First, Hasidism rejects the artificial distinction between the sacred and the profane:

The central example of the Hasidic overcoming of the distance between the sacred and the profane point to an explanation of what is to be understood by the fact that Hasidism has its word to speak in the crisis of Western man. (Buber, *Hasidism and Modern Man*, 38, hereafter referred to as *HMM*)

Over and against the growing secularized vision of modern culture, "Hasidism sets the simple truth that the wretchedness of our
world is grounded in its resistance to the entrance of the holy into
lived life" (*HMM*, 40). While the modern age knows how to talk
about things and beings, we have lost sight of Hasidism's "great
insight that our relations to things and beings form the marrow of
our existence" (*HMM*, 40). Insisting on "the holy intercourse with
all existing beings," Hasidism "opposes this corrosion of the living
power of meeting" (*HMM*, 40).

The Hasidic myth of the sparks, as described in chapter 2, teaches
the ubiquity of the sacred. Insofar as divine sparks are everywhere,
there is no dimension of our lives in which we do not encounter the
divine. We thus relate to the divine not by withdrawing from our
everyday encounters but by meeting life in all of its fullness and by
adopting an open, hallowing stance to those beings that cross our
paths. Conversely, whenever we retreat from the immediacy of
lived encounters to the seclusion of our religious institutions, we
forsake the everyday opportunities to encounter the divine.

Hasidism, as Buber read it, contained an implicit critique of institutional religion. Insofar as divine sparks permeate all reality, when
we circumscribe religion within fixed boundaries we limit our access to the divine. Emphasizing such concepts as intentionality,
ecstasy, and devotion, which concern the spiritual state of the
believer, Hasidism sowed the seeds for a critique of religious forms
and structures.

"The Way of Man According to the Teachings of Hasidism" is one
of Buber's most succinct discussions of religious life and faith.[4]
Although in that essay, as in all of his Hasidic writings, Buber did
not explicitly use the philosophical categories of *I and Thou*, they
are implied throughout. Accordingly to arrive at a comprehensive
understanding of his views on religious life and faith, we must read
"The Way of Man" and *I and Thou* intertextually.[5] Whereas *I and
Thou* provides the conceptual framework for Buber's mature interpretation of Hasidism, the Hasidic tales concretize, through narrative, the categories of his relational philosophy.

Faith, as depicted in "The Way of Man," begins with an awareness of being addressed. God's question to the first man in the
Garden of Eden, "Where are you?" is addressed to each individual

in every age, in order "to awaken man and destroy his system of hideouts" (HMM, 134). By reflecting on our current situation and examining where we stand on our life's journey, we set the stage for unifying the forces that operate within us.

Yet, if we become immersed in self-concern, we block the path to genuine faith. The purpose of turning inward is not to focus on ourselves but to prepare ourselves to reach out and relate to others. While self-examination is a first step, the end is to establish genuine relations with others and, through them, with the divine. The authentic religious quest, therefore, does not begin with systematized doctrines or institutionalized patterns of behavior but in our encounter with the immediate environment:

> The environment which I feel to be the natural one, the situation which has been assigned to me as my fate, the things that happen to me day after day, the things that claim me day after day—these contain my essential task and such fulfillment of existence as is open to me. (HMM, 172)

In his early writings on Hasidism, Buber had emphasized the individual's spiritual condition, while only alluding to the importance of relating to others. Only after the publication of I and Thou did interhuman relationships become pivotal to his interpretation of Hasidism and of religion in general.

Through the process of self-reflection followed by turning to others, we help to reunite the fragmented sparks:[6]

> For the Hasidic conception springs from the realization that the isolation of elements and partial processes from the whole hinders the comprehension of the whole, and that real transformation, real restoration, at first of the single person and subsequently of the relationship between him and his fellow men, can only be achieved by the comprehension of the whole as a whole. (HMM, 156)

Buber found in Hasidism an implicit critique of the modern, fragmented, atomistic view of reality, "in which a man sees himself only as an individual contrasted with other individuals, and not as a genuine person whose transformation helps toward the transformation of the world." This atomistic view is "the fundamental error which Hasidic teaching denounces" (HMM, 157). The following passage offers a succinct statement of Buber's views concerning human existence.[7]

The Baal Shem teaches that no encounter with a being or a thing in the course of our life lacks a hidden significance. The people we live with, the animals that help us with our farm work, the soil we till, the materials we shape, the tools we use, they all contain a mysterious spiritual substance which depends on us for helping it towards its pure form, its perfection. If we neglect this spiritual substance sent across our path, if we think only in terms of momentary purposes, without developing a genuine relationship to the beings and things in whose life we ought to take part, as they in ours, then we shall, ourselves, be debarred from true, fulfilled existence. (*HMM*, 173)

As this passage suggests, each being is in a continuing state of becoming; we actualize ourselves though our encounters with others; to actualize ourselves and to help actualize those around us, we must act in such a way as to help them grow into that which they are intended to be; we fulfill this responsibility in and through the quality of the relationships that we establish. Just as the fulfillment of the other depends upon these relationships, so, too, does our own fulfillment as human beings.[8]

Insofar as the power of the Hasidic tales, like the power of myth in general, derives partly from the sense of immediacy that the narrative form evokes, translating them into fixed concepts only dilutes their power. Nevertheless, although evoking a sense of immediacy and deep spirituality, the stories fail to provide us with an explicit understanding of what the genuine religious life entails.[9] For example, while the tales teach responsibility for "developing a genuine relationship to the beings and things in whose life we ought to take part" (*HMM*, 173), we are never told the criteria by which we can evaluate such relationships. What is the exact nature of such relationships and how do we go about developing them? Similarly, while the tales teach that "the true love of God begins with the love of men" (*HMM*, 237) and the commandment to love our neighbor means to act lovingly, we are given only a vague impression of what that entails. Does love mean emotional attachments? Does it entail a prescribed set of actions and obligations?

To clarify these ambiguities, Buber, as indicated in chapter 4, turned to philosophical discourse. The concepts developed in *I and Thou* and subsequent philosophical works provide a more precise understanding of the Hasidic teachings. From these philosophical writings, we learn that "genuine relationship to the beings and things around us" means an I-You, dialogical or confirming relationship.

Redeeming the sparks through holy converse with the beings and things around us is the mythic analogue of dialogue. Each human encounter, insofar as it contains the seed of dialogue, is potentially a sacred, hallowing event. In Buber's reading of Hasidism, the sharp division between the sacred and the profane disappears. Consequently, insofar as the path to the divine is through encounters with other beings, the love of God depends upon our love for other persons. This idea is philosophically expressed in Buber's powerful metaphor:

Extended, the lines of relationships intersect in the eternal You. Every single You is a glimpse of that. Through every single You the basic word addresses the eternal You. (Buber, *I and Thou*, 123)

Hasidism teaches that all genuine relations converge in the eternal You; whenever persons genuinely relate to one another, they also relate to God. The key to religious life, therefore, is the I-You relation. Daily life is hallowed by entering into I-You relations with the world and with other persons.

The modes of relationship through which persons actualize their humanity and the modes through which the divine is actualized as an active force in daily life are one and the same. Whenever persons enter into direct, nonexploitative relations with other persons, they not only actualize themselves and others but also the divine. Thus, to Buber, being religious and being human are synonymous:

Man cannot approach the divine by reaching beyond the human; he can approach Him through becoming human. To become human is what he, this individual man, has been created for. This, so it seems to me, is the eternal core of Hasidic life and of Hasidic teaching. (*HMM*, 43)

The myth of the sparks also implies the unity of all creation. From this, Buber inferred that whatever persons do to others they also do to themselves: "for he who thrusts away his comrade, thrusts himself away: he who thrusts away a particle of the Unity, it is as if he thrusts away the whole" (*HMM*, 243). Accordingly, everyday relationships have cosmic significance. Through dialogical relations, the world is redeemed and the divine reunified.[10]

Like the Hasidim, Buber used stories to convey root experiences that had shaped his religious thinking. The story of his meeting with an unnamed young man in early years of World War I serves to explain how he arrived at his nonspecialized view of religion. Still under the influence of a mystical experience, Buber was unable to be wholly present to the young man and neglected to sense the questions that were left unasked. The young man, obliged to leave with these questions unanswered, died shortly thereafter.[11] As Buber tells it, the powerful impact of this event led him to revise his understanding of religion.[12]

Since then, I have given up the "religious" which is nothing but the exception, extraction, exaltation, ecstasy; or it has given me up. I possess nothing but the everyday out of which I am never taken. . . . I know no fullness but each mortal hour's fullness of claim and responsibility. Though far from being equal to it, yet I know that in the claim I am claimed and may respond in responsibility, and know who speaks and demands a response.

I do not know much more. If that is religion, then it is everything, simply all that is lived in its possibility of dialogue. (Buber, *Between Man and Man*, 14)

Buber concluded that moments of private religious experience only impede our genuine relation to the divine. Insofar as the relation to the human You and the eternal You intersect, all genuine meeting, regardless of time and place, is, by definition, religious. Thus, in Buber's usage, *religion* is an all-embracing term which refers to any situation that bears the potential for dialogue:

Either religion is a reality, rather the reality, namely the whole existence of man in the real world of God, an existence that unites all that is partial; or it is a phantom of the covetous human soul, and then it would be right promptly and completely to replace its rituals by art, its commands by ethics, its revelations by science. (Buber, *Believing Humanism*, 111)

God—The Eternal You

Buber rejected the philosophers' efforts to understand God through objective categories. He believed that objectivistic thought and language distort our understanding of religion. When a distancing, objective stance is taken toward the divine, as Buber said, we analyze, categorize, and measure the "You that in accordance with its nature cannot become It" (Buber, *I and Thou*, 123).

The key to our knowledge of the divine is genuine dialogue, arising from a direct, preconceptual encounter.[13] To emphasize this point, Buber told yet another story, this one concerning his meeting with a Protestant minister.[14] In response to the minister's query, "Do you believe in God?" Buber, hesitating, responded yes. However, immediately after taking leave of the minister, Buber realized that "if to believe in God means to be able to talk about him in the third person, then I do not believe in God. If to believe in him means to be able to talk to him, then I believe in God" (*PMB*, 24).

Nevertheless, Buber was not willing to eliminate all talk of God. He insisted, however, on using God language that adequately reflected his relational view of the divine. In his early lectures, between 1909 and 1918, he had used terms such as *unconditional* (Unbedingten) and *absolute*.[15] However, these abstract terms were inconsistent with his relational philosophy. Thus, in *I and Thou*, Buber coined the term *eternal You*. Unlike *absolute* and *unconditional*, the personal metaphor *eternal You* indicates that our relationship to the divine parallels our relationship to other persons, and our relation to other persons is the paradigm for our relationship to the divine.

Yet referring to God as the eternal You does not imply that God is person. Eternal You is simply "the proper metaphor for the relation to God" (Buber, *I and Thou*, 151). This metaphor served to correct the philosophical tendency to view God in abstract terms: "The designation of God as a person is indispensible for all who, like myself, do not mean a principle when they say 'God' " (Buber, *I and Thou*, 151).

While the concept of personhood, like any concept, is inadequate when applied to the divine, it succeeds in conveying the fact that personhood is an aspect of our encounter with God:

The concept of personhood is, of course, utterly incapable of describing the nature of God: but it is permitted and necessary to say that God is also a person. . . . It is as Absolute Person that God enters into direct relationship to us. (Buber, *I and Thou*, 181–82)

The metaphor *eternal You* also indicates that, in our relationship to God, as in our relationship to other persons, the effort to possess or dominate conflicts with genuine relation. Whenever we attempt to capture the divine in abstract concepts and images, we remove ourselves from the immediacy of genuine relation. Similarly, when philosophers attempt to deduce God from a given or to prove His existence by means of logic, they succeed only in distancing themselves from the divine.

It is not as if God could be inferred from anything—say from nature as its cause, or from history as its helmsman, or perhaps from the subject as the self that thinks itself through it. It is not as if something else were "given" and this were then deduced from it. This is always what confronts us immediately and first and always, and legitimately can only be addressed, not asserted. (Buber, *I and Thou*, 129)

To Buber, all attempts to prove the existence of the divine are misguided and misleading. Insofar as the You-ness of God, in contrast to all other beings, is eternal, all efforts to capture it in objective language are futile. Consequently, the enterprise of rational theological speculation is misplaced. Just as we cannot know another person by assuming an objective stance, we cannot know the eternal You in this way either; we know it only through relation.[16]

Moreover, all efforts to prove that mutuality between persons and God exists are in vain. All that the believer can do is precisely what Buber did, that is, he or she "bears witness and invokes the witness of those whom he addresses—present or future witness" (Buber, *I and Thou*, 182). In addition, he or she can endeavor, through edifying discourse, to persuade.

In *I and Thou*, therefore, Buber revised the individualistic and mystical discourse that had informed his earlier discussions of religion. Although mystics had rightly proclaimed the inadequacy of language and the distorting effect of institutions, Buber believed they failed to attribute adequate significance to social relations. Whether advocating withdrawal from the world through meditation or unification with the universe or God, mystics deny the reality of everyday social relations, thereby diverting our attention from the social core of religious life.[17]

In contrast to the mystics' tendency to unite the self and the divine, Buber insisted that to encounter God, we must preserve our unique individual selfhood. If people surrender or suppress their independent beings, no genuine divine-human encounter can occur.

In contrast to mystical religions, Buber confirmed the reality of the everyday world:

What is greater than all enigmatic webs at the margins of being is the central actuality of an everyday hour on earth, with a streak of sunshine on a maple twig and an intimation of the eternal You. (Buber, *I and Thou*, 135–36) [18]

In his attempt to revise misleading conceptions of faith, Buber said virtually nothing about individual religious experience. Suspicious that individual religious experiences impede genuine relation to other persons, he appears to have left little, if any, room for private meditation. [19] We actualize the divine and transform it into a genuine force in our lives through our relations to others.

Nevertheless, Buber did not deny the possibility of a direct divine-human encounter: "I regard it as unqualifiedly legitimate when a man again and again, in an hour of religious fervor, adoring and praying, enters into a direct, 'world-free' relation to God" (Rome and Rome, *Philosophical Interrogations*, 86). [20]

To indicate the moral problem inherent in the use of the term God, Buber told the story of an encounter with the philosopher Paul Nartrop, who asked: [21]

How can you bring yourself to say "God" time after time? How can you expect that your readers will take the word in the sense in which you wish it to be taken. What you mean by the name of God is something above all human grasp and comprehension, but in speaking of it, you have lowered it to human conceptualization. What word of human speech is so misused, so defiled, so desecrated as this? All the innocent blood that has been shed for it has robbed it of its radiance. All the injustice that it has been used to cover has effaced its features. When I hear the highest called "God," it sometimes seems almost blasphemous. (Buber, *Eclipse of God*, 7) [22]

Buber admitted that the term *God* had been used to justify the most horrible deeds. Nevertheless, in spite of the fact that generations have both murdered and been murdered in the name of God whom they addressed as "You," Buber refused to abandon the term. No other term, he insisted, has the power to "capture the presence of Him whom the generations of men have honoured and degraded with their awesome living and dying" (Buber, *Eclipse of God*, 8). While respecting those who protest against the injustices perpetrated in its name, he argued: "We cannot cleanse the word 'God' and we cannot make it whole; but, defiled and mutilated as it is, we can raise it from the ground and set it over an hour of great care" (Buber, *Eclipse of God*, 8–9).

In spite of his criticism of institutionalized religion, Buber rejected the reductionistic critique of psychologists like Freud and Jung. He considered all efforts to reduce religious phenomena to psychological experiences misleading.[23] By reducing God to a psychic experience, these psychologists distort the ontic reality of our encounter with the other which is the basis of religious faith.

For Buber, all encounters with the divine entail both the self and other; neither can be eliminated. Moreover, although feelings inform the divine-human relationship, the relation, itself, is the primal reality.

All modern attempts to reinterpret this primal actuality of dialogue and to make of it a relationship of the I to the self or something of that sort, as if it were a process confined to man's self sufficient inwardness are in vain and belong to the abysmal history of deactualization. (Buber, *I and Thou*, 133)

Although in contrast to Freud's obvious antireligious bias, Jung appeared to have a positive regard for religion, Buber considered Jung's position far more dangerous to religious faith. Jung "oversteps with sovereign license the boundaries of psychology in its most essential point" by claiming that religion is to be understood as "a living relation to psychical events" (Buber, *Eclipse of God*, 79). By reducing religion to a psychic event, Jung "implied by this that it is not a relation to Being or Reality which, no matter how fully it may from time to time descend to the human soul, always remains transcendent to it. More precisely, it is not the relation of an I to a You" (Buber, *Eclipse of God*, 79). Accordingly, for Jung, "what the believer ascribes to God has its origin in his own soul" (Buber, *Eclipse of God*, 80).

While acknowledging that all statements about God are human statements, Buber denied that they are merely psychological projections. Distinguishing between psychic statements to which a metapsychic reality corresponds, and psychic statements to which none corresponds (Buber, *Eclipse, of God*, 135), Buber insisted that when the recipient of revelation speaks in the name of God, it is no illusion. Although we can offer no objective proof for this metapsychic reality and the language that we use is human in both conception and meaning, revelatory statements "witness to Him who stimulated it and to His will."[24] When psychologists pass judgment on the referent of such statements, they transgress the borders between science and religion and engage in "an illicit overstepping of boundaries":

Neither psychology nor any other science is competent to investigate the truth of the belief in God. It is the right of their representatives to keep aloof; it is not, within their disciplines, their right to make judgements about the belief in God as about something which they know. (Buber, *Eclipse of God*, 136)

Faith as Trust

Besides revising the conventional understanding of religion and God, Buber also undertook to revise what he perceived to be the common understanding of faith. Conventionally, faith is often taken to mean belief in the truth of propositions that cannot be logically validated. Seen in this light, a person of faith is one who acknowledges the truth of certain claims, such as those made about Moses or Jesus, that Moses was commissioned by God or that Jesus was sent by God to redeem humanity.

Buber, however, basing his interpretation on the Hebrew Bible, characterized faith as a fundamental attitude of existential trust actualized in the individual's and the community's life. According to the Hebrew Bible, the person of faith is the one who develops a trusting relationship with the divine. Contrasting the Hebrew concept *emunah* and the Christian concept *pistis*, Buber argued that *emunah* refers to a basic attitude of trust. Seen in that light, *to believe* means to trust in and be faithful to. Such a faith, which originates in the history of a community or a nation, "exists only in the actual realm of relationship between two persons." Only in the context of such a relationship can one be both loyal and trusting (Buber, *Two Types of Faith*, 28–29).

Buber found a different conception of faith actualized in Pauline Christianity.[25] This type of faith is represented by the claim, "I believe that it is so" and "originates in the history of individuals."

Pistis is represented by Paul's statement in Rom. 10:9–10, "This means the word of faith that we proclaim. For if on your lips is the confession Jesus is Lord and in your heart the faith that God raised him from the dead, then you will find salvation."[26]

Rooted in logical or noetic foundations, this kind of faith entails "the accepting and recognizing as true of a proposition pronounced about the object of faith (Buber, *Two Types of Faith*, 172). Rejecting the idea that genuine faith entails knowledge in the sense of *pistis*, Buber insisted that faith is a "factual event, lived life in dialogue" (Buber, *Believing Humanism*, 133). The person of faith, addressed by word and sign, responds by acting or refraining from acting.

Buber's religious faith is dialectically related to his philosophical anthropology. Although Buber placed his discussion of the divine-human relation in the third and final section of *I and Thou*, it was already presupposed in the first two sections. Ultimately, his fundamental vision of relationality is, although supported by psychological and anthropoligical evidence, grounded in religious faith:

In every sphere, through everything that becomes present to us, we gaze toward the train of the eternal You; in each we perceive a breath of it; in every You we address the eternal You, in every sphere according to its manner. (Buber, *I and Thou*, 57)

Revelation as Presence

Although denying that revelation is only a human projection, Buber acknowledged the human component in revelation. Insofar as we approach revelatory encounters with our own visions of the divine and our beholding is a "form giving beholding" (Buber, *I and Thou*, 166), we prefigure the experience:

But revelation does not pour into the world through its recipient as if he were a funnel; it confers itself upon him, it seizes his whole element in all of its suchness and fuses with it. Even the man who is "mouth" is precisely that and not a mouthpiece—not an instrument but an organ, an autonomous, sounding organ; and to sound means to modify sound. (Buber, *I and Thou*, 166)

In contrast to the interpretations of both theological traditional-ists and liberals, Buber focused on a revelatory process defined in terms of relation and dialogue. Revelation is neither a fixed body of teachings, as claimed by traditionalists, nor an inner experience or intuition, as maintained by theological liberals. Instead, revelation is an event in which one encounters and enters into a relationship with another. Common to all divine-human encounters is neither form nor content, but meeting and response.

The encounter with the divine, like the I-You relation to another person, yields presence rather than conceptual knowledge:

Man receives, and what he receives is not a "content" but a presence, a presence as strength. This presence and strength include three elements that are not separate but which may nevertheless be contemplated as three. (Buber, *I and Thou*, 158) [27]

Our meeting with the eternal You yields "the inexpressible con-firmation of meaning." We come away from the meeting convinced that life is meaningful:

It is guaranteed. Nothing, nothing can henceforth be meaningless. The question of the meaning of life has vanished. . . . You do not know how to point to or define the meaning, you lack any image or formula for it, and yet it is more certain for you than the sensations of your sense. (Buber, *I and Thou*, 159) [28]

Revelation also imparts a sense of being addressed. Far from mak-ing our lives easier, revelation elicits a heightened sense of respon-sibility and a felt need to respond through action. However, we alone can decide which action is called for; no one else has the right or the authority to prescribe that action:

The meaning we receive can be put to the proof in action only by each person in the uniqueness of his being and in the uniqueness of his life. No prescription can lead us to the encounter and none leads us from it. (Buber, *I and Thou*, 159) [29]

Moreover, we can only decide what response is called for at the moment of address.

Although Buber accepted the Bible as revealed scripture, he de-nied that Israel has a monopoly on revelation. [30] The claims of revelation invoked by the great religions and based on "the same quiet revelation that occurs everywhere and at all times" are valid.

At the same time, no one religion has a monopoly on truth: "Each religion is a human truth insofar as it represents the relationship of a particular community to the Absolute" (Buber, *Believing Humanism*, 115).

Buber also denied that all religions are equally valid. Once again, it is the existential experience of the individual and the community that is decisive. Insofar as the Jew experiences the world as unredeemed, he or she cannot accept the claims of Christianity. Similarly, insofar as Christians experience the truth of the claim of Christ's divinity and resurrection and actualize these truths in their daily lives, one who stands outside has no basis from which to criticize:

Pre-messianically our destinies are divided. Now to the Christian, the Jew is the incomprehensibly obdurate man, who declines to see what has happened; and to the Jew, the Christian is the incomprehensibly daring man, who affirms in an unredeemed world that its redemption has been accomplished. This is a gulf that no human power can bridge. (Buber, *Israel and World*, 40)

Buber distinguished his position from one that is based upon tolerance. His commitment to confirming others and acknowledging the validity of their existential stance precluded the idea of simply tolerating the errors of others. Each community should hold fast to its own faith. However, placing the relationship to God above all creedal truths, each community should recognize that "our Father's house is differently constructed than our human models take it to be" (Buber, *Israel and World*, 40).

Idolatry: A Revised Perspective

Buber's distinctive interpretation of religion entails a unique conception of idolatry. In their need for stability, permanence, and continuity, people create systems of dogma and moral principles. Thus, as is the case with all social institutions, organized religion is, like ancient idolatry, an expression of the desire to possess and control:

Man desires to have God; he desires to have God continually in space and time. He is loathe to be satisfied with the inexpressible confirmation of meaning; he wants to see it spread out as something that one can take out and handle again and again—a continuum unbroken in space and time that insures life for him at every point and moment. (Buber, *I and Thou*, 161–62)

The same anxieties that motivate people to formulate ideological and philosophical systems also lead them to transform God into an It, an object that can be analyzed, possessed and used. However, God, the "eternal You," "never ceases, in accordance with its nature, to be You for us" (Buber, *I and Thou*, 147). While every other You can revert to an It, the eternal You cannot. In the relation to the eternal You, latent "You-ness" is ever present.

As we have seen, Buber eschewed all efforts to talk of the divine in objectivistic terms. Moreover, he was highly suspicious of all attempts to formulate fixed principles and foundations upon which to ground our actions. Nevertheless, in sharp contrast to contemporary deconstructionists who, eschewing all talk of ground or foundation, view reality as an endless tapestry of signifiers, Buber, like Kierkegaard, ultimately reverts to the foundational claim of religious faith. Thus, for Buber, the eternal You is the ultimate ground for our relation to other persons and to nature. Without the eternal You, there is nothing upon which to ground the claim of the ultimate meaningfulness of our existence.

The eternal You also grounds our trust in the reality and primacy of relation. In the face of the overwhelming prevalence of the It world, only our faith and trust in the eternal You, and in the meaningfulness of life derived from it, enable us to go on:

In the great privilege of the pure relationship the privileges of the It world are annulled. By virtue of it, the You world is continuous; the isolated moments of relationships join for a world life or association. By virtue of it the You world has the power to give form: the spirit can permeate the It-world and change it. By virtue of it we are not abandoned to the alienation of the world and the deactualization of the I, nor are we overpowered by phantoms. (Buber, *I and Thou*, 148–49)

Buber readily acknowledged that there are no objective criteria by means of which one can demonstrate the reality of the eternal You. All efforts to transform this direct insight into rational discourse must fail. The claim for the primacy of relation does not rest upon logical argument but on a faith commitment expressed in the form of a fundamental, precritical insight. Ultimately, as with all such claims, it is a question of faith and experience. While we can never rationally demonstrate the truth of this faith experience, we can witness to it.[31]

I give no guarantees, I have no security to offer. But I also demand of no one that they believe. I communicate my own experience of faith to those whom I address. To those who have none, or imagine that they have none, I recommend only that they do not armor their souls with preconceived opinion. (Rome and Rome, *Philosophical Interrogations*, 96)

In light of Buber's resistance to rational theological discourse, his own effort to describe God as the You that cannot, in accordance with its nature, be anything other than a You, appears to be inconsistent. Buber seemed to be torn between his conviction that to speak about the divine in positive terms is to reduce it to an It, and the need to correct misinterpretations that distort our understanding of religious faith. In speaking of God as eternal You, Buber, rather than describing a metaphysical reality, is making what contemporary philosophers call a grammatical statement—that is, he is saying something about the conditions for talking about God. Therefore, when he speaks of God's nature, he is not saying that this is how God is, objectively speaking, but rather this is how God is manifest in our relationship to Him. Insofar as all God language is relational, when we speak of God, we speak not of an objective entity but of a relation as we experience it.

When viewed from Buber's perspective, blasphemy is not denying the objective reality of God but invoking the name of God out of a desire to possess Him or Her:

Whoever is dominated by the idol whom he wants to acquire, have and hold, possessed by his desire to possess, can find a way to God only by returning, which involves a change not only of the goal, but also of the kind of movement. . . . Woe unto the possessed who fancy they possess God! (Buber, *I and Thou*, 154–55)

Thus, idolatry is not, as Scheler and his disciples thought, the act of displacing God with the state, money, power, or knowledge. Not the what, but the how of the relation to the divine is essential; not that to which we relate, but the mode of relationship. To the extent that our relationship to the world and to others is informed by a utilitarian attitude, so is our relationship to God.

Organized religions, by seeking to translate spontaneous responses into fixed forms and structures, replace the immediacy of the divine-human encounter with reified, static forms:

And the cult, too, gradually becomes a substitute, as the personal prayer is no longer supported but pushed aside by communal prayer; and as the essential deed simply does not permit any rules, it is supplanted by devotions that follow rules. (Buber, *I and Thou*, 161)

Thus, from Buber's perspective, institutionalized religion entails the suppression of a unique, free, spontaneous, existential response. The very acts of designating specific spheres of our life as religious and establishing fixed forms of worship impede our encounter with the eternal You.[32] The divine-human encounter can only be actualized in the entirety of our lives and in the wholeness of our existence:

In truth, however, the pure relation can be built up into spatio-temporal continuity only by becoming embodied in the whole stuff of life. It cannot be preserved but only put to the proof in action; it can only be done, poured into life. Man can do justice to the relation to God that has been given to him only by actualizing God in the world in accordance with his ability and the measure of each day, daily. This is the only genuine guarantee of continuity. (Buber, *I and Thou*, 163)

As heretics and mystics have understood, to encounter the divine, we must depart from the fixed forms of tradition and recover the immediate actuality of relation. This relation, rather than the illusory objectivism of the tradition, is genuinely objective:

Subjectivism is psychologization while objectivism is reification of God; one a false fixation, the other a false liberation; both departures from the way of actuality, both attempts to find a substitute for it. (Buber, *I and Thou*, 167)

As previously discussed, Buber's faith that alienation could be overcome and life rendered meaningful is expressed by the idea of *teshuvah*. Although mired in the world of It, human beings have the capacity to liberate themselves from an alienated condition by entering into I-You relations. Although persons may step out of relation to another person or to the divine, they always have the potential to step back into relation.

The dual movement of persons toward and away from others, and toward and away from the eternal You, has its parallel in a twofold cosmic movement. As in human life, there is "a metacosmic primal form of duality that inheres in the world as a whole in its relation to that which is not world" (Buber, *I and Thou*, 149). In Hasidism, this twofold movement was expressed through the myth of the broken vessels. In that myth, creation is described as an original act of fragmentation and separation. The origin of the universe consists of an original breaking away. However, this break or rupture is not permanent. By turning back to its primal ground and entering into relation with it, the universe "redeems itself in being" (Buber, *I and Thou*, 149).

In spite of his strong antitraditionalist bias, Buber's position differed decidedly from that of liberal theologians. In contrast to theological liberals, he insisted that the genuine, nonrational meeting of the human and the divine is an event that precedes and transcends all theological concepts and moral principles. Being religious is not a matter of following a set of moral principles or adhering to a set of religious beliefs. In our relationship with others, we do not act to fulfill a moral code but to actualize the command that emerges out of our revelatory encounter.

Like Weber, who saw all religions as transforming the original charismatic moment into something routine, and like Simmel, who viewed institutionalized religion as the objectification of life forces, Buber believed that all religious groups transform relation into objecthood. Formal religion necessarily entails the loss of relational power. Dominated by objecthood, religions deprive people of the capacity to say You spontaneously with their whole being.

Evil as a Human Issue

Buber, like any religious thinker, was compelled to confront the problem of evil. While he did not shrink from this challenge, his interpretation of evil, grounded in his philosophy of relation and dialogue, differs significantly from others'. In contrast to traditional philosophy of religion and consistent with his own existentialist stance, Buber eschewed any metaphysical discussion of evil. Rather than attempt a rational inquiry into the problem of evil, he engaged in "a synthetic description of evil happenings, and so to assist in its understanding" (Buber, *Good and Evil*, 64). His concern was not evil as such but the way in which evil manifests itself in human existence.

Buber addressed the problem of evil on two levels. On one level, he engaged in a philosophical anthropological discussion of the place of evil in human life. Denying that we have any knowledge of evil "as such," or of a specific "locus of evil," Buber spoke of evil as "a condition and attitude in the life of individuals" (Rome and Rome, *Philosophical Interrogations*, 114). Accordingly, to understand evil we must understand the dynamics of human existence.

Buber carried on this discussion of the anthropological problem of evil through an examination of myths.[33] The myths teach us "what specifically happens in the life and soul of the man preoccupied with 'evil' and particularly, of him who is on the point of falling victim to it" (Buber, *Good and Evil*, 116). What we mean by evil "is revealed to the human person's retrospection, his cognizance of himself in the course of the life he has lived" (Buber, *Good and Evil*, 131).

Like Nietzsche, who, avoiding any substantive discussion of good and evil, inquired into the psychological conditions out of which these categories first arose, Buber analyzed good and evil by inquiring into the anthropological conditions from which our knowledge of good and evil emerges. However, in contrast to Nietzsche, Buber did not attempt to reduce good and evil to human attitudes. Viewing human decisions and actions in the context of his dialogical vision of life, he attributed cosmic significance to good and evil actions.

Analyzing biblical psalms and Iranian myths, Buber undertook to reveal the place of good and evil "in man's observation of the human world" (Buber, *Good and Evil*, foreword). What these myths reveal is "that in their anthropological reality, that is, in the factual context of the life of the human person, good and evil are not, as they are usually thought to be, two structurally similar qualities situated at different poles, but two qualities of totally different structure" (Buber, *Good and Evil*, 64).

It is usual to think of good and evil as two poles, two opposite directions, the two arms of a signpost pointing to right and left; they are understood as belonging to the same plane of being, as the same in nature, but the antithesis of one another. If we are to have in mind not ethical abstractions, but existent states of human reality, we must begin by doing away with this convention and recognizing the fundamental dissimilarity between the two in nature, structure, and dynamics within human reality. (Buber, *Good and Evil*, 121)

Viewed from this perspective, "evil is lack of direction, and that which is done in it and out of it as the grasping, seizing, devouring, compelling, seducing, exploiting, humiliating, torturing and destroying of what offers itself" (Buber, *Good and Evil*, 130). Evil does not stem from a decision to do evil but from indecision. Like I-It encounters, "evil cannot be done with the whole soul." Conversely, "good can only be done with the whole soul" (Buber, *Good and Evil*, 130). In our encounters with others, we act in an evil way when we grasp, seize, devour, compel, seduce, exploit, humiliate, torture, or destroy.

Buber rejected the view that evil is a fixed part of our being. Human existence is dynamic. Just as we move toward and away from others, we move toward and away from decision, from decision to indecision. Thus, the human being is "in an eminent sense good and evil; he is fundamentally twofold" (Rome and Rome, *Philosophical Interrogations*, 114).[34]

Alongside his inquiry into the anthropological dimension of evil, Buber also confronted the religious problem of evil, especially as posed by the destruction of six million Jews under the Nazis. Fifteen years before the emergence of "Holocaust theology," Buber raised the question of the implications of Auschwitz for the religious believer:[35]

In our time, one asks again and again: how is a Jewish life still possible after Auschwitz? I would like to frame this question more correctly: how is a life with God still possible in a time in which there is an Auschwitz? The estrangement has become too cruel, the hiddenness too deep. (Buber, *On Judaism*, 224)

Consistent with his existential orientation, Buber did not attempt to resolve rationally the theological problems posed by the Holocaust. Unlike theologians such as Richard Rubenstein, Buber did not view the Holocaust as a challenge to a particular conception of God.[36]

Instead, he defined the problem existentially in terms of the divine-human relationship:

One can still "believe" in the God who allowed those things to happen, but can one still speak to Him? Can one still hear His word? Can one still, as an individual and as a people, enter at all into a dialogic relationship to Him? Can one still call to Him? (Buber, *On Judaism*, 224)

To Buber, the post-Holocaust age is an age of the "eclipse of God." This biblical notion, which conveyed the experience of an interruption in the divine-human relationship, expresses the condition of the post-Holocaust believing Jew:

God seems to withdraw Himself utterly from the earth and no longer to participate in its existence. The space of history is then full of noise, but empty of the divine breath. For one who believes in the living God, who knows about Him, and is fated to spend his life in a time of His hiddenness, it is very difficult to live. (Buber, *On Judaism*, 223)

Like Job, the modern Jew can expect neither an explanation nor a justification. As in God's final appearance to Job, "nothing is explained, nothing adjusted; wrong has not become right, nor cruelty kindness" (Buber, *On Judaism*, 224). While Job was answered, the answer, like all revelation, took the form of presence rather than information. Similarly, the post-Holocaust Jew, avoiding all objectivistic theological discussion, can do nothing more than affirm a relationship in the face of catastrophe:

In such a state we await His voice, whether it comes out of the storm or out of a stillness that follows it. Though His coming appearance resembles no earlier one, we shall recognize again our cruel and merciful Lord. (Buber, *On Judaism*, 225)

Buber viewed the Holocaust as essentially a human problem. In a discussion late in his life with a group of young Israelis he observed: "I am inclined to the opinion that not only the holocaust, but all wars are to be understood in terms of the nature of the human being" (Ben Ezer, *Unease in Zion*, 107).

This view was already implied in his only novel, *Gog u'Megog*, which he began during the First World War but only completed for publication in 1943.[37] In the novel, Buber counterposed two views of war and catastrophe. Over and against those religious believers who view catastrophe in cosmic, eschatological terms, Buber juxtaposed a protagonist who focused on the human dimension. The book's central theme is contained in the words of a disciple who says of Gog, the embodiment of evil, "He can exist in the outer world only because he exists within us. . . . It is our betrayal of God that has made Gog to grow so great."[38]

In Buber's view, the modern Jew, while appealing to the hidden and hiding God, must continue to struggle to bring about redemption on Earth. Accordingly, Buber's response to the evils of Nazism also took the form of action. In the early 1930s, he assumed a position of leadership in the Jewish educational movement in Germany. Under the eyes of the Nazis, Buber organized courses and lectured to Jewish communities throughout Germany. In the words of Ernst Simon, Buber was one of the leaders of the movement for spiritual resistance among German Jews.[39]

Following the war, Buber was one of the first Jewish intellectuals to confront the German people directly. While most Jews avoided such a confrontation, Buber, although severely criticized, traveled to Germany to accept the Peace Prize of the German Book Trade in 1953. Speaking only eight years after the attempted destruction of European Jewry had been brought to a halt, he forthrightly voiced his feelings about the German people. Unwilling to assign blanket blame, Buber distinguished between those who remained passive, those who sought to help the Jews, and those who actually participated in the murder process. The last had

so radically removed themselves from the human sphere, so transposed themselves into a sphere of monstrous inhumanity inaccessible to my conception, that not even hatred, much less the overcoming of hatred, was able to arise in me. And what am I that I could here presume to forgive. (Buber, *Pointing the Way*, 232)

To Buber, the battle between human and antihuman forces that began with the Second World War still continues. However, rather than war precipitating the current crisis, it was the crisis of humanity that "brought forth the total war and the unreal peace which followed" (Buber, *Pointing the Way*, 236). The challenge, therefore, is to address the human situation that brought about the war, a situation that had its roots in the alienated condition Buber sought to confront in all of his writings:

Men are no longer able to speak directly to their fellows. They are not able to speak directly because they no longer trust one another, and everybody knows that the other no longer trusts him. (Buber, *Pointing the Way*, 237)

The inability of people to carry on authentic dialogue with one another "is not only the most acute symptom of the pathology of our time, it is also that which most urgently makes a demand on us" (Buber, *Pointing the Way*, 238). The task for the postwar generation, therefore, is not theological but anthropological. In the face of the mistrust that pervades the international world and precludes genuine dialogue between nations, our responsibility is to work for the recovery of dialogue. The post-Holocaust Jew, like all people, is responsible to foster dialogue wherever possible.[40]

The name, Satan, means in Hebrew the hinderer. That is the correct designation for the anti-human in individuals and in the human race. Let us not allow this Satanic element in men to hinder us from realizing man. Let us release speech from its ban. (Buber, *Pointing the Way*, 238–39)

In spite of his encounter with radical evil, Buber did not cease to believe in the possibility of *teshuvah* (return) and renewal. "The power of turning that radically changes the situation" can be revealed in the depths of crisis. However, Buber acknowledged that his faith in the possibility of renewed dialogue and restored trust was not subject to proof:

Can such an illness be healed? I believe it can be. And it is out of this, my belief, that I speak to you. I have no proof for this belief. No belief can be proved; otherwise it would not be what it is, a great venture. Instead of offering proof, I appeal to that potential [for] belief of each of my hearers which enables him to believe. (Buber, *Pointing the Way*, 238)

Like the dialogue between individuals, the dialogue between nations requires that each of the partners "heeds, affirms, and confirms his opponent as an existing other" (Buber, *Pointing the Way*, 238). While such dialogue may not eliminate conflict, it can begin the human conversation that could lead to overcoming it. As with all our commitments, this commitment to dialogue entails faith and risk: "Let us dare, despite all, to trust!" (Buber, *Pointing the Way*, 238–39).

8

Living as a Jew

As I have repeatedly emphasized, Buber viewed his Jewishness and his humanness as inextricably related. Consequently, his ideas about Judaism and his ideas about society in general are intertwined. Just as he derived many of his insights regarding the human condition from the writings of the prophets and Hasidism, his interpretation of Judaism and Jewish life are grounded in his philosophical anthropology and his social theory.

Buber's view of Jewish existence is a dialectic of responsibility to and participation in a particular community and responsibility to humanity as a whole. While the individual Jew is committed to the life and future of the Jewish people, the content and parameters of that commitment are shaped by his or her responsibility to humanity in general. At the same time, a Jew's contribution to and participation in the world at large is shaped and nurtured by his or her membership in the Jewish people. For Buber, humanness and Jewishness are dialectically linked.[1]

Buber's personal vision of humanity was shaped and nurtured by his Jewishness. He found in the teachings of Judaism unique insights into the human condition. Particularly in the writings of the prophets and Hasidism, he discovered the means through which to address the "crisis of Western man" (*HMM*, 38). While wishing to render these teachings accessible to humanity as a whole, Buber spoke as a Jew whose point of origin was the life situation of the Jewish people: "In order to speak to the world what I have heard, I am not bound to step into the street. I may remain standing in the door of my ancestral house; here too the word that it uttered does not go astray" (*HMM*, 42).

Buber viewed the problems confronting the Jewish people as a specific form of the problems confronting all humanity. He saw the life situation of his own people as the crucible in which to test the truth of his teachings. Truth, as Buber understood it, is not to be found in abstract teachings but is to be actualized in life situations. The significance of biblical Israel and Hasidism derived from the fact that they, more than other Jewish communities, succeeded in actualizing their teachings in concrete social and communal forms.

Buber did not regard truth as an ideal vision to be actualized in the future. People actualize truth in the situation in which they stand at any particular moment and cannot formulate in advance how to act in a future situation. In Buber's words, concerning the truth, people must ask, How can we accomplish it from where we are?[2]

While believing that ultimately truth is absolute and one, Buber acknowledged that, from the human perspective, it is forever situational and pluralistic. The Jew, therefore, like all persons, must discover truth as it emerges in the context of concrete communal life. In the case of the Jew, the community is that of the Jewish people.

For Buber, being Jewish means that one's consciousness is shaped by the actions and teachings of previous generations of Jews. Being a Jew is an existential given. One who is Jewish lives out his or her life and makes choices within the context of the past, present, and future of the Jewish people.

Unlike those secular Zionists who denied the uniqueness of the Jewish nation, Buber insisted that the Jews are not a nation like all other nations. In the course of its history, the Jewish people received upon itself a unique task. Its historical fate, shaped by the dialogue between Israel and the eternal You, can only be understood in the light of this task:[3]

If we really are Jews, meaning the bearers of a tradition and a task, we know what has been transmitted to us. We know that there is a truth which is the seal of God, and we know that the task we have been entrusted with is to let this one truth set its stamp on all the various facets of one's life. (Buber, *Israel and the World*, 235)

Although adopting the discourse of philosophy and social theory, Buber's fundamental orientation to life was religious. Notwithstanding his critical stance toward rabbinic Judaism, he shared the rabbis' view that the meaning of life is grounded in ultimate truths. Whereas the rabbis sought to concretize those truths through an imposed system of norms and practices, Buber, rejecting this system, believed that these truths could only be actualized through everyday activities and modes of relationship.

Like the traditionalist, Buber insisted that the first questions a Jew must ask are, What is the truth? and, what has God commanded us to do? However, eschewing all formulae and predetermined systems of behavior, he rejected the claim of rabbinic tradition to be normative for all Jews. The question of truth can be answered neither by prescribed norm nor by intellectual inquiry, but only through decision and action.

Unlike the traditionalists, who believe that each new situation could be adequately addressed through the framework of halakhah, Buber insisted that each situation requires a new decision and a new response. Unlike liberal religious Jews, he rejected all prescribed sets of moral principles and theological concepts. Like any other person, the Jew must discover that truth anew in every particular situation. In each situation, the Jew, like all persons, is responsible to listen for the signs of address, to decide, and to act.

For the people of Israel, as for any people, truth is actualized in historical situations. The testing ground of truth is the everyday life of the individual lived within the context of his community. Throughout his career, Buber continually sought to awaken the Jewish people to its responsibilities in the concrete life of the community.

Judaism and the Philosophy of Relation

The process of concept revision that I have discussed with regard to Buber's general philosophical writings is also evident in his writings on Judaism. Throughout his later years, the questions that he had formulated in his early addresses continued to occupy him: What do we mean when we call ourselves Jews? What, precisely, does living a Jewish life entail?

Following the publication of *I and Thou*, Buber reformulated his interpretation of Judaism in the light of his relational philosophy.[4] This new interpretation reflects the shift in focus from individual religious experience to interhuman relations and community. The beginnings of this shift, as I have shown, were already evident in "The Holy Way" and "Herut." However, these lectures contained only a preliminary sketch of his mature conception of Judaism. Not until the 1920s and 1930s did his mature conception clearly emerge.

The sociopolitical context within which Buber struggled with these questions had a decisive influence in shaping his answers. The audience Buber addressed in the 1920s and 1930s differed from the audience to whom he had presented his early lectures. His earlier audience had been composed primarily of young, Jewish intellectuals struggling to find their way among existing Jewish ideologies. In presenting Judaism to them as a powerful alternative to the alienated forms of life prevailing in Western society, Buber spoke in terms of existential religiosity and national renewal. During this period, his thought was oriented to the individual's quest for actualization, while the social implications of his philosophy of Judaism remained undeveloped.

During the 1920s and 1930s, the bulk of Buber's work on Jewish affairs revolved around Zionism.[5] In contrast to his earlier audience, there was no need to persuade his Zionist audience of the validity of being Jewish. For them, the issue was not whether or not to live in a Jewish way, but rather what strategies should be employed in seeking to carry out the Zionist dream.

Following Buber's immigration to Palestine in 1938, his context shifted to that of a community struggling to attain an autonomous existence in its historic homeland. For the last decades of his life, his efforts to clarify the meaning of Jewish life were shaped by the sociopolitical realities of the Arab-Jewish confrontation. This conflict, as Simon has observed, became the essential internal problem around which Buber defined the central issues of Jewish existence.[6]

Buber wrote as a critic of official Zionist ideology. As he viewed it, this ideology, based on an erroneous and destructive conception of Judaism, resulted in a program that distorted the actual needs of the Jewish people. To counter this situation, Buber formulated a revised interpretation of the goals and purposes of Zionism.

In contrast to his earlier writings, Buber's post-1923 writings reflect a less hostile attitude to traditional rabbinic Judaism. Even in "The Holy Way," Buber, approaching the age of forty, vented his anger and antagonism toward Orthodoxy, referring to the Orthodox as "you who are safe and secure, you who take refuge behind the bulwark of the law in order to avoid looking into God's abyss" (Buber, *On Judaism*, 137).[7]

However, during the 1920s, Buber's antagonism toward rabbinic Judaism receded, and his tone shifted from hyperbole to moderate reflection. For the first time, he acknowledged the positive contribution of the rabbis.[8] While continuing to regard rabbinic Judaism as a distortion of the authentic Jewish ethos, he nevertheless admitted that the rabbis had contributed important insights to that ethos:

In Hasidism I see merely a concentrated movement, the concentration of all those elements which are to be found in a less condensed form everywhere in Judaism, even in "rabbinic Judaism." Only, in rabbinic Judaism this movement is not visible in the structure of the community, but holds sway over the inaccessible structure of the personal life. (Buber, *Israel and the World*, 13)

During this period, Buber also revised his interpretation of the religious character of Judaism. In keeping with his new philosophical perspective, the concept of dialogue became basic to that interpretation. At the same time, the communal emphasis became more pronounced. Henceforth, he spoke of the task of the Jewish people in terms of their responsibility to establish an authentic community in the land of Israel.

The development in Buber's discussion of Judaism is clearly reflected in his writings on Hasidism and the Bible. In his Hasidic writings, the themes of relation and community now assume a central position. Unlike his earlier anthologies, which were comprised of complete stories, his work now consisted of extensive collections of brief, anecdotal tales. Moreover, Buber undertook a more active revision of these stories in an effort to bring out their religious meaning for the modern world and recover the existential truths reflected in the Hasidic sources. As the Bible presented the original paradigm of Jewish existence, Hasidism reflected the most successful effort by diaspora Jewry to actualize Judaism in communal life.[9]

As early as "Herut," published in 1919, Buber had stressed the need for a renewed Jewish teaching rooted in the Hebrew Bible. Just as the Renaissance had bypassed the Middle Ages in an effort to recover its roots in the literature of Greece and Rome, Israel had to move beyond rabbinic Judaism and recover its authentic roots in the Hebrew Bible. However, the current generation of Jews was alienated from the teachings of the Bible. To bridge this gap and restore the Bible to its rightful place at the center of the Jewish renewal, it was necessary to instruct the younger generation in the art of reading the Bible. Through a series of lectures, books, essays, and translations, Buber responded to this challenge.

Recovering the Bible

The return to the Bible was a common theme among Jewish nationalists. The Bible, in contrast to rabbinic literature, was viewed as the product of the nation's creative growth in its own land. Accordingly, the Bible served to provide the Jewish nationalists with new folk heroes and inspiration.

To Ahad Haam, the Bible was the source of the unique Jewish national spirit. In the writings of the prophets, Ahad Haam found the ideal of absolute righteous justice.[10] However, in contrast to traditional readers, Ahad Haam perceived the source of this ideal not in a divine revelation but in an event of moral inspiration.

Buber's approach to the Bible differed from that of most Jewish nationalists including Ahad Haam. To Buber, the Bible was more than a source of national, historical, and literary ideals; it also offered "normative primal forces" that have the power to shape the nation and set the direction for its life. Thus, the renewal and future of the Jewish nation and the recovery of its authentic task presupposes a renewal of the community's bonds to the text that nurtured its original emergence. "A Hebrew humanism can rise only from a sensitive selection that out of the totality of Judaism discerns the Hebrew person in his purest state. Thus, our humanism is directed to the Bible" (Buber, *On the Bible*, 212).

In contrast to Ahad Haam and other secular nationalists, Buber viewed the Bible as the record of Israel's ongoing relationship to

God. In the Bible, the modern reader can find expressions and echoes of the divine-human encounter. However, Buber did not accept the Bible as an unimpeachable source of truth; to do so would be to flee from the responsibility for decision that falls to each person. Unwilling to surrender this existential choice, Buber refused to abdicate individual critical judgment:

I have not been able to accept either the Bible or Hasidism as a whole; in one and in the other I had to and have to distinguish between that which had become evident to me out of my experience and truth and that which had not become evident to me in this manner. (Schilpp and Friedman, *Philosophy of Martin Buber*, 744; hereafter referred to as *PMB*)

While viewing the Bible as a bridge between the modern Jew and the divine, Buber was well aware of the modern Jew's alienation from the biblical texts. Many modern Jews simply could not accept the religious claims of the Bible at face value. To such readers, the Bible was the product of a vastly different world and its views are incompatible with the modern view of reality. The problem, as Buber saw it, was to develop a mode of reading and interpretation that would renew the Bible's power to speak to today's Jew.

To many Jews living in a modern, scientifically oriented culture, the Bible seemed to offer little. Regarding the Bible as a collection of myths and legends that taxed the credibility of the modern reader, they found little in it to help shape a meaningful orientation to life. To the reader seeking inspiration and meaning, the Bible's theological teachings seemed archaic and its religious laws obsolete. While some read it for aesthetic pleasure, they did so, Buber believed, at the expense of its religious power.

It was not sufficient simply to advocate a return to the Bible. For the Bible to serve as the basis of the modern Jewish renaissance, Jews had to be taught how to read it so as to recover its religious power. Accordingly, Buber's problem was to formulate an approach that would preserve the Bible's religious force while simultaneously honoring each reader's unique existential situation. Moreover, he sought to synthesize a modern, critical perspective with a religious perspective.

In a series of interpretative studies on the Bible, he sought to demonstrate the way in which it should be read in the hope of removing the impediments that prevent the modern Jew from experiencing its existential relevance.[11] Underlying these studies is the awareness of the "complete chasm between the Scriptures and the man of today" (Buber, *Israel and the World*, 94). The basic problem was, "How can we mediate between this man and the biblical message? Where is the bridge?" (Buber, *Israel and the World*, 101).

Buber's writings on the Bible are grounded in his philosophy of a dialogue. One important premise, discussed earlier, is that language expresses our direct response to reality and conveys our deepest existential experiences. To Buber, the biblical writers were poets who poured their feelings and emotions into word vessels. Through an encounter with their words, the modern reader can recover a sense of the existential situation in which the writings first emerged.

In contrast to the prevailing biblical scholarship of his day, Buber believed that the original words of the biblical poets were formulated orally. Only later were they subjected to a systematic process of writing, revision, and editing. Like all creative texts, the Bible arose in the context of living, relational situations. Thus, the Bible is a creative expression of living people in actual life situations. Insofar as the Bible arose out of a living dialogue between person and person, person and world, and person and God, conventional biblical scholarship errs in focusing its attention on the various strata of written sources.

To understand the biblical texts truly, the reader must approach them in the spirit of dialogue. If one is to recover the life situation in which the Bible was produced, one must grasp the basic rhythm and the spoken nuances of its language. Buber advised his readers to employ the same kind of creative imagination with the biblical text that he had employed with Hasidic writings.[12] Like all reading, reading the Bible is a personal, existential act. Thus, the reader must adopt an open, accepting attitude while divesting himself or herself of all presuppositions and prejudices:

He must face the Book with a new attitude as something new. He must yield to it, withhold nothing of his being, and let whatever will occur between himself and it. He does not know which of its sayings will overwhelm him and mold him, from where the spirit will ferment and enter into him, to incorporate itself anew in his body. But he holds himself open. He does not believe anything a priori, he does not disbelieve anything. (Buber, *Israel and the World*, 93)

Insofar as the highest, most intimate knowledge is attained not by assuming a detached, subject-object stance but by being open and fully present to the other, we should, Buber insisted, approach sacred scriptures in the same way that we approach other persons. In both instances, we gain knowledge by entering into direct relation, making ourselves fully present, and withholding nothing of ourselves.

The Bible translation, which was begun by Buber and Rosenzweig in 1925 and was completed by Buber several decades after Rosenzweig's death, was a part of Buber's overall effort to overcome the alienation that characterized the modern Jew's relationship to this basic source of Jewish religious teaching.[13] This translation was based on the assumption, referred to previously, that the Bible was originally spoken rather than written. Originating in actual life situations, the words were first formulated in the form of spoken human dialogue:

Speech means words spoken in specific situations. One must not remove the biblical word from the situation in which it was spoken, for to do so is to cut it off from its concreteness and its materiality. . . . Prophecy is the speech of a person, who speaks as one sent to address the community at a particular time and in a particular situation. (Buber, *Darko shel Mikra*, 363)

Insofar as language is rooted in existential situations, the texts must be approached existentially: "The important thing is to ask the text that we hold in our hand to tell us of its unique relation to the situation" (Buber, *Darko shel Mikra*, 364). The conventional historical approach, subsuming situations under the categories of time and causality, neglects the existential reality of situations.

Conventional biblical scholarship, viewing the Bible as a collection of literary documents, seeks to decode these documents and to catalogue them according to literary sources. From this perspective, biblical scholarship entails discerning the various sources and situating them according to time and place. However, when the Bible is seen as an oral document set to writing, the task of the scholar is not to divide and catalogue but to recover the life situation out of which the text was produced.

For Buber and Rosenzweig, the primary issues were not scholarly but religious and existential. Their translation arose out of a deep concern over the way in which Christian translators had distorted the teachings of the Bible. Thus, Buber and Rosenzweig viewed their translation as a critical activity that would liberate the biblical text from the strait-jacket imposed upon it by translators like Luther.

The Luther translation, laden with dogmatic Christian preconceptions, had wrenched the biblical text out of its original Hebrew habitat and transformed it into a message of Christian theology:

This is the key: for Luther, the actual statement had been subjugated to the dogma of "logos," "the speech of God," and the primary purpose of translation is to render that which impelled it, that is, Christ, perceptible. We, however, felt compelled to liberate the actual spoken, speakable statement (maamar) enslaved in writing, so that its voice could again be heard; let it say whatever it has to say, the world will listen. (Buber, *Darko shel Mikra*, 353)

To Buber and Rosenzweig, language is the vehicle through which people express their spontaneous responses to reality and convey their deepest, existential experiences. Like poets, the biblical writers expressed their feelings and emotions through myth. As Buber formulated it:

The great poets show us in their way how the nascence of myths and sagas takes place. Each myth, even the myth we usually call the most fantastic of all, is creation around a memory core, around the kernel of the organically shaping memory. (Buber, *Israel and the World*, 120)

To recover the life situation from which the text emerged, Buber and Rosenzweig used several strategies including revising the conventional literary structure; providing alternative translations that conveyed the emotional tone and concrete materiality of the original Hebrew; emphasizing the recurring terms through which the key meaning of passages was conveyed; and replacing abstract nouns with verbs.[14]

In conventional versions of the Bible, the text is divided into chapters and verses. To Buber and Rosenzweig, this seemingly harmless practice masked the original situation out of which the text emerged. The Bible is not a narrative told by a third person, but a spontaneous creative outpouring of innermost feelings arising out of our encounter with the world and with the divine. To divide it according to literary conventions is to disrupt the spontaneity of the text and perpetuate the erroneous view of the Bible as a written document. Moreover, this method of division destroys any hope of recovering the power and rhythm of the original spoken text.

To counter this, Buber and Rosenzweig altered the overall literary form of the text, removing all chapter and verse notations and organizing the material thematically. As a result, the meaning the reader derives from the text is significantly altered. For example, when read as a poem, the text of the creation story sounds totally different than it does when read as a narrative. The current literary form, divided into chapters and verses and interspersed with the conjunction *and*, is the work of later interpreters who gave the text a form alien to the original intentions of the authors/speakers.

Buber and Rosenzweig regularly translated terms in accordance with their sensuous, or material, meaning. Eschewing abstractions, they endeavored to situate words in actual life situations, recovering their fundamental sensuousness and feeling tone. For example, the Hebrew term *mizbeah*, commonly translated *altar*, is translated by Buber and Rosenzweig as *slaughter place*. This graphic translation, which conveys a strong sense of the situational reality of the sacrificial act, is based upon the meaning of the root *zbh*, which means *to slaughter*. In addition, basing their translation on the root *krv*, which means *to draw near*, Buber and Rosenzweig translated the term *korban*, commonly rendered *sacrifice*, as *drawing near*. Again, by translating the abstract noun form into the dynamic verb form, they remained faithful to the original Hebrew.[15]

Instead of the common word *spirit*, which implies a spirit-body dichotomy foreign to the biblical Hebrew, Buber and Rosenzweig translated the term *ruah* as *Geist/Braust* (rushing spirit). Emphasizing the dialogical nature of the divine-human relation, they approach the Divinity not as an abstract entity to be contemplated but as a living presence with whom one could enter into relation and dialogue. Accordingly, Buber and Rosenzweig personalized the concept of the Divinity by using personal pronouns in place of terms such as *God* or *Lord*.

Another device utilized by Buber and Rosenzweig is that of *Leitwortstil*. In their view, the recurrence of key words is the secret to deciphering the meaning of biblical passages.[16]

A key word is a word or linguistic root which is repeated within a text or a sequence of texts or a larger context in a highly significant manner. If one investigates these repetitions, one of the meanings of the texts is deciphered or clarified, or at least reveals itself more forcefully. (Buber, *Darko shel Mikra*, 284) [17]

The concept of myth, which I have already discussed in relation to Buber's Hasidic writings, was also fundamental to his biblical hermeneutic. To him, the organically formed descriptions and narratives in the Bible are mythic accounts of events that had been experienced:

I have nothing against calling these narratives myths and sagas, so long as we remember that myths and sagas are essentially memories which are actually conveyed from person to person. . . . I say again, memory not imagination. We know of it today because occasionally, though in unlikely and indeed in incredible ways, the existence of great poets with such organic memories still extends into our time. (Buber, *Israel and the World*, 119–20)

Again challenging the prevailing antimythic scholarly view, Buber held myth to be a valid category of biblical interpretation. Mythic accounts of the liberation from Egypt or prophetic revelation represent more than the products of a writer's creative imagination; they express the spontaneous, enthusiastic response of participants. Encountering the unplanned, unexpected events of the everyday world, the Israelite narrator "transformed the historical situation of his community at a single stroke with a fundamental stirring of all the elements in his being" (Buber, *Moses*, 14).

While the original traditions were subsequently edited, they are, Buber believed, basically reliable. In the ancient Near East, narrators generally accepted and transmitted traditions without altering them:

The great narrator allows the events to drop into him as they happen, careless, trusting, with faith. And memory does its part: what has thus been dropped into it, it molds organically, unarbitrarily, unfancifully into a valid account and narrative; a whole on which a great deal of conscious work has to be done, but the distinguishing mark was put upon it by the unarbitrary, shaping memory. (Buber, *Israel and the World*, 120)

Thus, the Bible provides us with the unarbitrary testimony of the creative memory of the group. While, in the process of transmission, "differing religious, social and familiar tendencies" (Buber, *Israel and the world*, 120) may have been absorbed, the core of this material is authentic and original.

Prevailing biblical scholarship viewed the Bible as the product of a long process of compiling and synthesizing different literary sources. In contrast to the biblical critics, Buber envisioned a natural, organic process of oral transmission in which the original mythic material was ultimately crystallized. Thus, the interpreter's task is to strip away the layers of later accretions in an effort to "penetrate to that original nucleus of saga which was almost contemporary with the initial event" (Buber, *Moses*, 18).

Buber's approach also differed from that of the historian who, demanding confirming evidence, refuses to accept the claims of the text at face value. Scholars who insist on corroborative evidence and objective testimony are inclined to be skeptical about stories such as the liberation from Egypt and the revelation at Sinai.[18] Buber insisted, however, that there are no objective ways to ascertain what "actually" took place. Despite the historian's insistence on corroborative verification, there is no a priori reason to reject the accounts of these events.

Formulated poetically and preserved by the formative, creative memory of the generations, these experiences are transmitted to us as authentic testimonies to lived events. Thus, for Buber, experiences such as the liberation from Egypt and the revelation at Sinai are real, actual events occurring in the natural world. In no way are we required to believe in the reality of a supernatural realm or in miracles that violate the processes of nature as understood by science.

Although the people who participated in these events perceived them through their normal senses, they did not experience them as natural events:

The meeting of a people with events so enormous that it cannot ascribe them to its own plans and their realization, but must perceive in them deeds performed by heavenly powers is of the genuine substance of history. (Buber, *Moses*, 16)

Owing to their fundamental faith attitude, the participants perceived the events as revelation. Yet Buber insisted that their experiences were not illusory. They reflected what people actually saw. In other words, what the texts communicate is what the partici- pants actually saw, experienced, and subsequently preserved in the memory of generations—a spontaneous, enthusiastic, formative memory.[19]

Moreover, according to Buber, if we understand the term cor- rectly, the events recorded in the Bible are historical. Insofar as they play a decisive role in shaping the consciousness and activity of subsequent generations, they are historical in the deepest sense of the word. What they portray is not an unattainable, supernatural reality but everyday moments in the lives of people:

> Whether Sinai was a volcano cannot be determined historically, nor is it historically relevant. But that the tribes gathered at the "burning moun- tain" comprehended the words of their leader Moses as a message from their God, a message that simultaneously established a covenant between them and a covenant between him and their community, is essentially an historical process, historical in the deepest sense; it is historical because it derives from historical connections and sets off fresh historical connections. (Buber, *Moses*, 17)

Revising the prevailing conception of *historical*, Buber privileged lived experiences and their immediate expressions over the de- tached, objective, analytic accounts of the modern scholars.[20]

While the traditional Jewish mode of reading the Bible viewed the text through the eyes of the rabbis, Buber, bypassing the rab- binic tradition, returned to the Bible itself and privileged it above all subsequent interpretations. In so doing, he leaped over two thousand years of tradition in an effort to recover the original roots of Israel's teachings.[21] Alongside the Hasidic writings, Buber viewed the Bible as an authentic source of the uniquely Jewish worldview.

Buber sought to counter prevailing misperceptions in the modern reader's attitude to the biblical text. To some, the Bible, like any artistic creation, is simply the outpouring of the artist's inner con- sciousness or imagination. For such readers, the Bible is metaphor or allegory. However, Buber rejected this approach, popular among liberal Jews, for reducing the Bible to the level of mere literature. Consequently, it was no longer seen as having a unique claim upon us but only as a source of historical interest or aesthetic pleasure.

The traditionalist approach, which accepts the Bible as a literal rendering of God's word, was unacceptable to Buber insofar as it demands a "sacrifice of intellect" that would cut the life of the modern reader "irreparably in two" (Buber, *Israel and the World*, 97). This view, dividing the natural from the supernatural, abstracts religion from the rest of life.

Diverging from both traditionalists and liberals, Buber insisted that modern readers could take the text seriously as religious teaching, without surrendering their intellectual integrity. Buber believed that everyone experiences moments that confirm the validity of biblical accounts. By helping the reader to recover such moments and relate them to biblical accounts, we can help to close the gap. For example, recalling moments of sudden insight or apperception can help open the modern reader to the meaning of biblical accounts of revelation. As in moments of personal insight, the person experiencing revelation is aware of receiving something. Thus, readers are able to confirm the truth of biblical passages through their own existential experience and should only accept as truth whatever in the text corresponds to that experience.[22] Rejecting Nietzsche's dictum, "One takes, one does not ask who gives" (Nietzsche, *Ecce Homo*, 102), Buber insisted that "as we take it, it is of the utmost importance to know that someone is giving" (Buber, *Israel and the World*, 98).

Buber's dialogical approach to the Bible contrasted sharply with the prevailing objectivistic biblical scholarship.[23] As a result, his biblical interpretations, like his interpretation of Hasidism, were sharply criticized by biblical scholars. At the same time, Buber, in his biblical studies, employed the very scholarly apparatus that he so consciously avoided in his Hasidic writings. Accordingly, Buber's approach to the interpretation of Scripture is inconsistent with the more radical view of interpretation reflected in his Hasidic works.

In light of the discussion in chapter 2, it is obvious that Buber's understanding of the Bible and the expressivist conception of language on which it rests also conflict with the views of contemporary literary theorists.[24] Moreover, his assumption that one can successfully strip away social and cultural conditioning and engage the text directly conflicts with contemporary theories of reading espoused by such figures as Roland Barthes.[25] As these theorists argue, and as Buber himself acknowledged with regard to his interpretation of Hasidism, all readers filter texts through the framework of the discourse and meaning that they bring to it.

The Prophet as Social Critic

In the prophetic view of history Buber found an alternative to the prevailing Western view. In the West, history focuses on the successes of nations and individuals. History, in this sense, is related to power and achievement. In contrast, the Bible focuses on failures. However, from the perspective of biblical thought, failure and success are understood differently than they are in conventional Western readings of history.

Whereas Western history celebrates the conquests and victory of kings and nations, the prophets were, in conventional terms, failures. However, while kings and emperors succeeded in conquering territories and subjugating nations, it is the prophet, the figure hidden in the quiver, who truly affects the course of events:

The real work, from the biblical point of view, is the late-recorded, the unrecorded, the anonymous work. The real work is done in the shadow, in the quiver. Official leadership fails more and more, leadership devolves more and more upon the secret. The way leads through the work which history does not write down, and which history cannot write down. (Buber, On the Bible, 150)

Biblical heroes, such as Moses or David, are not portrayed as unqualified successes. Instead, they are revealed in all of their weakness as people who fail to accomplish their primary goals. Similarly, the prophets are figures "whose existence is failure through and through. They live in failure; it is for them to fight and not to conquer. It is the fundamental experience of biblical leadership" (Buber, On the Bible, 143).

The prophetic vision of history contradicts Western notions of history. In place of the manifest history, which is measured in terms of power, military victory, and material achievement, the Bible offers a hidden history. Rather than focus on the deeds of kings or rulers, the Bible highlights the pronouncements of the prophets.

In the prophetic conception of history and of life in general, dialogue, according to Buber, is the central category. The prophets, beginning with the protoprophetic figure of Abraham, stood in a unique, dialogical relation with God. Viewing all of reality as the realm of the divine, the prophet experienced life as an ongoing relationship of address and response. Feeling addressed, the prophet, suppressing his basic instinct to flee, responded to the call. Out of this process of address and response, the prophet came to perceive earthly reality as the kingship of God.

The notion of address and response is key to understanding how the prophets perceived the political events of the day. To them, dialogue provided the frame of meaning through which the history of Israel was to be interpreted. According to this view, the meaning of events in the life of the community is not adequately grasped through political or military categories. In the conquering armies of Persia and Babylonia, the prophet saw a sign of the community's failure to heed the address.

For what the Bible understands as history is a dialogue in which man, in which the people, is spoken to and fails to answer, yet where the people, in the midst of its failure, continually rises up and tries to answer. It is the history of God's disappointments, but this history of disappointments constitutes a way, a way that leads from disappointment to disappointment, and beyond all disappointments; it is the way of the people, the way of man, yes, the way of God through mankind. (Buber, *On the Bible*, 144)

Coming to the people as the proclaimer of God's address, the prophet seeks to awaken them to the divine address and to shake them out of false refuges. However, the prophet fails; and history, understood biblically, is a recurring pattern of such failures.[26]

In his earlier lectures, Buber had posited Judaism as an alternative to the prevailing purposive, goal-oriented ethos of the modern West. In *I and Thou*, he sought to undermine the prevailing Western view of effectiveness and power. To the I-It mode of existence exalted by Western culture, he juxtaposed the I-You mode, grounded in the myths of Hasidism. Now, he brought the circle around by grounding his critique of the prevailing Western values in the Hebrew Bible. Whereas the West emphasizes and rewards power and physical conquest, the Bible emphasizes inner strength and defines victory in a different way.

At this point, the relationship between Buber's overall vision of reality and his interpretation of the biblical vision is evident. Challenging the prevailing ideas of life and success, in *I and Thou* Buber argued that genuine life is built out of I-You moments. Similarly, in the biblical view of history, "the way, the real way, from the Creation to the Kingdom, is trod not on the surface of success, but in the deep of failure" (Buber, *On the Bible*, 150). Furthermore, just as it is the melancholy of our individual lot that every I-You relation reverts to an I-It relation, it is the melancholy of our communal lot that the successes of history recede in the face of its failures.

However, just as we break through the world of I-It in moments of love and relation in our individual lives, in history, there are recurring moments of divine-human dialogue. As the individual looks forward to and holds himself or herself open for future I-You encounters, the prophet awaits the "final, messianic overcoming of history" (Buber, *On the Bible*, 150).

Hebrew Humanism:
Judaism and the Quest for True Community

In his early writings, Buber had criticized the institutionalized structures of rabbinic Judaism and had challenged his audience to confront the existential realities of Jewish nationhood. In his later writings, seeking to clarify the nature of Jewish nationalism, he engaged in an extensive revision of the concepts of Zionism, Zion, nation, nationalism, exile, and mission:

Where does Zionism stand? What came to mind first and what derived from it? Did Zionism appear first as a form of pride, or as a mission. If it was a mission (and it is not essential how you define the source of the mission, as an idea, as history, as the nation or as society; so long as you know in your heart that the thing that you seek to do, is required of you), how did the Jews carry it out? How did the Zionists fulfill it? How have I fulfilled it? (Buber, *Te'udah ve-Ye'ud* 2:226)

Buber eschewed all efforts to limit the Jewish question to an ideological issue. Like his mentor Ahad Haam, he viewed Zionism as embracing Judaism in its entirety.[27] In his earliest writings on

Zionism, under the influence of Nietzsche and *Lebensphilosophie*, he had related the idea of a Jewish renewal to the renewal of individual creativity. At that time, his primary concern was the nation's contribution to the actualization of the individual's inner strength and creative potential. However, following his shift to a relational philosophy, he redefined the task of national renewal in terms of the renewal of community.

As early as 1921, Buber had endeavored to clarify the unique nature of Israel's national existence by analyzing the concept of nation.[28] He argued that, in the absence of primordial kinship, a group can become a people through a common sense of destiny arising out of an event in which they "were shaped into a new entity by a great molding fate they experienced in common" (Buber, *Israel and the World*, 217). In such a moment, kinship can arise:

The concept "people" always implies unity of fate. It presupposes that in a great creative hour, throngs of human beings were shaped into a new entity by a great molding fate they experienced in common. This new "coined form" which in the course of subsequent events "develops as living substance," survives by dint of the kinship established from this moment on. (Buber, *Israel and the World*, 217)

In the wake of such a moment, the group preserves its common identity by means of common memory, which shapes the language, experience, and way of life of successive generations. In Buber's view, when a group develops an awareness of difference from other groups, we can begin to speak of a nation: "The term 'nation' signifies the unit 'people' from the point of view of active and conscious difference" (Buber, *Israel and the World*, 218). This sense of difference, expressed through nationalism, usually arises in a time of decisive social or political crisis.

To Buber, nationalism emerges only when a nation becomes aware of a deficiency in its existence. This deficiency may be lack of territorial security, lack of freedom, or lack of unity. At this point, a program is created to overcome the deficiency.

In a healthy nation, nationalism will recede as the deficiency is corrected. In an unhealthy nation, however, nationalism exceeds its rightful limits and becomes a permanent principle. In this situation, nationalism is no longer a response to a disease "but is itself a grave and complicated disease" (Buber, *Israel and the World*, 218).

As long as the nation is not elevated to an end in itself, nationalism may still continue to be fruitful. However, "the moment national ideology makes the nation an end in itself, it annuls its own right to live" (Buber, *Israel and the World*, 221).

The Jewish nation, according to Buber, had not yet succeeded in distinguishing between healthy and unhealthy nationalism. Striving to become a normal nation in the modern sense of the word, it had lost sight of its responsibility to humanity as a whole:

He who regards the nation as the supreme principle, as the ultimate reality, as the final judge, and does not recognize that over and above all the countless and varied peoples there is an authority named or unnamed to which communities as well as individuals must inwardly render an account of themselves, could not possibly know how to draw this distinction, even if he attempted to do so. (Buber, *Israel and the World*, 220)

Israel's consciousness of its absent homeland, fragmented social life, and stagnant culture was healthy nationalism. However, by viewing the nation as an end in itself, Jewish nationalism now confronted a crisis. To a significant degree, this crisis resulted from a confusion as to Judaism's true nature.

Israel, from its origin, was not only a people, it was also a community of faith. Accepting upon itself the responsibility to live as a kingdom of God, Israel eventually became a nation. However, its national status can only be understood in terms of its status as a community of faith. To the extent that the community was drawn into the process of secularization, it lost sight of its true foundations:

For Israel cannot be healed, and its welfare cannot be achieved by severing the concepts of people and community of faith, but only by setting up a new order including both as organic and renewed parts. (Buber, *Israel and the World*, 223)

Like Ahad Haam, Buber agreed that in order to recover an authentic national life, the Jewish people had to return to its national homeland and effect a social and cultural renaissance. Implicit in the concept of renaissance is "the idea of affirming man and the community of man, and the belief that peoples as well as individuals could be reborn" (Buber, *Israel and the World*, 240).[29] However, finding the social and cultural concerns of Ahad Haam and his followers inadequate, Buber emphasized an existential renewal on both the individual and communal levels.

To distinguish his conception of Jewish nationalism from conventional Zionist ideology, Buber coined the term *Hebrew humanism:*

I am setting up Hebrew humanism in opposition to that Jewish nationalism which regards Israel as a nation like unto other nations and recognizes no task for Israel save that of preserving and asserting itself. . . . By opposing Hebrew Humanism to a nationalism which is nothing but empty self assertion, I wish to indicate that, at this juncture, the Zionist movement must decide either for national egoism or national humanism. (Buber, *Israel and the World*, 248) [30]

Hebrew humanism differs from European humanism in two distinct ways. First, it is concerned with the total life of the individual and seeks to transform all aspects of that life. Furthermore, Hebrew humanism seeks to effect a transformation in the life of the community as a whole. Ultimately, the inner and the outer, the individual and the communal, are intertwined: "The change in the external arrangements of our life must be reflected in and renew our inner life again and again" (Buber, *Israel and the World*, 245). To distinguish artificially inner from outer or public from private is to distort the true nature of human existence. The Zionist movement, insofar as it had emphasized the public arena at the expense of the inner life of the individual, had failed.

A second difference between Hebrew humanism and European humanism revolves around the sources of their humanistic ideal. In the classics of Greece and Rome, the leaders of the European Renaissance had found the source of moral meaning and aesthetic satisfaction, as well as their historic roots. The roots of the Jewish national renewal, on the other hand, spring from the Hebrew Bible. Thus, Hebrew humanism was, at one and the same time, biblical humanism:

Biblical humanism moves from the mystery of the Hebrew language to the mystery of the Hebrew being. Biblical humanistic education means fulfillment of the one in the other. Its intent is to lead the Jew of today back to his origins. But his origins are there where he hears the voice of the Unconditional resounding in Hebrew.

Biblical humanism is concerned with a "concrete transformation" of our total—and not alone our inner—lives. This concrete transformation can only follow upon a rebirth of the normative primal forces that distinguish right from wrong, true from false, and to which life submits itself. The primal forces are transmitted to us in the work, the Biblical word. (Buber, *On the Bible*, 213)

Yearning to recover national roots, Jewish nationalists like Ahad Haam had turned to the Bible as a primary literary source. In the teachings of the prophets, they found validation for the Jewish national renewal and the longing for Zion. For Ahad Haam and other Jewish nationalists, the Bible was the primary source of national values and ideals.[31]

Buber, as we have seen, criticized the secular nationalists for ignoring the religious character of the Bible. The Bible had defined the basic character of the Jewish nation in religious terms. From the outset, Israel accepted upon itself a unique religiohistorical role, reflected in the concept of the "election of Israel." According to Buber, election implied not inherent superiority but heightened responsibility.

In its early period, the nation of Israel had understood election as living under the kingship of God. At Sinai, the community accepted Yahweh as king and pledged to subordinate its entire life to the terms of the covenant:[32]

The striving to have the entirety of its life constructed out of its relation to the divine can be actualized by a people in no other way than that, while it opens its political being and doing to the influence of this relationship, it does not fundamentally mark the limits of this relationship in advance, but only in the course of realization experiences or rather endures these limits again and again. (Buber, *Kingship of God*, 118–19)

To Buber, the concept of the covenant implied two basic ideas: the kingship of God and the hallowing of the everyday. The laws of the Torah and the teachings of the prophets seek to actualize the rule of God in all spheres of communal life. In the Bible, any dichotomy between the realm of the sacred and that of the profane is invalid. To live as a nation of God, "a kingdom of priests and a holy people" (Ex. 19:6), the community had to order its life so that all relationships between persons were hallowed. Later, Hasidism translated this idea into the concept of hallowing the everyday.

In contrast to the rabbinic tradition, which viewed the revelatory event at Sinai as the point of origin for authentic Judaism, Buber insisted that the event at Sinai represented only one particular stage of the process. Although the faith of Israel was formed through the shaping event at Sinai, the soul of Israel was pre-Sinaitic. This soul expressed itself not as law or dogma but in the fundamental faith attitude, which is already found in the patriarchal narratives:

In proclaiming its faith, its emunah, the soul only proclaimed that it put its trust in the everlasting God, that He would be present to the soul, as had been the experience of the patriarchs, and that it was entrusting itself to him, who was present. (Buber, *Israel and the World*, 29)

As early as 1918, Buber had characterized the relationship between Israel and Yahweh as an I-Thou relationship.[33] In subsequent writings, he utilized the concept of divine-human dialogue as the root metaphor of his interpretation of Judaism. In the I-Thou relationship, Buber saw the foundation of biblical faith and of all authentic Jewish teaching.

Yahweh, in encountering the community, also encountered each person individually. According to Buber, the commandments at Sinai were formulated in the singular to show that they were addressed to each person and to indicate each individual Israelite's responsibility to respond. While rabbinic tradition perceived Sinai as the event in which the group was given a specific body of law, Buber interpreted it as a dialogical event in which God addressed each You individually as well as collectively:[34]

In this dialogue, God speaks to every man through the life which he gives him again and again. Therefore, man can only answer God with the whole of life—with the way in which he lives this given life. . . . The whole of life is required, every one of its areas and every one of its circumstances. There is no true human share of holiness without the hallowing of the everyday. (Buber, *Israel and the World*, 33)

In the biblical understanding of the world genuine relationships between individuals are fostered and actualized in communities. In order to actualize the goals of creation, Yahweh turned to a specific group. In Abraham, we have the progenitor of the group that is to carry out the divine plan for humanity.

According to the biblical concept of the election of Israel, the divine plan can only be carried out by a community. Only a nation can actually model the modes of relationship required by the covenant:

For only an entire nation, which comprehends peoples of all kinds, can demonstrate a life of unity and peace, of righteousness and justice to the human race, as a sort of example and beginning. A true humanity, that is, a nation composed of many nations, can only commence with a certain definite and true nation. Only the fulfillment of this truth in the relations between the various sections of this people, between its sects and classes, capable of serving as a commencement of international fulfillment of the truth and of the development of a true fellowship of nations, a nation consisting of nations. (Buber, *Israel and the World*, 186–87)

The concepts of relation, dialogue, and community provided Buber with the foundations for his later interpretation of the people Israel and of Judaism. To actualize itself as a nation, Israel must live a life characterized by genuine relation and community. Israel fulfills its responsibility as a nation to the extent that it actualizes in its group life genuine, nonexploitative, confirming relations between persons. To hallow the everyday, one must foster genuine relations. In this way, the divine is actualized in daily life.

For the people of Israel, the land of Israel serves as the necessary precondition to fulfilling its task in the world. To actualize just and true relations fully in its everyday life, the nation requires a land of its own where it can establish communities that enjoy a full life.

How is it given to fulfill this truth if not by building the social pattern of our own people in Palestine all the way, from the pattern of family, neighborhood and settlement to that of the whole community? For it is no real community if it is not composed of real families and real neighborhoods and real settlements, and it is not a real nation if it does not maintain its truthfulness in true relations as well, the relationships of a fruitful and creative peace with its neighbors. (Buber, *Israel and the World*, 193)

Thus, to live as a Jew, individually and collectively, means to dedicate one's life to actualizing genuine relation in all spheres of life. This could be achieved most effectively in the Jewish homeland, where Jewish community is concretized in the social and cultural framework. As the Bible and Hasidism understood, Jewish living is a comprehensive mode of life encompassing national consciousness and devotion to the nation's historic vocation. Being a member of the nation in no way relieves the individual of responsibility for daily decisions. Above one's responsibility to the group stands one's responsibility to God. By hiding behind nationalistic slogans or high-minded principles, the individual Jew evades this responsibility.

Although Jewish goals could be concretized most fully in the Jewish homeland, where Jews lived as an autonomous community, Buber did not negate the possibilities of Jewish living outside of the homeland. As Hasidism had demonstrated, Jews could actualize their Jewishness wherever they lived. By hallowing the everyday relationships, Jews everywhere could actualize their unique task:

The higher, the decisive principle, which alone can knit together the relationship to God and the relationship to man—the principle of love— requires neither organizations nor institutions but can be given effect at any time, at any place. . . . Within the communal forms adopted in place of a state—that is, the local communities—active love, in the guise of mutual help, recurs as a basic social element. (Buber, *On Judaism*, 212)

As we have already noted, Buber refused to formulate responsibility into specific principles and actions. To his critics, this posed the danger of anarchy.[35] Nevertheless, Buber consistently rejected packaged solutions. Neither the individual nor the group can decide which is the right action prior to the actual situation.

Contrary to all ideologies and moral systems that prescribe normative patterns of behavior and coherent value systems, Buber insisted that the life of the individual and the community was based upon ongoing decision making. Everyday, the community had the responsibility of reexamining its choices and of drawing anew the "line of demarcation" separating the just action from the unjust action:

The fatal question does not take the form of a fundamental Either-Or; it is only a question of the right line of demarcation that has to be drawn ever anew—the thousandfold system of demarcation between the spheres which must of necessity be centralized and those which must operate in freedom; between the degree of government and the degree of autonomy; between the law of unity and the claim of community. (Buber, *Paths in Utopia*, 134)[36]

Testing the Teachings:
Buber as Social Critic

In Buber's own life, the truth of his teachings was tested in three distinct historical situations. In the earliest period of his life, he confronted the crisis of personal alienation and doubt. As we saw in chapter 3, he responded to this crisis by revising the teachings of Judaism in search of a way out of his alienation. As a writer and educator, he inspired a generation of young Jews and awakened them to the power of Judaism to renew the Jewish people and its culture.

Dissatisfied with abstract moralizing, Buber actively applied his ideas to the social and political situations in which he lived. During the 1930s, his philosophy was tested in the critical circumstances of the beleaguered German Jewish community. Buber responded by leading the effort to help the community find the inner spiritual power that would enable it to withstand the terror and oppression. Through personal teaching and communal leadership, Buber served as a pivotal point of German Jewry's spiritual resistance.[37]

Organizing schools, delivering lectures, publishing scholarly and inspirational tracts, and defending Judaism against the attacks of anti-Semitic critics, Buber played a vital role in helping the German Jewish community to maintain its morale in a time of growing fear and intimidation. Repeatedly, he urged Jews to adhere to their people and to embrace the teachings of Judaism by accepting the prophetic demand of choice and responsibility.[38]

Through teaching and writing, he undertook to bolster the sagging morale of German Jewry, serving as a source of strength in the face of growing violence, terror, and oppression.[39] In spite of ongoing harassment and threats, Buber refused to yield to the physical power of the Nazis. Throughout the period, he sought to comfort and sustain the community by drawing upon the teachings of the prophets and by advocating spiritual power. As the prophets had taught, what might appear on the surface to be failure and defeat is, when viewed in the proper perspective, a victory of the spirit.

However, not until his arrival in the land of Israel when the various strands of his social and religious thought converged with social reality, did Buber clearly emerge as a social critic. Criticizing those intellectuals who subordinated themselves to the prevailing forms of power, Buber insisted that the responsibility of intellectuals, like all people, was to transform ideas into reality by critically engaging the issues of everyday social and political life:

The intellect can be redeemed from its last lapse into sin, from the desecration of the word, only if the word is backed and vouched for with the whole of one's life. . . . No matter how brilliant it may be, the human intellect which wishes to keep a plane above the events of the day is not really alive. It can become fruitful, beget life, and live only when it enters into the events of the day. (Buber, *Land of Two Peoples*, 103) [40]

In addition to articulating his critique in articles and books, Buber engaged in public debate with the leaders of the Zionist movement and, after 1948, with the leaders of the newly established state of Israel. Buber continually confronted the Jewish community in Israel with the standards derived from his reading of the Bible. The return of the Jewish people to its homeland was not simply a venture in the rebirth of national power. Israel, from the time of its emergence, had perceived of its history in terms of a unique task, the establishment of a just community. Accordingly, Israel had continually to apply to itself different standards from those other nations used.

In the land of Israel, the truth of Buber's religious faith and commitment received its most serious test. There, his criticisms of the Zionist leadership acquired a practical force not possible in Europe where Jews as a community lacked political power. Living in the midst of a sizable Jewish population, which, as a community, exercised a distinct political, social, and economic influence in the country, Buber's criticisms acquired a social import previously missing. No longer addressing an ideological movement with virtually no political power, Buber's critical statements were now directed to the social and political realities of an emerging state.

As the dream of a Jewish homeland changed from ideal to reality, new challenges arose. Confronted with a Jewish state struggling to survive, Buber found himself challenged by conditions that daily threatened his own Zionist vision. With only a small group of colleagues and disciples to share his concept of Zion, he endeavored to carry out in practice the humanistic vision espoused in his writings.[41]

The challenges that confronted Buber in the Jewish homeland assumed several forms. First, there was the struggle between competing visions of Zion. On the one side stood David Ben Gurion and other political leaders, who elevated the nation and the state to the level of an ultimate value. On the other side was a small group that, in the spirit of Ahad Haam, considered the Jewish people to be the bearers of a unique moral responsibility and task to which all political strivings had to be subordinated.[42] Buber participated in this struggle, as we have seen, by articulating his unique conception of Hebrew humanism.

A second conflict, directly related to the first, concerned the character of Judaism. In Israel, the protaganists in this conflict were the religious traditionalists and the secular nationalists. As we have seen, Buber's interpretation of Judaism diverged from both of these camps. Refusing to concede to either camp the right to define Judaism, Buber argued vehemently for a unique synthesis of personal religious faith and communal consciousness.

A third conflict that challenged Buber's vision was the debate over the character of the newly emerging society in Israel. Only a small group endorsed Buber's socialist-humanist vision, which I have discussed in chapter 6. In contrast to Buber's concept of a federation of small communes, Israeli society developed around urban centers and private enterprise. The kibbutzim, which Buber regarded as the most successful experiment to date in communal living, were few in number and limited in influence.[43]

However, the most severe and demanding test for Buber's conception of Judaism and Jewish nationhood was the conflict between Jews and Arabs. In its relationship with the Arabs, the Jewish people faced the most serious test of its ability to actualize the prophetic vision of a just society. For Buber, this tragic conflict was the ultimate testing ground of Judaism and Zionism.[44]

The problem of how to relate to the Arabs had constituted an ongoing dilemma for the leaders of the Zionist movement. Among Jewish leaders, four basic positions emerged concerning the Arabs prior to the establishment of the Jewish state.[45] At one end of the spectrum, advocating a position of separatism and political domination, were the Revisionists led by Vladimir Jabotinsky. Acknowledging the force of Arab nationalist aspirations, Jabotinsky and his followers argued that only military control over the Arabs could ensure the survival of a Jewish homeland.

A more moderate, liberal position was adopted by leaders of the gradualist wing of practical Zionism, such as Haim Weizmann and David Ben Gurion. However, although espousing a humane policy toward the Arabs in Palestine, the liberals tended to deny the legitimacy of the Palestinian Arabs' nationalist aspirations. Convinced that the nationalist aspirations of Palestinian Arabs would decline as their socioeconomic position improved, they continually insisted on a Jewish homeland with a Jewish majority.

The left-wing Socialist-Zionists, including Ha-Shomer ha-Za'ir and Poelei Zion, identified with the Arab workers who were being exploited by the feudal effendis. Dedicated to helping a strong proletarian movement to emerge among the Arabs, they considered Zionism to be the major force for progress and Socialism in the Middle East. Nevertheless, the Socialist Zionists of the revolutionary left did not cease to advocate ongoing Jewish immigration and settlement, both of which were anathema to the Arabs.

The fourth group, representing the altruistic-integrative approach, was the group with which Buber identified and whose position he played an instrumental role in formulating. As early as 1921, Buber offered a resolution to the Twelfth Zionist Congress on the Arab question on behalf of the party, Hitahdut ha-Poel ha-Za'ir u'Ze'irei Zion. The resolution declared that the Jewish homeland would not be achieved at the expense of the rights of the Arab population:[46]

We do not aspire to return to the Land of Israel with which we have inseparable historical and spiritual ties in order to suppress another people or to dominate them. . . . Our return to the land of Israel, which will come about through increasing immigration and constant growth, will not be achieved at the expense of other people's rights. By establishing a just alliance with the Arab peoples, we wish to turn our common dwelling-place into a community that will flourish economically and culturally, and whose progress would bring each of these peoples unhampered independent development. (Buber, *Land of Two Peoples*, 61)

This statement contained Buber's basic views on the Arab-Jewish struggle. Although defending the right of the Jews to their homeland, he simultaneously acknowledged a similar right for the Palestinian Arabs. Accordingly, Buber insisted that Zionism reject any approach to settlement of the land that suppressed or dominated the Arab population.

Buber was adamant that Jewish settlement encompass an actual living together with the Arabs rather than merely living in physical proximity. The formulation of the Jewish claim and the way in

which it was to be actualized had to be shaped by a recognition of
the validity of the Arab claim to the land. In contrast to the majority of Zionists, he rejected the idea that the Jews could only fulfill
their task as a nation through a Jewish state. The validity of the
Arab claims precluded the possibility of a state in which Jews would
exercise political control. Instead, Buber, until 1948, advocated a
binational state in which Jews and Arabs could live "on the basis of
absolute political equality of two culturally autonomous peoples"
(Buber, *Land of Two Peoples*, 74).

A bi-national social-political entity, with its areas of settlement defined
and limited as clearly as possible, and with in addition economic cooperation to the greatest possible extent; with complete equality of rights between the two partners, disregarding the changing numerical relationship
between them; and with joint sovereignty founded upon these principles—
such an entity would provide both peoples with all that they truly need.
(Buber, *Land of Two Peoples*, 199)

This binational state would eventually form part of a federation of
Middle Eastern states.

Nevertheless, Buber never denied the claim of the Jewish people
to the land of Israel. Historic links to the land, the reclamation of
the land by the Jewish settlers, and the Jewish people's right to
fulfill its task among the nations of the world all served, in his view,
to validate the Jewish claim.[47]

We considered it a fundamental point that in this case two vital claims are
opposed to each other, two claims of a different nature and origin, which
cannot be pitted one against the other and between which no objective
decision can be made as to which is just or unjust. We considered and still
consider it our duty to understand and honor the claim which is opposed to
ours and to endeavor to reconcile both claims. (Buber, *Land of Two Peoples*, 120)[48]

Viewing the Arab-Israeli crisis within the framework of his overall social philosophy, Buber argued that Jewish-Arab relations had
fallen victim to politicization. Rather than confirm the basic humanity of the Arabs and recognize the validity of their aspirations
to national autonomy, the Zionist leaders had dehumanized the
Arabs through political slogans. The task, as he saw it, was to
depoliticize the Arab-Jewish conflict and restore it to the realm of
everyday relations between persons:

We must fight against the excessive growth of politics, must fight it from within, from a position within politics' own domain. Our objective is to eliminate the political surplus conflict, the imaginary conflict, to bare the real interests, to make known the true bonds of the conflict between interests. . . . The only hope is to establish institutions which accord supremacy to the demands of life over the demands of politics and which thereby provide us with a real and substantial base from which to explain the truth. (Buber, *Land of Two Peoples*, 188)

Buber's writings on Zionism and the Jewish state can only be understood in relation to his understanding of the Bible. The teachings of the prophets were not relics of a distant past but the foundations for life in the present. The meaning of modern Israel could only be understood in light of these teachings. Consequently, as previously discussed, the recovery of the Bible constituted one of the major tasks for the Jewish people in its quest for renewal. To Buber, this recovery meant a constant dialogue between the realities of the present and the teachings of the past.

Buber refused to yield to the politicians the right to set the conditions for the fulfillment of the Zionist dream. Continually, through public and private debate, he sought to persuade the leaders of the nation that the way they had chosen was disastrous.[49] If the Arab-Jewish conflict was to be resolved, the discussion had to be shifted from the framework of power politics to the sphere of human relationships. Only if that were accomplished would a solution be forthcoming. One prerequisite for the discussion, which derives directly from the philosophy of dialogue, was for Jews to make the Arabs present by imagining the situation as it appeared to them. This entailed a recognition of the Arabs as a people which, like the Jews, had a valid claim to the land. Moreover, it necessitated abolishing the false categories and stereotypes that shaped the Arab-Jewish confrontation and recognizing the basic humanity of the Arabs.

Insofar as living in a Jewish way entails striving to actualize genuine dialogue and genuine community in all facets of life, the Jewish community in its homeland must structure its social life in such a way that dialogue and community become real. The principles of justice and righteousness that were the basis of the Bible's understanding of the Jewish people's task had to become manifest in all of the dimensions of community life.

To the overwhelming majority of Jews living in Palestine, Buber and his colleagues were guilty of ignoring social, political, and military realities. To these Jews, the Arab attacks were violent criminal acts perpetrated against a guiltless minority who wanted nothing more than to live in peace. According to the prevailing Jewish view, Arab violence against the Jews derived from the Arabs' ignorance of authentic Zionist aspirations and/or from the violent, uncivilized Arab character.

Buber and his colleagues vehemently dissented from the conventional wisdom. According to Buber, if the Arabs of Palestine were reacting violently to Jewish settlement then much of the responsibility belonged to the Jews:

We have not settled Palestine together with the Arabs but alongside them. Settlement "alongside" [neben], when two nations inhabit the same country, which fails to become settlement "together with" [mit] must necessarily become a state of "against." (Buber, Land of Two Peoples, 91)

According to Buber, Arab attacks on Jews had to be understood in light of the Zionists' failure to establish a relationship of "genuine togetherness [Miteinanderleben] with the Arabs" (Buber, Land of Two Peoples, 93).

In the face of continued violence, Buber espoused the justice of the Arab claim. In the wake of the 1929 riots, he contended that "perhaps we ourselves provided the motive for the religious fanaticism of the [Arab] masses" (Buber, Land of Two Peoples, 94), a position most Jews viewed as nothing short of treason. At the same time, he continually criticized the Jewish community for employing physical violence.

Buber insisted that the means adopted by the Jews had a profound influence on the ends achieved:

Herein lies the foulest and the most fraudulent deception of all: that it is possible to achieve redemption through sin, if the sin is at all intended from the beginning to redeem. If the people justifies the murder, identifies with the perpetrators, and thus accepts responsibility for the sin as its own, we will bequeath to our children not a free and pure land but a thieves' den to live in and raise their children in. (Buber, Land of Two Peoples, 133)

Consequently, opposing all calls for violence against the Arabs and against the British Mandate authorities, Buber insisted that the community adhere to the policy of *havlagah* (restraint) espoused by most of the Jewish leaders.

Buber's views were bound to arouse violent responses. Even in 1948, as the newly formed Jewish state struggled to survive the Arab attack, he refused to acquiesce to the conventional wisdom that the Jews were the victims of an unprovoked attack. According to his reading of history, the Jewish claim that their settlement of the land had been peaceful was a distortion. The Arabs who were attacking the Jews "felt that they had been attacked by us, namely, by our peaceful conquest" (Buber, *Land of Two Peoples*, 227). Acknowledging the validity of this perception, Buber insisted that

the truth of the matter is that, when we started our infiltration into the country, we began an attack "by peaceful means." We did so because we were forced to, in order that we might reestablish an independent productive and dignified life for our people. (Buber, *Land of Two Peoples*, 227) [50]

Buber's metaphor of peaceful invasion was based upon several assumptions. First, the Jews had failed to attempt to reach an agreement with the Arabs regarding the terms of ongoing Jewish settlement. In addition, they had failed to convince the Arabs of their common interests through mutually beneficial economic activity. Instead, the Jews purchased land from wealthy land owners and took over the dominant economic positions at the expense of the Arab population at large. Finally, instead of deferring all political actions and proclamations until the foundation for a binational state had been established, the Jews insisted on establishing a Jewish state.[51] According to Buber, these factors created and fortified among the Palestinian Arabs a view of Jews as invaders bent upon dispossessing the Arab masses.

When the state of Israel was proclaimed in 1948, Buber and his supporters, admitting their failure to achieve a binational state, somewhat reluctantly embraced the new Jewish state. Buber recognized that the destruction of six million Jews in Europe and the need of masses of Jewish refugees for a home created pressures that were virtually impossible to resist. Still, he insisted that "our historical re-entry into our land took place through a false gateway" (Buber, *Land of Two Peoples*, 291). However, once he emphatically proclaimed that he "accepted as mine the State of Israel," he had "nothing in common with those Jews who imagine that they may contest the factual shape which Jewish independence has taken" (Buber, *Land of Two Peoples*, 292–93).

Following the emergence of the state of Israel, Buber sustained an ongoing dispute with the government leaders. In a series of debates with prime minister David Ben Gurion, Buber continually protested the politicization of Zionism and the elevation of the state to a supreme value.[52] Unwilling to allow the debate to remain on the level of generalities, he criticized specific governmental actions and policies.[53]

Buber and his colleagues in *Ichud* demanded the repatriation of Arab refugees who had fled from Israel in 1948. In addition, he campaigned vehemently for the abolition of the military controls that had been imposed on Israeli Arabs, who were "deprived of the rule of civil law that applies to the rest of the population" (Buber, *Land of Two Peoples*, 284). Moreover, Buber spoke out publicly in several instances when Israeli military forces had killed Arab civilians.[54] Similarly, Buber criticized the government for confiscating Arab lands in order to build a Jewish development town (Buber, *Land of Two Peoples*, 301).

Responding to Ben Gurion's argument concerning the economic, social, and educational benefits that the Arabs of Israel enjoyed, Buber insisted that such benefits did not justify the loss of equality and dignity that the Arabs suffered. Buber acknowledged that the Jewish state, like any state, could not avoid injustice. Like the will to power and domination, injustice is an intrinsic part of human society:

It is indeed true that there can be no life without injustice. The fact that there is no living creature which can live and thrive without destroying another existing organism has a symbolic significance as regards our human life. (Buber, *Land of Two Peoples*, 86)

However, the inevitability of injustice did not give the Israeli government the right to abdicate its responsibility to strive for justice. Ultimately, any nation is responsible to live in such a way as to limit injustice to the absolute minimum amount necessary for it to exist:

A person commences to be truly human when he pictures to himself the results of his actions and, accordingly, attempts to encroach upon other creatures as little as necessary. . . . We cannot refrain from doing injustice altogether, but we are given the grace of not having to do more injustice than absolutely necessary. And this in none other than the grace which is accorded to us: humanity. (Buber, *Land of Two Peoples*, 170)

Accordingly, the Jewish people must daily confront the responsibility of redrawing the line of demarcation between just and unjust acts. In the face of this ongoing responsibility, political slogans were totally inadequate. Nor would abstract principles suffice. Every day, leaders and citizens alike must accept their human responsibility and choose.

Buber rejected the conventional view, which saw the problem of Israel's survival solely in physical and military terms. To him, the true test of the Jewish people was moral and religious and revolved around the Jews' ability to achieve a genuine peace with the Arabs:

There can be no peace between Jews and Arabs that is merely a cessation of war; there can only be a peace of genuine cooperation. Today, under circumstances so manifoldly aggravated, the command of the spirit is to pave the way for the cooperation of peoples. (Ben Ezer, *Unease in Zion*, 120)

Concluding Reflections

My discussion of Buber's activities as a social critic in Israel is an appropriate place to conclude my analysis of his social and religious thought. Buber the philosopher cannot be understood independently of Buber the social critic. Just as his philosophical writings provide the conceptual underpinnings to his social thought, his social criticism represents the culmination of his philosophical teachings. If the force of Buber's philosophical anthropology most clearly emerges in the work of those who seek to heal the pain of mental suffering, the implications of his social thought are most clearly evident in his own efforts to address the ills of the society in which he lived.

Buber did not regard truth as an ideal vision to be actualized in the future. People actualize truth in the situation in which they stand at any particular moment. Concerning the truth people must ask, how can we accomplish it from where we are? To paraphrase a comment Buber once made about Judaism, not truth as idea nor truth as shape or form, but truth as deed is our task. Accordingly, one best understands Buber's thought when one recognizes that its appropriate testing ground is not to be found in university classrooms or the scholar's study; Buber tested his ideas in the laboratory of everyday human relationships, in the daily encounters between persons.

As a citizen of Israel, Buber insisted that he and his fellow citizens draw anew the line of demarcation every day. Although Buber consistently refused to prescribe the precise way that one should draw that line, his philosophical writings provide the orientation or framework through which to approach such decisions. Although recognizing the inescapability of injustice, he insisted that people do all in their power to confirm the basic humanity of the other, and to remain perpetually open to the possibility of genuine dialogue.

Since Buber's death in 1965, the political situation in his homeland, Israel, has become far graver. To many people, Israel's staggering victory in 1967, two years after Buber's death, appeared to confirm the illusory nature of Buber's vision. For a brief moment it seemed as if peace could be secured through military means.

However, the Palestinian uprising that began in December 1987, and that continues as these words are being written, confirms Buber's skepticism of the efficacy of military and political solutions. Nurtured by twenty-one years of occupation and humiliation, a new generation of Palestinians has arisen. Their pent-up frustration has exploded into violent acts of protest realizing Buber's worst fears. Young Israeli men and women, the youth to whom Buber felt particularly close during the last years of his life, are being called upon to repress the Palestinian population and to quell its nationalist yearnings.

While many see the uprising as further proof that military strength alone can assure the security of the Jewish state, others acknowledge the inviability of a Jewish state whose existence depends upon the continued control of a resistant population of more than one million people. As Buber had anticipated, this situation has a devastating impact on the moral fiber of the state. Nonetheless now, as during his lifetime, those Israelis who are drawn to Buber's teachings experience a profound sense of frustration. Wishing to enter into dialogue with their Arab brothers and sisters, these Israelis find few Palestinians in positions of leadership willing to respond. Consequently, those who advocate military or political solutions appear to hold a more realistic position. With all the difficulties that they entail, military and political solutions seem to be far more attainable than genuine dialogue between peoples.

Yet, there is a growing number of people who see recent events as validating Buber's claim that "there can be no peace between Jews and Arabs that is merely a cessation of war." To such people, the outbreaks of violence in the West Bank and Gaza are ample proof that an imposed peace, one that does not rest upon the mutual recognition of the humanity of the other, is illusory. Notwithstanding what takes place in the corridors of international diplomacy and regardless of the solutions effected through the exercise of force and power, the strife between peoples can only be resolved if we direct our attention to the realm of the interhuman—person with person.

Were Buber still alive, he would undoubtedly respond to today's problems as he did to those in his own time. As he wrote four months before his death, it is time to take the decision out of the hands of the politicians and the military:

It is indeed necessary that spiritual [intellectual as opposed to political] representatives of the two peoples enter into a true dialogue with one another, a dialogue based on shared sincerity and mutual recognition alike. . . . If here and now a dialogue between such persons will come about, its significance will spread far beyond the boundaries of the Near East; it may show whether in this late hour of history the spirit of humankind can influence our destiny. (Buber, *Land of Two Peoples*, 305)

Notes

1. One notable exception in the social sciences is Turner, *Ritual Process*, 125–45. See also Turner's *Dramas, Fields, and Metaphors*, 46–47, 251, and 274. Turner's use of Buber is discussed in chapter 6.
2. On Buber's influence on contemporary psychotherapists see chapter 5, 157–64.
3. Buber, *I and Thou*.
4. Schilpp and Friedman, *Philosophy of Martin Buber*, 693 (hereafter referred to as *PMB*); Friedman, "Interrogation of Martin Buber," in Rome and Rome, *Philosophical Interrogations*, 17.
5. Buber's name does not appear in the indices of the seminal work by Guttmann, *Philosophies of Judaism*, or in Rotenstreich, *Jewish Philosophy*. In Rotenstreich's earlier two-volume Hebrew work, *Jewish Thought in Modern Times* (Tel Aviv: Am Oved, 1945), a predecessor to the English edition, mention is made of Buber's contribution to Jewish nationalist thought. Brief references to Buber's religious philosophy appear only in the context of his discussion of Rosenzweig.

   For recent comments on this dilemma see the brief remarks of Robert Gordis in *Judaism* 27, no. 2 (spring 1978): 131–32 and Simon, "Builder of Bridges," 148–60, originally published in Hebrew in 1958.
6. Buber's position within Israeli society is discussed by Ben Chorin, "Buber in Jerusalem." The problem is also discussed by several of the participants in the symposium held at Ben Gurion University of the Negev, in January 1978. See Bloch and Gordon, *Martin Buber*, especially xvii. In the same volume, see Walter Kaufmann, "Buber's Failures and Triumph," 3–8; Haim Gordon, "The Sheltered Aesthete: A New Appraisal of Martin Buber's Life," 25–39; and Menahem Dorman, "Martin Buber's Address 'Herut' and Its Influence on the Jewish Youth Movement in Germany," 233–51. For a recent discussion supportive of Buber see Paul Mendes-Flohr, "Martin Buber's Reception among Jews."

7. For Buber's influence on the kibbutz movement see the article by Dorman, referred to above, n. 6. See also Shlomo Lilker, *Kibbutz Judaism*. Buber's interaction with young kibbutzniks during the last few years of his life is discussed by Avraham Shapira in "Meetings with Buber." The Hebrew reader is referred to "Buber's Meeting with Second Generation Kibbutzniks," in Shapira, *Khan ve-'Akhshav*, 44–51; and in the same volume, Menahem Gerson, "Buber and the Kibbutz of Today," 36–43.

8. Jacob Agus, *Modern Philosophies*. Agus, one of the earliest, if not the earliest American Jewish thinker to treat Buber seriously, nevertheless observed that "uprooted from the soil of German philosophy, Buber's influence has waned considerably in recent years" (ibid., 214). By the time the volume was reissued in 1970, Agus had occasion to note in the foreword, "Buber's influence has grown immensely and the fertility of his basic intuition has been amply demonstrated" (ibid.). In *Judaism and Modern Man*, a work permeated with Buber's influence, Will Herberg noted: "To Martin Buber and Franz Rosenzweig, I owe not only my basic 'existentialist' approach but also—and here I can never sufficiently express my gratitude—my understanding of how to establish my religious existence in the modern world" (x). In the following decade, Cohen, *The Natural and the Supernatural Jew*, and Borowitz, *A New Jewish Theology*, each included lengthy discussions of Buber, although primarily from a theological perspective.

9. "The State of Jewish Belief: A Symposium," *Commentary* 42, no. 2 (August 1966): 72. The symposium was reprinted as a separate volume, the editors of *Commentary* magazine, *The Condition of Jewish Belief* (Toronto: Macmillan, 1966).

10. These criticisms and Buber's response to them are discussed in chapter 2. See also my article, "The Buber-Scholem Debate."

11. This approach characterizes the writings of Maurice Friedman. See Maurice Friedman, *Martin Buber*. Friedman, the first to publish an extensive study of Buber in English, based his work on the centrality of dialogue in Buber. While making Buber available to an English-reading public, Friedman's work suffers from a lack of critical perspective, a sense of development, and historical contextualization. These last two shortcomings have been corrected to a degree in Friedman's recent three-volume biography, *Martin Buber's Life and Work*. However, while providing historical background and tracing the stages of Buber's thought, the biographical interpretation is grounded in a teleology that views everything in Buber's early writings as leading up to *I and Thou*.

Ernst Simon, an astute student of Buber, also considered the category of dialogue as fundamental to Buber's thought. See Simon, "From Dialogue to Peace." In focusing on the concept of dialogue, Simon was simply following Buber's own summary in *PMB*, 743–44. One of the few discussions to emphasize the motif of alienation in Buber is Kaplan,

"Buber and Otherness." See also Walter Kaufmann's introduction to Schacht, *Alienation*, xviii.

12. Lukes, "Alienation and Anomie," 140.
13. Taylor, *Hegel and Modern Society*, 90.
14. The problems associated with the concept of intentionality have been discussed by many contemporary literary critics. For a convenient summary of the contemporary objections from a Marxist perspective see Eagleton, *Literary Theory*, 67–88. See also Culler, *Pursuit of Signs*, chaps. 2–3; and Culler, *On Deconstruction*, 122–28. For some philosophical considerations of the problem see Stout, "Meaning of Text" and Dworkin, "Law." Dworkin has some interesting things to say about the effect of a writer's later writings on our reading of his or her earlier works on pp. 257–61.
15. A recent exception is Bernard Susser's *Existence and Utopia*. In Hebrew, see Yasour, *Buber's Social Philosophy*, and his essay, "Buber's Social Thought and Kibbutz Research." See also the Hebrew collection, *Martin Buber and the Kibbutz*. In the recently reprinted Hebrew edition of Buber's *Paths in Utopia (Netivot be-'Utopia,* 276–314), Avraham Shapira's essay, "Hevrutot Mithavot ve-Tikkun Olam," provides an illuminating interpretation of Buber's social thought. However, Shapira's work emphasizes the Zionist dimension of Buber's thought. Yasour, who discusses Buber's grounding in German social theory, relates this to his overall philosophical enterprise only in passing.
16. Barrett, *Irrational Man*, 36.
17. Simon is one of the only interpreters of Buber to pay attention to the relationship between Buber and Weber, see Simon, "Buber and German Jewry."
18. Rorty, *Mirror*. The ensuing discussion is indebted to Rorty. I discuss the concept of edifying philosopher as it relates to Buber in chapter 4, 104–7.
19. Rorty, *Mirror*, 12.
20. Ibid., 360. A similar conception of philosophizing is discussed by Cavell in "Existentialism" and by Pitkin in *Wittgenstein and Justice*; see especially chap. 14 in the latter.
21. Culler, *On Deconstruction*, 180. Modern writers on deconstruction agree that Nietzsche's writings are a basic source of this movement. See, for example, Norris, *Deconstruction*, chap. 4; and Spivak's preface to her translation of Jacques Derrida's *Of Grammatology*. On Buber's early attraction to Nietzsche's deconstructionist tendencies, see chapter 1, 25–29.
22. In his afterword to *I and Thou*, Buber wrote of the need to "sometimes step out of our habits of thought" (177). However, in contrast to Nietzsche, Buber, as we shall see, not content to unmask the inconsistencies and disjunctures in Western culture, wished to find a way to move beyond them.

23. For the analogy of edifying philosophy and conversation see Rorty, *Mirror*, 373: "Edifying philosophy aims at continuing a conversation rather than at discovering truth."

24. Rome and Rome, *Philosophical Interrogations*, 84–85. As Robert Wood observes, "Buber's fundamental position is an 'ism' and yet not an 'ism'. It is an 'ism' because it is a position that stands against other positions; it is not an 'ism' because it points to a place and calls for an action, but it claims no exhaustive insight into ultimates—indeed, it denies that such insight is even possible" (Wood, *Buber's Ontology*, 110). The reactive nature of Buber's thought and his rejection of any possible knowledge of ultimates are additional characteristics of the edifying philosopher.

25. See Bloom, *Anxiety*; Bloom, *Kabbalah*; and Bloom, *Agon*. See chapter 3 for further clarification of this concept. For readers familiar with the history of Zionism, it should be obvious that this use of the term *revisionist* has no connection to the militant Revisionist Zionism of Vladimir Jabotinsky and his followers, which Buber detested.

26. On the concept of strong reader, see chapter 2, and the references cited there in n. 2.

27. See above, n. 25.

28. See the discussion of dialogue and community in Bernstein, *Beyond Objectivism*, preface, 223–31; and Bernstein, *Philosophical Profiles* (Philadelphia: University of Pennsylvania Press, 1986), 94–114, 260–72. In his introduction to the former volume Bernstein comments, "Playing off the strengths and weaknesses of Gadamer, Habermas, Rorty and Arendt, I show how an underlying common vision emerges, one that illuminates the dialogical character of our human existence and our communicative transactions, and that points to the practical need to cultivate dialogical communities" (xv). Although Bernstein's conception of dialogue differs significantly from Buber's, a critical comparison of these two interpretations could yield valuable results.

29. See Carol Gilligan, *In a Different Voice: Psychological Theory and Women's Development* (Cambridge: Harvard University Press, 1982). Gilligan finds that women tend to define identity "in the context of relationship and judged by a standard of responsibility and care. Similarly, morality is seen by these women as arising from the experience of connection and conceived of the problem of inclusion rather than one of balancing claims" (160). Nel Noddings, *Caring: A Feminine Approach to Ethics and Moral Education* (Berkeley and Los Angeles: University of California Press, 1984). Noddings, who attempts to develop an ethic of caring rooted in relation, refers to Buber throughout the book. Jean Baker Miller, *Toward a New Psychology of Being* (Boston: Beacon Press, 1976). Miller argues that a women's sense of self is organized around the ability to maintain relationships and affiliations, and that the "disruption of an affiliation is perceived not as just a loss

of a relationship, but as something closer to a total loss of self" (83). See also Marilyn French, *Beyond Power: On Women, Men and Morals* (New York: Summit Books, 1985). A theory of development and learning based upon caring and relationship is formulated in Mary Field Belenky, Blyth McVicker Clincy, Nancy Rule Goldberger, and Jill Matlock Tarule, *Women's Ways of Knowing: The Development of Self, Voice and Mind* (New York: Basic Books, 1986).

CHAPTER ONE

1. For a critical discussion of the concept of alienation, see Schacht, *Alienation*; Taylor, *Hegel and Modern Society*, chap. 2; and Avineri, *Hegel's Theory*, chap. 5. An inclusive selection of writings on alienation is found in Josephson and Josephson, *Man Alone*. For a systematic analysis of the concept see Lukes, "Alienation and Anomie." See also Feuer, "What is Alienation?"
2. Heinemann, *Existentialism*, 9.
3. In no way is this intended as a representation of Buber's conscious intention. As Bloom and others have shown, multiple factors contribute to the development of a persons' intellectual position. On the problem of intention in writing and thought see above, Introduction, n. 14. Insofar as all reading is interpretive, my interpretation is but one of the many viable ways one can read Buber. The question is not whether any particular interpretation is the "right reading," but rather, which interpretation provides the reader with insights into Buber's thought.
4. Lukes, "Alienation and Anomie," 140.
5. Buber discussed this estrangement from Jewish tradition in "My Way to Hasidism," in *Hasidism and Modern Man* (hereafter referred to as *HMM*). For a critical analysis of Buber's relationship to Jewish tradition by a close friend and colleague, see Simon, "Buber and the Faith of Israel," in Simon, *Aims, Junctures, Paths*, 87–142.
6. For a discussion of the radical change in values among the fin de siècle generation, see the fine study by Schorske, *Vienna*. Additional insight into the cultural environment of the period is found in Janik and Toulmin, *Wittgenstein's Vienna*. See also Zweig, *World of Yesterday*.
7. Schorske, *Vienna*, xxvi.
8. For an English translation, see Buber, "Viennese Literature." Buber's early intellectual background is discussed in Hans Kohn, *Martin Buber: Sein Werk und Seine Zeit*, chaps. 1–2; and Friedman, *Buber's Life and Work*, vol. 1, chap. 1.
9. For Buber's relationship to Von Hofmannsthal, see Buber, *Briefwechsel*, vol. 1, letters 88, 93–95, 102–3; vol. 2, letters 210, 214–15, 219, 234–35, 273.

10. Wolfram Mauser, *Bild und Gebarde in der Sprach Hofmannsthals* (Vienna: Hermann Bohlaus, 1961), 58; cited in Janik and Toulmin, *Wittgenstein's Vienna*, 116. According to Janik and Toulmin, "to be a fin de siècle Viennese artist or intellectual, conscious of the social realities of Kakania, one had to face the problem of nature and limits of language, expression and communication" (*Wittgenstein's Vienna*, 117).

11. Janik and Toulmin, *Wittgenstein's Vienna*, 118. For Buber's influence on Musil see Dietmar Goltschnigg, *Mystische Tradition im Roman Robert Musils: Martin Buber's "Ekstatische Konfessionen" im "Mann Ohne Eigenschaften"* (Heidelberg: Lothar Stiehm Verlag, 1974); and Luft, *Robert Musil*, 187–88, 261.

12. Buber knew Mauthner and invited him to write one of the volumes of the series *Die Gesellschaft*, which Buber edited between 1906 and 1912. See also Buber, *Briefwechsel* vol. 1, letters 96–7, 100. Mauthner's influence on Landauer is clearly evident in Landauer's book, *Skepsis und Mystik*; see Lunn, *Prophet*, 130. For Buber's own form of language skepticism see chapter 4.

13. Fritz Mauthner, *Beiträge zu einer Kritik der Sprache* (Stuttgart: J. G. Cotta, 1901–03), xi, cited in Janik and Toulmin, *Wittgenstein's Vienna*, 122. Mauthner's conception of language is discussed by Weiler in *Mauthner's Critique*. Janik and Toulmin make a convincing case for the influence of Mauthner on Ludwig Wittgenstein, see *Wittgenstein's Vienna*, 120–32, 178–82, 196–201.

14. Schorske, *Vienna*, 167.

15. For Buber's relationship to Herzl see Simon, "Buber and German Jewry," 21–27; and Schaeder, *Humanism*, 226–40.

16. Barrett, *Irrational Man*, 34. For the impact of World War I on Buber see Friedman, *Buber's Life and Work* 1:178–202; and Paul R. Flohr, "The Road to *I and Thou*." The general disillusionment of the post–World War I generation is discussed by, among others, Wohl in *1914*; Zweig in *World of Yesterday*, 192–237; Luft in *Robert Musil*, 121–39; and, in relation to European social thought, Hughes in *Consciousness*, chap. 9.

17. See Erikson, *Childhood*, chap. 7. The yearning for relation and the necessity of genuine relation for the actualization of the self are basic ideas in Buber's mature philosophy (see chapter 5). Walter Kaufmann has called attention to the fact that the early loss of a parent is a common element in the lives of several modern philosophers of alienation; see his introductory essay to Schacht, *Alienation*, xxxiii–xxxiv. While Buber's mother didn't die during his youth, she was absent from his life during his childhood and played no role in his upbringing following the breakup of the marriage. See below, chap. 5, n. 59.

18. Buber's relationship with his father was never a close one. See Buber, *Briefwechsel* vol. 1, letters 124, 179, 215, 380. Their correspondence reflects the oedipal revolt that Schorske finds to be the characteristic of many young Viennese of that generation. See Schorske, *Vienna*, introduction.

19. See his "Biblical Leadership," in Buber, *Israel and the World*. For the significance of myth in Buber's thought see chapters 2, 3, and 8.
20. The positive relationship between Buber and his grandparents is clearly reflected in Buber, *Briefwechsel* vol. 1, letters 7–8, 84–85, 101, 108, 125, 130, 143. Buber also spoke of the strong security provided by his grandparents in "My Way to Hasidism"; see *HMM*, 55–57.
21. On Buber's changing attitude to rabbinic Judaism see the sources cited in chapter 8, nn. 4 and 8.
22. Buber's strong ties to Nietzsche are clearly reflected in an unpublished essay, "Zarathustra," and in an early encomium entitled "Ein Wort über Nietzsche und die Lebenswerte." Simon refers to Buber's intellectual struggle to emancipate himself from Nietzsche in "Buber and German Jewry." See also Schaeder, *Humanism*, 31–38; and Friedman, *Buber's Life and Work* 1:26–32. For Nietzsche's powerful impact on Buber's friend and mentor Gustav Landauer see Lunn, *Prophet*, 17–48. On Nietzsche see Walter Kaufmann, *Nietzsche*; Stern, *Nietzsche*; Hollingdale, *Nietzsche*; and Hayman, *Nietzsche*. See also the provocative study by Nehamas, *Nietzsche*, which perceptively addresses some of the issues discussed in chapter 2.
23. Nietzsche, "On Truth and Lie in an Extra-Moral Sense," in Nietzsche, *Portable Nietzsche*, 46–47. This passage is frequently cited in works on semiotics and deconstruction.
24. See Nietzsche, *Good and Evil*, part 1.
25. Nietzsche, *Twilight of the Idols*, in Nietzsche, *Portable Nietzsche*, 542.
26. Ibid., 494.
27. Ibid., 562–63.
28. Stern, *Nietzsche*, 83. See also Nietzsche, *Untimely Meditations*, 128–30, 143–46. Nietzsche gave *Ecce Homo* the subtitle *How One Becomes What One Is*.
29. Nietzsche, *Good and Evil*, 29.
30. Nietzsche, *Gay Science*, 25, 181.
31. "Zarathustra," 10. The file in the Buber Archives for "Zarathustra" bears the date 1895, which would make Buber seventeen at the time of its writing.
32. Unless otherwise noted, all translations from German and Hebrew texts are mine.
33. Buber, "Nietzsche und die Lebenswerte."
34. Buber, "Nietzsche und die Lebenswerte," 13, translated in Schaeder, *Hebrew Humanism*, 35.
35. Kaufmann, *Nietzsche*, 101.
36. On the idea of *agon* (conflict) as a primary factor in literary creativity see Bloom, *Anxiety*; Bloom, *Kabbalah*; and Bloom, *Agon*. See also Said, "Interview." This idea is elaborated by Rorty in *Consequences*, 139–159.
37. *PMB*, 12.
38. Bloom develops the idea in *Anxiety* and in *Kabbalah* that, in order to

emerge as a creative thinker or writer, one must "swerve" from the ideas of one's original precursor.

39. See chap. 6, 174–77.
40. See chapters 4 and 5. Buber described his intellectual development in the afterword to *I and Thou*, 171, and in *PMB*, 11–15, 689–91, and 711–12.
41. The influence of Tonnies, already evident in the lecture "Alte und Neue Gemeinschaft," is clearly expressed in Buber's 1919 essays, *Worte an die Zeit*, discussed in chapter 4. Simmel, one of Buber's teachers in Berlin, wrote one of the volumes in the series *Die Gesellschaft* edited by Buber. See the references to Kohn and Friedman cited previously, n. 8. On Tonnies's influence, see Yasour, *Buber's Social Philosophy*, chap. 3.
42. Marx, *Early Writings*, 127. For a thorough discussion of Marx's theory of alienation see Ollman, *Alienation*. See also Tom Bottomore, ed., *A Dictionary of Marxist Thought*, s.v. "alienation," 9–15.
43. Marx, *Early Writings*, 129.
44. Mitzman, *Sociology and Estrangement*, 13.
45. Tonnies, *On Sociology*, 76.
46. Tonnies, *Community*, 37.
47. Ibid., 252.
48. Ibid., 42.
49. Ibid., 77.
50. Ibid., 130.
51. Ibid., 202.
52. Ibid.
53. Tonnies, *On Sociology*, 316–17.
54. On Simmel see Weingartner, *Experience and Culture*; Coser, *Georg Simmel*; and Simmel, *Sociology*. The influence of Simmel on Buber is discussed by Flohr in *Kulturmystik*, chaps. 1–2. See also Schaeder, *Humanism*, 46–53; Kohn, *Martin Buber*, 59–67.
55. Simmel, *Conflict*, 12. This conflict between the pulsating life force and the objectified forms also characterized Buber's thinking as we shall see in chapters 3, 5, and 7.
56. Simmel refers to Nietzsche in *Conflict*, 13.
57. Simmel, *Sociology*, 58–59.
58. Ibid., 422. Compare Buber's description in *Daniel* discussed in chapter 4.
59. Weber, *Protestant Ethic*, 182.
60. Dennis Wrong, Introduction to Wrong, *Max Weber*, 26.
61. Neue Gemeinschaft served as a forum for young Viennese intellectuals dissatisfied with the prevailing social and cultural ethos. See Kohn, *Werk und Zeit*, 28–31; Lunn, *Prophet*, 141–47; and Flohr and Susser, "Alte und Neue Gemeinschaft," an article which includes the first published version of Buber's lecture together with an introduction. See also Flohr's dissertation, *Kulturmystik*.

62. On *Lebensphilosophie* (philosophy of life), see Weingartner, *Experience and Culture*, chap. 1; Gier, *Wittgenstein*, chap. 3. As we shall see in the next three chapters, Buber's early writings were rooted in concepts borrowed from *Lebensphilosophie*. Barukh Kurzweil has discussed the influence of Nietzsche and *Lebensphilosophie* on turn-of-the-century Hebrew writers in *Sifruteinu ha-Hadashah*, 225–60. See also Biale, *Gershom Scholem*, chap. 3.

63. Neue Gemeinschaft marked the beginning of Buber's lifelong relationship with Gustav Landauer, a socialist and anarchist who became his close friend and mentor. Buber's relationship with Landauer was extremely close. Their influence on one another is discussed by Lunn, *Prophet*, 144–147, 172–74, 224–26, 246–53, 266–73.

64. See Flohr and Susser, "Alte und Neue Gemeinschaft."

65. On the emergence of Zionism see Vital, *Origins of Zionism*, and Laqueur, *History of Zionism*, chaps. 1–4. Shlomo Avineri discusses the intellectual roots of Zionism in *Modern Zionism*. Buber's early relationship to the Zionist movement is discussed by Kohn, *Werk und Zeit*, 28–55, and Friedman, *Life and Work*, vol. 1, chaps. 3–4.

66. For a discussion of the fundamental views of rabbinic sages see Urbach, *Sages;* and Moore, *Judaism*.

67. Buber's early studies of mysticism include his dissertation, "Individuationsproblems," and an essay "Über Jakob Boehme," which appeared in 1901. Buber's most comprehensive statement on the nature of mysticism is found in his introduction to his anthology *Ecstatic Confessions*. See also his comment on Troeltsch's paper, "Mystik als religioser Solipsismus."

68. Buber, "Zur Geschichte des Individuationsproblems." Buber originally considered calling his dissertation a study in Renaissance psychology. Individuationsproblems (MS. var. 350/A2, Martin Buber Archives, Jerusalem) is marked "material for a psychology of the Renaissance." For the turn-of-the-century conception of psychology see the editor's introduction to Kierkegaard, *Concept of Anxiety*, xiii–xiv. On Buber's study of psychiatry, cf. Jochanan Bloch, *Die Aporie des Du*, 300–302, n. 35. Buber's psychological orientation is also apparent in his interpretation of Judaism, cf. Buber, *On Judaism*, 22–33, 56–62.

69. In light of Buber's later social orientation, it is interesting to note that at this early stage in his development, he favored Boehme's mystical orientation over Feuerbach's social orientation. Whereas Feuerbach depicted the divine as emerging out of the relations between individuals, between the I and the Thou, Buber still preferred Boehme's concept of the underlying unity of creation. Although, in his later writings, Buber continued to emphasize a mystical predilection for unity and wholeness, the themes of community and interhuman relation became dominant, as we shall see in chapters 5 and 6.

70. The concept of entelechy, basic to Aristotle, is fundamental to Buber's philosophy as indicated by his extensive use of the term *Verwirkli-*

chung (actualization). *Verwirklichung*, discussed in chapter 4, presupposes the basic tendency within each being to grow and actualize its own inner potential. Although Buber, in *I and Thou*, replaced the term *Verwirklichung*, as used in his earlier work *Daniel*, with *Beziehung*, the idea of entelechy continued to play a major role in his thought.

71. Buber, *Ecstatic Confessions*, 1–11. On *Erlebnisse*, a term connoting the basic life experience, the fundamental stratum of experience, see Ermath, *Wilhelm Dilthey*, 93–139.

72. Compare Feuerbach's projectionist conception of religion in *Essence of Christianity*. On Nietzsche's projectionist views see *Genealogy of Morals: The Antichrist* anthologized in Nietzsche, *Portable Nietzsche*, 565–656; and, in that same volume, *Zarathustra*, 103–439, especially 197–200.

73. As we shall see in chapters 4 and 7, the view of experience as antecedent to language and of the inability of language to fully capture this experience remain basic to Buber's thought. The relationship of language and mysticism is the fundamental theme of Landauer's book *Skepsis und Mystik*, which Buber had read. For a discussion of views of language in the early twentieth century see Janik and Toulmin, *Wittgenstein's Vienna*; and Weiler, *Mauthner's Critique*. On Von Hofmannsthal's view of language see Hamburger, *Hofmannsthal*, 3–16. For a critique of the idea of a prelinguistic stratum of experience held by mystics and most existentialists see the essays in Katz, *Mysticism*, especially 22–169, and Paul Van Buren, *Edges of Language*, chaps. 2 and 3.

CHAPTER TWO

1. "I could not become a Hasid. It would have been an unpermissible masquerade had I taken on the Hasidic manner of life—I who had a wholly other relation to Jewish tradition, since I must distinguish in my innermost being between what is commanded me and what is not commanded me" (Buber, *Hasidism and Modern Man*, 24 [hereafter referred to as *HMM*]).

2. The category of misreading, formulated by such contemporary literary critics as Paul de Man and Harold Bloom, refers to the fact that any act of reading is necessarily an interpretative act, and that one can never simply replicate a meaning that supposedly inheres in a text. It is related to Nietzsche's observation: "No. Facts is precisely what there is not, only interpretations" (Nietzsche, *Will to Power*, 267). For a lucid discussion of this concept, see Culler, *On Deconstruction*, 175–79.

The idea of "strong misreading" and "creative misreading" is argued by Harold Bloom in *Anxiety* and *Kabbalah*, especially 93–126 of the latter. "A strong reading can be defined as one that itself produces other readings" (Bloom, *Kabbalah*, 97). See also Bloom, *Breaking of the Vessels*, 7–40, where, drawing upon Nietzsche and Emerson, Bloom advocates a pragmatic theory of reading. Rorty provides a philosophical context for the difference between "strong reading" and "weak reading" in "Nineteenth-Century Idealism and Twentieth-Century Textualism," in Rorty, *Consequences*, 139–59. Referring to Bloom, Rorty describes strong misreading as occurring when "the critic asks neither the author nor the text about their intentions but simply beats the text into a shape that will serve his purpose. He does this by imposing a vocabulary —a 'grid', in Foucault's terminology—on the text which may have nothing to do with any vocabulary used in the text or by its author, and seeing what happens" (Rorty, *Consequences*, 151).

3. Buber never fully resolved the tension between conventional historical scholarship and his revisionist mode of interpretation. Thus, while defending himself against Scholem's criticisms, Buber refrained from following Nietzsche's lead and challenging the validity of conventional historical inquiry. Instead, Buber simply contrasted his "mythic" way of reading the past with Scholem's historical orientation. See Buber, "Interpreting Hasidism." Unlike Nietzsche, Buber never totally dissociated himself from conventional Western scholarship. Instead, he considered the human sciences, including anthropology, psychology, history, and sociology, as appropriate contexts in which to study Judaism. See Buber, Feivel, and Weizmann, *Jewish School*. In his later studies on the Bible, which are discussed in chapter 8, Buber integrated the methods of conventional biblical scholarship, including historical, philological, and archaeological research, with his distinctive "mythic" orientation.

4. See Buber, "My Way to Hasidism," in *HMM*, 47–69.

5. Buber's study of non-Jewish mysticism resulted in the publication of two works. The first, *Ekstatische Konfessionen*, is an anthology of primarily non-Jewish mystical writings, both Eastern and Western. The second, *Reden und Gleichnisse des Tschuang Tse*, is a selection of chapters from the well-known Taoist text. Buber's introduction to that work is available in English translation in Buber, *Pointing the Way*, 31–58, as "The Teaching of the Tao."

6. On Hasidism see *Encyclopedia Judaica* 7:1390–1426; Weiss, *Studies*; Scholem, *Major Trends*, 325–50; Jacobs, *Hasidic Prayer*; and Jacobs, *Seeker of Unity*. On Haskalah see *Encyclopedia Judaica* 7:1434–52; Dawidowicz, *Golden Tradition*, introduction and 113–68, 273–333; and Mendes-Flohr and Reinharz, *Jew in the Modern World*, 310–28.

7. For examples of the prevailing view of Hasidism by Western scholars see Graetz, *History of the Jews*, chap. 9. See also Biale, *Gershom Scholem*, chap. 1. The bias of German Jews against eastern European Jewry at the beginning of the twentieth century is reflected in Franz Rosenzweig's letters, see Glatzer, *Franz Rosenzweig*, 73–80. Glatzer's work

and Scholem's *From Berlin to Jerusalem*, chaps. 1–2, describe the ethos that pervaded German Jewry during the early part of the century.

8. This is the basis of one of Scholem's major criticisms of Buber. See "Martin Buber's Interpretation of Hasidism," in Scholem, *Messianic Idea*, 227–50. Buber defended his emphasis on myths and stories and his disregard of theoretical works in "Interpreting Hasidism" (see n. 3); *HMM*, 21–43; *Origin and Meaning*, chap. 1; and Schilpp and Friedman, *Philosophy of Martin Buber*, 731–41 (hereafter referred to as *PMB*).

9. The Lurianic version is discussed by Tishby, *Torat ha-Ra ve-ha-Kelipah* and by Scholem. See Scholem, *Major Trends*, lecture 7; Scholem, *Messianic Idea*, 37–48; and Scholem, *Kabbalah*, 128–44. For the Hasidic interpretation of the Lurianic myth see Jacobs, "Uplifting of Sparks"; Jacobs, *Seeker of Unity*, chap. 3; and *Encyclopedia Judaica*, s.v. "Hasidism," 7:1403–14.

10. On *devekut* see Scholem, *Messianic Idea*, 203–27.

11. For Nietzsche's emphasis on person as creator see *Zarathustra* in Nietzsche, *Portable Nietzsche*, 163–66, 172–77.

12. On the potential of any encounter for being a redemptive act see Menahem Nahum of Chernobyl, *Upright Practices*, 39, 237–38, and editor's introduction, 16; Scholem, *Messianic Idea*, 216, 232; *Encyclopedia Judaica*, s.v. "Hasidism," 7:1405–10; Jacobs, "Uplifting of Sparks," especially 115–25; and Zeitlin, *Be-Fardes ha-Hasidut*, 25–30.

13. Buber's description of Hasidism as Kabbalah become ethos, first stated in Buber, *Rabbi Nachman*, 10, and elaborated in Buber, *Origin and Meaning*, 252, was, with reservations, accepted by Scholem. See Scholem, *Major Trends*, 342.

14. For this distinction see Kierkegaard, *Concluding Unscientific Postscript*, 181–82.

15. On the concept of *kavanah* in Hasidism, see Weiss, *Studies*, 95–125; and Jacobs, *Hasidic Prayer*, 70–92.

16. According to the rabbis, even the carrying out of a commandment without the proper motivation or intention could lead to one's fulfilling it with the proper intention. See Urbach, *Sages*, 392–99.

17. See Scholem's critique of Buber's existential interpretation in Scholem, *Messianic Idea*, 228–50. Scholem rejected Buber's reading as a violation of the canons of objective, historical scholarship.

18. In a letter to Max Brod dated 1913, Buber explicitly referred to numerous places in his earlier writings where he spoke of social concerns. At the same time, he indicated to Brod that he was not satisfied with his previous treatment of the social dimension of life and that he hoped to correct this in a future work. See Buber, *Briefwechsel* vol. 1, letters 226–27. For further indications of this social concern see n. 60.

19. This is Buber's earliest reference to the realm of "the between," which he first formulated as a technical concept in 1906 in "Geleitwort" and elaborated in such post–World War I writings as *I and Thou*, "Dia-

logue" (in Buber, *Between Man and Man*, 1–39), and "Elements of the Interhuman" (in Buber, *Knowledge of Man*, 72–88).

20. In this idea, we see a preliminary formulation of the notion, developed fully in *I and Thou*, that genuine relation entails mutuality—that is, experiencing a situation from the perspective of the other. See chapter 4.

21. Scholem objected to this reading, claiming that it ignored the nihilistic dimension of Hasidism. In response, Buber, arguing uncharacteristically along historical lines, distinguished different trends within Hasidism.

22. The metaphor of the abyss recurs in Buber's writings. See, for example, *HMM*, 67; *PMB*, 11; and Buber, *On Judaism*, 159, 194, 201.

23. For the concept of "trope" as a defensive move against one's precursor, see Bloom, *Map of Misreading*, 75–78, 93–95; and Bloom, *Breaking of the Vessels*.

24. Buber, "Interpreting Hasidism," 224.

25. For a discussion of the concept of myth see Nietzsche, *Birth of Tragedy*, 102–12, 136–40; and Nietzsche, *Advantage and Disadvantage*, 37–47. See also White, *Metahistory*, 335; McNeil, "Make Mine Myth." Kohn discusses the role of myth in turn-of-the-century thought in Kohn, *Martin Buber*, 86–89. See also Liebert, "Mythus und Kultur," 397–445.

26. For Nietzsche's comments on the metaphorical nature of language see Nietzsche, *Portable Nietzsche*, 42–47; and Nietzsche, *Good and Evil*, 23–32.

27. Buber's language is reminiscent of the language used by the writers and philosophers of fin de siècle Europe who belonged to the school of *Lebensphilosophie*, a movement deeply influenced by Nietzsche. See also chapter 1, n. 62.

28. Nietzsche, *Birth of Tragedy*, 136. For a similar view expressed by a modern historian, see McNeil, "Make Mine Myth." See also n. 53.

29. In his earliest lectures on Judaism delivered between 1909 and 1919, he distinguished between the authentic, mythic monotheistic stream within Judaism and the rationalist monotheistic stream. See Buber, *On Judaism*, 95–107.

30. Until recently, Buber's translations constituted one of the few available sources of Hasidic texts for the non-Hebrew–reading public. Frequently, one finds Buber's interpretations cited as sources for the Hasidic teachings instead of the original Hasidic texts. Harold Bloom has spoken of the phenomenon of the ephebe so eclipsing the precursor that the later interpreter appears to beget the original text, which he refers to as *apophrades* (Bloom, *Anxiety*, 141), and *transumption* (Bloom, *Breaking of the Vessels*, 73–107).

31. Virtually all scholars in the field of Jewish studies consider Scholem's works to be authoritative and acknowledge his major contribution to our understanding of Jewish history. While some of his specific interpre-

tations have been called into question, no one questions his preeminent place among modern Jewish scholars.

32. Scholem, *Messianic Idea*, 236.
33. See, for example, Scholem's essay on the concept of *devekut* in Scholem, *Messianic Idea*, 203–27. On Scholem's idealistic orientation to Hasidism see Schatz, "Interpretation of Hasidism." The inadequacy of the conceptual approach to religious phenomena and the need to see religious teachings in their social, experiential, and ritual contexts is argued by Ninian Smart in *Philosophy of Religion:* "We must obey the rule that concepts should be seen in context. The context is not just linguistic, but extra linguistic. Religious concepts, therefore, need to be seen in the context of the forms of religious life—and even more broadly, in as much as religions provide one set of answers to what we have called problems of living meaning" (96–97).
34. Scholem, *Messianic Idea*, 234.
35. Ibid., 247–48. Scholem also criticized Buber for failing to include footnotes in his works on Hasidism, thereby violating the canons of historical scholarship. Buber partially acquiesced to Scholem by publishing under separate cover a set of references to his work, *Der Grosse Maggid.* However, these references were not included in later editions of the work. For Scholem's observations on this, see his essay, "Martin Buber's Conception of Judaism," in Scholem, *On Jews and Judaism*, 165–66. For an insightful critical analysis of the function of footnotes in scholarly works see Nimis, "Fussnoten." I am grateful to my colleague Amy Richlin for calling my attention to this article.
36. Scholem, *Messianic Idea*, 242.
37. Ibid.
38. Ibid., 244.
39. Ibid., 243.
40. Ibid., 245.
41. *Ibid.* This charge of religious anarchism is somewhat ironic given Scholem's own admitted propensity for anarchism.

> Anarchism held many attractions for me, especially its positive utopianism. But it, too, always filled me with terror. I knew that it stood no chance of realization, given the data of the human race, in history. This is a kind of messianic vision to which the transition is not possible with the forces functioning in history.
>
> To this day I would say that the only social theory that makes sense— religious sense too—is anarchism, but it is also—practically speaking—the least possible theory. It doesn't stand a chance because it doesn't take the human being into consideration: it is based on an extremely optimistic assessment of the human spirit; it has a messianic dimension, a transhistorical one. (Scholem, *On Jews and Judaism*, 32–33)

See also Scholem's Hebrew essay, "Jewish Mysticism Today," in Scholem, *Devarim be-Go* 1:71–83, where Scholem argued that contemporary Jewry is, from a religious perspective, anarchistic. However, while Scholem empathized with the anarchist tendencies that he uncovered in Kabbalah, he was apprehensive of their destructive quality. On this subject see Biale, "Scholem and Anarchism."

Buber, on his part, denied that the term anarchism accurately described his position, insisting that he never rejected law in principle, as one would expect from an anarchist, but believed that by legislating religious behavior, a society deprives the individual of the fundamental human responsibility to choose.

42. Scholem, *Messianic Idea*, 247–48.
43. Buber, "Interpreting Hasidism." See also Buber's reply to Rivkah Schatz-Uffenheimer in *PMB*, 731–41.
44. See Buber, "Interpreting Hasidism," 222.
45. Actually, as Scholem, himself, indicated, his original reasons for undertaking the study of Kabbalah were no less pragmatic than Buber's. "I wanted to enter the world of kabbalah out of my belief in Zionism as a living thing—as the restoration of a people that had degenerated quite a bit" (Scholem, *On Jews and Judaism*, 18). In the same interview Scholem indicated that the survival of Judaism was at the heart of his concern with Kabbalah: "I was interested in the question: Does halakhic Judaism have enough potency to survive? This question was tied up with my dreams about the kabbalah, through the notion that it might be kabbalah that explains the survival of the consolidated force of halakhic Judaism. That was certainly one of my obvious motives" (ibid., 19).
46. From Buber's 1918 essay, "My Way to Hasidism."
47. In spite of the fact that he emphasized Hasidism as a mode of life, unlike the social theorist, Buber did not explore the communal forms and patterns of relationship in the Hasidic community. Instead, he focused on the myths as the most immediate expression of those forms. This clearly separates him from such writers as Tonnies, Simmel, and Weber and aligns him more closely with Nietzsche and Kierkegaard. Interestingly, in his philosophical writings, Buber criticized the latter for neglecting the social dimension of human life. See Buber, "What is Man?" in Buber, *Between Man and Man*, 65–82; 148–56. See also chapter 4.
48. The antimythic attitude is epitomized in the writings of Yehezkel Kaufmann, one of the leading Jewish Bible scholars of Buber's generation: "There is no mythological or magical stratum in Biblical literature. . . . Fossil remains of ancient myths stemming from before the rise of Israelite religion are to be found in the Bible, but living myths—whether Israelite or foreign—are absent" (Kaufmann, "Biblical Age," 13). This passage reflects a fundamental argument of Kaufmann's monumental study of Israelite religion, *Toledot ha-Emunah ha-Yisraelit*, 8 vols. (Jerusalem: Mosad Bialik, 1956). See also the abridged transla-

tion, Kaufmann, *The Religion of Israel*, trans. Moshe Greenberg (Chicago: University of Chicago Press, 1969).

49. On antimythic motifs in nineteenth-century Jewish thought see Rotenstreich, *Jewish Philosophy*, chap. 5; and Moshe Schwartz, *Language, Myth, Art*, parts 1 and 2.

50. Stout, "Relativity of Interpretation," 112.

51. This attitude is clearly reflected in Yehezkel Kaufmann's four-volume study, *Golah ve-Nekhar*. In his introduction, Kaufmann, one of the first Zionist thinkers to undertake a historical interpretation of Judaism, distinguished his historical, objectivist approach from the theological or metaphysical approaches of previous generations. See my "Historical Sociology and Ideology."

52. For a critical description of this conception of historical inquiry see Harvey, *Historian and Believer*, 38–101; Patrick Gardiner, *Historical Explanation*; W. B. Gaillie, *Philosophy and Historical Understanding*; and Leff, *History and Social Theory*, 3–137.

53. See, for example, the critical comments of Ismar Schorsch in his introduction to Graetz, *Structure*; and Baron, *History and Jewish Historians*, 65–106. For a contemporary Jewish historian's doubts concerning the privileging of the historical orientation to the past, see Yerushalmi, *Zachor*, 77–103. On p. 98, Yerushalmi states: "I am far from immune to the seductions of myth, and I fancy myself more aware than most of its place in the healthy life of a people. I freely admit that there are times when I myself question the value of studying the past, disturbing thoughts that come usually 'when sleep wanders,' and occasionally during the day."

54. For examples of this reading of the controversy see Rivkah Schatz Uffenheimer, "Man's Relation to God and World in Buber's Rendering of the Hasidic Teaching," in *PMB*, 403–34; Biale, *Gershom Scholem*; Louis Jacobs, "Aspects of Scholem's Study of Hasidism," in *Modern Judaism* 5 (1 February 1985): 95–103; and Schatz, "Interpretation of Hasidism."

55. This view was expounded in Germany by Heinrich Graetz in *Structure of Jewish History* and in Eastern Europe by Simon Dubnow. See Dubnow, *Nationalism and History*. With the emergence of Zionism and the return of the Jews to Israel, history became a dominant means of uncovering the past glories of the emerging nation and served to legitimate its nationalist claims. On reconstructing history according to nationalist categories, see the brief discussion by Kedourie, *Nationalism*, 73–81.

56. The strongest argument for history as a form of literary discourse is found in White, *Tropics of Discourse*. See also his *Metahistory*. The constructivistic nature of historical discourse and its inadequacy for recovering existential reality are discussed by Chiaromonte in *Paradox*. General works in contemporary literary theory supporting this critique of history include Eagleton, *Literary Theory*; and Culler, *On Decon-*

struction. See also Leitch, *Deconstructive Criticism;* and Lentricchia, *After the New Criticism.* A philosophical perspective on current literary interpretation is found in Rorty, *Consequences,* especially chaps. 6 and 8. See also Rorty, *Mirror,* chaps. 7 and 8.

57. This position is forcibly argued by White and Chiaromonte; see n. 56.

58. Included in this group are Rorty, White, Foucault, Lentricchia, and Bloom. For a general discussion of literary theory and the interpretation of Judaism, see my article "Textualism."

59. Most scholars who recognize that Buber and Scholem were engaged in different activities assume that only Scholem's interpretation of Hasidism is valid.

60. As indicated in chapter 1, Buber's concern with altering the prevailing forms of social relations was already evident in his earliest works. Further expressions of this social concern include his activities as the editor of the series *Die Gesellschaft–Sammlung Sozialpsychologisches Monographien,* vols. 1–40 (Frankfurt: Rütten & Loening, 1906–12), which was devoted to social and political theory; his lecture, "The Holy Way" (in *On Judaism,* 108–48), delivered in 1918; *Worte an die Zeit,* published in 1919; and *I and Thou.* See also n. 18.

61. Rorty, *Consequences,* 153. The question of relativism and the pluralistic nature of interpretation has been discussed by Stout in "Relativity of Interpretation," where he modifies Rorty's interpretation of reading.

62. Holtz, *Back to the Sources,* 20.

63. Scholem, *Messianic Idea,* 300.

64. Scholem, *Sabbatai Sevi,* xi.

65. Among the proponents of this view are Fish, *Is There a Text?;* Bloom, *Kabbalah,* especially 93–126, a chapter entitled "The Necessity of Misreading"; and Bloom, *Map of Misreading.* For a philosophical perspective, see Rorty, *Consequences,* 139–59.

66. White, *Metahistory,* 7.

67. Claude Levi-Strauss, *La Pensée sauvage,* quoted in Chiaromonte, *Paradox,* 37.

68. Levi-Strauss, *La Pensée sauvage,* quoted in Chiaromonte, *Paradox,* 38.

69. The term "Christianity," for example, is not the name for any single unit of the type for which the historian of specific ideas looks. I mean by this not merely the notorious fact that persons who have equally professed and called themselves Christians have, in the course of history, held all manner of distinct and conflicting beliefs under the one name, but also that any one of these persons and sects has, as a rule, held under that name a very mixed collection of ideas, the combination of which into a conglomerate bearing a single name and supposed to constitute a real unity was usually the result of historic processes of a highly complicated and curious sort. (Lovejoy, *Great Chain,* 6)

See also Max Weber, *The Methodology of the Social Sciences,* trans. and ed. Edward A. Shils and Henry A. Finch (New York: Free Press, 1949), 85–112; and Gordon Leff, *History and Social Theory,* 117–69).

70. Biale, *Gershom Scholem*, 6.
71. Scholem, "With Gershom Scholem: An Interview," in Scholem, *On Jews and Judaism*, 1–48. Scholem discusses his relationship to Zionism and other intellectual currents preceding his involvement with the study of Kabbalah in *From Berlin to Jerusalem*, 36–82.
72. Scholem, *On Jews and Judaism*, 19.
73. Biale, *Gershom Scholem*, 79.
74. Ibid., 102. Biale clearly recognizes that Scholem's historiography is deeply rooted in ideological and theological concerns. However, according to Biale, Scholem has succeeded where Buber has failed. In contrast to what Biale refers to as "Buber's ahistorical mysticism," Scholem formulated a dialectical, counterhistory that included "the totality of the contradictory principles that make up Jewish history" (ibid., 111). Scholem, unlike Buber, was able to strike a "balance between applying categories from his own experience to his historical material and letting the sources speak for themselves" (ibid., 202). Like most historians, Biale ignores the claim of philosophers and literary critics cited above that sources can never speak for themselves. Yet, in a later response to the criticisms of Yosef Dan, Biale criticizes the positivistic view of historical writing, insisting that "there is a necessary interaction between the historian's contemporary philosophical position and his research." Nevertheless, Biale contrasts Scholem's ability to balance faithfulness to sources and interpretive judgments to Buber's use of "historical texts to buttress philosophical positions" (Biale, "Ten Unhistorical Aphorisms," 91, nn. 5, 6). Thus, Biale appears to advocate a middle position between the constructivistic view of historical writing, as formulated by Hayden White and Chiaromonte, and the positivist view that he attributes to Dan. Unlike Biale, I would agree with White that the difference between a historian like Scholem and a philosopher like Buber is not one of a kind but one of degree.
75. Stout, "Relativity of Interpretation," 111. The relationship of literary interpretation to particular styles of life is discussed by Nehamas in *Nietzsche*, 62–73.
76. Kaufmann, "Buber's Religious Significance," in *PMB*, 680. In response to critics who insist on reading Buber's Hasidic works through the lens of objectivistic historiography, Kaufmann further argued:

> The reply to such criticisms is implicit in the comparison with the Gospels which, no doubt, will strike some readers as blasphemous. What saves Buber's work is its perfection. He has given us one of the great religious books of all time, a work that invites comparison with the great Scriptures of mankind. This estimate must seem fantastic to those who have not read *The Tales of the Hasidim*. But if it should be justified, then the criticism that Buber is not an impartial historian can be accepted cheerfully without being considered very damning. (*PMB*, 680)

77. In fairness to Scholem, titles such as *The Origin and Meaning of Hasidism*, as well as the style utilized by Buber in several of the essays in that book, do serve to convey to the uninformed reader a false impression that the work belongs to the genre of historiography. It must be pointed out, however, that the original German title was *Das Botschaft des Chassidismus*, (The Message of Hasidism). However, by allowing the English title to stand, Buber, knowingly or unknowingly, contributed to the misreading of his own works. Consequently, Buber is not totally innocent of having provided some justification to the claims of Scholem and his disciples that he offered a distorted picture of Hasidism. Moreover, Buber could have taken greater care to emphasize, especially in the volume just mentioned, that he was not engaged in a historical inquiry. Nevertheless, this in no way invalidates Buber's approach.

78. To many scholars, this perspectival, constructivist orientation appears to do away with all evaluative criteria and leads only to anarchy. However, this criticism is itself grounded in the assumption that a nonselective representation of the world is possible: "Choosing, selecting, and simplifying do not amount to falsifying what is before us, unless we believe that there can be a representation of the world that depends on no selection at all, and that this representation constitutes the standard of accuracy" (Nehamas, *Nietzsche*, 56).

79. Rorty, *Consequences*, 92.

80. Stout, "Relativity of Interpretation," 103. Further on in this essay, Stout gives a concrete example to show that the issue of "right" reading is often beside the point:

> Take, for example, Michael Walzer's interpretation of Thucydides' *History of the Peloponnesian War* [in *Just and Unjust Wars*]. Walzer refers to the statement about force Thucydides "seems in fact to be making," but it becomes clear that whether Thucydides really meant to make such a statement is not the issue. "This is certainly the way Hobbes read Thucydides and it is the reading with which we must come to grips." Why is it the Hobbist reading that matters? It is not that Walzer seeks an explanatory account of Hobbes' use of Thucydides. Walzer is writing moral philosophy. He wants an interpretation of Thucydides that will pose a possibility for moral reflection. If Thucydides meant nothing of the kind—indeed, if Hobbes found no such possibility in Thucydides—it wouldn't matter. Walzer's interpretation would serve its normative purpose nonetheless. (Ibid., 111)

81. In contrast to Rorty, who views culture as an ongoing conversation, Alisdair MacIntyre depicts it as an ongoing debate or argument:

> For what constitutes a tradition is a conflict of interpretations of that tradition, a conflict which itself has a history susceptible of rival interpretations. If I am a Jew I have to recognize that the tradition of Judaism is partly constituted by a continuous argument over what it means to be a Jew. (MacIntyre, "Epistemological Crises," 62)

82. A common response to the argument being set forth here is that it presumes an interpretative anarchy. While the present situation does not allow for rendering cross-perspectival epistemological judgments concerning the validity of interpretations, the position argued in this chapter does not presume that we are obliged to accept all interpretations as equally valid. As Nietzsche recognized, every interpretation, "every view of the world makes possible and promotes a particular kind of life and therefore presupposes and manifests specific interests and values" (Nehamas, *Nietzsche*, 64–65).

83. Stout, "Relativity of Interpretation," 114. See also the discussion of perspectivalism by Nehamas, *Nietzsche*, chap. 2.

CHAPTER THREE

1. Among the most important critics are Franz Rosenzweig, whose debate with Buber we shall discuss below, and Scholem, whose basic criticisms I analyzed in the previous chapter. In addition to the works cited there, see also Scholem's essay, "Martin Buber's Conception of Judaism," in Scholem, *Jews and Judaism*, 126–71. On the Buber-Scholem debate, see the penetrating observations of Ernst Simon, a man close to both of them, in *Aims, Junctures, Paths*, 245–56, 314–26. Simon wrote some of the most important critiques of Buber's views on Judaism. See his seminal essay "Martin Buber and the Faith of Israel," ibid., 87–125. For a traditionalist critique of Buber see Eliezer Berkovitz, *Major Themes*, 68–148. See also the theological critique of Arthur Cohen in *Natural and the Supernatural Jew*, 149–78, and the same author's *Martin Buber*.

2. As indicated in the Introduction, my use of the term *revisionism* is indebted to the writings of Harold Bloom. See, in particular, Bloom, *Map of Misreading*, especially 3–6. Among the paradigmatic revisionists, Bloom identifies the Lurianic Kabbalists (Bloom, *Kabbalah*) and Ralph Waldo Emerson. See Bloom, *Agon*, chap. 6; and Bloom, *Breaking of the Vessels*, chap. 1. There is a strong connection between Bloom's concept of revisionism, his theory of misreading, and the concept of edifying philosopher discussed in chapter 4. In *Consequences*, Rorty endorses Bloom's concept of "strong reading," while Bloom affirms Rorty's concept of interpretation in *Agon*, chap. 1.

3. Bloom, *Map of Misreading*, 34.

4. Ibid., 3–4.

5. Kierkegaard, *Present Age*, 33.

6. Kierkegaard, "The Point of View for My Life as an Author," in Kierkegaard, *Anthology*, 328.

7. Kierkegaard, *Attack Upon Christendom*, 283–84.

8. "The Established Church has hitherto let nothing be heard from it, has not in the remotest way showed a disposition to make known how

remotely it is related to New Testament Christianity, and it is not even possible to say of it with truth that it is an effort in the direction of coming close to the Christianity of the New Testament" (Kierkegaard, *Attack Upon Christendom*, 19). "Official Christianity is not the Christianity of the New Testament" (ibid., 41). This distinction is reiterated on pp. 15–55 and throughout the work.

9. Kierkegaard, *Concluding Unscientific Postscript*, 182.

10. Ibid., 182.

11. Mackey, *Kierkegaard*, 198.

12. On the alienation of European Jewish youth see Scholem, *From Berlin to Jerusalem*, chaps. 1–3; Scholem, *On Jews and Judaism*, 1–7; and Glatzer, *Franz Rosenzweig*, 1–31. These feelings of alienation are also reflected in Hans Kohn's introduction to *Vom Judentum*, a volume published by the group before which Buber delivered his first lectures on Judaism beginning in 1909.

13. Kohn, Introduction to *Vom Judentum*, v. This anthology of writings by many of the men associated with the Prague Bar Kokhba group is a convenient compendium of the views of young Jewish intellectuals of the period.

14. "Unless he belonged to the strictly orthodox minority, the thoughtful German Jew of the First World War generation, groping for inner direction and orientation, sought to find his bearing in an intellectual field delimited by the ideas and aspirations of Herzl, Hermann Cohen and Buber" (Simon, "Buber and German Jewry," 27). Simon discusses the controversy between Cohen and Buber on pp. 27–33. Buber's critique of Cohen is found in his *Völker, Staaten und Zion*. A Hebrew translation may be found in Buber, *Te'udah ve-Ye'ud* 1:147–62. For an English excerpt from Cohen's response, see Cohen, *Reason and Hope*, 163–71. Buber's response is translated in Arthur Cohen, ed., *The Jew*, 85–96. For an English selection of Hermann Cohen's writings on Judaism see Cohen, *Reason*, and Cohen, *The Religion of Reason*.

15. A selection of reformist views may be found in Mendes-Flohr and Reinharz, *Jew in the Modern World*, 145–76; Phillipson, *Reform Movement*; and Plaut, *Rise of Reform Judaism*.

16. See Ahad Haam's critique of Western assimilationists in "Slavery in Freedom," in Ahad Haam, *Nationalism*, 44–65.

17. Nietzsche first described his conflict view of history in *Birth of Tragedy*. A similar model of history was later adopted by Scholem. See Biale, *Gershom Scholem*, chaps. 2 and 9.

18. A selection of Ahad Haam's writings may be found in Ahad Haam, *Nationalism* and *Selected Essays*. The views of Ahad Haam and Buber with regard to German Zionism are discussed in Reinharz, "Ahad Haam, Buber and Zionism." See also Israel Klausner, *Herzl's Opposition*. For a discussion of Ahad Haam's revision of rabbinic tradition see my article, "Secular System of Meaning."

19. Kohn, *Living in a World Revolution*, 67. See also Kohn's introduction to Ahad Haam, *Nationalism*, and Kohn's essay, "Zion and the Jewish National Idea," in *Zionism Reconsidered*, ed. Michael Selzer, 175–212. A classic critique of Western Zionism is Ahad Haam's essay, "The Jewish State and the Jewish Problem," in Ahad Haam, *Nationalism*, 66–89. For a general discussion of the critics of Western Zionism see Laqueur, *History of Zionism*, 384–440. On the general quest for ethnic roots during the early decades of the century see Laqueur, *Young Germany*; and Mosse, *Germans and Jews*, 77–115.

20. Ahad Haam, "The Law of the Heart," in Hertzberg, *Zionist Idea*, 252.

21. On the eastern European Enlightenment's critique of rabbinic Judaism see Patterson, *Hebrew Novel*; Dawidowicz, *Golden Tradition*, 14–49; Kurzweil, *Sifruteinu ha-Hadashah*, 11–171; and Mendes-Flohr and Reinharz, *Jew in the Modern World*, 310–26.

22. Ahad Haam, *Collected Writings*, vi.

23. Ahad Haam, *Nationalism*, 208.

24. Ibid., 209.

25. Ibid., 194.

26. For Buber's later views on Ahad Haam see the Hebrew essays in Buber, *Te'udah ve-Ye'ud* (Destiny and Mission), 243–45; and Buber, *Israel and Palestine*, 143–47.

27. The invitation to deliver a series of lectures to the group of Jewish intellectuals in Prague, known as Bar Kokhba, presented Buber with an opportunity to formulate his thoughts on the meaning of Judaism. In three lectures, delivered between 1909 and 1911, and in a series of subsequent essays and lectures spanning the period to 1919, Buber elucidated his views on Judaism and sought to reveal to his audiences the spiritual power hidden within Judaism. On the background of Buber's lectures to Bar Kokhba see the introduction by Robert Weltsch to the Hebrew collection of Buber's writings, Buber, *Te'udah ve-Ye'ud* 1:7–14. See also Weltsch's introduction to the German edition of Buber's writings on Judaism, Buber, *Der Jude und Sein Judentum*, xxiii–xxvii; Nahum Glatzer, editor's postscript in Buber, *On Judaism*, 237–42; and Friedman, *Buber's Life and Work*, vol 1, chap. 7.

28. As I shall discuss in chapter 4, this method was characteristic of Buber's lecture style as reflected in his lectures "Religion als Gegenwart" and "Martin Buber Abende." The former has been published in Horowitz, *Buber's Way to I and Thou*. "Abende," delivered in 1923, shortly after the publication of *I and Thou*, remains unpublished.

29. Compare Kierkegaard, "For without risk there is no faith, and the greater the risk, the greater the faith; the more objective security the less inwardness (for inwardness is precisely subjectivity), and the less objective security the more profound the possible inwardness" (Kierkegaard, *Concluding Unscientific Postscript*, 188).

30. Kohn's introduction to *Vom Judentum* and various essays in that vol-

ume make it clear that the group's concerns were primarily existential rather than scholarly.

31. Buber took terms conventionally used in one way and demonstrated the problem of this usage. As we shall see in the following pages concerning his discussion of religion and religiosity and nation, he often replaced conventional terms with alternative ones that served to undercut the premise upon which the conventional usage was based. Buber utilized a similar strategy in his critique of official Zionism (see chapter 8), in his discussion of I-You and I-It (see chapter 4), and in his analysis of community (see chapter 6). In applying the term *deconstructive* to Buber I in no way wish to imply that his approach is similar to that of Jacques Derrida. As I shall discuss later, Buber's logocentric and expressivist theory of language was exactly the kind of theory Derrida rejects. See chapter 6, n. 55; and chapter 8, n. 24.

32. For a contemporary critique of the concept of tradition see Frank Lentricchia, *Criticism and Social Change* (Chicago: University of Chicago Press, 1983), 124–27; and MacIntyre, "Epistemological Crises," 54–74, especially 60–65. A similar view of tradition as ongoing argument or debate by a contemporary Jewish writer is Oz, *Land of Israel*, 136–38. Radical critiques of tradition are also found in the volumes by Rorty and Bloom referred to in chapter 2, n. 2.

33. This remains Buber's view of evil, which he treats not as a substantive force but as an existential stance. See chapter 7.

34. Buber's *religion* and *religiosity* distinction closely resembles Kierkegaard's distinction between *Christendom* and *Christianity* discussed earlier. See Kierkegaard, *Attack Upon Christendom*, 28–42, 117–24, 210–16; and Kierkegaard, *Concluding Unscientific Postscript*, 537–44. While Kierkegaard, too, had employed the term *religiosity*, he, unlike Buber, used it as a general term for religious life. Although Grete Schaeder has suggested that Buber's use of the term *religiosity* derives from Simmel, Simmel's descriptive use of the term lacks the critical edge that Buber assigns to it. See Georg Simmel, *The Sociology of Religion*, trans. Curt Rosenthal (New York: The Philosophical Library, 1959), 11 passim.

35. Kierkegaard, distinguishing between the what and the how of faith, spoke of authentic faith in terms of the relationship between the individual and God. See, for example, Kierkegaard, *Concluding Unscientific Postscript*, 540. In this early lecture, the term *Unbedingten* has been translated by Glatzer as unconditioned (Buber, *On Judaism*, 12). In later passages, Glatzer has translated it as unconditional. See Buber, *On Judaism*, 69, 150, 154, 168–69, 171.

36. Buber's style of language criticism or, as he later called it, *Begriffskritik* (concept criticism), was not dissimilar to the approach of his friend and mentor Gustav Landauer. Landauer, a disciple of the Viennese philosopher Fritz Mauthner, stressed the inadequacy of language and

the need to carry on an ongoing critique of language. According to Janik and Toulmin, Mauthner's writings had a significant impact on Ludwig Wittgenstein. See Janik and Toulmin, *Wittgenstein's Vienna*, 121–33, 196–99.

37. See the discussion of Buber's edifying strategy in chapter 4.

38. For earlier statements of Buber's hostility to the rabbis see chapter 2. As I shall discuss in chapter 8, Buber's attitude to rabbis softened somewhat during the 1920s. See the sources cited in chapter 8, n. 4.

39. For general discussions of rabbinic Judaism see Moore, *Judaism*, and Urbach, *Sages*. A good discussion of the institutional structure of rabbinic Judaism among European Jews on the eve of the Western Enlightenment is Katz, *Tradition*, 3–209. For the dialectical role of religion as a legitimating force in traditional societies see Berger, *Sacred Canopy*.

40. See Buber, "My Way to Hasidism," in Buber, *Hasidism and Modern Man*, 56–58 (hereafter referred to as *HMM*); and Buber's letter to Franz Rosenzweig, in Rosenzweig, *On Jewish Learning*, 110.

41. For sources on *Lebensphilosophie*, see chapter 1, n. 62.

42. The concept of *Erlebnis* is discussed in Ermath, *Wilhelm Dilthey*, chap. 2.

43. Simmel, *Conflict*, 20.

44. The philosophy of life was also reflected in the works of Wilhelm Dilthey, who, like Simmel, was one of Buber's professors. Dilthey constructed a theory of the human sciences based upon the idea of immediate life experience *(Erlebnis)*. Synthesizing history and psychology, Dilthey combined an intuitive study of forms of life and objectified spirit with a comparative, rational analysis. In contrast to Nietzsche and Simmel, however, Dilthey refrained from social and cultural criticism, seeking instead to create a new method for interpreting human culture and its historical development. Dilthey's relationship to *Lebensphilosophie* is discussed by Ermath in *Wilhelm Dilthey*, 108–39. For a brief selection of Dilthey's writings in English see Dilthey, *Selected Writings*.

45. Simmel, *Conflict*, 12.

46. Coser, *Georg Simmel*, 141.

47. "The Janusian process, although it may occur dimly and in a moment of time, consists of interest in opposites, formulating opposites, recognizing the salience or impact of particular opposites with respect to a particular problem, task or field, and conceiving or postulating the opposites simultaneously" (Rothenberg, *Emerging Goddess*, 251). Rothenberg also argues that "creative people do not use opposition consciously to accomplish any set purpose, but they are drawn to opposition and they tend to formulate opposites because such a procedure is useful, and often critical, in making discoveries and producing artistic creations" (ibid., 250).

48. Walter Kaufmann criticized Buber for such simplified bifurcation. See chapter 4, n. 56.

49. On the conflict of life and form see chapter 1. An early effort by Buber to struggle with this issue is found in his somewhat confusing essay "Das Gestaltende," in *Jüdische Bewegung* 1:204–15.

50. The concept of blood is utilized by Buber in his pre–World War I writings to refer to the "innermost stratum" of a person's identity and is composed of those elements, transmitted from the past, that make the person aware of being a part of a group or nation. For a discussion of this concept see Glatzer's editor's postscript in Buber, *On Judaism*, 239–40. In the period after World War I, Buber modified his use of the concept of blood. In 1921, in a speech to the Twelfth Zionist Congress in Karlsbad, Buber clarified his concept of nationhood. Insisting that biological bonds are not essential to a nation, Buber emphasized the necessity of a unity that resulted from "a great molding fate they experienced in common" (Buber, *Israel and the World*, 217). There, as in subsequent writings and lectures, he vehemently attacked all forms of national chauvinism. See Buber, *Israel and the World*, 214–26 and "The Power of the Spirit" (1934), 173–82 in the same volume. See also Buber's later observations in Rome and Rome, *Philosophical Interrogations*, 78.

In the Hebrew edition of *Reden über das Judentum*, published in 1959, Buber added the following note:

> Several years after these words were written, evil men arose and perverted the concept, "blood" which I found it necessary to use here. Therefore, I hereby announce that every place I used the concept, "blood," I in no way intended it as a racial term, which, in my opinion, has no basis, but as a term that indicates the continuity of generations, which is the backbone which preserves a people's essence. (Buber, *Te'udah ve-Ye'ud* 1:29)

For a critical perspective on Buber's usage see Mosse, *Germans and Jews*, 77–115.

51. On the concepts of exile and redemption see Halpern, *Idea of the Jewish State*, 95–104; and Yizhak Baer, *Galut*. The most extensive discussion of the concept of exile and its significance for Jewish history is found in Yehezkel Kaufmann, *Golah ve-Nekhar*. For a discussion of Kaufmann's views, see my articles "Exile and Alienhood" and "Religion, Ethnicity and Jewish History." For a recent discussion of the concept of exile in Zionist writings see Arnold Eisen, *Galut*.

52. For Ahad Haam's complex view on the negators of the diaspora, see Ahad Haam, "The Negation of the Diaspora."

53. For Ahad Haam's views on the renewal of Judaism see Ahad Haam, *Nationalism*, 66–89; and my essay, "Secular System of Meaning."

54. Nietzsche's approach to the past is most clearly seen in such works as *Birth of Tragedy, Genealogy of Morals*, and *Advantage and Disadvantage of History*. For a discussion of Nietzsche's orientation to history see White, *Metahistory*, chap. 9; and Kaufmann, *Nietzsche*, chap. 4.

55. To Buber, the life of a group is analogous to that of an individual. What the individual experiences in his or her own psychic life, the group experiences on a broader scale:

> The life story of a people is, after all, nothing more than the life story of any member of that people, in large projection; and whatever the history of Judaism teaches us can be complemented and affirmed through self observation, by every individual Jew, if only he is sufficiently unafraid, clearsighted, and honest. (Buber, *On Judaism*, 24)

Like an individual, a group struggles to actualize its inherent life forces and its innate predispositions.

56. During the 1920s, Buber increasingly adopted a positive attitude toward the rabbinic sources; see chapter 8 and the writings cited there in n. 4. In "Imitatio Dei" (Buber, *Israel and the World*, 66–77), written in 1926, Buber cited extensively from rabbinic sources.

57. Buber, *On Judaism*, 88–93, 32, 43.

58. For basic ideas of nineteenth-century German nationalism see Berlin, *Vico and Herder*, Introduction and 143–216. Changing German views of nationalism in the nineteenth century are discussed by Iggers in *German Conception of History*, chap. 2. For other critical discussions see Minougue, *Nationalism*; Kedourie, *Nationalism*, chaps. 1–5; and Shaefer, *Nationalism*, especially chaps. 1–4 and chap. 12.

59. As we shall see, Buber's interpretation of the basic ethos of Judaism changed as his overall philosophical position became clarified. In his earliest writings, he spoke of Judaism's prédisposition to unity, deed, and future redemption, as well as religiosity and myth. In his mature writings, particularly after *I and Thou*, he emphasized Judaism's striving for genuine community and dialogical existence. See chapter 8.

60. For a discussion of the concept of *teshuvah* as employed in rabbinic literature see Urbach, *Sages*, 462–71.

61. See, for example, Hirsch, *Nineteen Letters*, 106–11. See also Mendes-Flohr and Reinharz, *Jew in the Modern World*, 140–81. For criticisms of Zionism for being incompatible with European values by both liberals and traditionalists see ibid., 427–28 and 432–33. For other criticisms of Zionist ideology see Selzer, *Zionism Reconsidered*, 1–22, 49–64.

62. The "turn to the East" was a common motif among German and Viennese intellectuals of the day, as reflected in the work of Hermann Hesse. Buber had a high opinion of the writings of Rudolph Kassner on this topic and also held Indian religion in high regard. See Buber, *Briefwechsel* 1:237. On Buber's own relation to the religion of China see chapter 4, 136–39.

63. As Rivkah Horowitz has argued, Buber's revision of his earlier position may have been precipitated in part by the critical arguments of Franz

Rosenzweig, whose article criticizing Buber's views had not been accepted for publication in *Vom Judentum*. On this, see Horowitz, *Buber's Way to I and Thou*, 187–89, and n. 69.

64. In a few other places, Buber spoke of ritual in positive terms. See "The Pharisees," in Cohen, *The Jew*; and "On National Education," in Buber, *Israel and the World*, 161–63. Buber also spoke of "the structures of the life of a people" (ibid., 210). See also the comments of Simon in *Aims*, 128–34.

65. Wilhelm Dilthey, with whom Buber studied in Berlin, considered symbols, cultural forms, and social structures as a key to understanding the basic experience of an age *(Erlebnis)*. See Dilthey, *Selected Writings*, 159–263. See also H. P. Rickman, *Wilhelm Dilthey: Pattern and Meaning in History* (New York: Harper and Row, 1961), 113–58. It is worth noting that Dilthey spoke of historical-cultural understanding *(Verstehen)* in terms of I and Thou.

> Understanding is a rediscovery of the I in the Thou: the mind rediscovers itself at ever higher levels of complex involvement: this identity of the mind in the I and the Thou, in every subject and community, in every system of a culture and finally, in the totality of mind and universal history, makes successful cooperation between different processes in the human studies possible. (Dilthey, *Selected Writings*, 208)

Buber, however, makes no mention of Dilthey as one of those who influenced his philosophy of dialogue. See Buber, *Between Man and Man*, 209–24. For a recent attempt to situate Buber within the hermeneutic tradition of Dilthey see Steven D. Kepnes, "A Hermeneutic Approach to the Buber-Scholem Controversy," in *Journal of Jewish Studies* 38, no. 1 (Spring 1987): 81–98. My reading of this controversy, discussed in chapter 2, differs significantly from Kepnes'.

66. The concept of Hebrew humanism is discussed at length in chapter 8. Grete Schaeder has utilized this concept as the root metaphor of her study, *Humanism*.

67. In his earlier lectures, Buber had alternately viewed Hasidism in terms of religiosity, myth, and the actualization of the three-fold ethos of unity, deed, and future. Community became a central motif in his interpretation of Hasidism only after World War I.

68. This mention of model community is from a 1914 lecture; Buber only began to utilize it as a fundamental concept in 1918.

69. Franz Rosenzweig, in the essay "Atheistische Theologie," originally submitted to but never published in *Vom Judentum*, had criticized Buber's conception of God as articulated in his earliest lectures on Judaism. A Hebrew translation is available in Franz Rosenzweig, *Naharaim*, 70–79. In his 1923 preface to his lectures on Judaism, Buber, responding to Rosenzweig's criticism, took great pains to stress that he never intended to suggest that God actually undergoes change. Al-

though admitting to inexactitude in his original wording, Buber insisted that he never intended to reduce God to an idea or symbol but only to describe the way in which God is perceived in human society. See Buber, *On Judaism*, 5–6.

70. For Rosenzweig's critique see his essay "The Builders," in Rosenzweig, *On Jewish Learning*, 72–92. The debate was continued in correspondence between Buber and Rosenzweig, included in the same volume, 109–24. See also Simon, "Buber and German Jewry," especially 33–39; and Simon, *Aims, Junctures, Paths*, especially 87–103, 120–42, where Simon, whose view of halakhah was close to that of Rosenzweig, criticizes Buber's position. Simon sees the Buber-Rosenzweig debate mirrored in Buber's novel *For the Sake of Heaven*. For a recent discussion of the Buber-Rosenzweig debate see Mendes-Flohr, "Law and Sacrament."

71. Genuine affirmation of the law must be anchored in this certitude of the fact of revelation and that its content has been faithfully preserved in the 613 mitzvot and their framework. Indeed, such affirmation has religious value only insofar as it is supported by this certitude. The legitimacy of the life of the man whose observance of the law is grounded on this basis is unassailable, the legitimacy of what, to him, is truth, irrefutable. . . . But if he lacks this certitude, his sacrificial spirit, whether a result of piety or of habit, loses its religious import and hence its special sanctity.

Observance of commandments because one know or feels that this is the only way in which to live in the name of God has a legitimacy all its own, essentially inaccessible to all outside criticism, whose criteria it can reject. (Buber, *On Judaism*, 165)

72. See, for example, Austin, *How to Do Things with Words*; Katz, *Mysticism*; and Paul Van Buren, *Edges of Language*. If, as these works claim, language is a form of activity, Buber's distinction between actions (halakhah) and texts (Bible) cannot be sustained. Language, once uttered, cannot be reversed any more than can other forms of behavior. Accordingly, the Bible is another form of institutionalized religion and is susceptible to Buber's critique. Buber's response to this challenge would undoubtedly be predicated on his expressivist view of language and the romantic views of myth and poetry discussed earlier. The contemporary literary theorists discussed in chapter 2, who reject the expressivist view of language, would reject Buber's claim that biblical teachings are a true expression of the divine-human encounter. See chapter 8, n. 24, and chapter 6, n. 55.

CHAPTER FOUR

1. Schilpp and Friedman, *Philosophy of Martin Buber*, 689 (hereafter referred to as *PMB*). The paradox of trying to philosophically discuss insights and experiences that are metaphilosophical is insightfully dis-

cussed by Jochanan Bloch in "The Justification and the Futility of Dialogical Thinking" and more extensively in *Die Aporie des Du*, particularly chap. 1.

2. See Rorty, *Mirror*, 11–12, 365–70. See also Richard Bernstein, *Philosophical Profiles* (Philadelphia: University of Pennsylvania Press, 1986), chaps. 1 and 2. For critical examinations of Rorty see Christopher Norris, *The Contest of Faculties: Philosophy and Theory after Deconstruction* (London: Methuen, 1985), chaps. 1 and 6; Cornell West, "The Politics of American Neo-Pragmatism," in John Rajchman and Cornell West, eds., *Post Analytic Philosophy* (New York: Columbia University Press, 1985), 259–75; and John D. Caputo, "The Thought of Being and the Conversation of Mankind: The Case of Heidegger and Rorty," in Robert Hollinger, ed., *Hermeneutics and Praxis* (Notre Dame, Ind.: University of Notre Dame Press, 1985), 248–71.

3. Rorty, *Mirror*, 360.

4. Ibid., 361.

5. Ibid., 377.

6. Ibid., 362.

7. Ibid., 358–59.

8. Ibid., 360.

9. Ibid.

10. My orientation to Buber's philosophy as edifying and social differs significantly from that of other authors whose works situate Buber's thought in the context of Western philosophy. By overlooking or minimizing the social concerns underlying Buber's work, studies such as Theunissen's *The Other*, Bloch's *Die Aporie des Du*, and Wood's *Martin Buber's Ontology* divert our attention from the edifying task that Buber set for himself and from the concrete social issues that he addressed. Moreover, several of these works tend to overlook the development in Buber's thinking in the years after *I and Thou*, a development that I shall discuss in the following chapters.

11. For an insightful discussion of Buber's adumbration of antiobjectivistic and antifoundational themes in contemporary philosophy, see Emanuel Levinas, "Martin Buber, Gabriel Marcel, and Philosophy," in Bloch and Gordon, *Martin Buber*, 305–21.

12. Rorty, *Mirror*, 360.

13. Like Buber, the psychiatrist Albert Rothenberg describes creativity as an ongoing process in which an artist or thinker clarifies an original insight or vision. "Much of the creative process consists of elaboration, execution and the attempt to differentiate and to clarify through language, symbols and tangible constructions. Much of creation arises from hard, systematic labor, the drive to perfect an entity roughly produced" (Rothenberg, *Emerging Goddess*, 134).

However, according to Bloom, this developmental view overlooks the struggle and reversal that revision entails. Although Buber, in the

passage from *I and Thou*, spoke in terms of clarification and elaboration, his later philosophy, to which Buber referred as a process of
"radical self correction" (*PMB*, 714), represented a swerve away from
and a struggle against his earlier views. Moreover, as discussed in
chapter 1, Buber described his early intellectual development with
metaphors more appropriate to Bloom's conflict model of creativity.

14. The resemblance between Buber's *Daniel* and Nietzsche's *Zarathustra*
was immediately apparent to Landauer. Upon reading the first proofs
of Buber's book, Landauer indicated how happy he was that the book
was more than a simple imitation of Nietzsche: "You have achieved
with this work, the proofs of which I have before me, what Nietzsche
did not achieve in *Zarathustra [Thus Spoke Zarathustra]*, and the *Di-
thyrambs*" (Buber, *Briefwechsel* 1:180). In several ways, *Daniel* evokes
images of *Thus Spoke Zarathustra*, the Nietzschean work that had
made such a profound impact on the young Buber. Like Nietzsche,
Buber couched his argument as a series of conversations, thereby utilizing indirect, quasi-poetic discourse in contrast to the systematic, analytic discourse of conventional philosophy. Also, Daniel, like Zarathustra, first appears to us as he descends from the mountain in order to go
out among the people. Moreover, like Nietzsche's work, Buber's *Daniel*
criticizes the prevailing rationalistic, instrumentalist mode of thought
for its stifling effect upon the individual and society.

15. Buber first learned about the structuring role of categories from Kant.
However, finding Kant's critique insufficient, Buber turned to Nietzsche
whose deconstruction of language and rational thought he found more
satisfying. See *PMB*, 12. See also Rome and Rome, *Philosophical Interrogations*, 21.

16. In "Metropolis," Simmel used the metaphor of an individual who, upon
arriving in a new city, sought vainly to orient himself through abstract
categories. In a similar vein, Wittgenstein spoke of philosophizing as
analogous to finding one's way out of a maze: "Our language can be
seen as an ancient city: a maze of little streets and squares, of old and
new houses, and of houses with additions from various periods; and
this surrounded by a multitude of new boroughs with straight regular
streets and uniform houses" (Wittgenstein, *Philosophical Investigations*, 8e, para. 18); "A philosophical problem has the form: I don't
know my way about" (Ibid., 49e, para. 123); and "What is your aim in
philosophy?—To shew the fly the way out of the fly-bottle" (Ibid.,
103e, para. 309).

17. As discussed in chapter 1, Nietzsche also spoke of intellectual systems
as hideouts to which we flee in an effort to avoid the freedom of choice
and the accompanying responsibility.

18. As Buber's letters from this period clearly reveal, he had, by 1913,
recognized the need to expand his discussion into the realm of social
relations. See Buber, *Briefwechsel* vol. 1, letters 226–27. Listing a series

of passages from his earlier writings that had strong social implications, Buber indicated his intention to spell out these implications in another work. However, not until 1923, with the publication of *I and Thou*, did he succeed in doing this.

19. To Buber, the self is not static but continually moves between orientation and actualization in a constant state of tension (Buber, *Daniel: Dialogues on Realization*, 142 [all references to *Daniel* are taken from 1964 English translation]). According to Buber, a person's life is characterized more by discontinuity than by continuity and stability:

> An actualizing kind of man, an orienting kind of man, do not exist. . . . Rather, actualization and orientation dwell close together, like conception and pregnancy, like knowledge and dissemination, like discovery and utilization. As in the life of the community, the attained reality must ever again be inserted in the structure of experience, so in the life of the individual, hours of inserting follow hours of actualization, and must so follow; the solitary reality is still not only the highest of blisses but also the heaviest of burdens. (Buber, *Daniel*, 70–71)

Echoing a Nietzschean theme, Buber suggested that there is an elite for whom the hours of actualization merge together into a "succession of summits." For such people, the moments of orientation are permeated by the "impulses of the actual" (Ibid., 70–71).

20. As indicated in the passage quoted in n. 19, Buber acknowledged that these categories were ideal types. Likewise, in *I and Thou*, Buber acknowledged that no person is either pure person or pure ego; see n. 58. For a comparison of *Daniel* and *I and Thou*, see Rivkah Horowitz, *Buber's Way to I and Thou*, 214–25.

21. This essay was written in 1914 and, together with four others published in that year, may be read as a commentary to *Daniel*. All five essays have been translated in Buber, *Pointing the Way*, 5–30. As discussed in chapter 2, Buber emphasized Hasidism's concern for the concrete and the everyday.

22. In form as well as content, Buber conveyed to the reader the importance of dialogue. In addition to being an important theme in *Daniel*, the concept of dialogue also shaped the book's literary structure. Unlike Nietzsche's *Zarathustra*, which is composed as a series of monologues, *Daniel* is written as a series of dialogues between the protagonist, Daniel, and several partners. As indicated in n. 26, in *I and Thou*, Buber used the concept *relation*. Dialogue emerged as a fundamental concept only in the years following *I and Thou*.

23. As I indicate in chap. 6, n. 17, Buber, beginning in 1906, had concerned himself with fundamental issues of social and political life as the editor of *Die Gesellschaft*, a monographic series on political, social, and cultural issues. However, not until 1923 did he address these issues extensively in his own writings.

24. See chap. 1, n. 16.
25. During World War I, Buber interpreted the war in redemptive terms, a position for which he was sharply criticized by Landauer. Mendes-Flohr [formerly Flohr] has argued that Landauer's sharp criticism of Buber's views of the war was the decisive factor leading to Buber's shift from *Lebensphilosophie* and mysticism to philosophy of dialogue. According to this view, Buber was so stunned by the severity of Landauer's criticism that he reconsidered his overall philosophical orientation. See Paul R. Flohr, "The Road to *I and Thou*"; and Flohr, *Kulturmystik to Dialogue*, 143–69. In contrast to Flohr's interpretation of "Buber's volte-face," I have argued that the shift in Buber's position is already evident in his earlier writings and represents the culmination of a gradual intellectual process. See, in particular, the letters referred to in n. 18. While Landauer's criticism may have served as a catalyst moving Buber to crystallize his social concerns, it is, I believe, exaggerating the importance of the criticism to isolate it as the major causal factor. Like many other intellectuals who adopted apocalyptic views of the war, Buber, in the wake of the war, experienced profound disillusionment.

In future works, Buber criticized the apocalyptic attitude which viewed war and revolution as redemptive. This is clearly spelled out in his novel *For the Sake of Heaven*, which Buber began during World War I, but which he did not complete until 1942. For an alternative rejoinder to Flohr see Friedman, *Buber's Life and Work* 1:200–201, 397–98, and chap. 9, n. E.
26. See Buber, *Briefwechsel*, vol. 2, letters 11, 17, and 53. Horowitz's *Buber's Way to I and Thou*, an important contribution to our understanding of the development of Buber's thought, focuses on the religious dimension of Buber's thought while neglecting his social concerns. Horowitz makes only a cursory reference to "The Holy Way" and *Grosse Maggid* and does not discuss *Worte* or the social themes in "Holy Way."

In attempting to argue the decisive influence of Rosenzweig and Ebner on *I and Thou*, Horowitz focuses on such terms as *dialogue*. The term *dialogue*, however, does not occur in *I and Thou*. As I shall show in chapter 5, dialogue becomes a central concept only in subsequent works. Moreover, it is not simply the term *dialogue* that is the significant contribution of Buber's work but the way in which he formulated it into a unique interpretation of the human condition. The problem in Horowitz's interpretation lies in the narrowness of the author's approach, which overlooks the basic social and edifying *Problemstellung* of Buber's writings, choosing instead to focus on limited literary and philological evidence. For a critique of Horowitz's thesis, see Friedman, *Buber's Life and Work* 1:415–27; and Maurice Friedman, "Martin Buber and Franz Rosenzweig: The Road to *I and Thou*," *Philosophy Today* (Fall 1986): 210–20. Unfortunately, while correctly arguing in his article for a more developmental interpretation, Friedman fails to do justice to Buber's social concerns.

27. For a discussion of the effect of this social turn on Buber's interpretation of Judaism, see chapters 3 and 8.
28. The original manuscript in the Martin Buber Archives bears the title "The Actualization of Judaism." Flohr discusses the lecture at length in *From Kulturmystik to Dialogue*, 160–74. According to Flohr, in "Road to *I and Thou*," the earliest indication of Buber's move away from *Lebensphilosophie* was the 1917 article "Vorbemerkung über Franz Werfel," in Buber, *Jüdische Bewegung* 2:104–10. However, it was not until "The Holy Way" that Buber clearly articulated the basic importance of the interhuman *(das Zwischenmenschliche)*.
29. On Buber's later views concerning the possibility of direct divine-human encounter see Rome and Rome, *Philosophical Interrogations*, 86; and *PMB*, 710.
30. This essay, still unavailable in English, was originally intended as the first in a series devoted to the emerging "people's revolution" *(Volkerrevolution)*, a revolution to be forged out of a synthesis of religiosity and community. Aligning himself with Tonnies, Tolstoy, Kropotkin, and Landauer, Buber distinguished this underground revolution—a revolution of the spirit—from the Marxist revolution rooted in sociopolitical upheaval.
31. See chapter 1 on Boehme.
32. The concept of human beings as creators, a theme that recurs in the writings of Nietzsche, was a significant factor in Buber's early attraction to Hasidism; see Buber, "My Way To Hasidism," in *Hasidism and Modern Man*, 47–69 (hereafter referred to as *HMM*).
33. As I show in chapter 6, the concept of education as drawing out the potential of the other was basic to Buber's social thought.
34. For a comprehensive analysis of Landauer's social and political philosophy, a philosophy with which Buber largely identified, see Lunn, *Prophet*. For Buber's sympathetic view of Landauer's social philosophy see Buber, *Paths in Utopia*, 46–57. After Landauer's death, Buber edited and published many of his works. See also Flohr, *From Kulturmystik to Dialogue*, 160–69.
35. As I discuss in chapter 6, Buber expanded this critique of Marxian socialism in *Paths in Utopia* and in his essay "Prophecy, Apocalyptic, and the Historical Hour," in Buber, *Pointing the Way*, 192–207.
36. See Introduction, n. 15. Buber's social and political thought is also analyzed by Ernst Simon in *Kav ha-Tihum* (The Line of Demarcation). See also the brief discussion by Robert Weltsch, "Buber's Political Philosophy," in *PMB*, 435–49.
37. As stated previously, I do not claim that Buber was a "deconstructionist" in the manner of Derrida. His philosophy differs in basic ways. Clearly, Buber's philosophy was logocentric. He fully believed that

there are preconceptual experiences and that language reflects these experiences. However, Buber was also, as indicated earlier, a language skeptic who was sensitive to the arbitrariness of language and its inadequacy in communicating human experience.

38. For further discussions of concept clarification see *PMB*, 696–97, 706–7; Rome and Rome, *Philosophical Interrogations*, 17–18, 67; and Buber, *Believing Humanism*, 31, 87, 134, 153–65. In his 1950 Hebrew essay "Adult Education," Buber wrote:

> The first task [of education] is the clarification of concepts, especially in the social, economic and political realms. Beginning with the reading of the morning paper through participation in evening meetings, the young person is flooded with a plethora of concepts which he accepts and utilizes, without giving an accounting as to their actual meaning for him or for others who use them. Examination and clarification are essential conditions to cognition. (Buber, *Te'udah ve-Ye'ud* 2:404–5)

39. These lectures, delivered in 1924 in Vienna, are MS. var. 350/B, 47d, Martin Buber Archives, Jewish National Library, Jerusalem.

40. Buber, "Abende," 3. The pages in the original manuscript are unmarked.

41. As many commentators have observed, the It world of *I and Thou* corresponds to the world of orientation discussed in Buber's earlier meditation on the human condition in Buber, *Daniel*.

42. Buber used the term *experience (Erfahrung)* to denote this I-It mode of existence/relation. However, his primary concern was to argue that *Erfahrung*, the I-It mode of relation, constitutes only one way of being in the world. In later writings, Buber used the term *experience* in a more conventional way; see, for example, *PMB*, 689.

43. Franz Rosenzweig was one of the first to criticize Buber for presenting a distorted vision of the It world. To Rosenzweig, Buber was guilty of accepting the straw man that European rationalism had created. See Buber, *Briefwechsel*, vol. 2, letters 103–5. For a translation and discussion of some of the relevant correspondence, see Horowitz, *Buber's Way*, 226–31. Buber, referring to this criticism more than forty years later, readily acknowledged his neglect of the It world. However, he explained that neglect in terms of the purpose at hand, which was, as I have argued, to combat the alienation that pervades modern life:

> Indeed it does not [do] justice to the It: because I am born in the midst of this situation of man and see what I see and must point out what I have seen. In another hour it would perhaps have been granted to me to sound the praises of the It; today not: because without a turning of man to his Thou no turn in his destiny can come. (*PMB*, 704)

44. In the remainder of this book, I adopt the translation of Walter Kaufmann who has made a convincing case that in *I and Thou* and in Buber's subsequent writings, the German word *Du* is best rendered in

English by *You* rather than *Thou*. See Kaufmann, Prologue in Buber, *I and Thou*, 14–15. Like Kaufmann, I shall retain the traditional translation of the title *I and Thou*, since this is the way that the work is known in the English-speaking world. For a critique of Kaufmann's position see Friedman, *Buber's Life and Work* 1:428–29.

45. For other criticisms by Buber of Marx, see Buber, *Paths in Utopia*, 80–98; Buber, *Pointing the Way*, 192–207. See also chapter 6.

46. Kierkegaard, *Concluding Unscientific Postscript*, 109.

47. Heinemann, *Existentialism*, 35.

48. This is in marked contrast to his earlier position on Feuerbach expressed in his 1901 essay on Boehme (see chapter 1). Whereas the 1901 essay reflects Buber's early identification with mystical doctrines, the 1938 discussion shows his shift to relational, or dialogical, philosophy.

49. "On the map of Nietzsche's philosophical interests and concerns, the domain of inquiry which lies at its center is what might be called philosophical anthropology; for it is above all upon 'man'—upon human nature, human life, and human possibility—that his attention focuses" (Richard Schacht, *Nietzsche*, 267).

50. Hollingdale, *Nietzsche*, 176.

51. Nietzsche, *Untimely Meditations*, 127.

52. Ibid., 128.

53. Although defining a person in terms of relation, Buber did not deny a person's unique, individual qualities. As Hasidism had taught him, while the self depends for its full actualization on its relationship to other selves, to relate to others, we must unify our own selves. For Buber's dialectical view of self-actualization see chapter 5.

54. The idea that language generates or constitutes the framework through which we see and experience reality has been developed by philosophers such as Wittgenstein, J. L. Austin, and Norman Malcom. See Pitkin, *Wittgenstein and Justice*, and sources cited in chapter 3, n. 72. The constitutive force of language is also argued by David Bohm in *Wholeness*. Although Bohm, a physicist whose ideas are firmly rooted in Eastern religions, never mentions Buber, there is a definite affinity between their views. On Bohm, see also chapter 8, n. 15.

55. As Rivkah Horowitz points out (*Buber's Way to I and Thou*, 35), while terms such as *It world* and *You world* were used in Buber's 1922 lectures ("Religions als Gegenwart"), the lectures were primarily concerned with theological and metaphysical issues. Buber first introduced the basic words *I-You* and *I-It* in *I and Thou*. In that book Buber focused on modes of relationship. Horowitz provides a detailed comparison of *I and Thou* and the 1922 lectures. See n. 26.

56. Buber, as we have repeatedly seen, utilized polar concepts, such as relation/experience, religiosity/religion, education/propaganda, dialogue/monologue, official/underground Judaism. Walter Kaufmann criticized this polar approach in his introduction to Buber, *I and Thou*,

insisting that it oversimplified the complexities of human relationships, a position that he reiterates in *Discovering the Mind*, 257–72, and in "Buber's Failures and Triumph." In *Emerging Goddess*, Rothenberg argues that polar thinking, which he refers to as Janusian thinking, is an essential tool of creative thinkers and artists. See Rothenberg, *Emerging Goddess*, chap. 7. Kaufmann acknowledged that Buber's later writings are less open to his charge of romanticism and manicheanism (Kaufmann, *Discovering the Mind*, 265). As I shall argue in chapters 5 and 6, the romanticism of *I and Thou*, to which Kaufmann objects, is increasingly absent from Buber's later discussions of dialogical relations. See, in particular, Buber, *Knowledge of Man*, 59–88.

57. Kaufmann has observed that Buber's work appeared in 1923, the same year as Freud's *Das Es und das Ich* (*The Ego and the Id*, trans. and ed. James Strachey. [New York: W. W. Norton, 1960]). While commonly translated as *The Ego and the Id*, translated literally it means: *The It and the I*. See Kaufmann's prologue to Buber, *I and Thou*, 15–16.

58. "No human being is pure person, and none is pure ego; none is entirely actual, none entirely lacking in actuality. Each lives in a twofold I. But some men are so person-oriented that one may call them persons, while others are so ego-oriented that one may call them egos" (Buber, *I and Thou*, 114–15). Thus, ego and person represent what Weber called "ideal types." On several other occasions, Buber warned against taking his categories literally. See Buber, *Daniel*, 70–71; and n. 19.

59. Buber subsequently expressed his regret over this choice of words which immediately call to mind the opening verse of Genesis and of the Gospel of John. As he later explained, it was never his intention to assert the temporal priority of relation, but simply to prioritize the steps essential to human becoming. See *PMB*, 706.

The concept of entelechy is basic to Buber's philosophy. See chap. 1, n. 70; and Buber, *Knowledge of Man*, 84–85. Whether talking of individuals or communities, Buber assumed the existence of inherent, primal forces that yearned to be actualized. Through this process of actualization, the individual being realizes its own unique potential. This concept, which is basic to the writings of psychologists like Horney, Maslow, and Rogers, has been recently discussed by Yalom in *Existential Psychotherapy*, 279–85. The influence of Buber on Yalom is discussed in chapter 5. For a critique of the concept of entelechy as it is used by contemporary psychology see Rosenthal, *Words and Values*.

60. See Buber, *I and Thou*, 111–15. In asserting the pendulum-like nature of life, Buber emphasized the discontinuity that characterizes human existence, a theme that has roots in the writings of Nietzsche and is common to many poststructuralist literary theorists.

61. I find this passage somewhat confusing. I am not sure why Buber did not say that all actual life is relation and that relation *(Beziehung)*, not encounter *(Begegnung)*, is a matter of grace. After all, we can, to

a degree, plan encounters with the other, but we can never plan relation. Accordingly, it is relation, not encounter, that occurs through grace. On the problematics surrounding the terms *Beziehung* and *Begegnung*, see the remarks of Gabriel Marcel in *PMB*, 41–48. Buber's response appears in *PMB*, 705–7.

62. Buber depicted Napoleon as the epitome of evil in his novel *For the Sake of Heaven*.

63. Whereas, in *PMB*, *Beziehung* is translated as relationship, I consistently translate it as relation, which, as I have shown, represents a particular kind of relationship.

64. The organic interrelationship of nature was discussed by Buber in his early essay on Boehme and in his dissertation. In 1901, Buber identified with this mystical orientation. Later, however, he privileged the existential individuation of the person, a motif already evident in his dissertation. In direct relation, the individuated quality of the self is preserved. In his writings on Hasidism, Buber emphasized that the liberation of the spark did not result in the annihilation of the concrete, individual life of each being, as some Hasidic sources claim. See chapter 2, 46–50.

65. Although Buber insisted that his views differed from those of mystics, the sense of organic wholeness, immediacy, and ineffableness that characterizes the I-You relation clearly resembles the experiences conveyed in the writings of many mystics. To convey a sense of wholeness and unity, Buber employed the analogy of music, an image frequently used by mystics. Thus, he argued, when we hear a melody or read a poem, we do not first see the individual tones or words. Instead, we see or hear the totality, the organic whole. Only when we step back and assume a detached stance do we analyze the poem or melody, breaking it down into component parts. Similarly, when we step back and assume a distance in our relations with other beings, we fragment the wholeness of the other and destroy the immediacy of relation. On this, see the discussion by Malcolm Diamond, *Martin Buber*, chap. 2.

66. See chapter five, where Buber's concept of *inclusion* is discussed.

67. From Buber, "My Way to Hasidism," first published in 1918.

68. Buber first elaborated the concept of the "hallowing of the everyday" in his introduction to the 1921 work *Der Grosse Maggid*. This essay may be found in English translation in Buber, *Origin and Meaning of Hasidism*; see, in particular, 149.

69. The Taoist writings also confirmed Buber's skeptical attitude toward language. Dissatisfied with conventional Chinese views of morality, the teachers of Tao had, like the edifying philosophers of the West, endeavored to liberate people by challenging conventional concepts and values: "Lao Tsu ushers me, far more deeply than Hume, into the problematics of conceptuality; he discloses to me, as Hume does not, the abyss beneath the concepts; he helps me to do what Hume will not

and cannot do—see through the indispensible logizing of reality" (Rome and Rome, *Philosophical Interrogations*, 17).

70. For English translations of the Taoist texts under discussion see Lao Tsu, *Tao Te Ching*, trans. D. C. Lau (New York: Penguin Books, 1963); and *Chuang Tzu: Basic Writings*, trans. Burton Watson (New York: Columbia University Press, 1964). In 1910 Buber published a selection from the writings of Chuang Tzu, entitled *Reden und Gleichnisse des Tchuang Tse*. The introduction to these lectures is translated in *Pointing the Way*, 31–58. In that essay, Buber still emphasized the mystical experience of unity. In August 1924, Buber delivered a series of unpublished lectures in Ascona, Switzerland, on the *Tao Te Ching*. In those lectures, "Besprechungen mit Martin Buber über Lao-tse's *Tao-te-king*," Buber extensively discussed the Taoist concepts that he found to be compatible with his own thought and elaborated on the relationship of those concepts and his own philosophy of relation. See also Buber, "Religion als Gegenwart," in Horowitz, *Buber's Way to I and Thou*, 113. For further discussion of the Taoist influences in Buber's thought see Robert Wood, "Buber and the Far East," in Bloch and Gordon, *Martin Buber*, 331–35.

71. Munro, *Concept of Man*, 142.

72. Watson, *Chuang Tzu*, 6. For a slightly different interpretation see Welch, *Taoism*, 13–14.

73. Munro, *Concept of Man*, 144.

74. Ibid., 145, 151, 155.

75. Ibid., 158–59.

76. Among those scholars who discuss this social motif in Taoism see Kuang-ming Wu in *Chuang Tzu: World Philosopher at Play*, American Academy of Religion Studies in Religion, 26 (New York: Crossroad Publishing; Chico, Calif.: Scholars Press, 1982), especially 91–137; and Norman Girardot, "Behaving Cosmogonically." See also Girardot, *Myth and Meaning*, 84. These interpretations, which highlight the social orientation of Taoist writings, lend support to Buber's effort, in his unpublished lectures on Lao Tsu, to integrate Taoist teachings with his philosophy of relation. For a highly suggestive discussion of Chuang-tzu as an edifying philosopher, see Yearly, "Perfected Person," 125–39. I am grateful to Professor Girardot for providing me with a prepublication draft of his lecture.

77. This idea has its parallel in the Hasidic teaching emphasized by Buber, that we help to liberate the divine spark in others by honoring that which is unique in them; see chap. 2, 47–51 and chap. 7, 207–11. The concepts of dialogue and confirming the other, which will be discussed at length in the next chapter, represent a further development in Buber's application of the ideas implicit in the Taoist vision.

CHAPTER FIVE

1. In light of this ongoing revision, Kaufmann, who focuses his critique on the categories of *I and Thou*, does Buber a disservice. See chap. 4, n. 56.
2. The shorter works referred to by Buber, as listed in the German edition of *I and Thou*, include "Dialogue," "Questions to the Single One," and "What Is Man," reprinted in Buber, *Between Man and Man*. The later works include "Elements of the Interhuman" and "Distance and Relation," both reprinted in Buber, *Knowledge of Man*.
3. As I shall discuss later, these include the Americans Carl Rogers and Irvin Yalom, the Scottish psychiatrist R. D. Laing, and the English psychiatrist Robert Hobson.
4. On the differences between the approach taken here and other works on Buber written in the Continental philosophical tradition, see chap. 4, n. 10.
5. This question, as mentioned earlier, was the title of a 1919 essay by Buber.
6. Kaufmann, Buber's translator and admirer, insisted that there are many other modes of I-You relations besides those discussed by Buber. Rejecting Buber's dichotomous way of speaking, Kaufmann insisted, "Man's world is manifold and his attitudes are manifold." While people, in search of simplicity, like to be told that there are only two worlds and two ways, this is deceptive. See his preface to Buber, *I and Thou*, 9–17. See also Kaufmann, *Discovering the Mind* 2:257–65; and his critical assessment in Bloch and Gordon, *Martin Buber*, 3–24. See also above, chap. 4, n. 56.
7. Although scholars such as Friedman and Horowitz speak of *I and Thou* as a philosophy of dialogue, this is not precise. As I have shown, the dominant concept in that work is relation. The concept of dialogue, however, does not become central to Buber's writings until several years later. It is first discussed extensively in his 1925 essay, "Reden über das Erziehische" (education) published in 1926 (now in Buber, *Between Man and Man*, 83–103) and is elaborated in his essay, *Zwiesprache* (dialogue), published in 1929 and expanded into book form in 1932 (now in ibid., 1–39). Buber continued to revise and elaborate on the concept of dialogue in later essays; for example, in "Distance and Relation," originally published in German in 1950, and in "Elements of the Interhuman," published in 1954 (now in Buber, *Knowledge of Man*).
8. As Friedman has noted, Buber's thinking had influenced a number of European psychotherapists. See *Life of Dialogue*, chap. 21; and Friedman, *Buber's Life and Work* 2:225–30. In recent years, a school of existential sociology has emerged that focuses on the preconceptual,

prelinguistic moment or experience, as did Buber. See Douglas and Johnson, *Existential Sociology*, chaps. 1 and 2. There is no indication, however, that Buber's writings had any influence on this school.

9. The essays "Distance and Relation" and "Elements of the Interhuman" were first presented as lectures at the Washington School of Psychiatry in 1957. See Farber, "Introductory Remarks," 95–96.

10. See Leslie H. Farber, "Martin Buber and Psychotherapy," in *PMB*, 577–602. On Buber's interactions with psychiatrists and psychologists in the later years of his life, see Friedman, *Buber's Life and Work* 3:205–29.

11. Buber, "Elements of the Interhuman" (1957), in Buber, *Knowledge of Man*, 75. Earlier Buber had written: "The dialogical situation can be adequately grasped only in an ontological way. But it is not to be grasped on the basis of the ontic of personal existence, or of that of two personal existences, but of that which has its being between them and transcends both" (Buber, *Between Man and Man*, 204).

12. Thus Buber objected that the German philosopher Max Scheler's emphasis on the category of "sympathy" was insufficient and misleading insofar as it privileged feeling over relation. For Buber's criticism of Scheler see Buber, *Between Man and Man*, 181–96. For Scheler's views see Scheler, *The Nature of Sympathy* (New Haven, Conn.: Yale University Press, 1954).

13. In *Between Man and Man* (4–5), Buber described a meeting of eight representatives of different countries in Potsdam in 1914 that exemplifies this form of dialogue. For more on the meeting of this group, known as the Forte Kreis, see Friedman, *Buber's Life and Work* 1:178–85, 197–99.

14. On the concept of entelechy, see chap. 4, n. 59 and chap. 1, n. 70. As indicated in chapter 1, Nietzsche had emphasized the individual's obligation to actualize his or her full potential, even making this idea the subtitle of his work *Ecce Homo: How One Becomes What One Is*. See also the introduction to Nietzsche, *Ecce Homo*, 14–15. Similarly, Kierkegaard emphasized the obligation of each person to become an individual. However, in contrast to these precursors, Buber insisted that one actualizes oneself only through relations to others.

15. For more on Buber's views on acceptance see his public debate with Carl Rogers (Buber, *Knowledge of Man*, 166–84).

16. See the critique of this concept by Nathan Rotenstreich in *PMB*, 97–132.

17. This passage is from Buber's 1957 Afterword. Earlier, in *I and Thou* (57–60), Buber had distinguished between the various levels of relationship (inanimate, animate, spiritual, and human) according to their use of language.

18. Once again, Buber appealed to "the testimony of your own mysteries, my reader, which may be buried under debris, but are presumably accessible to you" (Buber, *I and Thou*, 174).

19. This seems to indicate that the teacher-student, therapist-patient relationships, in which full mutuality is unattainable, are not genuine dialogues. Yet, Buber refers to them as examples of I-You relations. This appears to confirm the fact, disputed by Kaufmann, that for Buber, there are different levels of genuine dialogue, of which the teacher-student, therapist-patient relationships represent one.

20. Buber's interest in psychotherapy can be traced back to his student days when he attended several courses in that field. See Buber, *Knowledge of Man*, 167–68. His early writings, as we saw in chapters 2 and 3, reflect a psychological orientation. Although critical of what he termed the reductionistic "psychologizing" tendency in modern culture, Buber maintained a lifelong interest in psychotherapy and engaged in many exchanges with psychotherapists. See Friedman, *Buber's Life and Work* 1:345–53; and Bloch, *Die Aporie des Du*, 300, n. 35.

21. For an acerbic critique of Buber's interpretation of guilt see Haim Gordon, "The Sheltered Aesthete: A New Appraisal of Martin Buber's Life," in Bloch and Gordon, *Martin Buber*, 215–32.

22. See Laing, *Self and Others*, 98–107; Yalom, *Existential Psychotherapy*, especially chaps. 8–9; the dialogue between Buber and Carl Rogers in Buber, *Knowledge of Man*, 166–84; and Hobson, *Forms of Feeling*.

23. In *Martin Buber: The Life of Dialogue*, Friedman devoted a chapter to Buber's influence on European psychotherapists. In *Buber's Life and Work*, he discussed Buber's relationship to Carl Rogers. To my knowledge, there is no existing discussion of Buber's influence on the contemporary psychotherapists discussed here.

24. Yalom, in contrast to the somewhat optimistic American humanistic psychologists like Maslow and Rogers, grounds his views in the ideas of European existentialists like Heidegger and Sartre and, like them, emphasizes such themes as death and anxiety. See Yalom, *Existential Psychotherapy*, chaps. 1–5. Insofar as Buber spoke of the "melancholy of our lot" and the necessary reversion of every I-You relationship to an I-It relationship, he did not share the optimistic attitude of the humanistic psychologists. However, unlike Yalom, Buber says little about death and its psychological impact.

25. Yalom, *Existential Psychotherapy*, 401.

26. Ibid., 401.

27. For Buber's discussion of this distinction see chapter 6.

28. Yalom, *Existential Psychotherapy*, 408.

29. Ibid., 409.

30. Ibid., 411.

31. To Yalom, the Freudian model of transference, rationalizing the therapist's concealment of his own person, precludes an authentic therapist-patient relationship and, consequently, impedes effective therapy. Instead of viewing the therapist-patient relationship as inherently significant, Freudians view it instrumentally, as a means to understanding other, more important relationships. Over and against this view, Yalom

stresses the dialogical nature of the therapeutic relationship. See Yalom, *Existential Psychotherapy*, 401–15.

32. Ibid., 355.
33. Ibid., 363.
34. Ibid., 373.
35. Ibid., 367, 373. Insofar as Yalom's description of need-less love is far
more lucid than Buber's, the contemporary American reader is better
able to grasp the applicability of Buber's categories from Yalom's discussion than from the more obscure language of *I and Thou*.
36. Ibid., 485.
37. Ibid., 439. Yalom cites Buber's observation, " 'What for? What am I to
find my particular way for? What am I to unify my being for?' The
answer is: 'Not for my own sake,' " (Buber, *Hasidism and Modern Man*,
163).
38. In his autobiography, Laing describes the prejudice against talking
with mental patients that prevailed during his medical training. Referring to Buber's category of relation, Laing observes, "Whatever else it
[treatment of mental patients] has to do with, the issue has to
do with human relationships" (Laing, *Wisdom, Madness and Folly*,
31).
39. Laing, *Self and Others*, 99.
40. Ibid.
41. Ibid., 99. This concurs with Buber's position that one can confirm an
opponent with whom one disagrees. See Buber, *Knowledge of Man*, 69,
85–88.
42. Laing, *Self and Others*, 101.
43. See Buber, *Knowledge of Man*, 75–78.
44. Laing, *Self and Others*, 109.
45. Ibid., 110.
46. Ibid., 111.
47. Hobson, *Forms of Feeling*.
48. Hobson mentions I. T. Ramsey, D. W. Hamlyn, R. S. Peters, H. McCabe,
Wittgenstein, and Austin.
49. As I have repeatedly emphasized, Buber continually advocated an existential analysis of concepts.

> An ever renewed analysis of basic concepts appears to me to be a central task of
> thought because it is the presupposition for an ever renewed confrontation with
> reality. Concepts, the grandiose instruments of human orientation, must repeat-
> edly be clarified; a final validity can never be accorded them, although each of
> the great explanations claims for itself the character of final validity, and
> clearly must claim it. (Rome and Rome, *Philosophical Interrogations*, 17)

In his book *Believing Humanism*, 153–73, Buber applied his critique of
language to the categories of contemporary psychiatry.
50. As discussed in chapter 2, the categories of myth and story were basic
to Buber's thinking. See chapter 7 for Buber's use of personal stories.

51. Hobson, *Forms*, 26.
52. Ibid., 27.
53. Ibid., 28.
54. Ibid., 21.
55. Ibid., 22.
56. Ibid., 46–47.
57. Ibid., 137.
58. Ibid., 191.
59. The fear of separation and loss that Hobson, following Bowlby, locates in our initial experience of separation from the mother helps to shed light on Buber's own life experience and his overriding concern for direct, nonpurposive, loving relations. As I discussed in chapter 1, one of Buber's earliest memories was his sudden separation from his mother. This separation, which lasted until his adult years, had a profound impact on his vision of reality. See *PMB*, 3–4. In pointing out the importance of this loss to Buber's subsequent thinking, I in no way wish to reduce the meaning and significance of his work to this one moment. There is little reason to doubt, however, that the early separation from his mother played a significant role in the development of his world-view. See chapter 1, n. 17; and Freidman, *Buber's Life and Work* 1:1–7.
60. In 1929, Buber had spoken of the artist as an "onlooker" who assumes an objectivist, rather than a dialogical, stance; see Buber, *Between Man and Man*, 9. For a fuller discussion of Buber's philosophy of art, see the article by Louis Z. Hammer in *PMB*, 609–28; and Moshe Schwartz, "Martin Buber's Aesthetic Thought," in Schwartz, *Language, Myth, Art*, 309–32.

CHAPTER SIX

1. Walter Kaufmann, Prologue to Buber, *I and Thou*, 38. As stated in chapter 5, this focus on the edifying, social orientation of Buber's thought differentiates my approach from those who seek to situate Buber in the context of Continental, transcendental philosophy. See the references cited in chap. 4, n. 10.
2. Kaufmann, Prologue to Buber, *I and Thou*, 38. As I shall show in chapter 7, Kaufmann's comment notwithstanding, *I and Thou* did address religious concerns, but in terms of a revised conception of religion. See also Buber, *Believing Humanism*, 111; and Schilpp and Friedman, *Philosophy of Martin Buber*, 741–42 (hereafter referred to as *PMB*).
3. Although, as I shall show in chapter 7, there is an underlying religious premise to *I and Thou*, Buber's social thought stands on its own and can be read independently of that religious premise. In a similar way Michael Walzer argues that the biblical book of Exodus, while ostensibly a religious text, has served throughout history as a paradigm of

revolutionary politics: "The Exodus is an account of deliverance or liberation expressed in religious terms, but is also a secular, that is, a this-wordly and historical account" (Walzer, *Exodus and Revolution*, 9). In chapter 8, I shall discuss Buber's activity as a social critic in Israel during the last three decades of his life.

4. "Martin Buber had spoken of *Verfremdung* in his long discussion of 'the proliferation of the It-world' in Part Two of *Ich und Du* (1923). In retrospect, we can even say that most of Part Two deals with alienation" (Walter Kaufmann in Schacht, *Alienation*, xviii).

5. Tonnies formulated that position in a speech delivered to the First German Congress of Sociology in 1910. Buber had attended that conference and participated in the discussions. See Buber, "Mystik als Religioser Solipsismus."

6. At the University of Frankfurt Buber had lectured under the auspices of the faculties of theology and religion. Originally, the administration of the Hebrew University had wanted to appoint him to a chair in religion studies *(Religionswissenschaft)*. The trustees, however, responding to pressures from the Orthodox community, rejected this plan and finally agreed to appoint him to a chair in social philosophy. See Friedman, *Buber's Life and Work* 2:252–56, and the note to chap. 13, 366–67.

7. Robert Friedrichs, in describing the sociologist's attitude of engagement with his subjects, states: "Martin Buber has provided our generation with a vocabulary that, although in a poetic mode, speaks poignantly to the stance we describe" (Friedrichs, *Sociology*, 257). For other contemporary discussions of social theory see Bernstein, *Social and Political Theory*; and Giddens, *Central Problems*.

8. The concern for concept clarification, which we encountered in chapter 3, is a recurring theme in Buber's writings. In "Religion als Gegenwart," Buber's lectures from 1922 translated and published in Horowitz, *Buber's Way to I and Thou*, he focused on the concept of religion. In "Abende," the concept under analysis is community. See also Buber, *Believing Humanism*, 57, 87, 134, 153; *PMB*, 310, 314, 689f., 696–97, 701, 706–7; and Rome and Rome, *Philosophical Interrogations*, 17, 34, 67, 83, 100.

9. See Weber, "Politics as a Vocation" and "Science as a Vocation," in Weber, *From Max Weber*, 77–156. For rebuttals to the conventional view that Weber endorsed a "total disjunction between knowledge and values," see Introduction to Wrong, *Max Weber*, 16–17; Gouldner, "Anti-Minotaur"; and Bendix and Roth, *Scholarship and Partisanship*, chap. 2.

10. For the concept of meaning as a central category in the interpretation of human society and culture, see Berger and Kellner, *Sociology Reinterpreted*; Berger, *Sacred Canopy*; and Geertz, *Interpretation of Cultures*, especially 52 and 212.

11. In *Interpretation*, Walzer argues that, unlike intellectuals who assume

a detached stance of critical analysis, the people to whom we generally apply the label social critic are active members of the community that they are criticizing. Rather than stand without and apply an abstract standard, social critics draw upon their communities' own moral principles as the bases for their critiques.

12. For a critique of the objectivist stance in sociological thought see the essays by Wrong and Gouldner referred to in n. 9 and Gouldner's *Coming Crisis*, especially 481–512. See also the writings of C. Wright Mills in Mills, *Power, Politics and People*. A recent philosophical discussion of the problem of objectivity is Bernstein, *Beyond Objectivism*. See also Rorty, *Mirror*, part 3.

13. In *Interpretation and Social Criticism*, Michael Walzer speaks of the biblical prophet as a model of the social critic. To Walzer, a social critic is one who stands within, although frequently on the margins of, the community that he or she is criticizing. In many respects, Walzer's interpretation is similar to Buber's. In a recent interview, Walzer indicated that he was revising his forthcoming expanded study of modern social critics to include a chapter on Buber. See Michael Walzer, *The Company of Critics: Social Criticism and Political Commitment in the Twentieth Century* (New York: Basic Books, 1988). The discussion of Buber is on pp. 67–79.

14. In light of the discussion surrounding Buber's appointment at the Hebrew University (see n. 6), his concern to distinguish the sociologist's role from that of the religious leader may be read as a commentary on his position as a professor of social philosophy.

15. Gouldner, *Coming Crisis*, 484. See also Buber's essay "The Demand of the Spirit and Historical Reality," in Buber, *Pointing the Way*, 177–91.

16. See chap. 8, 253–63.

17. Throughout his life, Buber actively engaged in activites aimed at altering the prevailing social forms and attitudes. In addition to his short-lived participation in Neue Gemeinschaft and his editing of *Die Gesellschaft*, Buber participated actively in the religious socialist movement in Germany during the twenties; see n. 59. In Israel, as I shall discuss in chapter 8, he was one of the leaders of a group critical of the prevailing Jewish attitude toward the Arabs.

18. Unlike Nietzsche, Buber, in the spirit of Lurianic Kabbalah and Hasidism, accepted as a given the primordial cosmic condition of unity and wholeness. Transposing the myth of the broken vessels into an existential key, Buber appropriated the broken vessels and scattered sparks as metaphors for the human condition. Scattered throughout the world and embedded in all things, the sparks offer a person the opportunity to counter fragmentation and recover unity. Through our relations with others, we can liberate the sparks and bridge the abysses. See also chap. 2, 47–51.

In contrast to Buber, Scholem emphasized the catastrophic implications of the Lurianic myth. See Scholem, *Major Trends*, 244–86; and Scholem, *Kabbalah*, 128–43. Scholem read the myth as a response to and commentary on the expulsion of Spanish Jewry at the end of the fifteenth century. Harold Bloom, emphasizing the catastrophic motif of the myth, transformed it into a paradigm of poetic (and other) creativity. See Bloom, *Kabbalah*.

19. Paul Mendes-Flohr has reviewed the various interpretations of the "center" in "Community and Renewal: Dialogue as a Metasociological Principle." See also Yasour, *Buber's Social Philosophy*, 125–28; and Susser, *Existence and Utopia*, 52–53, 145–47, 160.

20. I have altered the current translation slightly in keeping with the original German and the Herbrew translation in *Netivot be-'Utopia*, 185, of Buber's 1931 essay, "Bemerkungen zur Gemeinschaftsidee," where the statement originally appeared. See also Buber, *Nachlese*, 76. While, in Buber's view, the originality of the center derives from its capacity to render the divine manifest to the community, the more earthly, creaturely, and attached the center is the truer it is and the more capable of manifesting the divine. Compare with his 1918 lecture, "The Holy Way" (Buber, *On Judaism*, 110), where the center does not yet appear in his definition of community.

21. See Buber, "Abende." Other unpublished materials from which I have drawn include "Staat und Gemeinschaft," "Erziehung zur Gemeinschaft," and "Vortrag des Hernn Dr. Martin Buber am 24. Jan. 1931, über Individuum und Person-Masse und Gemeinschaft."

22. Buber, "Erziehung zur Geimeinschaft," 10–13.

23. In this essay, "Elements of the Interhuman," Buber referred to his fifty-year effort to elucidate this existential dimension of social relations. See Buber, *Knowledge of Man*, 72–73.

24. Although he entitled his most extensive discussion of social theory *Paths in Utopia*, Buber denied being a utopian in the conventional sense. He simply wished to identify with that group of socialist thinkers whom Marx disparagingly referred to as Utopian Socialists. Unlike apocalyptic socialists such as Marx, who saw a catastrophic revolutionary event as a prerequisite to the new society, Buber viewed himself as a meliorist believing that social progress results from the ongoing gradual improvement of everyday relationships.

25. A similar position is advocated by Paul and Percival Goodman in *Communitas*.

26. See Weber, *Social and Economic Organization*, 136.

27. See "Wie kann Gemeinschaft werden," in Buber, *Kampf um Israel*, 255–57.

28. Turner, *Ritual Process*, 96.

29. Ibid., 127.

30. Ibid.

31. Ibid.

32. Ibid., 131–32.
33. Ibid., 128.
34. Turner, *Dramas, Fields, and Metaphors*, 244. On 231–71, Turner situates the idea of communitas in the contexts of such theorists as Levi-Strauss, Weber, and Durkheim.
35. The term *Verfremdung* (alienation) actually appears in several places in part 2 of Buber, *I and Thou*, 107, 111, 120–21, and in "Wie kann Gemeinschaft werden," in Buber, *Kampf um Israel*, 265. However, even where the technical term *alienation* is not used, the idea of alienation pervades these works.
36. Weber, *Protestant Ethic*, 181.
37. See n. 24. This same attitude was personified in Buber's novel, *For the Sake of Heaven*, by the holy Yehudi, who rejected his teacher's efforts to hasten the messianic era through theurgic practices and advocated hallowing the everyday as the way to effect redemption.
38. Buber spoke of the Russian Revolution of 1917 in "Staat und Gemeinschaft," "Abende," and "Erziehung zur Gemeinschaft."
39. See also Buber, *Eclipse of God*, 129:

> One surely cannot swim against the stream, one says. But perhaps one can swim with a new stream whose source is still hidden? In another image, the I-Thou relation has gone into the catacombs—who can say with how much greater power it will step forth? Who can say when the I-It relation will be directed anew to its assisting place and activity!

40. For an analysis of Marx's concept of revolution see Avineri, *Karl Marx*, 134–49, 217–22. For a psychologically oriented interpretation see Tucker, *Philosophy and Myth*, 194–202; for Tucker's critique of Marx see 233–43.
41. Avineri, *Karl Marx*, 251.
42. This portrayal of the prophetic position is rooted in the myth of the broken vessels discussed in chapter 2, 47–51, in which one participates in the redemptive process through everyday actions and relationships. Redemption is, according to this view, a gradual process.
43. See "Prophecy, Apocalyptic and the Historical Hour," in *On the Bible*, 183–87. In *For the Sake of Heaven*, Buber personified these two attitudes to social change in the form of two Hasidic leaders and their followers. This work, which Buber began toward the end of World War I, but which he did not complete until 1943, comprises his most comprehensive discussion on the problem of our response to social and political evil. For an alternative interpretation of this novel, see Simon, *Aims, Junctures, Paths*, 74–76. Simon interprets the debate between the Yehudi and Yeshaya (Buber, *For the Sake of Heaven*, 98–103) as a commentary on the Buber-Rosenzweig debate over the law.
44. The concept of education played a major role in Buber's writing, and he devoted several lectures and essays to this topic. See "Education"

and "Education of Character," in Buber, *Between Man and Man*, 83–117; and "Education and World View," in Buber, *Pointing the Way*, 98–105. See also the unpublished essay "Erziehung zur Gemeinschaft." Buber's views on education are discussed by Simon in "Martin Buber, The Educator," in *PMB*, 543–76. See also Hill, *Education*, 236–43, 253–66; Friedman, *Buber's Life and Work*, vol. 2, chap. 2; Zvi Kurzweil, *Martin Buber and Modern Educational Thought* (Jerusalem: Schocken, 1978); and Gordon, "Would Buber Endorse?" 215–23.

45. In his essay on the education of character, Buber wrote: "Genuine education of character is education for community" (Buber, *Between Man and Man*, 116). This idea also occurs in "Erziehung zur Gemeinschaft," 9, and in "Society and State" (1951), in Buber, *Pointing the Way*, 176.

46. Gustav Landauer, Buber's friend and mentor, also objected to the Marxist apocalyptic notion of revolution. Buber was most likely influenced in his socialist views by Landauer. On the differences between them, see n. 61.

47. See Buber, "On Education," in Buber, *Between Man and Man*, 83–103.

48. This is a later formulation of what Buber previously referred to as the "Innate You" *(Eigeborne Du)*. In Buber, *Between Man and Man*, Ronald Gregor Smith translates *Trieb der Verbundenheit* as *instinct for communion*. I prefer the term *drive for communion*, which is more consistent with Buber's socioexistential orientation. For a discussion of the problems surrounding the translation of Buber's writings, see Walter Kaufmann's prologue to Buber, *I and Thou*.

49. This meaning of *education* is reflected in the etymology of the German word *Erziehung*, which means drawing forth or drawing out. See Buber, "Worte," and Buber, *Israel and the World*, 149.

50. Buber translated the German word *Auferlegung*, meaning laying on or imposing, as *propaganda*.

51. The propaganda-education distinction parallels Buber's distinction between state and society. Whereas propaganda is the appropriate mode of discourse within the political structure of the state, education is the appropriate mode in society. Whereas the propagandist relates to others as Its, the educator approaches them as Yous.

52. On the relationship between Buber's own ideas and those of Dewey see the essay by Paul Pfeutze, "Buber and American Pragmatism," in *PMB*, 511–42. A view of education based upon dialogue is found in Freire, *Pedagogy of the Oppressed*. However, in contrast to Buber, Freire understands dialogue primarily in terms of intellectual dialogue. In recent feminist writings, one finds a conception of education that is closer to Buber's. See, for example, Mary Field Belensky et al., *Women's Ways of Knowing*, and Nel Noddings, *Caring*, both referred to in Intro., n. 29.

53. This is evident in Buber's discussions of the zaddik in his relationship to his followers. See Buber, *Tales of the Hasidim* 1:1–14; and "My Way

to Hasidism," in Buber, *Hasidism and Modern Man*. The concept of educational models is discussed by Buber in "On National Education," in Buber, *Israel and the World*, 149–63.

54. See Buber, *I and Thou*, 158–59:

   And this is second: the inexpressible confirmation of meaning. It is guaranteed. Nothing, nothing can henceforth be meaningless. The question about the meaning of life has vanished. But if it were still there, it would not require an answer. You do not know how to point to or define the meaning, you lack any formula or image for it, and yet it is more certain for you than the sensations of your senses.

55. There is an obvious contradiction between the skeptical view of language articulated here and the expressivist view of language contained in Buber's writings on Hasidism and the Bible. Buber's translations of Hasidic tales, and the Bible especially, were premised on a belief that language expresses the existential situation in which the words were first spoken. Seen in this light, language can draw us closer to that situation. These works appear to be grounded in a philosophy of presence in which the spoken word expresses the presence of the speaker. Yet, as the passage quoted here indicates, his work is permeated by a skeptical view of language. To my knowledge, Buber never recognized the inherent tension between these two views of language. On the problem of the relation between language and reality in recent discussion, see Saussure, *Course in General Linguistics*, 65–78. See also Leitch, *Deconstructive Criticism*, chap. 1. Leitch writes: "The word, 'tree', an assembly of four letters, is not the wooden object. This sign marks the absence of the object" (ibid., 57). See also Frank Lentricchia, *After the New Criticism*, 112–24. Lentricchia discusses existential and phenomenological approaches to language and reading in chaps. 2–4.

56. This metaphor, basic to Akiba Ernst Simon's interpretation of Buber's sociopolitical philosophy, is the title that he chose for his incisive analysis of that philosophy. See Simon, *Kav Ha-Tihum* (The Line of Demarcation).

57. For this aspect of Landauer's thought see Lunn, *Prophet*, chap. 4.

58. Buber delivered a lecture, "Staat und Gemeinschaft," to students at the University of Frankfurt in 1923. Later, he published a revised essay under the same name in *Pointing the Way*, 161–76.

59. Buber was an active participant in the religious socialist movement in Germany. See Friedman, *Buber's Life and Work* 2:95–103. See also Buber, "Three Theses on Religious Socialism," in Buber, *Pointing the Way*, 112–14; Buber, "Why the Land of Israel Must Be Socialistic" (Hebrew), in Buber, *Te'udah ve-Ye'ud* 2:258–67 (German original in Buber, *Kampf um Israel*, 283–302); and Buber, *Paths in Utopia*, chaps. 1, 10–11.

60. For Landauer's views see Lunn, *Prophet*, especially chap. 4. Lunn supports Buber's interpretation of Landauer (ibid., 224).

61. Landauer had emphasized the inner transformation of the individual: "The way in which we must proceed, in order to come to community with the world, leads not toward the external, but toward the internal. . . . We return wholly into ourselves and there we find the living world." Landauer, *Skepsis und Mystik*, cited in Lunn, *Prophet of Community*, 162. Buber, in contrast to Landauer, focused on the interhuman. True community, according to Buber, would only emerge when persons are educated to the relational nature of human life and to the social conditions necessary to engender such relationships. For Buber, the goal of education is to foster relation, dialogue, and, as a result, community. In "The Holy Way" (Buber, *On Judaism*, 108–48), which was dedicated to Landauer, Buber spoke of the establishment of genuine community in the land of Israel as "our revolution." See ibid., 145.

62. Referring to the kibbutz effort as "an experiment that did not fail" (Buber, *Paths in Utopia*, 139–49), Buber intentionally avoided calling it a success. Such a characterization would have been too static for Buber's dynamic, process-oriented perspective. Many kibbutz members who had been originally inspired by Buber grew disenchanted with his teachings. See Menahem Dorman, "Martin Buber's Address, 'Herut' and Its Influence on the Jewish Youth Movement in Germany," and the ensuing discussion in Bloch and Gordon, *Martin Buber*, 233–51.

63. Buber continued to place great hope in the kibbutz. Toward the end of his life he engaged in a series of converations with numerous kibbutz representatives. See Shapira, "Meetings With Buber," 48–54. A partial Hebrew transcript of some of these meetings edited by Shapira is found in Shapira, *Khan ve-'Akhshav*, 44–51; and in the Hebrew version of Martin Buber, *Paths in Utopia (Netivot be-'Utopia)*, 229–35. The latter volume also includes an illuminating interpretation of Buber's social thought by Avraham Shapira, 276–314. See also chap. 8, n. 43.

64. Many of Buber's essays on these issues have been reprinted in Buber, *Pointing the Way*; see, especially, 109–239. In his later years, Buber articulated many of these concerns in interviews. See, for example, the interview in the journal of kibbutz thought *Shedemot*, November 1962.

65. See chapter 4.

66. Kierkegaard, *The Present Age*, 53.

67. Ibid., 55–68.

68. Buber quoted from Kierkegaard's journals to support his interpretation; see Buber, *Between Man and Man*, 51. For a critique of Buber's reading of Kierkegaard see Robert L. Perkins, "Buber and Kierkegaard: A Philosophic Encounter," in Bloch and Gordon, *Martin Buber*, 275–303.

69. Kierkegaard's refusal to marry his fiancée, Regina Olsen, was, in Buber's view, a consequence of his erroneous conception of religion. Believing that assuming responsibility for another person would limit his capacity to respond to God, Kierkegaard understood his act of renuncia-

tion to be a religious act. To Buber, this contradicted the teachings of Kierkegaard's own master, Jesus. Consistent with Jewish teachings, Jesus had taught that relationships to others bridge the abyss separating the human and the divine. In the same spirit, Buber insisted that "God wants us to come to him by means of the Reginas he has created and not by renunciation of them" (Buber, *Between Man and Man*, 52). Robert Perkins challenges this interpretation in "Buber and Kierkegaard," in Bloch and Gordon, *Martin Buber*, 275–303.

70. See Buber, *Pointing the Way*, 192–239.
71. See "Hope for this Hour," Buber, *Pointing the Way*, 220–29.
72. In Buber, *I and Thou*, 120–23, Buber referred to these two illusory paths by means of which we futilely seek to escape from our condition of alienation.
73. See Buber, "Abstract and Concrete," in Buber, *Pointing the Way*, 230.
74. Hammarskjold, *Servant of Peace*, 186–87.
75. Ibid. Buber described his relationship with Hammarskjold in Buber, *Believing Humanism*, 57–59. See also Friedman, *Martin Buber's Life and Work* 3:303–20.

CHAPTER SEVEN

1. This is a translation of Buber's introduction to *Chassidische Bücher*, originally published in 1927.
2. See, for example, Buber, *Eclipse of God*, 14, 20.
3. As mentioned in chapter 2, Buber had referred to his writings on Hasidism as an effort "to help our age renew its ruptured bond with the Absolute" (Buber, "Interpreting Hasidism," 218). In his early writings on Hasidism and his lectures on Judaism, Buber simultaneously criticized the conventional understanding of religion and endeavored to reveal the power inherent in authentic faith.
4. Although Buber warned against identifying his interpretations of Hasidism with his own personal views (see Rome and Rome, *Philosophical Interrogations*, 88, 90), it is clear that he personally identified with the views expressed in "The Way of Man" (ibid.). It should be noted that the term *way* in the title most certainly parallels the Chinese *Tao*, also translated as *way*. The Tao represents the cosmic way of all things to which persons must accommodate themselves in order to be in tune with the ultimate rhythm of the cosmos. Buber defined Torah as "the instruction of an instructor in the right path of life, the teaching of a teacher about the true way" (Rome and Rome, *Philosophical Interrogations*, 100). Bloch sees "The Way of Man" as a critique of the psychological interpretation of religion, see Bloch, *Aporie des Du*, 300, n. 35.
5. For the importance of intertextuality to contemporary literary theory see Culler, *Pursuit of Signs*, chap. 5.

6. This twofold process parallels the two steps to "reflexion" and "dialogue," discussed in "Dialogue," in Buber, *Between Man and Man*, 21–24; and the movements of distancing and relating discussed in "Distance and Relation," in Buber, *Knowledge of Man*, 59–71.

7. While, as mentioned in n. 4, Buber endeavored to distinguish his own teachings from the teachings of Hasidism, concerning this passage he explicitly stated: "It is my conviction that this doctrine is essentially true" (Buber, *HMM*, 173–74).

8. In his pre–*I and Thou* interpretation of Hasidism, Buber spoke of our responsibility to set free the creatures and objects that we encounter, by cultivating and enjoying them in holiness. While he spoke, in that passage, of a person's responsibility to "his animals, and his walls, his garden and his meadow, his tools and his food" (*HMM*, 105), nothing is said about our responsibility to enter into relationships with the people we encounter or to help them to develop their own potential. By 1921, in an essay introducing *Der Grosse Maggid*, he spoke of the responsibility to love our neighbor and of the helping relationship between the *zaddik* and his followers. Only after Buber formulated his relational philosophy and his social intepretation of religion did the relationship to other persons become central to his interpretation of Hasidism.

9. On the primacy of myth in Buber's thought and Buber's relationship to the contemporary efforts at demythologizing see the insightful Hebrew essay by Moshe Schwartz in *Language, Myth, Art*, 216–49.

10. The messianic force of everyday relations is a basic theme of Buber's novel *For the Sake of Heaven*, published originally in Hebrew as *Gog u'Megog*. The Hebrew title, which refers to the mythic, eschatological battle described in chapters 38 and 39 of the biblical book of Ezekiel, more adequately reflects the messianic themes of the novel. See also chap. 6, n. 43.

11. Students of Buber disagree on the cause of the young man's death. Some, like Nahum Glatzer, attribute his death to suicide. Friedman, however, although acknowledging that he may have willed his own death, insists that the young man died in the war. On the various interpretations of the young man's death see Friedman, *Buber's Life and Work* 1:187–90; 396, chap. 9, n. C.

12. For other examples of decisive moments or events that had a formative effect on Buber's thought see his childhood conversation with the young girl concerning his mother (Schilpp and Friedman, *Philosophy of Martin Buber*, 23–24; hereafter referred to as as *PMB*) discussed in chapter 1; the story of his encounter with a horse (Buber, *Between Man and Man*, 11f.); Buber, *Eclipse of God*, 3–9; and Buber, "My Way to Hasidism," in *HMM*, especially 50–53.

13. Abraham Heschel, who, like Buber, grounded his philosophy of religion in the teachings of existentialism and Hasidism, also emphasized the

preconceptual, presymbolic ground of human experience; see Heschel, *God in Search of Man*, 114–16. See also Heschel, "Depth Theology." I have compared and contrasted Buber's and Heschel's philosophies of religion and interpretations of Judaism in Silberstein, "The Renewal of Jewish Spirituality: Two Views."

14. The minister, William Hechler, was a warm supporter of the Zionist movement. See Friedman, *Buber's Life and Work* 1:185–87.

15. *Unconditional* and *unconditioned* are alternatively used in Buber, *On Judaism*, to translate the term *Unbedingten*. The use of this term and the term *absolute* appear to be Buber's attempt to translate the Kabbalistic term *Ein Sof*, which may also be translated as unbounded, unlimited, or infinite. On the concept of *Ein Sof*, see Gershom Scholem, *Kabbalah*, 88–95. In his preface to the 1923 edition of his lectures *On Judaism (Reden über das Judentum)*, Buber revised the language he had originally used in the lectures to speak of God; see Buber, *On Judaism*, 3–10. Rosenzweig had criticized the early lectures in an essay, "Atheistische Theologie," Rosenzweig, *Kleinere Schriften* (Berlin: Schocken, 1937), 278–90 (Hebrew translation in Rosenzweig, *Naharium*, 70–79). The essay was unpublished until 1937. See Friedman, *Buber's Life and Work* 1:398–400; and Horowitz, *Buber's Way to I and Thou*, 187.

16. Buber acknowledged that what we need to know for practical purposes can be known through an objective stance. However, this knowing is qualitatively different from the direct, unmediated knowing of I-You. The latter mode of knowing provides the deepest knowledge of self, other persons, and the divine. However, in the case of the latter, objective knowledge for pragmatic purposes is "idolatry."

17. In 1910, Buber had argued that mysticism was not susceptible to a sociological approach and could only be grasped by social scientists through the categories of psychology.

18. Buber's rejection of mysticism was, as we saw in chapter 3, already underway in 1913 in *Daniel* and in other essays from that period. In *The Other*, Theunissen argues that Buber's interpretation of dialogue negates the everyday world. For a critique of Theunissen's position see Bloch, *Aporie des Du*, and Bloch, "Justification and Futility of Dialogical Thinking."

19. See Yalom's criticism in Yalom, *Existential Psychotherapy*, 367–68.

20. See also *PMB*, 710: "The direct relation to God is in no way contested; its actuality, indeed, is recognized in all that befalls us, hence addresses us, and in all with which we react, hence answer. It is only added that the essential relation to God must find its complement in the essential relation to man."

21. In telling autobiographical stories to demonstrate a fundamental point, Buber is being true to his overall view of the power of mythic discourse discussed in chapter 2. For other examples see the sources cited above

in n. 12 and Buber, *Kampf um Israel*, 171–77 (translated in *PMB*, 16–19, and *PMB*, 3–4). See also *PMB*, 31–33. While the systematic philosopher might be inclined to regard such stories as being of dubious value, they are reflective of Buber's deep conviction that our deepest insights arise out of existential situations and encounters rather than out of abstract contemplation.

22. In Buber, *I and Thou*, 123–24, Buber had formulated the criticism of God talk in a more abstract, philosophical form. The difference in formulation is indicative of the shift in focus to social concerns, a shift that I have discussed in chapter 4.

23. Buber leveled a similar critique at the efforts of Schleiermacher and Otto to speak of a unique religious experience; see Buber, *I and Thou*, 129.

24. Consistent with his existential, antiobjectivist orientation, Buber refrained from using such concepts as prove and demonstrate, and instead used the discourse of witness.

25. Buber's interpretation of Christianity is critically discussed from Protestant, Catholic, and Jewish perspectives in Bloch and Gordon, *Martin Buber*, 385–472.

26. *The New English Bible* (New York: Oxford University Press, 1971). Buber insisted that he was in no way implying that "Jews in general and Christians in general believed thus and still believe, but only that one faith has found its representative actuality among Jews and the other among Christians." At the same time, he acknowledged that "each of the two has extended its roots into the other camp also, the 'Jewish' into the Christian, but the Christian also into the Jewish" (Buber, *Two Types of Faith*, 11). See also Rome and Rome, *Philosophical Interrogations*, 108–9.

27. Buber's phenomenological conception of revelation differs from the content-oriented view commonly attributed to rabbinic Judaism. In rabbinic Judaism, revelation is spoken of as the "giving of Torah" or as the giving of "the Torah." The rabbis identified the traditional commandments as the content of revelation at Sinai. As discussed in chapter 3, Rosenzweig, while sharing Buber's existential orientation to revelation, nevertheless sought to validate the traditional rabbinic system of commandments. On Rosenzweig's criticism and Buber's response see chapter 3 and the sources cited there in n. 70.

28. Buber appears to be talking of the direct encounter with the divine rather than the encounter with the divine through our encounter with others. This derives from his desire to clarify the revelatory claims of historical religious faiths. As indicated earlier (see n. 20), Buber, while not denying the validity of direct encounters, emphasized the encounter with other persons.

29. See *HMM*, 142: "The way by which a man can reach God is revealed to him only through the knowledge of his own being, the knowledge of his

essential quality and inclination." The Hasidic notion that each individual is responsible for raising his own unique spark is subjected by Buber to a strong reading in which he transposed a concept that is fully compatible with the rabbinic structure into the language of religious pluralism: "What it is that can and shall be done by just this person and no other can be revealed to him only in himself" (ibid.). Views such as these provoked Scholem's criticism of Buber as a religious anarchist. See also chapter 2.

30. In spite of his resistance to all forms of institutionalized religion, Buber accepted the Hebrew Bible as sacred scripture. As noted in chapter 3, Rosenzweig, seizing upon this inconsistency, argued that Buber was no less obliged to remain open to the claim made for the sacredness of the rabbinic system of commandments.

31. Whereas Rorty's edifying philosopher eschews argument in favor of rational persuasive conversation, Buber utilized the religious discourse of witness and testimony. For a deconstructive interpretation of religion, see Mark Taylor, *Erring: A Post Modern A/theology* (Chicago: University of Chicago Press, 1984), and the anthology *Deconstruction and Theology* (New York: Crossroad Publishing, 1982).

32. See the discussion of Buber's debate with Franz Rosenzweig in chapter 3, 101–3.

33. See Buber, *Good and Evil*, especially 115–20.

34. Buber draws upon the rabbinic notion that within each person there dwell together inclinations to good and to evil. For Buber, evil has no fixed essence but is manifest existentially in the dynamic process of life.

35. Wiesel's autobiographical *Night* (New York: Hill and Wang, 1960), which preceded the systematic theological discussions of the Holocaust, first appeared in French in 1958. In the 1966 *Commentary* symposium on Jewish thought, the issue of the Holocaust was not raised by the editors. See *The Condition of Jewish Belief* (Toronto: Collier-Macmillan, 1966). On pp. 198–201 of the Symposium, Richard Rubenstein raised the question. He explored it more thoroughly in Rubenstein, *After Auschwitz: Essays in Contemporary Judaism* (Indianapolis: Bobbs-Merrill, 1968).

36. See Rubenstein, *After Auschwitz*. Rubenstein focused on the way in which the Holocaust affects what we are able to believe concerning God. In contrast to Buber, Rubenstein insisted that the link between Heaven and Earth was broken and that the possiblity of faith in a personal, caring God had been destroyed.

37. The book appeared in English bearing the title *For the Sake of Heaven* (see n. 10). The Hebrew title, which refers to the mythical apocalyptic battle at the end of days, reflects the confrontation with evil depicted in the book.

38. This passage from Buber, *For the Sake of Heaven*, 54, is cited by Buber

in *Good and Evil*, 65, in answer to the question of how to struggle against evil. In his note in *Good and Evil*, 65, Buber observed, "Fully to understand this passage, the reader must recall the time at which the novel was written." The novel, begun by Buber during the First World War, reflects a significant shift in his view of war. See the sources cited in chap. 1, n. 16.

39. See Simon, "Adult Education"; Baker, *Days of Sorrow*, 175–80; and Freidman, *Buber's Life and Work* 2:198–222. See also chapter 8, 253–55.

40. On Buber's efforts to combat the evils within Israeli society and his struggle in behalf of Arab-Jewish rapprochement, see chapter 8.

CHAPTER EIGHT

1. "Man cannot approach the divine by reaching beyond the human; he can approach Him through becoming human. To become human is what he, this individual man, has been created for. This, so it seems to me, is the eternal core of Hasidic life and Hasidic teaching" (Buber, *Hasidism and Modern Man*, 42–43; hereafter referred to as *HMM*).

2. In 1918 Buber wrote, "Not truth as idea nor truth as shape or form, but truth as deed is Judaism's task" (Buber, *On Judaism*, 113). In *HMM*, Buber emphasized that the starting point of our relation to the sacred is "the place on which one stands" (172).

3. The effort of early Zionist thinkers to deny the uniqueness of Israel and to insist that Israel is a nation like all the other nations is discussed by Rubinstein in *From Herzl to Gush Emunim*, chaps. 1–2.

4. See, in particular, Buber, "Two Foci of the Jewish Soul," and Buber, "The Faith of Judaism," in Buber, *Israel and the World*, 13–40; and Buber, "Pharisaism," in *The Jew: Essays from Martin Buber's Journal*, 223–31. Simon critically analyzed Buber's views on rabbinic Judaism in Simon, *Aims*, 87–103, 128–34.

5. See Friedman, *Buber's Life and Work* 2:chaps. 1 and 8. The writings directed to the condition of German Jewry under Nazism are an exception.

6. See Simon, *Kav Ha-Tihum*, 14–15.

7. Of course, Orthodoxy was not the only Jewish movement criticized by Buber. He also aimed his criticisms at the reformers and the assimilationists; see Buber, *On Judaism*, 36–38, 133–39. See also his extensive critique of liberal Judaism in his response to Hermann Cohen, originally published in *Der Jude* in 1916 and now available in English translation in Arthur Cohen, *The Jew: Essays from Martin Buber's Journal*, 85–96.

8. See n. 4. The change in Buber's attitude is discussed by Hans Kohn, *Martin Buber*, 273, n. 1; and by Ernst Simon in "Buber and the Faith of

Israel," in *Aims, Junctures, Paths*, 87–142. The modification of his attitude to rabbinic Judaism may be viewed as the result of a number of factors, including Rosenzweig's influence (see on this point Horowitz, *Buber's Way to I and Thou*, 226–58); the need to respond to hostile writings on Judaism by Christians (see Cohen's comments in *The Jew*, 223–24); Buber's role as a communal leader and spokesman during the period of the rise of Nazism; and Buber's concern for Jewish youth's growing secularism and estrangement from Jewish tradition (see Buber, *Israel and the World*, 137–63). In one of his letters to Rosenzweig, Buber indicated that, as he grew older, the Sabbath came to have added meaning in his life. This did not, however, lead Buber to observe the Sabbath according to halakhah. Haim Gordon mentions that Buber attended synagogue from time to time during the 1930s but attributed this less to religious motivation than to the desire to demonstrate solidarity with his fellow Jews in Germany. See Bloch and Gordon, *Martin Buber*, 36. See also Yehoshua Amir, "Buber u'Vet Ha-Kenesset" (Buber and the Synagogue), in Shapira, *Khan ve-'Akhshav*, 114–18.

9. Simon offers an insightful analysis of the development of Buber's interpretation of Hasidism in *Aims, Junctures, Paths*, especially 103–26.

10. See chap. 3, n. 18, for sources on Ahad Haam.

11. In contrast to the artistic orientation employed in his Hasidic writings, Buber utilized a method of close critical text study in his writings on the Bible. Also, whereas, in his Hasidic works, he frequently omitted and altered texts in order to convey the desired message, his biblical studies are characterized by faithful adherence to the received texts. Finally, his biblical works are accompanied by full scholarly documentation, including copious footnotes and bibliographic references.

12. Buber described his method, which he called "tradition criticism," in *Moses*, 15–19.

13. See, in particular, Buber, "The Man of Today and the Jewish Bible" in Buber, *Israel and the World*, 89–102.

14. The method employed by Buber and Rosenzweig is described in their German work, *Die Schrift*, especially 135–275. Many of these essays can be found in Hebrew in Buber, *Darko shel Mikra*, 272–309. For a discussion of the approach used by Buber and Rosenzweig to translate the scriptures, see Everett Fox, Introduction to *In the Beginning*. Fox's translation owes much to the Buber and Rosenweig translation. See also the essay by Uffenheimer, "Buber and Modern Biblical Scholarship," in Bloch and Gordon, *Martin Buber*, 163–211.

15. In Bohm, *Wholeness*, 27–47, the physicist-philosopher David Bohm employs a similar approach, focusing on the verbal roots of language in an effort to argue a dynamic, relational interpretation of reality and society. Like Buber, Bohm recognizes the constitutive force of language and advocates a change in the syntax and grammatical form of language "so as to give a basic role to the verb rather than to the noun" (ibid.,

29). Combining insights derived from Eastern religions and quantum physics, Bohm, like Buber, rejects the fragmentary, mechanistic view of the universe and human society and argues for its replacement by a processal, relational interpretation of reality. Although Bohm focuses on "wholeness," in contrast to Buber's "relation," I find many suggestive parallels between their views of reality. For a brief reference to modern physics in Buber's writings, see Buber, *Believing Humanism*, 167. There, in the middle of a discussion with psychiatrists on the therapeutic relationship, Buber stated: "New terminology is needed to express Niel Bohr's theory of complementarities—the one I think most important of the theories of our day."

16. This method is discussed by Uffenheimer in Bloch and Gordon, *Martin Buber*, 172–78.

17. The translation is taken from Uffenheimer's essay, ibid., 172.

18. The conflict between the historical mode of thought and that of the religious believer is discussed in an illuminating way by Harvey in *The Historian and the Believer*.

19. See Buber, *Moses*, 14–17 and 74–78. For a discussion on the relationship between myth and the religious way of "seeing" that owes much to Wittgenstein, see Barbour, *Myths, Models and Paradigms*.

20. For a discussion of an existential view of history similar to Buber's, see MacQuarrie, *Existentialism*, 220–35.

21. For comments regarding Buber's quest for originality, see Harold Bloom's introduction to Buber's *On the Bible*, ix–xxxii, especially xviii and xxxi–xxxii.

22. As indicated in my discussion of *I and Thou*, Buber looked to the experience of the reader for confirmation of the claims made in that work as well.

23. For critical but sympathetic discussions of Buber's biblical interpretation see Shemaryahu Talmon, "Buber's Path as an Interpreter of Bible" (Hebrew), in Shapira, *Khan ve-'Akhshav*, 124–39; Talmon, "Martin Buber"; Benjamin Uffenheimer, "Buber and Modern Biblical Scholarship," in Bloch and Gordon, *Martin Buber*, 163–211, especially 205–8; James Muilenberg, "Buber as Interpreter of the Bible," in *PMB*, 381–402; and Michael Fishbane, "Martin Buber." Hans-Georg Gadamer, a disciple of Buber's teacher Dilthey, espouses a theory that views reading as a dialogue between an I and a Thou, a theory that has some affinity to Buber's. However, unlike Buber, Gadamer acknowledges the futility of seeking to escape our historical and linguistic conditioning. See Gadamer, *Truth and Method* (New York: Continuum, 1975). For a discussion of the entire hermeneutical tradition from Schleiermacher through Dilthey to Gadamer see Richard Palmer, *Hermeneutics* (Evanston, Ill.: Northwestern University Press, 1969). See also Steven D. Kepnes, "A Hermeneutic Approach to the Buber-Scholem Controversy," *Journal of Jewish Studies* 38, no. 1 (spring 1987), 81–98. In contrast to his

interpretation of Hasidism, Buber's approach to the Bible is far more compatible with the hermeneutic tradition. See chap. 3, n. 65.

24. The privileging of the spoken over the written word has been sharply criticized by Jacques Derrida and his disciples. See, for example, Derrida, *Of Grammatology*, part 1 and 1xvii–1xxviii. Moreover, the expressivist view that language reflects the reality that it signifies has been sharply challenged by De Saussure and his successors. See Catherine Belsey, *Critical Practice*, chaps. 1 and 2; Eagleton, *Literary Theory*, chap. 4; and Leitch, *Deconstructive Criticism*, chap. 2. In fact, Buber himself, as mentioned previously, was skeptical of the power of language to reflect lived reality accurately. The primacy of oral over written expression is argued by Ong in *Orality and Literacy*. See also chap. 6, n. 55.

25. "The 'I' which approaches the text is already a plurality of other texts, of codes which are infinite, or, more precisely, lost." Barthes, *S/Z*, 10. See also, Culler, *Roland Barthes*, 81–83. For a collection of writings on the role of the reader in shaping the meaning of texts, see Tompkins, *Reader Response Criticism*.

26. This is yet another example of Buber's critique of the prevailing Western ethos of success from the perspective of an alternative, biblically rooted ethos.

27. To Ahad Haam, "Hibbat Zion is not merely a part of Judaism, nor is it something added on to Judaism; it is the whole of Judaism, but with a different focal point." (Ahad Haam, "The Law of the Heart," in Hertzberg, *Zionist Idea*, 255).

28. For other examples of Buber's efforts at concept clarification, see chap. 6, n. 8.

29. Buber attributed his concept of renaissance to the influence of Dilthey and the philologist Konrad Burdach. To Buber, these men "showed us that behind the Renaissance was the idea of affirming man and the community of man, and the belief that peoples as well as individuals could be reborn" (Buber, *Israel and the World*, 241).

30. Buber first introduced the concept of Hebrew Humanism in 1913 in Buber, Feivel, and Weizmann, *Jewish School*. See also Buber, "The Holy Way," in Buber, *On Judaism*, 140; and Buber, *On the Bible*, 211f.

31. See Ahad Haam's essays "Priest and Prophet," and "Moses," in Ahad Haam, *Selected Essays*, 125–38. I discuss Ahad Haam's secular reading of the Bible in "Secular System of Meaning."

32. *Kingship of God* was the title Buber chose for his first published book on the Bible, which appeared in German in 1931.

33. "Man's mind thus experiences the unconditional as that great something that is counterposed against it, as the Thou as such" (Buber, *On Judaism*, 150).

34. Scholem was highly critical of Buber's reading of the Bible, calling it "purely pneumatic exegesis, the subjectivity of which bewilders the

reader." Buber "loosens up the historical assertions he can no longer accept, and inserts a thoroughly mystical concept of revelation—albeit in modern formulation—into the historical one" (Scholem, *On Jews and Judaism*, 158). Scholem used the term *historical* to refer to the concrete social and cultural context in which specific laws were transmitted. In contrast to the prevailing historicism of his day, Buber operated with an existential conception of history. See his essay "Saga and History," in Buber, *Moses*, 13–19. See chapter 2 for a discussion of Buber's objection to the nineteenth century's privileging of history.

35. Hugo Bergman, one of Buber's disciples, demanded of his teacher specific guidance: "What way is being recommended? Contemporary men cannot escape the necessity of demanding from their teachers that they show them the way to follow. They ask, 'what then shall we do?'" (*PMB*, 304–5). Buber responded, "I oppose just this expectation. One shall receive the direction from the teacher, but not the manner in which one must strive for this direction. That each man must acquire for himself" (ibid., 717–18).

36. See chap. 6, n. 56. Buber had made this same statement in an earlier essay on community, written in 1932. See Buber, *Believing Humanism*, 88.

37. Buber's role in the life of German Jewry has been discussed by Simon in "Afbau im Untergang." An abbreviated version appeared as "Martin Buber and German Jewry." See also Simon's Hebrew essay introducing Buber, *Te'udah ve-Ye'ud* 1:25–27, reprinted in Simon, *Aims, Junctures, Paths*, 163–204. Buber's writings from the Nazi period appear in Buber, *Die Stunde und die Erkenntnis*. For selected essays in English, see Buber, *Israel and the World*, 78–82, 137–48, 167–82. For a discussion of Buber's life in Germany under the Nazis see Friedman, *Buber's Life and Work* 2:147–237.

38. Many of Buber's early disciples, inspired by his writings on Jewish nationalism, emigrated to Israel. Later, they were critical of the fact that he remained in Germany and only left in order to avoid arrest. See Simon, "Martin Buber and German Jewry"; and Scholem, *On Jews and Judaism*, 14, 71–92, 127. Scholem challenged the notion that a German-Jewish symbiosis ever existed. In his remarks at a ceremony honoring Buber for completing the German Bible translation, Scholem caustically characterized the translation as a *Gastgeschenk*, a parting gift of gratitude "which German Jewry gave to the German people." Scholem asked: "For whom is this translation intended and whom will it influence? Seen historically, it is no longer a *Gastgeschenk* of the Jews to the Germans but rather—and it is not easy for me to say this—the tombstone of a relationship that was extinguished in unspeakable horror. The Jews for whom you translated this are no more" (Scholem, *Messianic Idea*, 318).

39. In addition to lecturing on the Bible throughout Germany, Buber pub-

lished a series of studies and anthologies intended as sources of encouragement and consolation to the beleaguered community, including the consolation chapters from Deutero-Isaiah published as *Die Tröstung Israels* (The Consolation of Israel), and a selection of twenty-three psalms entitled, *Aus Tiefen rufe ich Dich* (Out of the Depths I Call to You).

40. See the comment by Walzer referred to in chap. 6, n. 11.

41. Buber's influence was primarily limited to a small circle of Jewish intellectuals, most of them European born, who participated with Buber in such groups as Brit Shalom, the League for Arab-Jewish Cooperation, and Ichud. These groups espoused the idea of a homeland in which the political and social rights of Arabs and Jews would be guaranteed. To a lesser degree, Buber influenced some of his university students and members of left-wing kibbutzim. See nn. 42, 43.

42. This group, of which Buber was a leader, included such people as Ernst Simon, Hugo Bergmann, Judah Magnes, Robert Weltsch and Gershom Scholem. See the succinct comments by Paul R. Mendes-Flohr in Buber, *Land of Two Peoples*, 72–73, 148–52 passim, as well as the references cited there on 31, n. 44.

43. Buber's relationship to the kibbutz movement is discussed by Yasour in *Buber's Social Philosophy*, 41–52, and in his Hebrew essay, "Buber's Social Thought and Kibbutz Research." See also the Hebrew collection, *Martin Buber and the Kibbutz* (Haifa: Center for Kibbutz-University Studies, 1980). For a critical perspective on this aspect of Buber's life see the article by Menahem Dorman, "Martin Buber's Address 'Herut' and Its Influence on the Jewish Youth Movement in Germany," and the ensuing discussion in Bloch and Gordon, *Martin Buber*, 233–51. See also Simon, "Buber and German Jewry." For a list of Buber's discussions with kibbutz members that have been published in various kibbutz newspapers and journals, see Yasour, *Buber's Social Philosophy*, 180–81. See also chap. 6, n. 63.

44. The most thorough treatment of Buber's view on the Arab-Jewish conflict in the context of his political and social philosophy is Simon, *Kav ha-Tihum* (The Line of Demarcation). See also Robert Weltsch, "Buber's Political Philosophy," in *PMB*, 435–50; Friedman, *Buber's Life and Work* 2:17–20, 287–94, and 3:332–71; and Paul Mendes-Flohr, Introduction to Buber, *Land of Two Peoples*, 3–33.

45. The most comprehensive analysis of these issues is found in Gorni's Hebrew work, *Jewish Question*. Gorni analyzes the several basic positions that developed within the Zionist movement prior to the establishment of the state. For other discussions of the views of Zionist leaders on the Arabs in Palestine, see Elon, *The Israelis*, 148–86; Amnon Rubinstein, *From Herzl to Gush Emunim*, 50–67; and Paul Mendes-Flohr's introduction to Buber, *Land of Two Peoples*, 4–12. See also Laqueur, *History of Zionism*, chap. 5; and Cohen, *Israel and the Arab*

World. On one Zionist leader's efforts to come to terms with the Arab population see Ben Gurion, *My Talks with Arab Leaders.*

46. The resolution that was finally presented was significantly diluted by a drafting committee in ways for which Buber was unprepared; see his later reflections on the affair in Buber, *Land of Two Peoples,* 65. For the ensuing discussion and outcome see ibid., 62–68. This book comprises a significant addition to the corpus of Buber's writings and makes Buber's developing views on the Jewish Arab struggle available to the English reader for the first time.

47. For a thorough statement of Buber's views on the Jewish claim to the land see ibid., 82–91. See also Buber's letter to Gandhi, ibid., 111–26.

48. These comments are from Buber's response to Mohandas K. Gandhi's sharp rebuke of the Jewish claims in Palestine. See ibid., 106–11.

49. See ibid., 237–44 and 298–303 for examples of Buber's encounters with Israeli leaders.

50. Buber's statement aroused the anger of one of his own disciples who felt that Buber had gone too far. See ibid., 228–35, and Buber's reply on 236–39.

51. According to Mendes-Flohr, Buber also alluded to covert actions by the Israeli military to encourage the flight of the Arabs. On this issue, see Tom Segev, *1949: The First Israelis* (New York: Free Press, 1986), chaps. 1–3.

52. Buber, *Land of Two Peoples,* 239–44, 294–97. See also Keren, *Ben Gurion,* 63–99, where the Buber–Ben Gurion debates are viewed in the context of Ben Gurion's debates with Israeli philosophers. See also the essay by Simon, "Buber or Ben Gurion."

53. See Buber, *Land of Two Peoples,* 239–44, 261–63, 283–88, and 294–303 for examples of Buber's confrontations with Israeli government leaders. In addition to the issues regarding the Arab-Jewish conflict discussed here, Buber also protested the execution of Adolph Eichmann and repeatedly spoke out on internal political issues such as the Lavon affair and the trial of Aaron Cohen. See Friedman, *Buber's Life and Work* 3:3–32, 332–71.

54. On Buber's statements concerning the attacks on the Jordanian village of Kibya in 1953 and the village of K'far Kassem in 1956, see Friedman, *Buber's Life and Work* 3:337–38, and the sources he cites on 455–57.

Bibliography

I. Works by Martin Buber

A. UNPUBLISHED WRITINGS

"Aus: 'Mitteilungen des Verbandes der jüdischen Jungendvereine Deutschlands', Heft 2/3, Berlin, April/Mai, 1918." Martin Buber Archives. Jewish National and University Library. Jerusalem.

"Besprechungen mit Martin Buber in Ascona, August, 1924, über Lao-tse's Tao-te-king." MS. var. 350,45/b. Martin Buber Archives. Jewish National and University Library. Jerusalem.

"Individualismus und Kollektivismus: Vortrag von Prof. Martin Buber gehalten am 7. Juli, 1947 bei Herrn Dr. med. Hans Trub, Schmelzbergstrasse 28, Zurich 7." MS. var. 350,47/c I/b. Martin Buber Archives. Jewish National and University Library. Jerusalem.

"Martin Buber Abende." MS. var. 350/B, 47d. Martin Buber Archives. Jewish National and University Library. Jerusalem.

"Rede Dr. Martin Bubers gehalten am Jugendmeeting am 25. Marz, 1920 in Prag." MS. var. 350, 32d. Martin Buber Archives. Jewish National and University Library. Jerusalem.

"Religion in the Land of Israel." MS. var. 350, 40a–5. Martin Buber Archives. Jewish National and University Library. Jerusalem. (Later published in Hebrew in Buber, *HaRuah v'Hameziut*. Tel Aviv: Mahbarot LaSifrut, 1942).

"Staat und Gemeinschaft." February 1924. MS. var. 350, 47e. Martin Buber Archives. Jewish National and University Library. Jerusalem.

"Vortrag des Herrn Dr. Martin Buber am 24 January, 1931, über Individuum und Person—Masse und Gemeinschaft." MS. var. 350, 47a,b. Martin Buber Archives. Jewish National and University Library. Jerusalem.

"Vortrag von Herrn Professor Martin Buber: Erziehung zur Gemeinschaft. (6. April, 1929)." MS. var. 350, 47a,b. Martin Buber Archives. Jewish National and University Library. Jerusalem.

"Zarathustra." MS. var. 350/B76. Martin Buber Archives. Jewish National and University Library. Jerusalem.

"Zur Geschichte des Individuationsproblems: Nicholaus von Cues und Jakob Boehme." Dissertation, 1904. MS. var. 350/A2. Martin Buber Archives. Jewish National and University Library. Jerusalem.

B. PUBLISHED WRITINGS

"Alte und neue Gemeinschaft." Edited by Paul R. Flohr and Bernard Susser. *Association for Jewish Studies Review* 1 (1976): 50–56.
Aus Tiefen rufe ich Dich. Berlin: Schocken, 1936.
A Believing Humanism—My Testament, 1902–1965. Translated by Maurice Friedman. Credo Perspectives. New York: Simon and Schuster, 1967.
Between Man and Man. New York: Macmillan, 1965.
Martin Buber: Briefwechsel aus sieben Jahrzehnten. (Letters.) 3 vols. Edited by Grete Schaeder. Heidelberg: Lambert Schneider, 1972.
"Buber's Meetings with Second Generation Kibbbutz Members." *Khan ve-'Akhshav: Iyyunim be-Haguto ha-Hevratit ve-ha-Datit shel M. M. Buber.* Jerusalem: Efrat, 1982, 44–51.
Die Chassidischer Bücher. Berlin: Schocken, 1932.
Daniel—Dialogues on Realization. Edited and translated by Maurice Friedman. New York: Holt, Rinehart and Winston, 1964.
Daniel: Gespräche von der Verwirklichung. Leipzig: Insel-Verlag, 1913.
Darko shel Mikra. (Hebrew.) Jerusalem: Bialik Institute, 1964.
Das dialogische Prinzip. Heidelberg: Verlag Lambert Schneider, 1979.
Drei Reden über das Judentum. Frankfurt: Rutten and Loening, 1911.
Eclipse of God. New York: Harper and Brothers, 1952.
Ecstatic Confessions. Collected and introduced by Martin Buber. Edited by Paul Mendes-Flohr. Translated by Esther Cameron. New York: Harper and Row, 1985.
Ekstatische Konfessionen—Gesammelt von Martin Buber. Jena: E. Diederichs, 1909.
Ereignesse und Begegnungen. Berlin: Schocken, n.d.
For the Sake of Heaven. New York: Meridian Books; Philadelphia: Jewish Society of America, 1945.
"Geleitwort." In Sombart, Werner, *Das Proletariat.* Vol. 1 of *Die Gesselschaft,* edited by Martin Buber. Frankfurt: Rutten and Loening, 1906, 14–15. For English translation see Flohr, *From Kulturmystik to Dialogue,* 193–98.
Good and Evil. New York: Charles Schribner's Sons, 1952.
Der Grosse Maggid und seine Nachfolge. Frankfurt: Rutten und Loening, 1922.
Hasidism and Modern Man. New York: Horizon, 1958.
Der Heilige Weg: Ein Wort über die Juden und die Volker. Frankfurt: Rutten und Loening, 1920.
I and Thou. Translated by Walter Kaufmann. New York: Scribners, 1971.
Ich und Du. Leipzig: Insel-Verlag, 1923.

"Interpreting Hasidism." *Commentary* 36, no. 3 (September 1963): 218–25.
"Interrogation of Martin Buber." In *Philosophical Interrogations*, edited by Beatrice and Sydney Rome. New York: Harper and Row, 1970.
Israel and Palestine. London: East-West Library, 1952.
Israel and the World. New York: Schocken, 1963.
Der Jude und Sein Judentum—Gesammelte Aufsätze und Reden. Cologne: J. Meltzer, 1963.
Die Jüdische Bewegung. Vols. 1 and 2. Berlin: Jüdischer Verlag, 1920.
Kampf um Israel—Reden und Schriften, 1921–1932. Berlin: Schocken, 1933.
Kingship of God. Translated by Richard Scheinmann. New York: Harper and Row, 1967.
The Knowledge of Man—Selected Essays. Edited by Maurice Friedman. Translated by Maurice Friedman and Ronald Gregor Smith. New York: Harper and Row, 1965.
A Land of Two Peoples: Martin Buber on Jews and Arabs. Edited by Paul Mendes-Flohr. New York: Oxford University Press, 1983.
The Legends of the Baal Shem. New York: Schocken, 1969.
Moses: The Revelation and the Covenant. New York: Harper and Brothers, Harper Torchbooks, 1958.
"Mystik als religioser Solipsismus—Bemerkungen zu einem Vortag von Ernst Troeltsch." *Verhandlungen des Ersten Deutschen Soziologentages vom 19–22 Oktober 1910 in Frankfurt a.M.* Frankfurt: Verlag Sauer und Auvermann K.G., 1969, 206–7.
Nachlese. Heidelberg: Verlag Lambert Schneider, 1966.
Netivot be-'Utopia. Edited by Avraham Shapira. Tel Aviv: Am Oved, 1983.
On the Bible. Edited by Nahum N. Glatzer. New York: Schocken, 1982.
On Judaism. Translated by Eva Jospe. Edited by Nahum Glatzer. New York: Schocken, 1967.
"On Viennese Literature." Edited by William Johnson. Translated from Polish by Robert A. Rothstein. *The German Quarterly* 47, no. 4 (November 1974): 559–66.
The Origin and Meaning of Hasidism. New York: Horizon Press, 1960.
"Our Greatness Is Bound to the Greatness of the Region: Interview with Professor Martin Buber." (Hebrew.) *Etgar* 1, no. 17 (2 November 1961): 4–5.
Paths in Utopia. Boston: Beacon Press, 1949.
"Pharisaism." In *The Jew: Essays from Martin Buber's Journal, Der Jude, 1916–1928,* edited by Arthur A. Cohen. Translated from German by Joachim Neugroschel. University, Ala.: University of Alabama Press, 1980.
Pointing the Way—Collected Essays. Translated from German and edited by Maurice Friedman. New York: Harper, 1957.
"Proximity and Relation in the Kibbutz Experience: The Meeting of Young Kibbutz Educators with Martin Buber." In Martin Buber, *Netivot be-'Utopia,* edited by Avraham Shapira. Tel Aviv: Am Oved, 1983, 229–35.

Reden über das Judentum. Frankfurt: Rutten und Loening, 1923.
Reden und Gleichnisse des Tschuang Tse. Leipzig: Insel-Verlag, 1910.
"Religion als Gegenwart." In *Buber's Way to I and Thou: An Historical Analysis and the First Publication of Martin Buber's Lectures "Religion als Gegenwart,* vol. 7 of *Phroneses: Eine Schriftreihe,* edited by Rivkah Horowitz. Heidelberg: Verlag Lambert Schneider, 1978.
Die Stunde und die Erkenntnis—Reden und Aufsätze, 1933–35. Berlin: Schocken, 1936.
Tales of Rabbi Nachman. Bloomington, Ind.: University of Indiana Press, 1956.
Tales of the Hasidim. 2 vols. New York: Schocken, 1947–48.
Te'udah ve-Ye'ud. 2 vols. Jerusalem: Ha-Sifriah Ha-Zionit, 1959.
Die Trostung Israels. Berlin: Schocken, 1933.
Two Types of Faith. New York: Harper and Brothers, 1961.
"Über Jakob Boehme." *Wiener Rundschau* 5, no. 12 (15 June 1901): 9.
Urdistanz und Beziehung: Beiträge zu Einer Philosophischen Anthropologie. Heidelberg: Verlag Lambert Schneider, 1978.
Völker, Staaten und Zion. Berlin: R. Lowit Verlag, 1917.
Worte an die Zeit. Erstes Heft, Grundsätze. Zweites Heft, Gemeinschaft. Munich: Dreilanderverlag, 1919.
"Ein Wort über Nietzsche und die Lebenswerte." *Die Kunst im Leben.* 1, no. 2, 12 (December 1900): 13.
"Zionism True and False." In *Unease in Zion,* edited by Ehud ben Ezer. New York: Quadrangle Books, 1974.
Zwiesprache. Berlin: Schocken Verlag, 1932.

C. WITH OTHERS

Buber, Martin, and Rosenzweig, Franz. *Die Schrift und ihre Verdeutschung.* Berlin: Schocken, 1936.
Buber, Martin, Feivel, Berthold, and Weizmann, Chaim. *A Jewish School of Higher Learning.* Translated from German by Shaul Esh. Jerusalem: Magnes Press of The Hebrew University, 1968.

II. Works by Other Authors

Agus, Jacob. *Modern Philosophies of Judaism.* New York: Behrman's Jewish Book House, 1941.
Ahad Haam. *Collected Writings.* (Hebrew.) Tel Aviv: D'vir, 1947.
———. *Ahad Haam: Nationalism and the Jewish Ethic.* Edited by Hans Kohn. New York: Schocken, 1962.
———. "The Negation of the Diaspora." In *The Zionist Idea,* edited by Arthur Hertzberg. New York: Atheneum, Temple Books, 1970.
———. *Selected Essays of Ahad Haam.* Translated from Hebrew and edited by Leon Simon. New York: Atheneum, 1970.

Austin, J. L. *How to Do Things with Words.* Edited by J. O. Urmson and Marina Sbisa. Cambridge, Mass.: Harvard University Press, 1962.

Avineri, Shlomo. *Hegel's Theory of the Modern State.* Cambridge, England: Cambridge University Press, 1972.

———. *The Making of Modern Zionism.* New York: Basic Books, 1981.

———. *The Political and Social Thought of Karl Marx.* Cambridge, England: Cambridge University Press, 1968.

Baer, Yizhak. *Galut.* New York: Schocken, 1947.

Baker, Leonard. *Days of Sorrow and Pain: Leo Baeck and the Berlin Jews.* New York: Oxford University Press, 1978.

Barbour, Ian. *Myths, Models and Paradigms: A Comparative Study in Science and Religion.* New York: Harper and Row, 1974.

Baron, Salo. *History and Jewish Historians.* Compiled by Arthur Hertzberg and Leon A. Feldman. Philadelphia: Jewish Publication Society, 1964.

Barrett, William. *Irrational Man.* New York: Doubleday, Anchor Books, 1958.

Barthes, Roland. *S/Z.* Translated by Richard Miller. New York: Hill and Wang, 1974.

Bellah, Robert. *Beyond Belief: Essays on Religion in a Post-Traditional World.* New York: Harper and Row, 1971.

Belsey, Catherine. *Critical Practice.* London: Methuen, 1980.

Ben Chorin, Schalom. "Martin Buber in Jerusalem." In *Martin Buber 1878–1978,* edited by Wolfgang Zink. Bonn-Bad Godesberg: Hochwacht, 1978.

Bendix, Reinhard, and Roth, Guenther. *Scholarship and Partisanship: Essays on Max Weber.* Berkeley and Los Angeles: University of California Press, 1971.

Ben Ezer, Ehud, ed. *Ein Shaananim be-Zion.* Tel Aviv: Am Oved, 1986.

———, ed. *Unease in Zion.* New York: Quadrangle Books, 1974.

Ben Gurion, David. *My Talks with Arab Leaders.* Jerusalem: Keter, 1962.

Berger, Peter. *The Sacred Canopy.* Garden City, N.Y.: Doubleday, Anchor Books, 1969.

Berger, Peter, and Kellner, Hansfried. *Sociology Reinterpreted: An Essay on Method and Vocation.* Garden City, N.Y.: Doubleday, Anchor Books, 1981.

Bergman, Samuel Hugo. *Dialogical Philosophy from Kierkegaard to Buber.* (Hebrew.) Jerusalem: Bialik Institute, 1974.

Berkovitz, Eliezer. *Major Themes in Modern Philosophies of Judaism.* New York: Ktav, 1974.

Berlin, Isaiah, "Does Political Theory Still Exist?" In *Concepts and Categories.* New York: Viking Press, 1979.

———. *Vico and Herder: Two Studies in the History of Ideas.* New York: Random House, Vintage Books, 1977.

Bernstein, Richard. *Beyond Objectivism and Relativism.* Philadelphia: University of Pennsylvania Press, 1983.

———. *Praxis and Action.* Philadelphia: University of Pennsylvania Press, 1971.

———. *The Restructuring of Social and Political Theory*. Philadelphia: University of Pennsylvania Press, 1978.

Biale, David. *Gershom Scholem: Kabbalah and Counter History*. Cambridge, Mass.: Harvard University Press, 1979.

———. "Gershom Scholem and Anarchism as a Jewish Philosophy." *Judaism* 32, no. 1 (winter 1983): 70–76.

———. "Gershom Scholem's Ten Unhistorical Aphorisms on Kabbalah: Text and Commentary." *Modern Judaism* 5, no. 1 (February 1985): 67–93.

Bloch, Jochanan. *Die Aporie des Du: Probleme der Dialogik des Martin Bubers*. Heidelberg: Lambert Schneider, 1977.

———. "The Justification and the Futility of Dialogical Thinking." In *Martin Buber: A Centenary Volume*, edited by Jochanan Bloch and Haim Gordon. New York: Ktav, 1984.

Bloch, Jochanan, and Gordon, Haim, eds. *Martin Buber: A Centenary Volume*. New York: Ktav, 1984.

Bloom, Harold. *Agon: Towards a Theory of Revisionism*. New York: Oxford University Press, 1982.

———. *The Anxiety of Influence*. New York: Oxford University Press, 1973.

———. *The Breaking of the Vessels*. Chicago: University of Chicago Press, 1982.

———. *Kabbalah and Criticism*. New York: Continuum, 1983.

———. *A Map of Misreading*. New York: Oxford University Press, 1975.

Bohm, David. *Wholeness and the Implicate Order*. London: Routledge and Kegan Paul, 1980.

Borowitz, Eugene. *A New Jewish Theology in the Making*. Philadelphia: Westminster Press, 1968.

Bottomore, Tom, ed. *A Dictionary of Marxist Thought*, Cambridge, Mass.: Harvard University Press, 1983.

Cavell, Stanley. "Existentialism and Analytic Philosophy." *Daedelus* 93 (summer 1964): 946–74.

Chiaromonte, Nicola. *The Paradox of History*. Philadelphia: University of Pennsylvania Press, 1985.

Cohen, Aaron. *Israel and the Arab World*. New York: Funk and Wagnalls, 1970.

Cohen, Arthur, ed. *The Jew: Essays from Martin Buber's Journal, Der Jude, 1916–1928*. Translated from German by Joachim Neugroschel. University, Ala.: University of Alabama Press, 1980.

———. *Martin Buber*. New York: Hillary House, 1957.

———. *The Natural and the Supernatural Jew*. New York: Pantheon Books, 1962.

Cohen, Hermann. *Reason and Hope: Selections from the Jewish Writings of Hermann Cohen*. Translated by Eva Jospe. New York: W. W. Norton, 1971.

————. *The Religion of Reason Out of the Sources of Judaism*. Translated by Simon Kaplan. New York: Frederick Ungar, 1972.

Cohn, Margot, and Buber, Raphael, comps. *Martin Buber: A Bibliography of His Writings, 1897–1978*. Jerusalem: Magnes Press, The Hebrew University, 1980.

The Condition of Jewish Belief: A Symposium. Compiled by the editors of *Commentary*. Toronto: Collier-Macmillan, 1966.

Coser, Lewis, ed. *Georg Simmel*. Englewood Cliffs, N.J.: Prentice-Hall, Spectrum Books, 1969.

Culler, Jonathan. *On Deconstruction*. Ithaca, N.Y.: Cornell University Press, 1983.

————. *The Pursuit of Signs*. Ithaca, N.Y.: Cornell University Press, 1981.

————. *Roland Barthes*. New York: Oxford University Press, 1983.

Dawidowicz, Lucy. *The Golden Tradition*. Boston: Beacon Press, 1957.

Derrida, Jacques. *Of Grammatology*. Translated by Gayatri Chakravorty Spivak. Baltimore: Johns Hopkins University Press, 1974.

Diamond, Malcolm. *Martin Buber, Jewish Existentialist*. New York: Harper and Row, 1968.

Dilthey, Wilhelm. *Pattern and Meaning in History*. Edited by H. P. Rickman. New York: Harper and Row, 1961.

————. *Selected Writings*. Edited by H. P. Rickman. New York: Cambridge University Press, 1978.

Douglas, Jack D., and Johnson, John M., eds. *Existential Sociology*. Cambridge, England: Cambridge University Press, 1967.

Dubnow, Simon. *Nationalism and History*. Edited by Koppel Pinson. Philadelphia: Jewish Publication Society; Cleveland: World Publishing Company, 1958.

Dworkin, Ronald. "Law as Interpretation." In *The Politics of Interpretation*, edited by W. J. T. Mitchell. Chicago: University of Chicago Press, 1982.

————. "My Reply to Stanley Fish (and Walter Benn Michaels): Please Don't Talk about Objectivity Any More." In *The Politics of Interpretation*, edited by W. J. T. Mitchell. Chicago: University of Chicago Press, 1982.

Eagleton, Terry. *Literary Theory: An Introduction*. Minneapolis: University of Minnesota Press, 1983.

Eisen, Arnold. *Galut*. Indianapolis: Indiana University Press, 1986.

Elon, Amos. *The Israelis: Fathers and Sons*. New York: Holt, Rinehart and Winston, 1971.

Encyclopedia Judaica. Vol. 7. S.v. "Hasidism" and "Haskalah."

Engels, Friederick, and Marx, Karl. *The German Ideology*. New York: International Publishers, 1947.

Erikson, Erik. *Childhood and Society*. New York: W. W. Norton, 1963.

Ermath, Michael. *Wilhelm Dilthey: The Critique of Historical Reason*. Chicago: University of Chicago Press, 1978.

Farber, Leslie. "Introductory Remarks." *Psychiatry* 20, no. 2 (1957): 95–96.

Feuer, Lewis. "What Is Alienation? The Career of a Concept." In *Sociology on Trial*, edited by Maurice Stein and Arthur Vidich. Englewood Cliffs, N.J.: Prentice-Hall, Spectrum Books, 1973.

Feuerbach, Ludwig. "Basic Principles on the Philosophy of the Future." In *The Worlds of Existentialism*, edited by Maurice Friedman. Chicago: University of Chicago Press, 1964.

———. *The Essence of Christianity*. Translated by George Eliot. New York: Harper and Row, 1957.

Fish, Stanley. *Is There a Text in this Class? The Authority of Interpretive Communities*. Cambridge, Mass.: Harvard University Press, 1980.

Fishbane, Michael. "Martin Buber as an Interpreter of the Bible." *Judaism* 27, no. 2 (spring 1978): 184–95.

Flohr, Paul R. *From Kulturmystik to Dialogue: An Inquiry into the Formation of Martin Buber's Philosophy of I and Thou*. Doctoral dissertation. Ann Arbor, Mich.: University Microfilms, 1974.

———. "The Road to *I and Thou*: An Inquiry into Buber's Transition from Mysticism to Dialogue." In *Texts and Responses: Studies Presented to Nahum N. Glatzer on the Occasion of His Seventieth Birthday by His Students*, edited by Michael A. Fishbane and Paul R. Flohr. Leiden: E. J. Brill, 1975.

Flohr, Paul R., and Susser, Bernard. "Alte und Neue Gemeinschaft: An Unpublished Buber Manuscript." *AJS Review* 1 (1976): 41–56.

Fox, Everett. *In the Beginning: A New English Rendition of the Book of Genesis*. Translated by Everett Fox. New York: Schocken, 1983.

Freire, Paolo. *Pedagogy of the Oppressed*. New York: Seabury Press, 1970.

Friedman, Maurice. *Martin Buber: The Life of Dialogue*. New York: Harper and Brothers, 1960.

———. *Martin Buber's Life and Work*. Vol. 1, *The Early Years, 1878–1923*. Vol. 2, *The Middle Years, 1923–1945*. Vol. 3, *The Later Years, 1945–1965*. New York: Dutton, 1981–83.

———. "Martin Buber's Theory of Knowledge." *Review of Metaphysics* 8, no. 2, 30 (December 1954): 264–80.

Friedrichs, Robert W. *A Sociology of Sociology*. New York: Free Press, 1970.

Gaillie, W. B. *Philosophy and Historical Understanding*. 2d ed. New York: Schocken, 1968.

Gardiner, Patrick. *The Nature of Historical Explanation*. Oxford, England: Oxford University Press, 1961.

Geertz, Clifford. *The Interpretation of Cultures*. New York: Basic Books, 1973.

Giddens, Anthony. *Central Problems in Social Theory*. Berkeley and Los Angeles: University of California Press, 1979.

Gier, Nicholas. *Wittgenstein and Phenomenology*. Albany: State University of New York Press, 1981.

Girardot, Norman. "Behaving Cosmogonically in Early Taoism." In *Cos-

mogony and Ethical Behavior, edited by Robin Lovin and Frank Reynolds. Chicago: University of Chicago Press, 1985.

———. *Myth and Meaning in Early Taoism*. Berkeley and Los Angeles: University of California Press, 1984.

Glatzer, Nahum. *Franz Rosenzweig: His Life and Thought*. New York: Schocken, 1953.

Goodman, Paul, and Goodman, Percival G. *Communitas*. New York: Alfred J. Knopf and Random House, Vintage Books, 1960.

Gordon, Haim. "Would Martin Buber Endorse the Buber Model?" *Educational Theory* 23, no. 3 (1973): 215–23.

Gorni, Yosef. *The Jewish Question and the Arab Problem (Hebrew.)* Tel Aviv: Am Oved, 1985.

Gouldner, Alvin. "Anti-Minotaur: The Myth of a Value Free Sociology." In *Sociology on Trial*, edited by Maurice Stein and Arthur Vidich. Englewood Cliffs, N.J.: Prentice-Hall, 1963.

———. *The Coming Crisis of Western Sociology*. New York: Basic Books, 1970.

Graetz, Heinrich. *History of the Jews*. vol. 5. Philadelphia: Jewish Publication Society, 1985.

———. *The Structure of Jewish History*. Translated and edited by Ismar Schorsch. New York: Jewish Theological Seminary of America, 1975.

Guttmann, Julius. *Philosophies of Judaism: A History of Jewish Philosophy from Biblical Times to Franz Rosenzweig*. Translated by David W. Silverman. New York: Holt, Rinehart and Winston, 1964.

Halpern, Benjamin. *The Idea of the Jewish State*. Cambridge, Mass.: Harvard University Press, 1961.

Hamburger, Michael. *Hofmannsthal: Three Essays*. Princeton: Princeton University Press, 1972.

Hammarskjold, Dag. *Servant of Peace: A Selection of Speeches and Statements of Dag Hammarskjold*. Edited by Wilder Foote. New York: Harper and Row, 1963.

Harvey, Van. *The Historian and the Believer*. New York: Macmillan, 1966.

Hayman, Ronald. *Nietzsche: A Critical Life*. New York: Penguin, 1980.

Heinemann, F. H. *Existentialism and the Modern Predicament*. New York: Harper and Brothers, 1953.

Herberg, Will. *Judaism and Modern Man*. New York: Farrar, Straus and Cudahy, 1951.

Hertzberg, Arthur, ed. *The Zionist Idea*. New York: Atheneum, Temple Book, 1970.

Heschel, Abraham. "Depth Theology." In *The Insecurity of Freedom*. New York: Farrar, Straus and Giroux, 1966.

———. *God in Search of Man*. New York: Meridian Books; Philadelphia: Jewish Publication Society, 1959.

Hill, Brian V. *Education and the Endangered Individual: A Critique of Ten Modern Thinkers*. New York: Dell, 1975.

Hirsch, Samson Raphael. *Nineteen Letters*. New York: Feldheim, 1960.

Hobson, Robert. *Forms of Feeling: The Heart of Psychotherapy*. London: Tavistock Publications, 1985.

Hollingdale, R. J. *Nietzsche*. London: Routledge and Kegan Paul, 1973.

Holtz, Barry. *Back to the Sources*. New York: Summit Books, 1984.

Hook, Sidney. *From Hegel to Marx: Studies in the Intellectual Development of Karl Marx*. Ann Arbor, Mich.: University of Michigan Press, 1962.

Horowitz, Rivkah. *Buber's Way to I and Thou: An Historical Analysis and the First Publication of Martin Buber's Lectures "Religion als Gegenwart."* Vol. 7 of *Phroneses: Eine Schriftreihe*. Heidelberg: Verlag Lambert Schneider, 1978.

———. "Discoveries Concerning the History of Martin Buber's *I and Thou*." (Hebrew.) *Proceedings of the Israel National Academy of Science* 5, no. 8 (1982): 161–87.

Hughes, H. Stuart. *Consciousness and Society*. New York: Random House, Vintage Books, 1958.

Iggers, Georg G. *The German Conception of History*. Middletown, Conn.: Wesleyan University Press, 1968.

Jacobs, Louis. *Hasidic Prayer*. New York: Schocken, 1972.

———. *The Seeker of Unity: The Life and Works of Aaron of Starosselje*. London: Vallentine, Mitchell and Co., 1966.

——— "The Uplifting of Sparks in Later Jewish Mysticism." In *Jewish Spirituality: From the Sixteenth Century Revival to the Present*, edited by Arthur Green. New York: Crossroad, 1987.

Janik, Allan, and Toulmin, Stephen. *Wittgenstein's Vienna*. New York: Simon and Schuster, 1973.

Josephson, Eric, and Josephson, Mary, eds. *Man Alone: Alienation in Modern Society*. New York: Dell, 1962.

Kaplan, Edward. "Martin Buber and the Drama of Otherness: The Dynamics of Love, Art, and Faith." *Judaism* 27, no. 2 (spring 1978): 196–206.

Katz, Jacob. *Tradition and Crisis*. New York: Schocken, 19, 1961.

Katz, Steven T. "Dialogue and Revelation in the Thought of Martin Buber. *Religion Studies* 14 (March 1978): 57–68.

———. *Post Holocaust Dialogues: Critical Studies in Modern Jewish Thought*. New York: New York University Press, 1985.

———, ed. *Mysticism and Philosophical Analysis*. New York: Oxford University Press, 1978.

Kaufmann, Walter. *Discovering the Mind*, vol. 2. New York: McGraw-Hill, 1980.

———. *Nietzsche: Philosopher, Psychologist, Antichrist*. 4th ed. Princeton, N.J.: Princeton University Press, 1974.

———. "Buber's Failures and Triumph." In *Martin Buber: A Centenary Volume*, edited by Jochanan Bloch and Haim Gordon. New York: Ktav, 1984, 3–24.

Kaufmann, Yehezkel. "The Biblical Age." In *Great Ages and Ideas of the*

Jewish People, edited by Leo W. Schwarz. New York: Random House, 1956.

———. *Golah ve-'Nekhar*. (Hebrew.) 4 vols. Tel Aviv: D'vir, 1928–1932.

———. *The Religion of Israel*. Translated by Moshe Greenberg. Chicago: University of Chicago Press, 1969.

Kedourie, Elie. *Nationalism*. New York: Praeger, 1960.

Keren, Michael. *Ben Gurion and the Intellectuals: Power, Knowledge, and Charisma*. De Kalb, Ill.: Northern Illinois University Press, 1983.

Kierkegaard, Soren. *Attack upon Christendom*. Translated by Walter Lowrie. Princeton, N.J.: Princeton University Press, 1968.

———. *The Concept of Anxiety*. Edited and translated by Reidar Thomte and Albert B. Anderson. Princeton, N.J.: Princeton University Press, 1980.

———. *Concluding Unscientific Postscript*. Translated by David F. Swenson and Walter Lowrie. Princeton, N.J.: Princeton University Press, 1941.

———. *A Kierkegaard Anthology*. Edited by Robert Bretall. Princeton, N.J.: Princeton University Press, 1946.

———. *The Present Age*. Translated by Alexander Dru. New York: Harper and Row, 1962.

Klausner, Israel. *Herzl's Opposition*. (Hebrew.) Tel Aviv: 1959.

Kohn, Hans. *Living in a World Revolution*. New York: Pocket Books, 1964.

———. *Martin Buber: Sein Werk und seine Zeit*. Wiesbaden: Fourier Verlag, 1979.

———. "Zion and the Jewish National Idea." In *Zionism Reconsidered*, edited by Michael Selzer. New York: Macmillan, 1970.

Kurzweil, Barukh. *Sifruteinu Ha-Hadashah: Hemshekh o'Mahapekhah?* (Modern Hebrew Literature: Continuity or revolt). Tel Aviv: Schocken, 1959.

Laing, R. D. *Self and Others*. Baltimore: Penguin Books, 1971.

———. *Wisdom, Madness and Folly: The Making of a Psychiatrist*. New York: McGraw-Hill, 1985.

Landauer, Gustav. *Skepsis und Mystik*. Cologne: Markan-Block Verlag, 1923.

Laqueur, Walter. *A History of Zionism*. New York: Holt, Rinehart and Winston, 1972.

———. *Young Germany: A History of the German Youth Movement*. New York: Basic Books, 1962.

Leff, Gordon. *History and Social Theory*. Garden City, N.Y.: Doubleday, Anchor Books, 1971.

Leitch, Vincent B. *Deconstructive Criticism*. New York: Columbia University Press, 1983.

Lentricchia, Frank. *After the New Criticism*. Chicago: University of Chicago Press, 1980.

Liebert, Arthur. "Mythus und Kultur." In *Kant-Studien*. Berlin: Verlag von Reuther und Reichard, 1922.

Lilker, Shlomo. *Kibbutz Judaism: A New Tradition in the Making*. New York: Cornwall Books, Herzl Press, 1982.

Lovejoy, Arthur O. *The Great Chain of Being*. New York: Harper and Row, 1965.

Lowith, Karl. *From Hegel to Nietzsche*. New York: Doubleday, 1967.

———. "Weber's Interpretation of the Bourgeois-Capitalistic World in Terms of the Guiding Principle of Alienation." In *Max Weber*, edited by Dennis Wrong. Englewood Cliffs, N.J.: Prentice-Hall, 1970.

Luft, David S. *Robert Musil and the Crisis of European Culture, 1880–1942*. Berkeley and Los Angeles: University of California Press, 1980.

Lukes, Steven. "Alienation and Anomie." In *Philosophy, Politics and Society*, 3d series, edited by Peter Laslett and W. G. Runciman. Oxford, England: Oxford University Press, 1969.

Lunn, Eugene. *Prophet of Community: The Romantic Socialism of Gustav Landauer*. Berkeley and Los Angeles: University of California Press, 1973.

MacIntyre, Alisdair. "Epistemological Crises, Dramatic Narrative, and the Philosophy of Science." In *Paradigms and Revolutions: Applications and Appraisals of Thomas Kuhn's Philosophy of Science*, edited by Gary Gutting. Notre Dame, Ind.: University of Notre Dame Press, 1980.

Mackey, Louis. *Kierkegaard: A Kind of Poet*. Philadelphia: University of Pennsylvania Press, 1971.

McNeil, William. "Make Mine Myth." *New York Times*, 28 December 1981.

MacQuarrie, John. *Existentialism*. Harmondsworth, England: Penguin Books, 1972.

Mandlebaum, Maurice. *History, Man and Reason: A Study in Nineteenth-Century Thought*. Baltimore: Johns Hopkins University Press, 1971.

Marcuse, Herbert. *Reason and Revolution: Hegel and the Rise of Social Theory*. Boston: Beacon Press, 1967.

Martin Buber and the Kibbutz. Haifa: The Kibbutz University Center, 1980.

Marx, Karl. *Karl Marx: Early Writings*. Translated and edited by T. B. Bottomore. New York: McGraw-Hill, 1964.

Menahem Nahum of Chernobyl. *Upright Practices, The Light of the Eyes*. Translated by Arthur Green. New York: Paulist Press, 1982.

Mendes-Flohr, Paul. "Community and Renewal: Dialogue as a Metasociological Principle." (Hebrew.) In *Khan ve-'Akhshav: Iyyunim ba-Haguto ha-Hevratit ve-ha-Datit shel M. M. Buber*, edited by Avraham Shapira. Jerusalem: Efrat, 1982.

———. "Law and Sacrament: Ritual Observance in Twentieth-Century Jewish thought." In *Jewish Spirituality from the Sixteenth Century Revival to the Present*, edited by Arthur Green. New York: Crossroad Publishing Company, 1987.

———. "Martin Buber's Reception Among Jews." *Modern Judaism* 6, no. 2 (May 1986): 111–26.

Mendes-Flohr, Paul, and Reinharz, Jehuda, eds. *The Jew in the Modern World*. New York: Oxford University Press, 1980.

Mills, C. Wright. *Power, Politics and People: The Collected Esssays of C. Wright Mills*. Edited by Irving Louis Horowitz. New York: Ballantine Books, 1963.

Minougue, K. R. *Nationalism*. Baltimore: Penguin Books, 1967.

Mitzman, Arthur. *Sociology and Estrangement: Three Sociologists of Imperial Germany*. New York: Alfred Knopf, 1973.

Moore, George Foote. *Judaism in the First Centuries of the Christian Era*. Cambridge, Mass.: Harvard University Press, 1954.

Mosse, George. *Germans and Jews*. New York: Grosset and Dunlap, 1970.

Munro, Donald J. *The Concept of Man in Early China*. Stanford, Calif.: Stanford University Press, 1969.

Nehamas, Alexander. *Nietzsche: Life as Literature*. Cambridge, Mass.: Harvard University Press, 1985.

Nietzsche, Friedrich. *Beyond Good and Evil*. Translated by Walter Kaufmann. New York: Random House, Vintage Books. 1967.

———. *The Birth of Tragedy*. Translated by Francis Golffing. New York: Doubleday, 1956.

———. *Ecce Homo*. Translated by R. J. Hollingdale. Harmondsworth, England: Penguin Books, 1979.

———. *The Gay Science*. Translated by Walter Kaufmann. New York: Random House, Vintage Books, 1974.

———. *On the Advantage and Disadvantage of History for Life*. Translated by Peter Preuss. Indianapolis, Ind.: Hackett Publishing Company, 1980.

———. *On the Genealogy of Morals*. Edited by Walter Kaufmann and translated by Walter Kaufmann and R. J. Hollingdale. New York: Random House, Vintage Books, 1967.

———. *The Portable Nietzsche*. Edited and translated by Walter Kaufmann. New York: Viking Press, 1968.

———. *Schopenhauer as Educator*. Translated by James W. Hillesheim and Malcolm R. Simpson. South Bend, Ind.: Regnery/Gateway, 1965.

———. *Untimely Meditations*. Translated by R. J. Hollingdale. Cambridge, England: Cambridge University Press, 1983.

———. *The Will to Power*. Edited by Walter Kaufmann and translated by Walter Kaufmann and R. J. Hollingdale. New York: Random House, Vintage Books, 1967.

Nimis, Steve. "Fussnoten: Das Fundament der Wissenschaft." *Arethusa* 17, no. 2 (1984): 105–34.

Nisbet, Robert. *The Sociological Tradition*. New York: Basic Books, 1966.

Norris, Christopher. *Deconstruction: Theory and Practice*. London: Methuen, 1982.

Ollman, Bertell. *Alienation: Marx's Conception of Man in Capitalistic Society*. 2d ed. Cambridge, England: Cambridge University Press, 1971.

Ong, Walter. *Orality and Literacy: The Technologizing of the Word*. London: Methuen, 1982.

Oz, Amos. *In the Land of Israel*. New York: Random House, Vintage Books, 1984.

Pappenheim, Franz. *The Alienation of Modern Man: An Interpretation Based upon Marx and Tonnies*. New York: Monthly Review Press, Modern Reader Paperbacks, 1968.

Patterson, David. *The Hebrew Novel in Czarist Russia*. Edinburgh: The University Press, 1964.

Petrovic, Gajo. "Alienation." In *A Dictionary of Marxist Thought*, edited by Tom Bottomore, Laurence Harris, V. G. Kiernan, and Ralph Miliband. Cambridge, Mass.: Harvard University Press, 1983.

Phillipson, David. *The Reform Movement in Judaism*. New York: Ktav, 1967.

Pitkin, Hannah. *Wittgenstein and Justice*. Berkeley and Los Angeles: University of California Press, 1972.

Plaut, Walter G. *The Rise of Reform Judaism*. New York: World Union for Progressive Judaism, 1963.

Pockock, J. G. A. *Politics, Language and Time: Essays on Political Thought and History*. New York: Atheneum, 1973.

Psychiatry 20, no. 2 (1957).

Reinharz, Jehuda. "Ahad Haam, Martin Buber and German Zionism." In *At the Crossroad: Essays on Ahad Haam*, edited by Jacques Kornberg. Albany: State University of New York Press, 1983.

Ringer, Fritz. *The Rise of the German Mandarins*. Cambridge, Mass.: Harvard University Press, 1969.

Rome, Beatrice, and Rome, Sydney, eds. *Philosophical Interrogations*. New York: Harper and Row, 1970.

Rorty, Richard. *Consequences of Pragmatism*. Minneapolis: University of Minnesota Press, 1982.

———. *Philosophy and the Mirror of Nature*. Princeton, N.J.: Princeton University Press, 1979.

Rosenthal, Peggy. *Words and Values*. New York: Oxford University Press, 1984.

Rosenzweig, Franz. *Naharaim: Selected Writings.* (Hebrew.) Translated by Yehoshua Amir. Jerusalem: Bialik Institute, 1960.

———. *On Jewish Learning*. Edited by Nahum Glatzer. New York: Schocken, 1955.

Rotenstreich, Nathan. *Jewish Philosophy in Modern Times from Mendelssohn to Rosenzweig*. New York: Holt, Rinehart and Winston, 1968.

———. *Tradition and Reality: The Impact of History on Modern Jewish Thought*. New York: Random House, 1973.

Rothenberg, Albert. *The Emerging Goddess: The Creative Process in Art, Science and Other Fields*. Chicago: The University of Chicago Press, 1979.

Rubinstein, Amnon. *From Herzl to Gush Emunim: The Zionist Dream Revisited*. New York: Schocken, 1984.

Said, Edward. "Interview." *Diacritics*, fall, 1976.

Saussure, Ferdinand de. *Course in General Linguistics*. New York: McGraw-Hill, 1959.

Schacht, Richard. *Alienation*. Garden City, N.Y.: Doubleday, 1971.

——— *Nietzsche*. London: Routledge and Kegan Paul, 1983.

Schaeder, Grete. *The Hebrew Humanism of Martin Buber*. Detroit: Wayne State University, 1973.

Schaefer, Boyd C. *Nationalism: Myth and Reality*. New York: Harcourt, Brace and World, 1955.

Schatz, Rivkah. "The Interpretation of Hasidism as an Expression of Gershom Scholem's Idealistic Outlook." (Hebrew.) In *Gershom Scholem, The Man and His Work: Lectures Marking the Thirtieth Day of His Passing*. Jerusalem: Magnes Press and Mosad Bialik, 1983.

Schilpp, Paul, and Friedman, Maurice, eds. *The Philosophy of Martin Buber*. Library of Living Philosophers. LaSalle, Ill.: Open Court, 1967.

Scholem, Gershom. *Devarim be-Go*. 2 vols. Tel Aviv: Am Oved, 1982.

———. *From Berlin to Jerusalem*. New York: Schocken, 1980.

———. *Kabbalah*. New York: New American Library, Meridian Books, 1978.

———. *Major Trends in Jewish Mysticism*. 3d rev. ed. New York: Schocken, 1971.

———. *The Messianic Idea in Judaism*. New York: Schocken, 1971.

———. *On Jews and Judaism in Crisis*. New York: Schocken, 1976.

———. *Sabbatai Sevi: The Mystical Messiah, 1626–1676*. Translated by R. J. Z. Werblowsky. Princeton, N.J.: Princeton University Press, 1973.

Schorske, Carl. *Fin-de-Siècle Vienna: Politics and Culture*. New York: Random House, 1981

Schwartz, Moshe. *Language, Myth, Art*. (Hebrew.) Tel Aviv: Schocken, 1966.

Selzer, Michael, ed. *Zionism Reconsidered*. New York: Macmillan and Company, 1970.

Shapira, Avraham. "Hevrutot Mithavot ve-Tikkun Olam: ha-Utopism ha-Hevrati Shel Martin Buber." In *Netivot be-'Utopia*, by Martin Buber. Tel Aviv: Am Oved, 1983.

———. "Meetings with Buber." *Midstream* (November 1978): 48–54.

———, ed. *Khan ve-'Akhshav: Studies in the Social and Religious Thought of Martin Buber*. (Hebrew.) Jerusalem: Efrat, 1982.

Silberstein, Laurence J. "The Buber-Scholem Debate Reconsidered: Modes of Discourse in Modern Judaism." *Soundings* 71, no. 4 (winter 1988).

———. "Exile and Alienhood: Yehezkel Kaufmann on the Nation." In *Texts and Responses: Studies Presented to Nahum N. Glatzer*, edited by Michael A. Fishbane and Paul R. Flohr. Leiden: E. J. Brill, 1975.

———. "Historical Sociology and Ideology: A Prolegomenon to Yehezkel Kaufmann's *Golah ve-Nekhar*." In *Essays in Modern Jewish History: A Tribute to Ben Halpern*, edited by Frances Malino and Phyllis Cohen Albert. East Brunswick, N.J.: Associated University Presses, 1982.

———. "Judaism as a Secular System of Meaning: The Writings of Ahad Haam." *Journal of the American Academy of Religion* 52, no. 3 (September 1984): 547–68.

————. "Martin Buber." In *Encyclopedia of Religion*, edited by Mircea Eliade. New York: Macmillan, 1986.

————. "Martin Buber: The Social Paradigm in Modern Jewish Thought." *Journal of the American Academy of Religion* 49, no. 2 (1981): 211–29.

————. "Religion, Ethnicity and Jewish History: The Contribution of Yehezkel Kaufmann." *Journal of the American Academy of Religion* 42, no. 2 (September 1974): 516–31.

————. "The Renewal of Jewish Spirituality: Two Views." In *Jewish Spirituality from the Sixteenth-Century Revival to the Present*, edited by Arthur Green. New York: Crossroad Publishing Company, 1987.

————. "Textualism, Literary Theory and the Modern Interpretation of Judaism." In *Approaches to Modern Judaism*, edited by Marc Raphael. Chico, Cal.: Scholars Press, 1984.

Simmel, Georg. *The Conflict in Modern Culture and Other Essays*. New York: Teachers College Press, 1968.

————. *The Sociology of Georg Simmel*. Edited and translated by Kurt H. Wolff. New York: Free Press, 1950.

Simon, Ernst. "Adult Education in Germany as a Manifestation of Spiritual Resistance." In *Yearbook of the Leo Baeck Institute*, vol. 1. London: East and West Publishers, 1956.

————. *Afbau im Untergang, Judische Erwachsenbildung in national-sozialistischen Deutschland als geistiger Widerstand*. Tübingen: J. C. Mohr, 1959.

————. *Aims, Junctures, Paths: The Thinking of Martin Buber* (Hebrew.) Tel Aviv: Sifriat Poalim, 1985.

————. "Buber or Ben Gurion" (Hebrew.) *Ner* 9–10 (1965): 3–8.

————. "The Builder of Bridges." Translated by David Wolf Silverman. *Judaism* 27, no. 2 (spring 1978): 148–60.

————. "From Dialogue to Peace." *Conservative Judaism* 19, no. 4 (summer 1964): 28–31.

————. *Kav ha-Tihum*. Arab and Afro-Asian Monograph Series. Givat Havivah: The Center for Arab Studies, 1973.

————. "Martin Buber and the Faith of Israel. (Hebrew.) *Iyyun: Revaon Pilosophi* 9, no. 1 (1958): 19–56, reprinted in Simon, *Aims, Junctures, Paths*.

————. "Martin Buber and German Jewry." In *Yearbook of the Leo Baeck Institute*, vol. 3. London: East and West Publishers, 1958.

Smart, Ninian. *Philosophy of Religion*. New York: Oxford University Press, 1979.

Spivak, Gayatri Chakravorty. Preface to *Of Grammatology*, by Jacques Derrida. Baltimore: Johns Hopkins University Press, 1974.

Stern, J. P. *Friedrich Nietzsche*. New York: Penguin, 1978.

Stout, Jeffrey. "The Relativity of Interpretation." *The Monist* 69, no. 1 (January 1986): 103–18.

———. "What Is the Meaning of a Text?" *New Literary History* 14, no. 1 (autumn 1982): 1–14.

Susser, Bernard. *Existence and Utopia*. East Rutherford, N.J.: Associated University Presses, 1981.

Talmon, Shemaryahu. "Martin Buber as an Interpreter of the Bible." In *Martin Buber, 1878–1978*, edited by Wolfgang Zink. Bonn: Hohwacht Verlag, 1978.

Taylor, Charles. *Hegel and Modern Society*. Cambridge, England: Cambridge University Press, 1972.

Theunissen, Michael. *The Other: Studies in the Social Ontology of Husserl, Heidegger, Sartre and Buber*. Translated by Christopher Macann. Cambridge, Mass.: MIT Press, 1984.

Tishby, Isaiah. *Torat ha-Ra ve-ha-Kelipah be-Kabbalat ha-'Ari*. Jerusalem: Akadamon, 1940.

Tompkins, Jane, ed. *Reader Response Criticism: From Formalism to Post Structuralism*. Baltimore: Johns Hopkins University Press, 1980.

Tonnies, Ferdinand. *Community and Society*. Translated and edited by Charles P. Loomis. New York: Harper and Row, 1963.

———. *On Sociology: Pure, Applied and Empirical: Selected Writings*. Edited by Werner J. Cahnman and Rudolph Heberle. Chicago: University of Chicago Press, 1971.

Tucker, Robert C. *Philosophy and Myth in Karl Marx*. Cambridge, England: Cambridge University Press, 1961.

Turner, Victor. *Dramas, Fields and Metaphors: Symbolic Action in Human Society*. Ithaca, N.Y.: Cornell University Press, 1974.

———. *The Ritual Process: Structure and Anti-Structure*. Ithaca, N.Y.: Cornell University Press, 1977.

Urbach, Ephraim. *The Sages: Their Concepts and Beliefs*. Cambridge, Mass.: Harvard University Press, 1987.

Van Buren, Paul. *The Edges of Language*. New York: Macmillan, 1972.

Vital, David. *The Origins of Zionism*. New York: Oxford University Press, 1975.

Walzer, Michael. *Exodus and Revolution*. New York: Basic Books, 1985.

———. *Interpretation and Social Criticism*. Cambridge, Mass.: Harvard University Press, 1987.

Wartofsky, Marx. *Feuerbach*. Cambridge, England: Cambridge University Press, 1977.

Watson, Burton, trans. *Chuang Tzu, Basic Writings*. New York: Columbia University Press, 1964.

Weber, Max. *From Max Weber: Essays in Sociology*. Translated and edited by H. Gerth and C. Wright Mills. New York: Oxford University Press, Galaxy Books, 1946.

———. "The Nature of Charismatic Domination." In *Max Weber: Selections*, edited by W. G. Runciman and translated by Eric Matthews. Cambridge, England: Cambridge University Press, 1978.

――――. *The Protestant Ethic and the Spirit of Capitalism.* Translated by Talcott Parsons. New York: Charles Scribner's Sons, 1958.

――――. *Theory of Social and Economic Organization.* Translated by Talcott Parsons. New York: Free Press, 1974.

Weiler, Gershon. *Mauthner's Critique of Language.* Cambridge, England: Cambridge University Press, 1970.

Weingartner, Rudolph H. *Experience and Culture: The Philosophy of Georg Simmel.* Middletown, Conn.: Wesleyan University Press, 1962.

Weiss, Joseph. *Studies in Eastern European Jewish Mysticism.* Edited by David Goldstein. New York: Oxford University Press, 1985.

Welch, Holmes. *Taoism: Parting of the Way.* Boston: Beacon Press, 1957.

White, Hayden. *Metahistory: The Historical Imagination in Nineteenth-Century Europe.* Baltimore: Johns Hopkins University Press, 1973.

――――. *Tropics of Discourse: Essays in Cultural Criticism.* Baltimore: Johns Hopkins University Press, 1978.

White, Morton. *The Intellectual Versus the City.* Cambridge, Mass.: Harvard University Press, 1962.

Wittgenstein, Ludwig. *Philosophical Investigations,* 3d ed. New York: Macmillan, 1958.

Wohl, Robert. *The Generation of 1914.* Cambridge, Mass.: Harvard University Press, 1979.

Wood, Robert E. *Martin Buber's Ontology.* Northwestern University Studies in Phenomenology and Existentialism. Evanston, Ill.: Northwestern University Press, 1969.

Wrong, Dennis, ed. *Max Weber.* Englewood Cliffs, N.J.: Prentice-Hall, 1970.

Wu, Kuang-ming. *Chuang Tzu - World Philosopher at Play.* American Academy of Religion Studies in Religion, 26. New York: Crossroad Publishing Company, Chico, Cal.: Scholars Press, 1982.

Yalom, Irvin D. *Existential Psychotherapy.* New York: Basic Books, 1980.

Yasour, Avraham. *Martin Buber's Social Philosophy.* (Hebrew.) Tel-Aviv: Hozaat ha-Sefarim, 1981.

――――. "Martin Buber's Social Thought and Kibbutz Research." (Hebrew.) Ha-Kibbutz 8 (1982): 183–212.

Yearly, Lee. "The Perfected Person in the Radical Tschuang Tsu." In *Essays on Tschuang Tsu,* edited by Victor H. Mair. Asian Studies at Hawaii, 29. Hawaii: University of Hawaii Press, 1983.

Yerushalmi, Yosef Haim. *Zachor.* Seattle: University of Washington Press, 1982.

Zeitlin, Hillel. *Be-Fardes Ha-Hasidut ve-ha-Kabbalah.* Tel Aviv: Yavneh, 1960.

Zweig, Stefan. *The World of Yesterday.* Lincoln, Neb.: University of Nebraska Press, 1964.

Index

Action
  concept of, in Buber, 137–39
Actualization *(Verwirklichung)*
  in Buber's early writings, 110–11
Address and response
  in Bible, 245
  in dialogical relationship, 144–45
Ahad, Haam, 246, 248
  on alienation in Jewish life, 77–79
  on the Bible, 78–79, 234, 250
  Buber's critique of, 79–80, 91, 248–50
  on exile, 77–78, 89
  on Jewish identity, 78–79
  on Jewish nationalism, 77–78, 246, 248–49
  on moral responsibility of Jewish people, 255
  on myth, 78–79
Alienation
  Buber's critique of, 5–8, 18–20, 37, 109–10, 115–17, 123, 173–77, 182–87
  in Buber's life, 7, 22–25
  Hasidic critique of, according to Buber, 45, 50–51, 57, 206–9
  institutionalized religion as source of, 205
  in Jewish life, 31–36, 72, 74–75, 78–79, 81–82, 89–90, 167, 182–87, 235
  in Kierkegaard, 73
  in Marx, 32
  in Simmel, 32, 35–36, 182–83
  in Tonnies, 32–35, 182–83
  in Weber, 36, 183
  See also Buber, Martin
Anarchy
  and Buber, 45, 54–56, 253, 280 n. 41
  and Scholem, 280 n. 41
Angelus Silesius, 39–40
Anxiety of influence
  Bloom, Harold, on, 14
Apocalyptic thinker
  contrasted with prophetic thinker, 188
Arab-Jewish conflict
  Buber's views on, 256–66
Arab refugees
  Buber's views on, 262
Arabs, Palestinian
  Zionist views on, 256–57, 265–66
Art
  Buber's views on, 135–36, 164–65

Bar Kokhba group, 81
Barthes, Roland, 243
Begegnung (meeting)
  contrasted with *Beziehung* (relation), 133
Ben Gurion, David
  Buber's critique of, 255–57, 262
  on Palestinian Arabs, 256–57
Bergmann, Hugo, 326 n. 35
Beziehung (relation)
  contrasted with *Begegnung* (meeting), 133

Biale, David, 67, 284 n. 74
Bible
   in Ahad Haam, 77–79, 234, 250
   Buber's views on, 234–44
Biblical humanism. *See* Buber, Martin,
   on Hebrew humanism
Biblical language
   Buber's views on, 236–40, 243–44
Biblical scholars
   Buber's critique of, 241
Biblical writers
   as poets, Buber's views on, 236, 238
Blasphemy
   Buber's views on, 221
Blood
   concept of, in Buber's early writings,
   89, 291 n. 50
Bloom, Harold
   on anxiety of influence, 14
   on creative misreading, 13–14
   on revisionism, 13–14, 72, 286 n. 2
   on struggle with precursor, 30, 273 n. 38,
   279 n. 30
Boehme, Jakob, 30, 40, 115, 134
Bohm, David, 323 n. 15
Broken vessels, myth of. *See* Buber, Martin, and myth of divine sparks
Buber, Martin
   on action, 137–39
   on actualization of self, 48, 132, 134
   on actualization-orientation dichotomy, 110–11, 297 n. 19
   and Ahad Haam, 77–80, 91, 234, 246,
   248–50
   on alienation in Jewish life, 19, 44, 72,
   81–82, 87, 89–90, 93–94
   alienation in life of, 7, 19, 22–25
   on alienation in modern society, 5–8,
   18–20, 37, 50, 57, 104, 106, 108–10,
   115–18, 123, 173–77, 182–87, 313 n. 35
   and American Jewry, 4, 268 n. 8
   and anarchy, 54–56, 253
   and Angelus Silesius, 39–40
   on apocalyptic-prophetic dichotomy,
   188–89
   on Arab-Jewish conflict, 17, 256–66
   on Arab refugees, 262
   on artistic creativity, 135, 164–65
   and Bar Kokhba group (Prague), 81,
   288 n. 27

   on *Begegnung-Beziehung* dichotomy,
   133
   on being and seeming, 152–53
   on being present, 129
   and Ben Gurion, 255–57, 262
   on the Bible, 234–42
   on biblical language, 236–40, 243–44
   on biblical scholarship, 241
   on biblical view of history, 244
   on biblical writers as poets, 236, 238
   on binational state in Palestine, 258
   on blasphemy, 221
   on blood as force in national existence, 89, 291 n. 50
   and Boehme, Jakob, 40
   on Chinese religion, 94–95, 136–39
   on Christianity, 216–17, 219
   on city as symbol of alienation, 109
   on community, 8, 37–39, 49, 97, 99–
   101, 111, 114–16, 124, 177–82, 193–
   94
   on community, renewal of, 37–39, 193–
   94
   on concept criticism *(Begriffskritik)*,
   10–11, 80–81, 83–85, 90–91, 118–20,
   169–70, 173, 177–80, 300 n. 38,
   303 n. 69, 308 n. 49, 310 n. 8
   on confirming the other, 145, 148–49,
   180, 228
   confusion over his writings, 1–2, 5, 12
   controversy over Jewishness of his
   thought, 2–3
   on covenant, 250–52
   and creative misreading, 13–14, 44, 47,
   51, 63–66, 71–72
   criticism of anarchy in thought of, 253
   as critic of Zionism, 232, 254–63
   on culture, 164–65
   deconstructive approach of, 11–12, 28–
   29, 83–85, 90–91, 107–8, 118–21,
   289 n. 31, 299 n. 37
   and Dewey, John, 190
   on dialectic of humanness and Jewishness, 229–30
   on dialogue, 112, 135, 143–154, 186, 201,
   212, 228, 298 n. 26
   on dialogue, impediments to, 152–53
   on dialogue, stages in, 290 n. 47, 301 n. 56
   and dichotomous thinking, 87, 129, 142,
   301 n. 56

on drive to commune, 145
on drive to relate, 189
on eclipse of God, 226
as edifying philosopher, 9–13, 15, 63,
    105–12, 140–41
on education, 187–93
on education-propaganda dichotomy,
    189
on election of Israel, 250–52
on entelechy, 40, 149, 164, 275 n. 70,
    302 n. 59, 306 n. 14
on *Erlebnis* (life experience) 37–39,
    41, 86–88, 110–11, 121–22
on eternal You, 212–14, 220–23
on European Jewish youth, 82–83
on evil, 84, 223–28
on exile, 79, 82, 89–90
and existentialism, 48–49, 57, 83–84
on existential mistrust, 200–202
on experience *(Erfahrung)*, 119–20,
    300 n. 42
on faith, 216–17
and feminism, 16, 270 n. 29, 314 n. 52
and Feuerbach, 123–25, 275 n. 69
on freedom, 191
and Freud, 155, 200–201, 215
and German social theory, 19, 31–34,
    114–16, 164, 169–70, 181–84, 223
and God language, 125, 212–16, 220–
    21
and grandparents, 24
on guilt, 156
on halakhah (Jewish law), 97–99, 101–
    3
on hallowing the everyday, 48, 99, 136,
    206–11, 253
and Hammarskjold, Dag, 203
on Hasidic critique of alienation, 45,
    50–51, 206–9
on Hasidic interpretation of divine
    sparks, 47–48, 50, 207–11
on Hasidic interpretation of redemp-
    tion, 47–50
on Hasidic interpretation of *zaddik*,
    50–51
on Hasidic tales, 46, 58, 209, 233
on Hasidic view of faith, 209–10
on Hasidic view of love, 49–50
on Hasidism and community, 49, 100–
    101

on Hasidism and renewal of Jewish
    myth, 51
on Hasidism as humanism, 47
on Hebrew humanism, 100, 234, 246–
    53, 256
on helping relationships, 115
and Herzl, 41
and historical scholarship, 43–44, 51–
    71, 241–42, 277 n. 3
on the Holocaust, 225–28
on idolatry, 219–21
on I-It mode of relating, 116–17, 119–
    21, 129, 131, 153–54
on imagining the real, 149
on inclusion *(Umfassung)*, 144, 192
on injustice in human society, 262
on institutionalized religion, 103, 205–
    6, 222
on the interhuman *(das Zwischen-
    menschliche)*, 6, 114, 127, 146–47,
    203
on international relations, 200–201
and Israel, state of, 261–62
on Israel as a community of faith,
    248
and Israeli Jewry, 3–4
on It world, 120, 174–77, 300 n. 43
on I-You mode of relating, 117, 119–
    21, 129, 131, 133–37, 307 n. 19
on I-You relation with nature, 134
on Jewish chauvinism, 79–80
and Jewish educational movement in
    Nazi Germany, 227, 254, 326 n. 39
on Jewish history, 59–60, 91–94
and Jewish homeland, 101, 252–53
on Jewish identity, 89–90, 95–96, 100,
    230–31
on Jewish mysticism, 45
on Jewish national renaissance, 248
on Judaism, changing interpretation
    of, 99–101
on Judaism, conflict of official and un-
    derground, 92–93
on Judaism, crisis of, 74–75, 93–99
on Judaism, ethos of, 93
on Judaism, existentialistic orienta-
    tion to, 83–84
on Judaism, mythic character of, 51–
    53, 58–59
on Judaism, rabbinic, early views, 38–

Buber, Martin *(Continued)*
  39, 48–49, 80, 85–88, 92–93, 98–99;
  later views, 233, 242, 250–51, 322 n. 8
on Judaism, Reform, 75–77, 80
on Judaism and community, 37–39,
  49, 97, 99–101, 114, 248, 252–53,
  259
on Jung's critique of religion, 215
on *kavanah*, 48
on kibbutz, 198
and Kierkegaard, 19, 72–74, 114, 123–
  25, 128, 199–200
on Kierkegaard's critique of totalitarianism, 200
on knowledge, 123–24, 166, 192–93,
  319 n. 16
and Landauer, 115–16, 194, 196–97,
  316 n. 61
on land of Israel, 252–53
on language, 10–11, 83–85, 90–91, 118–
  20, 128–29, 169–70, 177–80, 243–44,
  294 n. 72, 303 n. 69, 315 n. 55
as leader of spiritual resistance under
  Nazis, 254
and *Lebensphilosophie* (philosophy of
  life), 38, 85–88, 96, 110–12, 114, 121–
  22
on liberal, rationalist ethos, 45
on life as oscillating process, 131–32
on line of demarcation, 194, 253, 263
on love, 49–50, 150, 178
on Marx, 124, 170, 200–201
on Marxist thought, 187–89
as meliorist, 185, 202
on mismeeting *(Vergegnung)*, 23–24
on modernity, 5–8, 18–20, 57, 109–10,
  116–17, 173–77, 182–87
on modern reader's approach to Bible,
  242
on mutuality in dialogical relationship, 135, 150–51
on mysticism, 39–42, 45, 111–12, 114,
  134, 213–14, 303 nn. 64, 65
on myth, 41, 51–53, 57–59, 224–25, 240–
  41
and myth of divine sparks, 47–51, 136,
  207–11, 223, 311 n. 18, 320 n. 29
on nation, 88–89, 247–48
on national consciousness, 89

on nationalism, 247–48
and Nietzsche, 12, 14, 19, 25–31, 38,
  41, 50–53, 57, 72, 82, 85, 88, 91–92,
  108–9, 123–28, 176, 200, 206, 224,
  243, 247, 273 n. 22, 296 n. 14
and Nietzsche's *Thus Spake Zarathustra*, 30, 296 n. 14, 297 n. 22
on objectivistic discourse, 106, 116–17,
  123–25, 128, 152, 170–71, 192–93, 211–
  12
on Palestinian Arabs, 256–66
and parents' divorce, 7, 22–23, 272 n. 17,
  309 n. 59
and Peace Prize of German Book Trade,
  227
on peopleland, 247–48
on person, 49–50, 127–36
on person-ego dichotomy, 129–30
on philosophical anthropology, 122–
  36, 147–54
and philosophical discourse, 1, 6, 9–
  13, 104–7, 118, 209
on philosophy of religion, 211–13, 220–
  21
on poetry, 165
on political orientation to life, 116–
  17
on political revolution, 186–88, 195,
  299 n. 30
on political surplus, 190
on power, 16–17, 31, 116–17, 121, 132–
  33, 137–39, 174–77, 245
on primal movements in human interaction, 143–44
on prophet as social critic, 188–89, 244–
  46
on prophetic view of history, 244–46
on prophet–social-theorist dichotomy,
  172
on psyche, 154–55
on psychological illness, 122, 155
on psychologism, 121–22, 128
on psychology of religion, 215–16
and psychotherapy, 146, 154–64,
  275 n. 68
on redemptive action, 47–48, 50–51
on reflexion *(Ruckbiegung)*, 144
on relation *(Beziehung)*, 119–21, 129–
  31, 138

on relation, innate drive for, 130–32, 189
on religion-religiosity dichotomy, 84–85, 87–88, 289 n. 34
on religions, 218–19
and religious anarchism, 55–56
on religious forms and symbols, 84–88, 96–97, 101–3
on responsibility of individual, 49, 84
on responsibility of intellectuals, 254
on revelation, 217–18, 241–42
as revisionist, 13–16, 52, 59, 71–74, 80–91, 94, 202–3
on romantic religion, 95–96
and Rosenzweig, Franz, 101–3, 237–40, 293 n. 69, 294 n. 70, 300 n. 43
on sacred and profane, 98–99, 206–11
and Scholem, Gershom, 4–5, 53–70
on secularization, 98–99
and Simmel, Georg, 86–87, 108–9, 164, 181, 223, 296 n. 16
on Sinaitic revelation, 250–51
as social critic, 89, 173, 253–65, 328 n. 53
on social-political dichotomy, 185
on social theory, 8, 168–73
on society-community dichotomy, 179
on sociology, 168–73
on speech, 128–29
on state, 193–95
and story as literary device, 210–12
as strong reader, 44, 47, 51, 63–66, 71
on study of past, 57–58
on success and failure, 137–39, 244–46
and Taoism, 136–39, 303 n. 69, 304 nn. 70, 76, 77, 317 n. 4
on teacher-student relationship, 192
on teaching, 190–92
on teshuvah (turning), 94, 144, 202, 222, 228
on textual interpretation, 13–14, 44, 47, 51, 63–66, 71, 166
and Thus Spake Zarathustra, 30
on tolerance, 219
and Tonnies, 114–15, 169–70, 181
on Torah as law and teaching, 97–99, 101–3, 294 n. 71
on totalitarianism, 200
on tradition, 83–84, 97–98, 101, 103

on traditionalist approach to Bible, 242–43
on truth, 153, 230–31, 264, 322 n. 2
and Turner, Victor, 181–82
and twelfth Zionist Congress, 257
on unconscious, 154–55
on utopian socialism, 193–98
and Weber, 170, 181, 223
on word pairs, 129
Works: Daniel, 108–12; "Herut," 95–99, 101–3, 232, 234; "The Holy Way," 114; "Hope for This Hour," 203; I and Thou, 136–39, 142–43, 168–69, 207–11; "Nietzsche und die Lebenswerte," 29; "The Task," 114, 116; "Way of Man," 207–11; "What Is to Be Done," 116; Worte an die Zeit, 114–16; "Zarathustra," 28
and World War I, 22, 113, 298 n. 25
on zaddik, 50–51
and Zionism, 37–38, 44, 79–80, 232, 246–53
Buber-Rosenzweig Bible translation, 237–40
concept of language in, 237–38
division of chapters and verses in, 238–39
key words as interpretive device in, 239–40
as response to Christian translations, 237–38
Buber-Scholem debate over Hasidism, 53–70
"Builders, The," Rosenzweig's essay, 101

Capitalism, 197
Center, in Buber's concept of community, 177
China, religions of, 94–95, 136–39
Christianity. See Buber, Martin, on Christianity
Chuang Tsu, 137
City, as symbol of alienation, 109
Community
and Buber's early encounter with Hasidism, 100
in Buber's early writings, 97, 99–101
in Buber's social theory, 114–16, 177–82

Community *(Continued)*
  contrasted with society, in Buber, 179–
    80
  education for, 187–93
Community, quest for, in German social
    theory, 31–32
Community, renewal of
  in Buber, 8, 37–39, 193–94
Community, yearning for, in fin de siècle
    Vienna, 21–22
Concept criticism *(Begriffskritik)*. *See*
  Buber, Martin, on concept criticism
Confirming the other
  in Buber, 145, 148–49, 180
Covenant
  Buber's concept of, 250–52
Creative misreading. *See* Misreading,
  creative
Creativity
  Buber's views on, 135, 164–65
Culture
  Buber's views on, 164–65

Daniel, Buber's book, 108–12
  compared with Nietzsche's "Zarathus-
    tra," 108
Descartes, René, 122
Devekut, 46
Dewey, John, 190
Dialogue, 112, 143–54, 305 n. 7
  in Buber's *Daniel*, 112
  in contemporary philosophy, 16,
    270 n. 28, 314 n. 52
  human capacity for, 186
  impediments to, 152–53
  and international relations, 201, 228
  and key to knowledge of the divine,
    212
  and making present, 149–50
  and mutuality, 135, 150–52, 192
  stages in, 144, 307 n. 19
Dilthey, Wilhelm, 290 n. 44, 293 n. 65,
    325 n. 29
Discourse, objectivistic
  Buber's critique of, 106, 116, 123–24,
    128, 170–71, 192–93
Divine sparks, myth of
  and Scholem's critique of Buber, 53–
    55, 311 n. 18

See also Buber, Martin, and myth of
  divine sparks
Drive to commune *(Betrieb der Verbundenheit)*, 145
Drive to relate, innate. *See* Buber, Martin, on relation, innate drive for

Edifying philosopher
  Buber as, 9–13, 63, 105–12, 140–41
Edifying philosophy
  Rorty, Richard, on, 10, 105–6
Education, 189
  in Buber, 187–93
  impediments to, 192
  and rational discourse, 193
Election of Israel
  in Buber, 250–52
Encounter *(Begegnung)*, contrasted with
  relation, 133–34
Entelechy. *See* Buber, Martin, on ente-
  lechy
Erikson, Erik, 23
Erlebnis (life experience)
  Buber's critique of, 121
  in Buber's early writings, 37–39, 86–
    88, 109–11
  See also Buber, Martin, on *Erlebnis*
Eternal You
  foundational concept in Buber, 220
  metaphor for God, 211–14, 220–23
Evil
  in Buber, 84, 223–28
Exile
  in Ahad Haam, 77–78, 89
  in Buber, 79, 82, 89–90
  in Herzl, 89
Existentialism, 48–49, 57
Existential mistrust
  in Buber, 200–202
Experience *(Erfahrung)*. *See* Buber, Martin, on experience

Faith. *See* Buber, Martin, on faith; Kier-
  kegaard, Soren, on religion
Feminism, 16, 270 n. 29, 314 n. 52
Feuerbach, Ludwig, 30, 123–25, 166
Fourier, Charles, 196
Freedom
  in Buber, 191

See also Buber, Martin, on freedom
Freire, Paolo, 314 n. 52
Friedman, Maurice, 268 n. 11
Freud, Sigmund, 122, 200–201
  Buber's critique of, 155
  on religion, 215

Gadamer, Hans Georg, 324 n. 23
Gemeinschaft. See Tonnies, Ferdinand,
  on *Gemeinschaft* and *Gesellschaft*
German social theory. *See* Buber, Mar-
  tin, and German social theory
Gesellschaft. See Tonnies, Ferdinand, on
  Gemeinschaft and *Gesellschaft*
Ginsberg, Asher. *See* Ahad Haam
God
  eclipse of, in Buber, 226
  as eternal You, 211–14, 220–23
  language, 212–16, 220–21
  objectivistic interpretation of, Buber's
    critique of, 211–12, 220
Goethe, Johann von, 132
Gog u'Megog, Buber's novel
  as response to the Holocaust, 226–27
Gouldner, Alvin, 173
Guilt. *See* Buber, Martin, on guilt

Halakhah (Jewish law). *See* Buber, Martin, on halakhah
Hallowing the everyday. *See* Buber, Martin, on hallowing the everyday
Hammarskjold, Dag, 203
Hasidic tales
  in Buber, 46, 58, 209, 233
  contrasted with abstract theological
    concepts, 209
  and Scholem's critique of Buber, 54
Hasidism
  Buber-Scholem debate over, 53–70
  and community, 49, 100–101
  as critique of institutionalized reli-
    gion, 48–49, 207
  as critique of social alienation, 45, 50–
    51, 206–7
  and love, 49–50
  and redemption, 47–50
  and religious faith, 209–10
  and Western utilitarian ethos, 42, 45

Haskalah, 44–45
Hebrew humanism. *See* Buber, Martin,
  on Hebrew humanism
Heidegger, Martin, 123
Herberg, Will, 268 n. 8
"Herut" (Freedom), Buber's lecture
  Rosenzweig's critique of, 101–3
Herzl, Theodor, 22, 37, 41, 89
Historical inquiry
  Buber's critique of, 51–53, 59–70, 241–
    44
  and literary theory, 59–70
  and myth in Buber's thought, 52
  and objectivity, 59–70
  White, Hayden on, 65
History
  Buber's concept of, 91–95, 241–46
  prophetic view of, 245–46
Hobson, Robert F.
  and Buber, 157, 161–64
  on concept of story, 162
  on dialogue, 163
Holocaust, the. *See* Buber, Martin, on
  the Holocaust
"Hope for This Hour." *See* Buber, Mar-
  tin, Works
Horowitz, Rivkah, 298 n. 26, 301 n. 55
Human interaction
  primal movements in, 143–44
Husserl, Edmund, 123

I and Thou
  as critique of modern society, 168–69
  mythic roots of, 136–39
  problems in, 142–43
  and "The Way of Man," 207–11
Ichud
  organization for Arab-Jewish rap-
    prochement, 262
Idolatry
  in Buber, 219–21
I-It mode of relating, 120–21, 128–35
  Buber's later views on, 153–54
  inevitability of, 131–32
  proliferation of, 174–77, 184
  See also Objectivistic thought; It world
Imagining the real, 149
Inclusion *(Umfassung)*

Inclusion *(Continued)*
in dialogical relation, 144
and education, 192
Influence, anxiety of. *See* Bloom, Harold, on anxiety of influence
Intellectuals
responsibility of, 254
Interhuman *(das Zwischenmenschliche)*, 6, 146–47, 173, 203
contrasted with community and society, 179
and critique of alienation, 183–84
in Turner, Victor, 182
International relations
in Buber, 200–201
Interpretation
Buber's revisionistic approach to, 72–74
and contemporary literary theory, 59–70
pragmatic view of, 69–70
See also Bloom, Harold; Buber, Martin, on textual interpretation; Rorty, Richard; Textual interpretation
Israel
as community of faith, 248
as homeland, 252–53
state of, 261–62
It world
proliferation of, 174–77, 184
See also Alienation; I-It mode of relating
I-You mode of relating, 119–21, 124, 128–39
and art, 135–36
and encounter, 134–35
and grace, 133–34
innate capacity for, 130–31
and mutuality, 135, 142
and nature, 134–35
as preconceptual, 135
and presentness, 129
and reciprocity, 134–35, 142
and religion, 210–11
and *wu wei*, 137–38
See also Dialogue; Confirming the other

Jesus, 132
Jewish historical scholarship

and Buber, 51–70, 241–42
and myth, 281 n. 48, 282 n. 53
See also Scholem, Gershom
Jewish history
Buber's interpretation of, 59–60, 91–94
Jewish identity
Ahad Haam on, 78–79
Buber on, 89–90, 95–96, 100, 230–31
Judaism
alienation of young Jews from, 31–36, 72, 74–75, 78–79, 81–82, 89–90, 167, 182–87, 235
crisis of, in Ahad Haam, 77–79
essentialist view of, 64
See also under, Buber, Martin
Judaism, rabbinic. *See* Buber, Martin, on Judaism, rabbinic
Judaism, Reform. *See* Buber, Martin, on Judaism, Reform
Jung, Carl, 122, 215
Jung Wien, 20

Kafka, Franz, 21
Kant, Immanuel, 30, 123
Kaufmann, Walter
on Buber's *Tales of Hasidim*, 68, 284 n. 76
on *I and Thou*, 168–69, 305 n. 6, 307 n. 19
Kavanah. See Buber, Martin, on *kavanah*
Kibbutz
in Buber, 198
Kierkegaard, Soren, 19, 30, 48
on Christendom-Christianity distinction, 73
and critique of totalitarianism, 199–200
on philosophical anthropology, 124–25
on religion, 72–74
as revisionist, 73–74
See also Buber, Martin, and Kierkegaard
Knowing
biblical conception of, 123–24
Knowledge. *See* Buber, Martin, on knowledge
Kraus, Karl, 21
Kropotkin, Peter, 196

Laing, R. D., 159–61
Landauer, Gustav, 21, 115–16, 194–97, 316 n. 61
Language
  in Buber-Rosenzweig Bible translation, 237–38
  skeptical view of, in fin de siècle Vienna, 20–21
  See also Buber, Martin, on language
Lao Tsu, 137.
  See also Buber, Martin, and Taoism
Law and commandment
  in Rosenzweig, 102
Lebensphilosophie (philosophy of life), 25–27, 35–39, 57, 85–88, 290 n. 44
  See also Buber, Martin, and *Lebensphilosophie*; Nietzsche, Friedrich; Simmel, Georg
Life
  conflict of, with form, 26, 35–36
  as oscillating process, 131–32
  See also *Lebensphilosophie*; *Erlebnis*
Line of demarcation. *See* Buber, Martin, on line of demarcation
Literary theory, contemporary
  and Buber-Scholem debate, 59–70
  and historical inquiry, 61–70
  See also Historical inquiry
Love
  in Buber, 150, 178
Luria, Isaac, 46
Lurianic Kabbalah, 46–47, 50

Marx, Karl, 170, 183
  alienation, theory of, 32
  Buber's critique of, 187–89, 200–201
  on political revolution, 187–89
Mauthner, Fritz, 21, 272 n. 12
Meeting. *See* Encounter
Meister Eckhart, 40
Mendes-Flohr, Paul, 298 n. 25
Mismeeting *(Vergegnung)*
  in Buber, 23–24
Misreading, creative
  in Buber, 13–14, 44, 63–66, 71–72
  as essential characteristic of all reading, 64, 276 n. 2
  in Jewish tradition, 63

  in Kabbalah, 63–64
  and Scholem, 63–64
Modernity. *See* Buber, Martin, on modernity
Musil, Robert, 21
Mutuality. *See* Buber, Martin, on mutuality in dialogical relationship; Dialogue, and mutuality
Mysticism. *See* Buber, Martin, on mysticism
Mysticism, Jewish. *See* Buber, Martin, on Jewish mysticism
Myth. *See* Buber, Martin, on myth; Nietzsche, Friedrich, on myth
Myth, Jewish. *See* Buber, Martin, on Judaism, mythic character of

Napoleon
  as epitome of evil, 132–33
Nartrop, Paul, 214
Nation. *See* Buber, Martin, on nation
National consciousness. *See* Buber, Martin, on national consciousness
Nationalism. *See* Buber, Martin, on nationalism
Neue Gemeinschaft, 37, 274 n. 61
Nicholas of Cusa
  in Buber's early writings, 39–40
Nietzsche, Friedrich
  Buber's critique of, 126
  and Buber's interpretation of history, 91
  as critic of European culture, 25–28
  on death of God, 25, 27–28, 206
  on good and evil, 224
  on history, 27, 91–92
  on language, 25–26
  and literary theory, 61–62
  on morality, 26
  on myth, 27, 52
  and nihilism, 27, 29–30
  and philosophical anthropology, 125–28
  on psychology, 26–27
  on truth, 25–26
  See also Buber, Martin, and Nietzsche
"Nietzsche und die Lebenswerte," Buber's essay, 29

Nihilism
  Hasidism as alternative to, 51

Objectivistic thought
  and historical inquiry, 59–70
  as impediment to dialogue, 152–53
  Kierkegaard on, 124–25
  and religion, 211–12
  and social theory, 170–71
  See also Buber, Martin, on objectivis-
    tic discourse; Historical inquiry, and
    objectivity; Buber, Martin, on psy-
    chologism
Orientation
  contrasted with actualization, 110–11

Palestinian Arabs. See Arabs, Palestinian
Palestinian uprising
  in light of Buber's teachings, 265–66
Pauline Christianity
  and faith, 216–17
Peoplehood. See Buber, Martin, on peo-
  plehood
Person. See Buber, Martin, on person
Philosophical anthropology. See under
  Buber, Martin; Kierkegaard, Soren;
  Nietzsche, Friedrich
Philosophical discourse
  normal and edifying, 9–13, 105–6
  See also Buber, Martin, on philosoph-
    ical discourse
Philosophy of religion. See Buber, Mar-
  tin, on philosophy of religion
Political dimension of life. See Buber,
  Martin, on political orientation to
  life
Political principle
  contrasted with social principle, 185–
  86
Power
  Buber's critique of, 16–17, 137–39, 176–
    77, 244–46
  See also Buber, Martin, on power;
    Buber, Martin, on success and fail-
    ure; I-It mode of relating
Propaganda
  contrasted with education, 189
Prophet
  contrasted with apocalyptic thinker,
    188

  contrasted with social theorist, 172
  and history, 244–46
  as social critic, 188–89, 244–46
  See also related topics under Buber,
    Martin; on prophet
Proudhon, Pierre Joseph, 196
Psyche. See Buber, Martin, on psyche
Psychological illness. See Buber, Martin,
  on psychological illness
Psychologism. See Buber, Martin, on psy-
  chologism
Psychotherapy, 154–64
  See also Buber, Martin, psychotherapy

Rabbinic Judaism. See Buber, Martin, on
  Judaism, rabbinic
Reading. See Textual interpretation;
  Misreading, creative
Reciprocity. See I-You mode of relating,
  and reciprocity
Redemption. See Hasidism, and redemp-
  tion; Buber, Martin, on redemptive
  action
Reflexion (Ruckbiegung). See Buber,
  Martin, on reflexion
Relation (Beziehung). See I-You mode
  of relating
Religion, institutionalized
  Buber's critique of, 84–85, 87–88, 103,
    205–6, 219, 222–23
  and objectivistic thought, 211
  psychological interpretation of, 214–
    15
  romantic, Buber's critique of, 96
  as source of alienation, 205
Religions of China. See Buber, Martin,
  on Chinese religion; Buber, Martin,
  Taoism
Religiosity. See Buber, Martin, on reli-
  gion-religiosity dichotomy
Religious forms. See Buber, Martin, on
  religious forms and symbols
Religious symbols. See Buber, Martin, on
  religious forms and symbols
Renaissance, Jewish national, 248
Responsibility of individual, 84
Revelation. See Buber, Martin, on reve-
  lation
Revisionism. See Bloom, Harold, on re-
  visionism; Buber, Martin, as revi-

sionist; Kierkegaard, Soren, as revisionist
Revolution, political. See Buber, Martin, on political revolution; Marx, Karl, on political revolution
Rilke, Rainer Maria, 21
Rorty, Richard, 10, 63, 105–6
on textual interpretation, 68–69, 277 n. 2
Rosenzweig, Franz
and bible translation, 237–40
as critic of Buber, 101–3, 293 n. 69, 294 n. 70, 300 n. 43
Rothenberg, Albert
on polar or dichotomous thinking, 87, 290 n. 47, 295 n. 13
Rubenstein, Richard, 225, 321 n. 36
Russia, 197

Saint Francis, 134
Scheler, Max, 128, 221, 306 n. 12
Schnitzler, Arthur, 20
Scholem, Gershom
and anarchism, 280 n. 35
on Buber's interpretation of Bible, 325 n. 34
and Buber's interpretation of Hasidism, 53–70, 280 n. 35
and creative misreading, 63–64
and dialectical view of history, 66–67, 284 n. 74
on German Jewry, 326 n. 38
Secularization. See Buber, Martin, on secularization
Self-actualization. See Buber, Martin, on actualization of self
Simmel, Georg, 31, 86–88, 108, 164, 181
on alienation, 35–36, 182–83
on antithesis of life and form, 86–87
on community, 181
on conflict of life and form, 35–36
on religion, 223
See also Lebensphilosophie
Simon, Akiba Ernst
Sinai. See Buber, Martin, on Sinaitic revelation
Social principle
contrasted with political principle, 185–86
Social theory, German, 31–36

See also Buber, Martin, on social theory
Society
contrasted with community, 179
oscillation of, between social and political principles, 185–86
Sociology. See Buber, Martin, on sociology; Social theory, German
Socrates, 132
State, the. See Buber, Martin, on state
Stein, Lorenz von, 196
Story. See Buber, Martin, and story as literary device
Stout, Jeffrey, on textual interpretation, 67, 69–70, 285 n. 80
Strong reader. See Buber, Martin, as strong reader; Misreading, creative
Success. See Buber, Martin, on success and failure
Symbols, religious. See Buber, Martin, on religious forms and symbols

Taoism. See Buber, Martin, and Taoism
Tao Te Ching, 137
See also Buber, Martin, on social theory
Teacher-student relationship. See Buber, Martin, on teacher-student relationship
Teaching. See Buber, Martin, on teaching
Teshuvah (turning). See Buber, Martin, on teshuvah
Textual interpretation
in contemporary literary theory, 63–70, 72, 277 n. 2, 285 n. 78
See also Buber, Martin, and creative misreading; Buber, Martin, on textual interpretation
"Thus Spake Zarathustra"
influence of, on young Buber, 30
Thus Spake Zarathustra
and Buber, 30
and Buber's Daniel, 108
Tikkun (repairing), in Lurianic kabbalah, 46
Tolerance. See Buber, Martin, on tolerance
Tonnies, Ferdinand, 31, 115, 169–70
on alienation, 32–35, 182–83

Tonnies, Ferdinand *(Continued)*
on *Gemeinschaft* and *Gesellschaft*, 33–35, 181
Torah
as law and teaching, 97–99, 101–3, 294 n. 71
in Rosenzweig, 101–3
Tradition, 68–69, 285 n. 81
See also Buber, Martin, on tradition
Truth. *See* Buber, Martin, on truth
Turner, Victor, 181–82

Unconscious. *See* Buber, Martin, on unconscious
Utopian socialism. *See* Buber, Martin, on utopian socialism

Vergegnung (mismeeting), 23–24
Vienna, fin de siècle, 20–21
Von Hofmannsthal, 20–22

Walzer, Michael, on social criticism, 310 n. 11, 311 n. 13
"Way of Man, The," Buber's essay
and *I and Thou*, 207–11
Weber, Max, 170, 181
on alienation, 36, 183
on religion, 223
Weizmann, Haim
on Palestinian Arabs, 256–57
White, Hayden, 65

Wittgenstein, Ludwig, 108, 296 n. 16
Word pairs. *See* Buber, Martin, on word pairs
World War I
and Buber, 113
cultural impact of, 22
Worte an die Zeit, Buber's book, 114–16
Wu wei, Taoist concept
in *I and Thou*, 137–39

Yalom, Irvin, 157–59

Zaddik
in Buber's interpretation of Hasidism, 50–51
Zionism
as alternative to Nietzschean vision, 38
Buber's critique of, 232, 246–63
Buber's early views on, 37–38
and Palestinian Arabs, 256–57
See also Ahad Haam; Herzl, Theodor
Zionist Congress, twelfth
Buber's address to, 257
Zivaat HaRibesh (The testament of Rabbi Israel Baal Shem)
influence on Buber, 47
Zweig, Stefan, 20
Zwischenmenschliche. *See* Interhuman; Buber, Martin, on the interhuman